Land of the Blindfolded

By Tsukuba Sakura

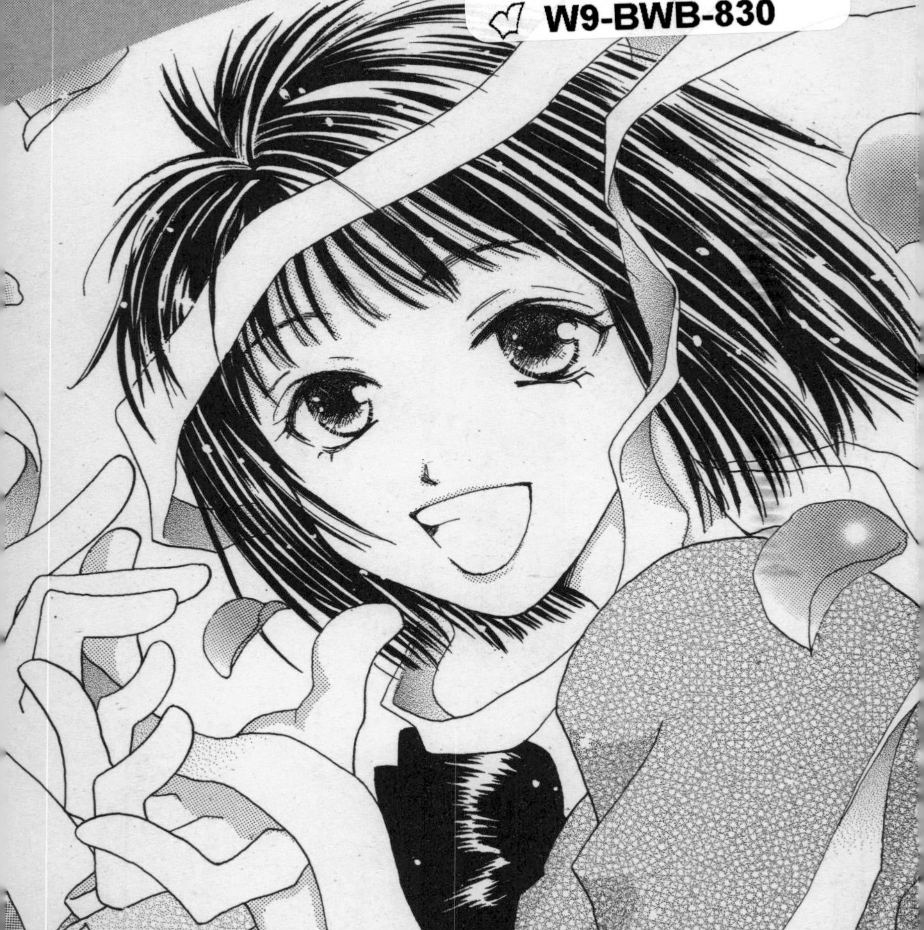

contents

Land of the Blindfolded **1**

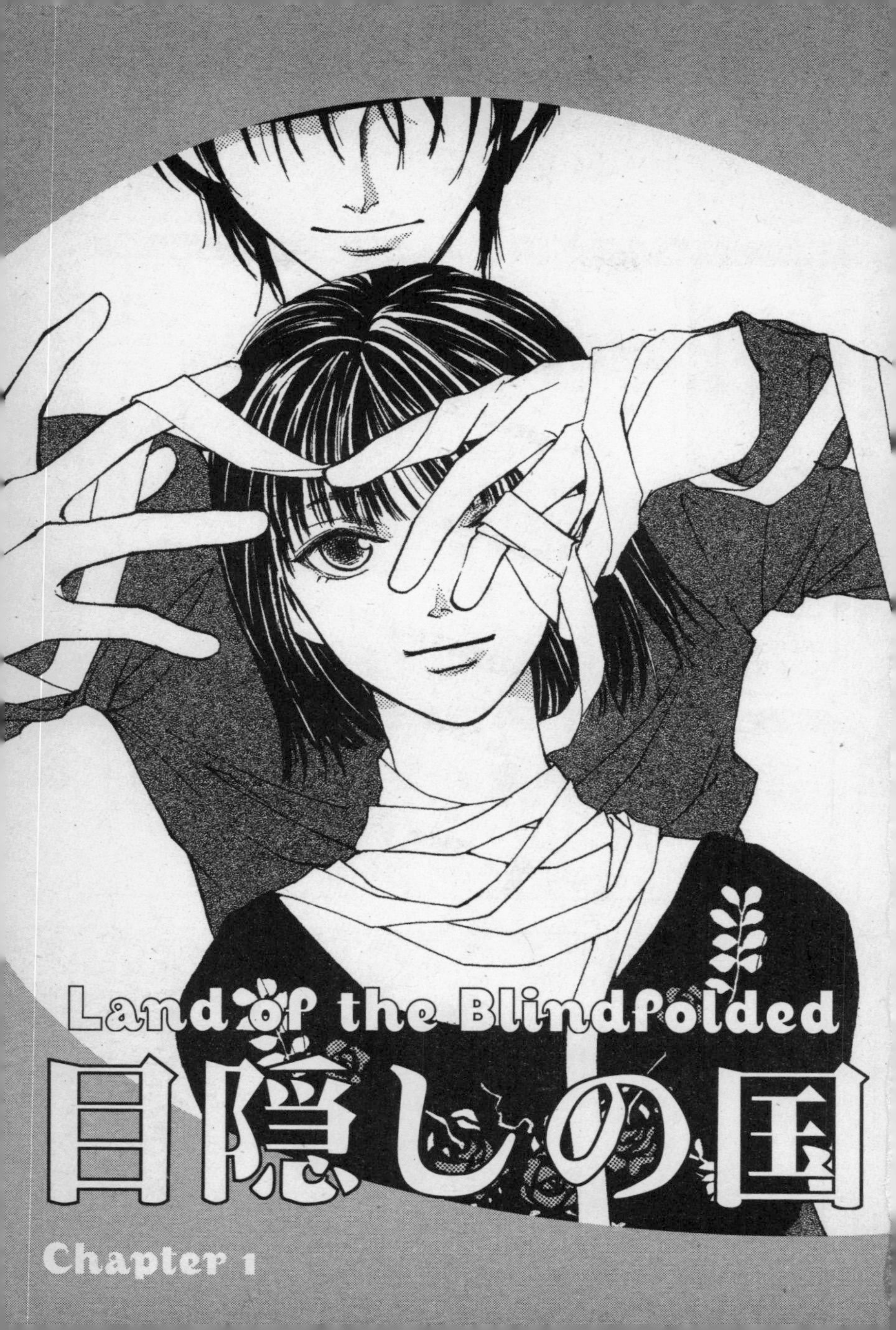

Land of the Blindfolded

目隠しの国

Chapter 1

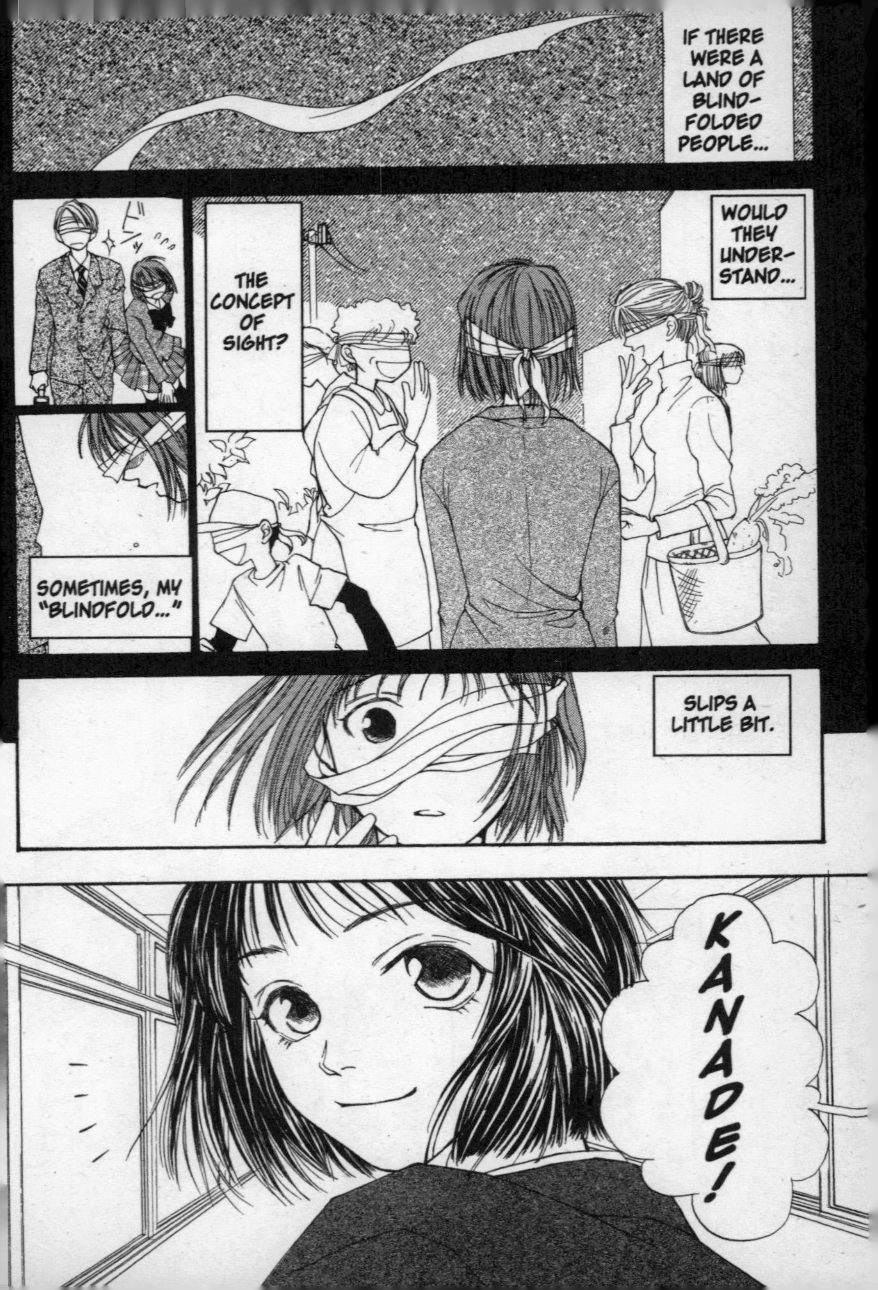
IF THERE WERE A LAND OF BLIND-FOLDED PEOPLE...
WOULD THEY UNDER-STAND...
THE CONCEPT OF SIGHT?
SOMETIMES, MY "BLINDFOLD..."
SLIPS A LITTLE BIT.
KANADE!

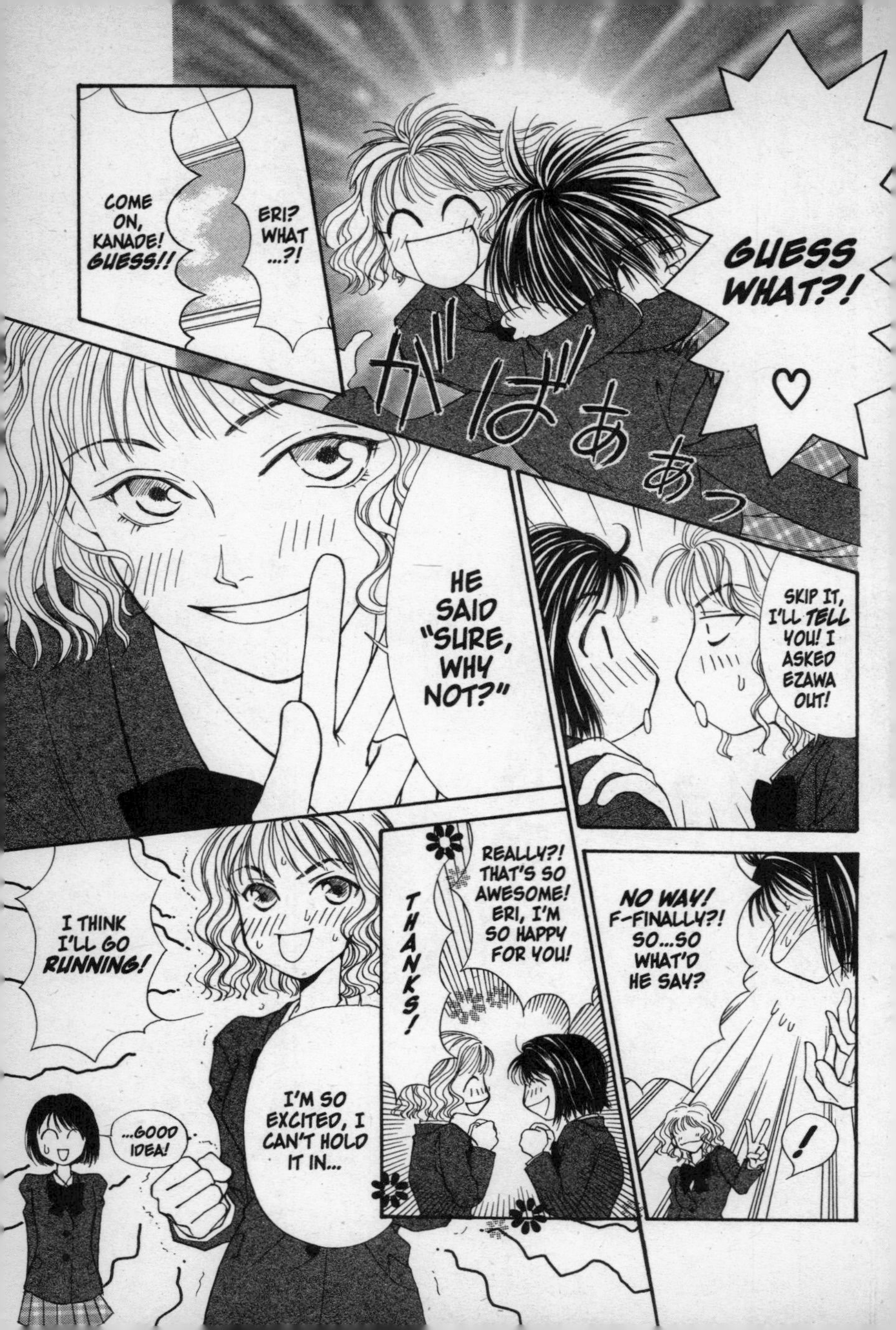
GUESS WHAT?! ♥
がばぁあっ
ERI? WHAT ...?!
COME ON, KANADE! GUESS!!
SKIP IT, I'LL TELL YOU! I ASKED EZAWA OUT!
HE SAID "SURE, WHY NOT?"
NO WAY! F-FINALLY?! SO...SO WHAT'D HE SAY?
!
REALLY?! THAT'S SO AWESOME! ERI, I'M SO HAPPY FOR YOU!
THANKS!
I'M SO EXCITED, I CAN'T HOLD IT IN...
I THINK I'LL GO RUNNING!
...GOOD IDEA!

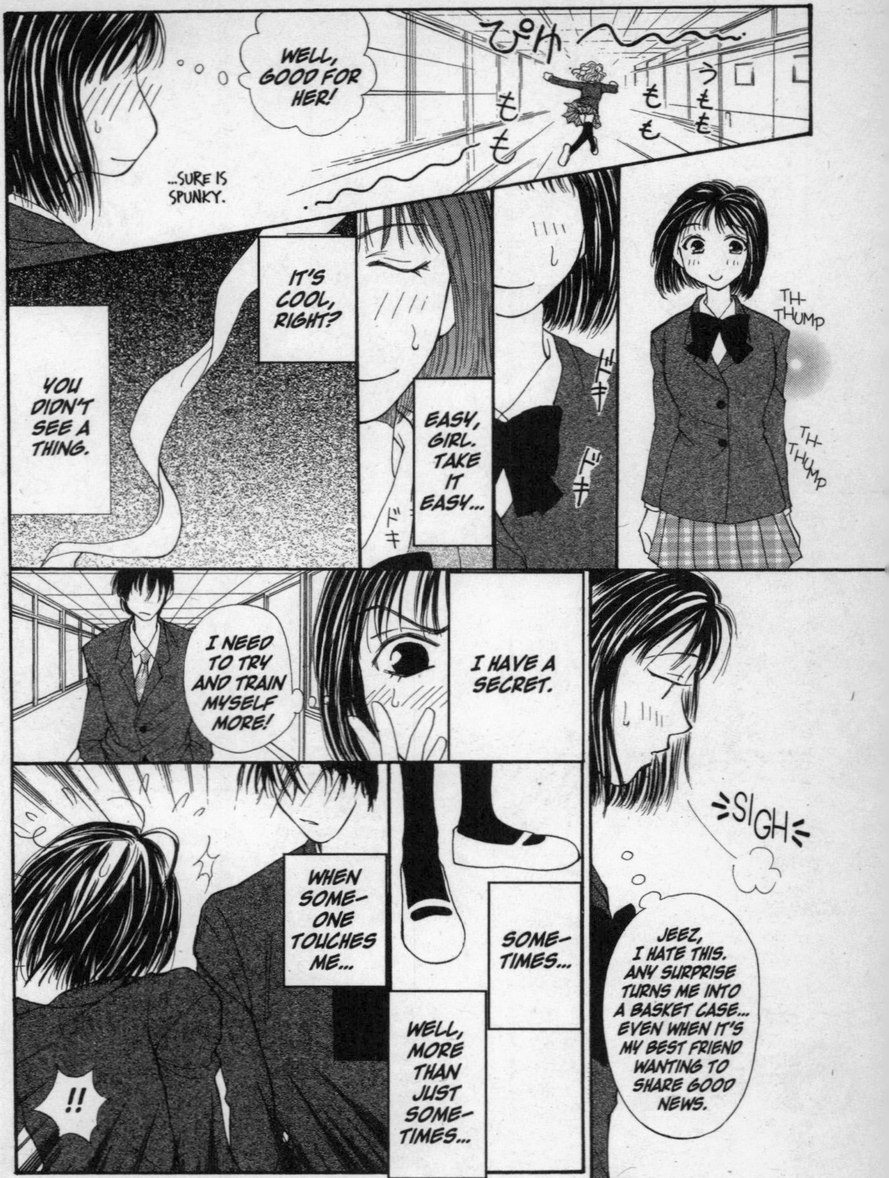
ぴゅ～
うもも
もも
もも
WELL, GOOD FOR HER!
...SURE IS SPUNKY.
TH-THUMP
TH-THUMP
ドキ ドキ
EASY, GIRL. TAKE IT EASY...
IT'S COOL, RIGHT?
ドキ
YOU DIDN'T SEE A THING.
SIGH
JEEZ, I HATE THIS. ANY SURPRISE TURNS ME INTO A BASKET CASE... EVEN WHEN IT'S MY BEST FRIEND WANTING TO SHARE GOOD NEWS.
I HAVE A SECRET.
I NEED TO TRY AND TRAIN MYSELF MORE!
WHEN SOME-ONE TOUCHES ME...
SOME-TIMES...
WELL, MORE THAN JUST SOME-TIMES...
!!

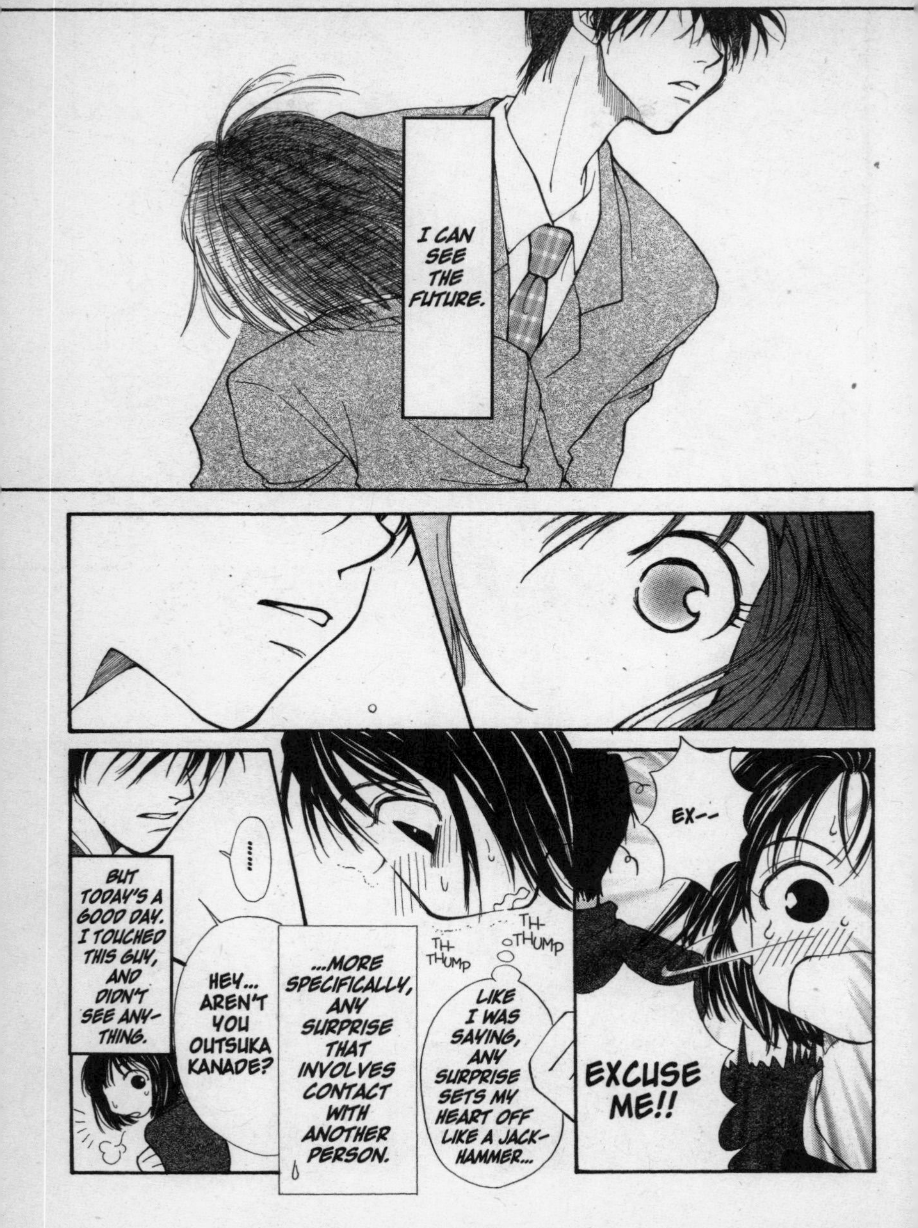

I CAN SEE THE FUTURE.
EX--
EXCUSE ME!!
TH THUMP
TH THUMP
LIKE I WAS SAYING, ANY SURPRISE SETS MY HEART OFF LIKE A JACK-HAMMER...
...MORE SPECIFICALLY, ANY SURPRISE THAT INVOLVES CONTACT WITH ANOTHER PERSON.
......
BUT TODAY'S A GOOD DAY. I TOUCHED THIS GUY, AND DIDN'T SEE ANY-THING.
HEY... AREN'T YOU OUTSUKA KANADE?

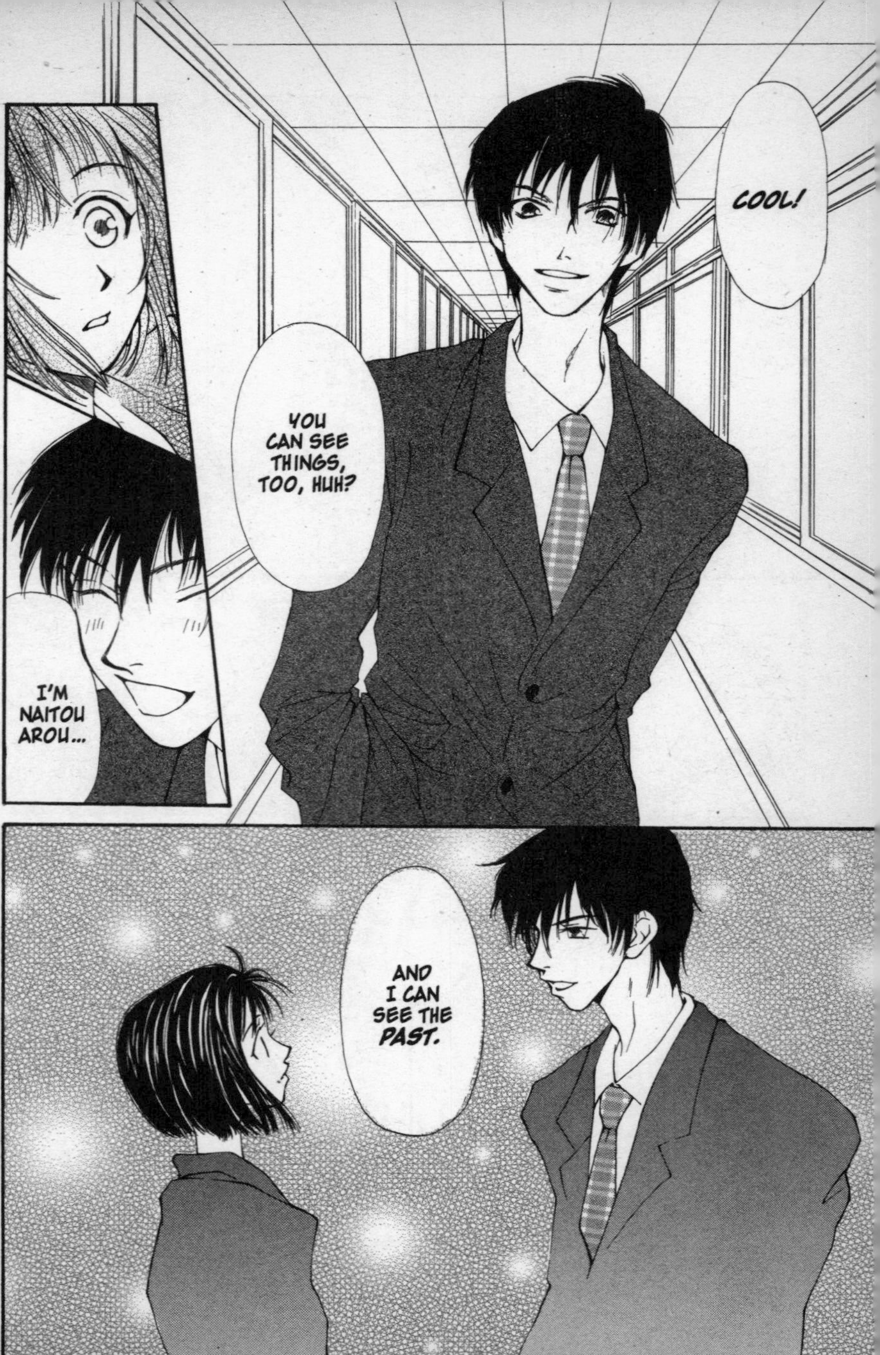
COOL!
YOU CAN SEE THINGS, TOO, HUH?
I'M NAITOU AROU...
AND I CAN SEE THE PAST.

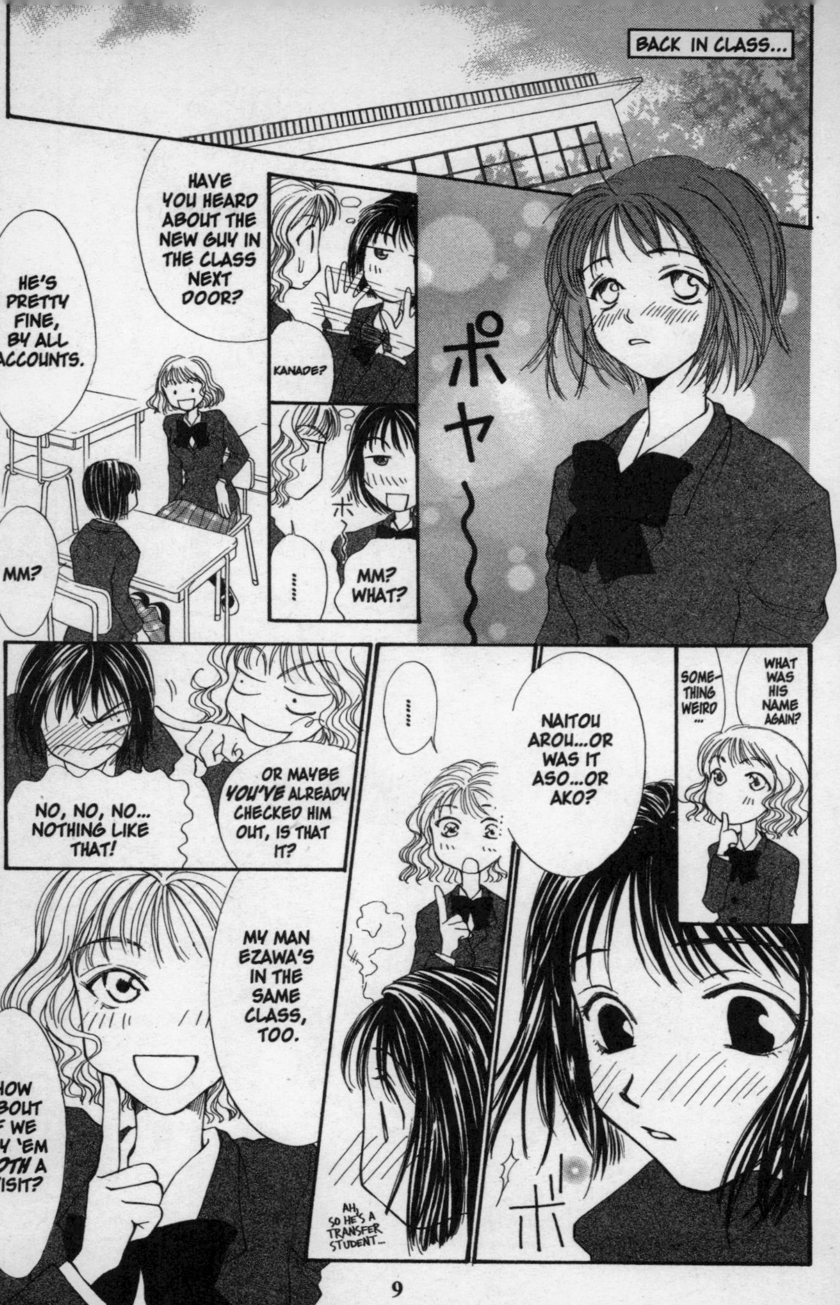
BACK IN CLASS...
ポヤ〜
HAVE YOU HEARD ABOUT THE NEW GUY IN THE CLASS NEXT DOOR?
HE'S PRETTY FINE, BY ALL ACCOUNTS.
MM?
KANADE?
......
ポ
MM? WHAT?
WHAT WAS HIS NAME AGAIN?
SOMETHING WEIRD...
NAITOU AROU...OR WAS IT ASO...OR AKO?
......
OR MAYBE YOU'VE ALREADY CHECKED HIM OUT, IS THAT IT?
NO, NO, NO... NOTHING LIKE THAT!
ボ
AH, SO HE'S A TRANSFER STUDENT...
MY MAN EZAWA'S IN THE SAME CLASS, TOO.
HOW ABOUT IF WE PAY 'EM BOTH A VISIT?

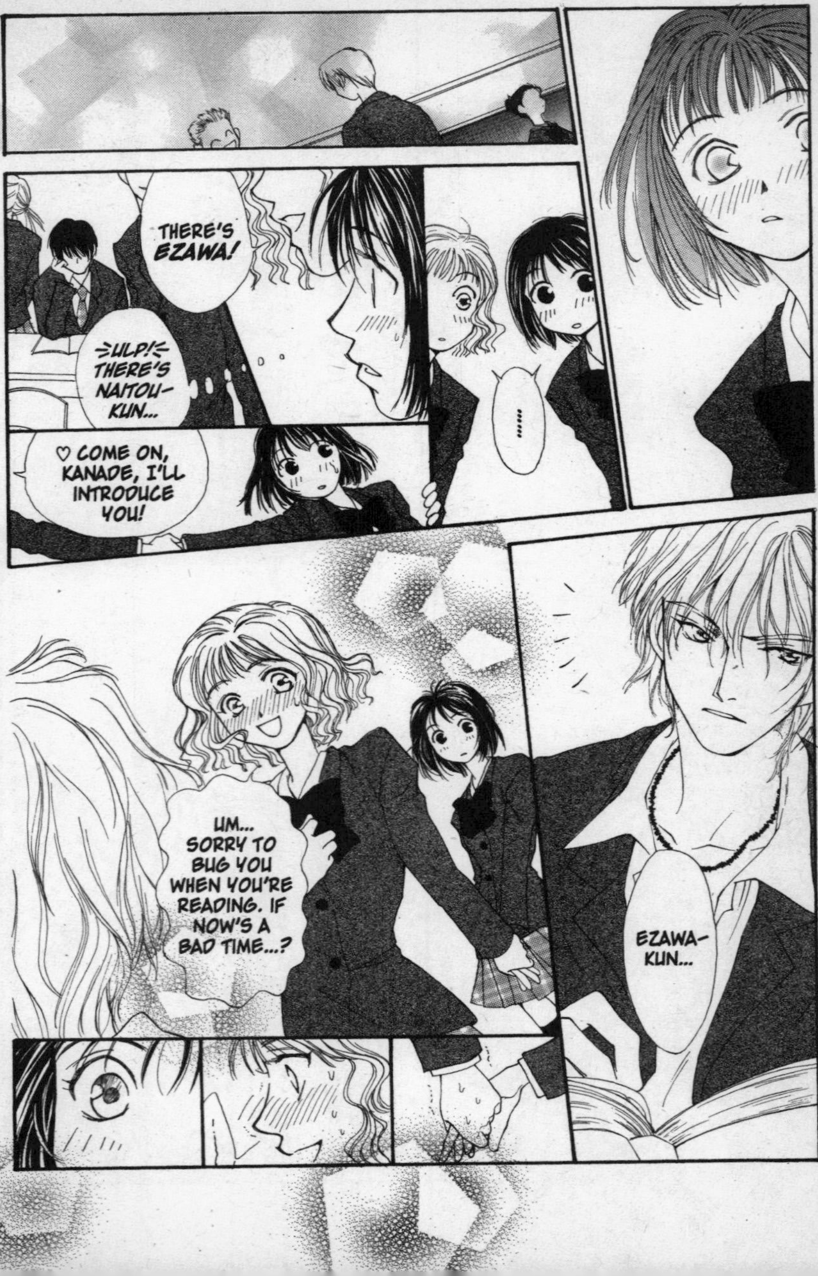

THERE'S EZAWA!
......
⚞ULP!⚟ THERE'S NAITOU-KUN...
♡ COME ON, KANADE, I'LL INTRODUCE YOU!
EZAWA-KUN...
UM... SORRY TO BUG YOU WHEN YOU'RE READING. IF NOW'S A BAD TIME...?

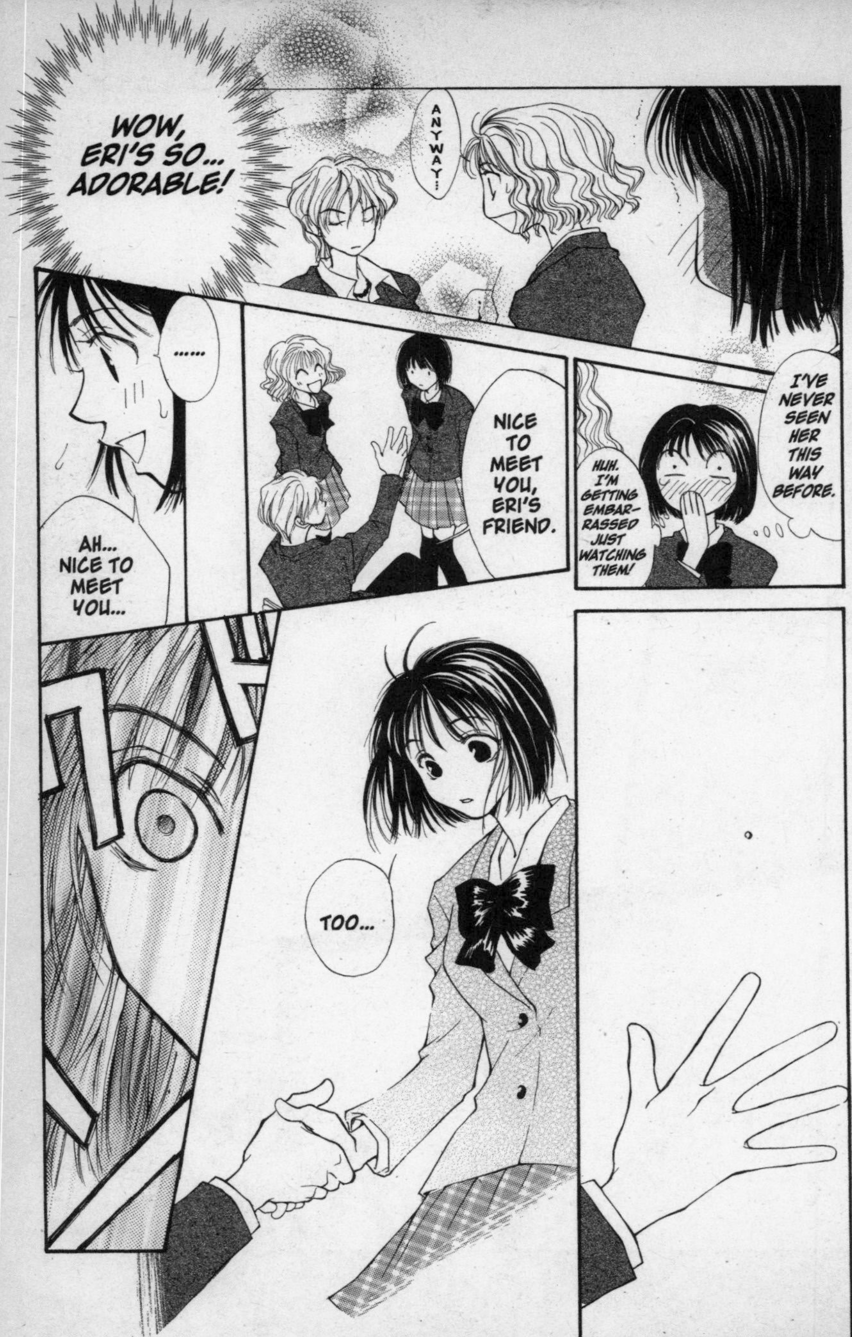
ANYWAY...
WOW, ERI'S SO... ADORABLE!
I'VE NEVER SEEN HER THIS WAY BEFORE.
HUH. I'M GETTING EMBARRASSED JUST WATCHING THEM!
NICE TO MEET YOU, ERI'S FRIEND.
......
AH... NICE TO MEET YOU...
TOO...

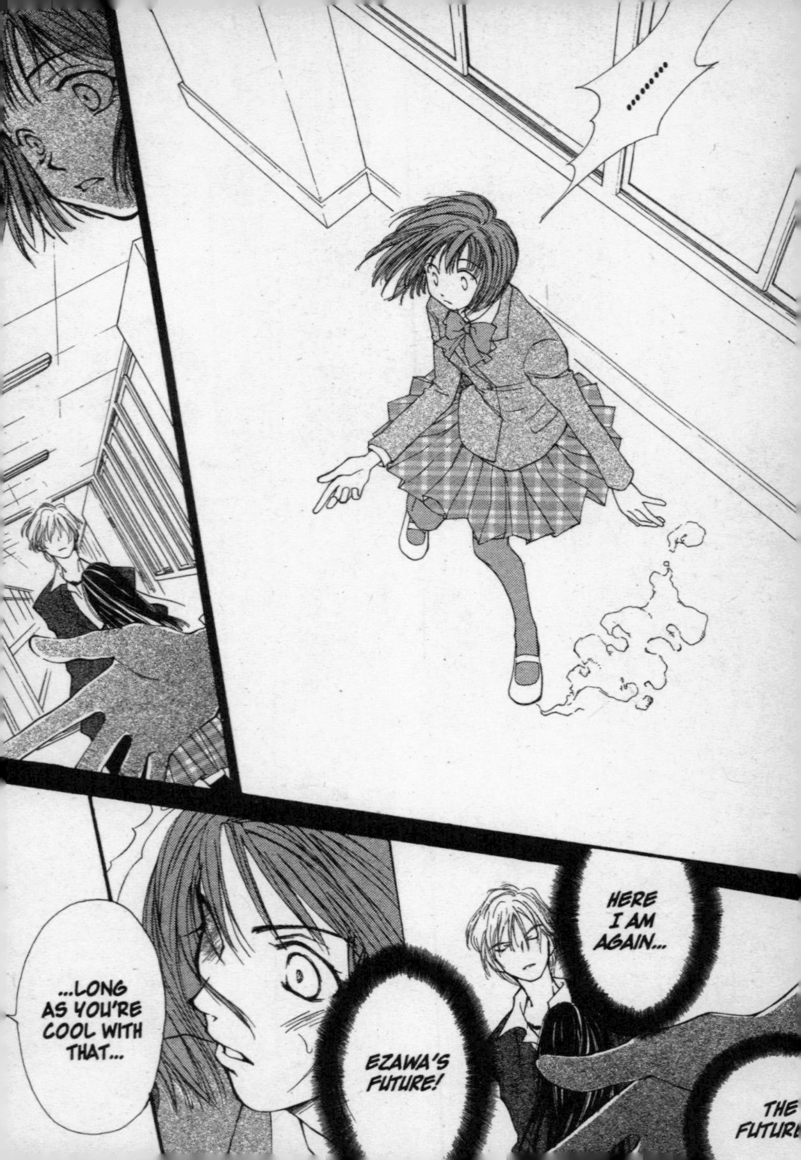
....
HERE I AM AGAIN...
THE FUTURE
EZAWA'S FUTURE!
...LONG AS YOU'RE COOL WITH THAT...

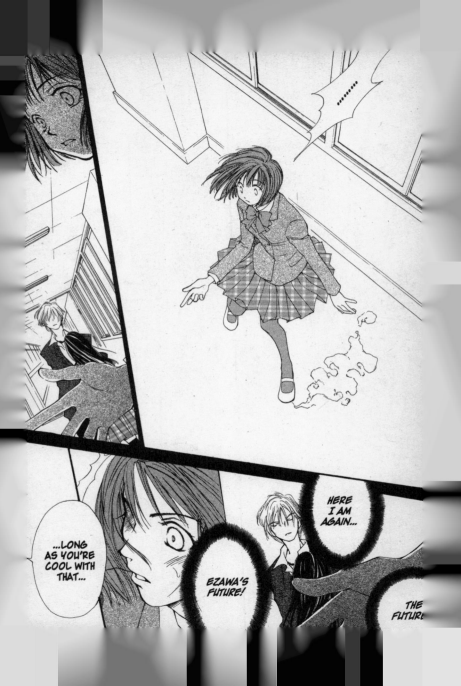

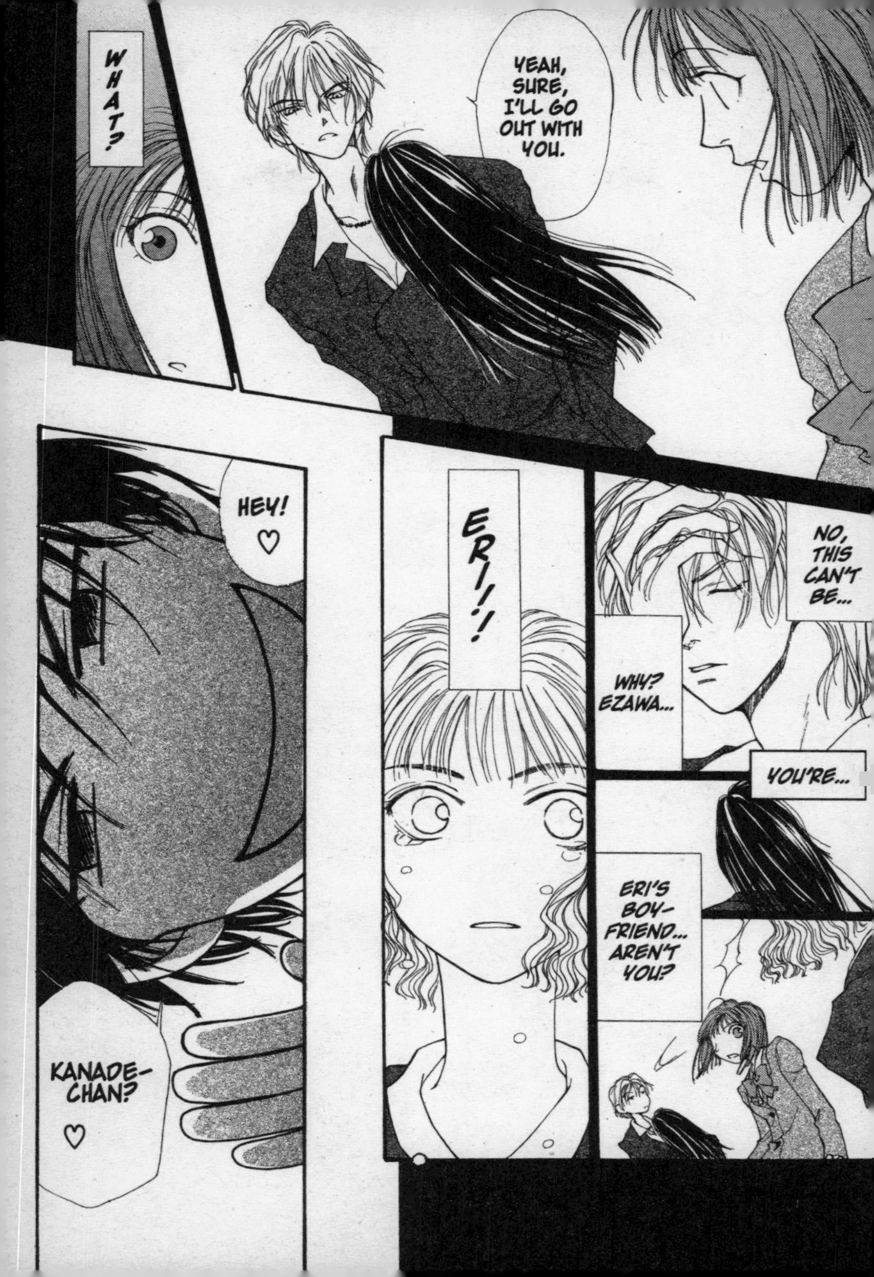
YEAH, SURE, I'LL GO OUT WITH YOU.
WHAT?
NO, THIS CAN'T BE...
WHY? EZAWA...
YOU'RE...
ERI'S BOY-FRIEND... AREN'T YOU?
ERI!!
HEY! ♡
KANADE-CHAN? ♡

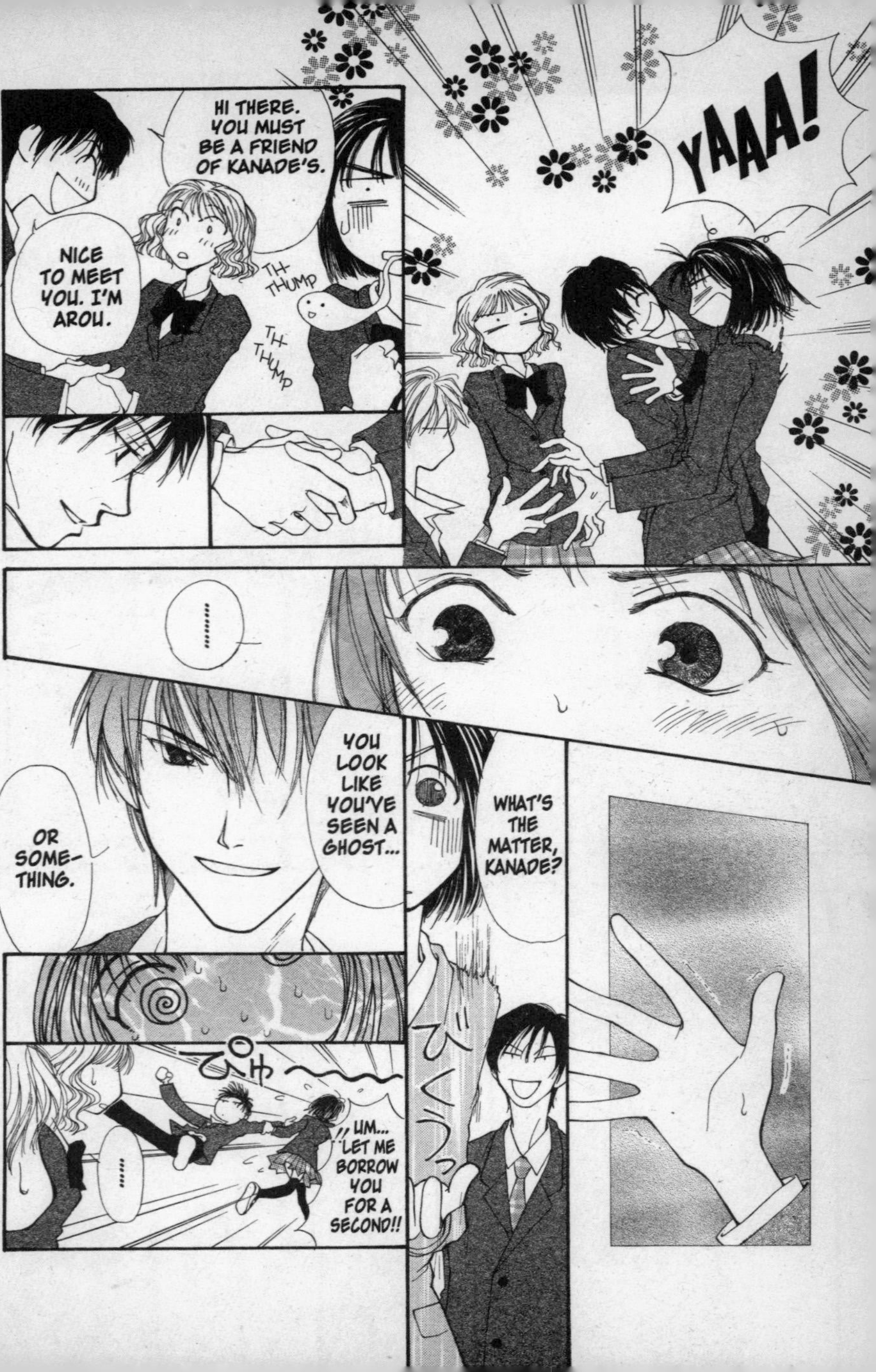
YAAA!
HI THERE. YOU MUST BE A FRIEND OF KANADE'S.
NICE TO MEET YOU. I'M AROU.
TH THUMP
TH THUMP
......
WHAT'S THE MATTER, KANADE?
びくっ
YOU LOOK LIKE YOU'VE SEEN A GHOST...
OR SOME-THING.
ぴゅ〜〜
UM... LET ME BORROW YOU FOR A SECOND!!
......

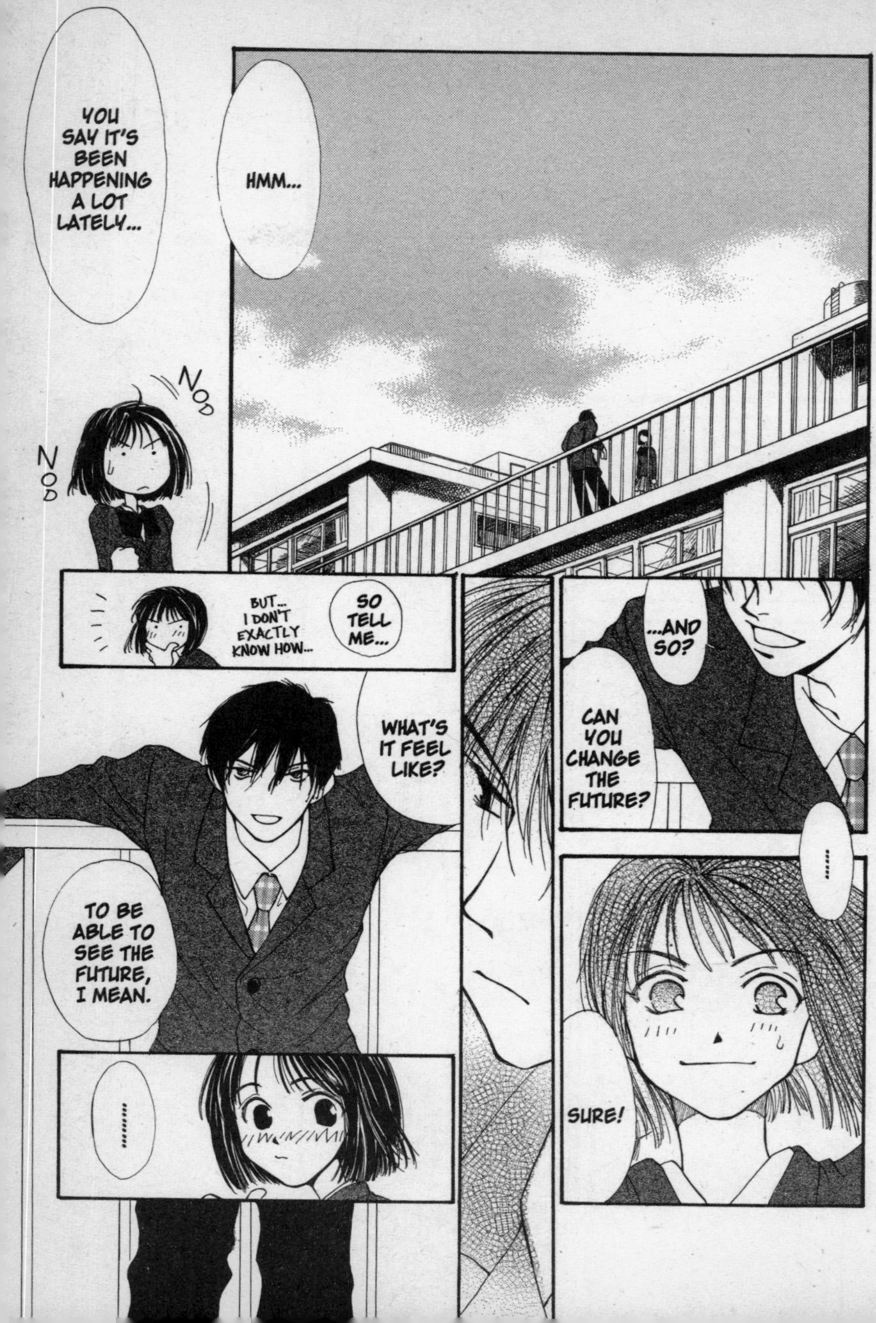
HMM...
YOU SAY IT'S BEEN HAPPENING A LOT LATELY...
NOD
NOD
...AND SO?
CAN YOU CHANGE THE FUTURE?
......
SURE!
SO TELL ME...
BUT... I DON'T EXACTLY KNOW HOW...
WHAT'S IT FEEL LIKE?
TO BE ABLE TO SEE THE FUTURE, I MEAN.
......

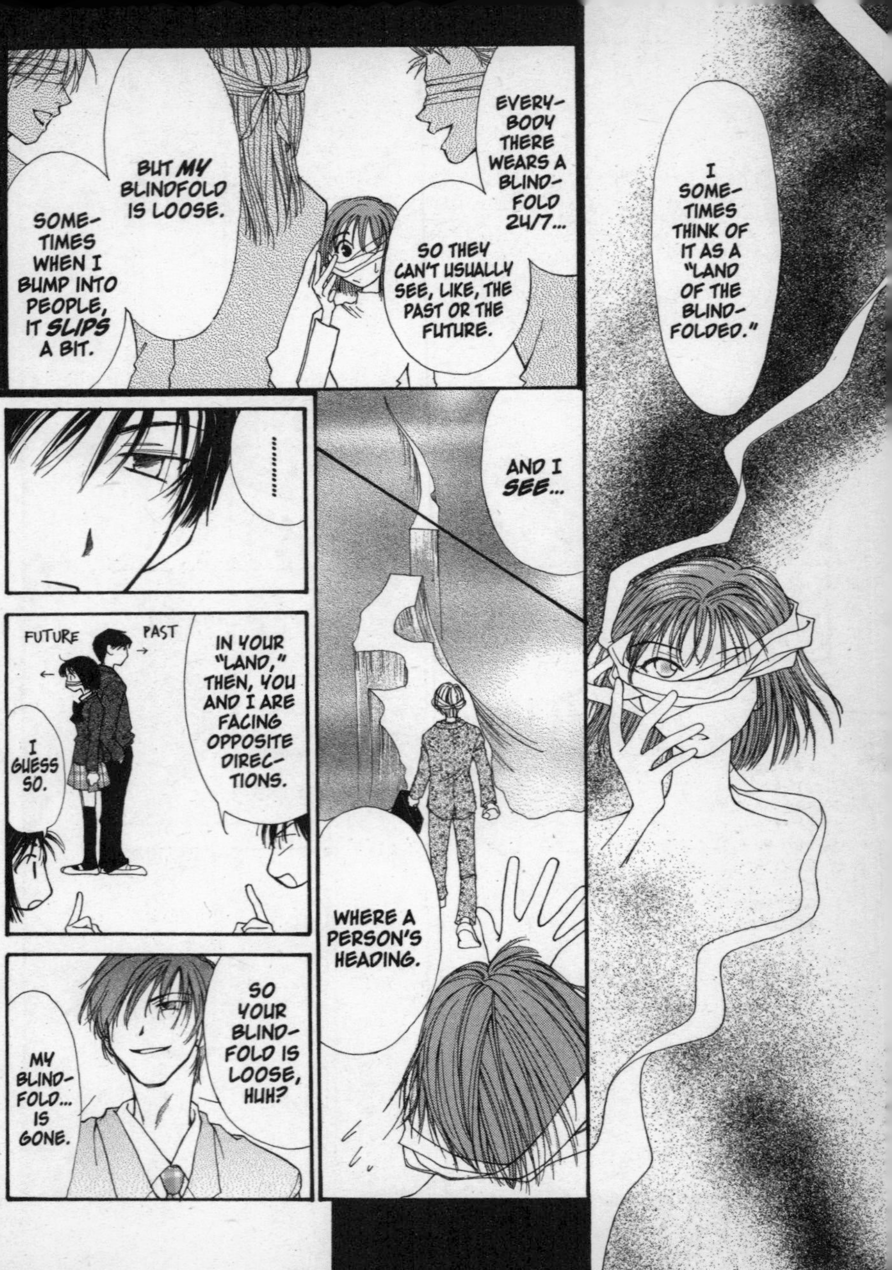
I SOMETIMES THINK OF IT AS A "LAND OF THE BLINDFOLDED."
EVERYBODY THERE WEARS A BLINDFOLD 24/7...
SO THEY CAN'T USUALLY SEE, LIKE, THE PAST OR THE FUTURE.
BUT MY BLINDFOLD IS LOOSE.
SOMETIMES WHEN I BUMP INTO PEOPLE, IT SLIPS A BIT.
AND I SEE...
WHERE A PERSON'S HEADING.
......
IN YOUR "LAND," THEN, YOU AND I ARE FACING OPPOSITE DIRECTIONS.
PAST
FUTURE
I GUESS SO.
SO YOUR BLINDFOLD IS LOOSE, HUH?
MY BLINDFOLD... IS GONE.

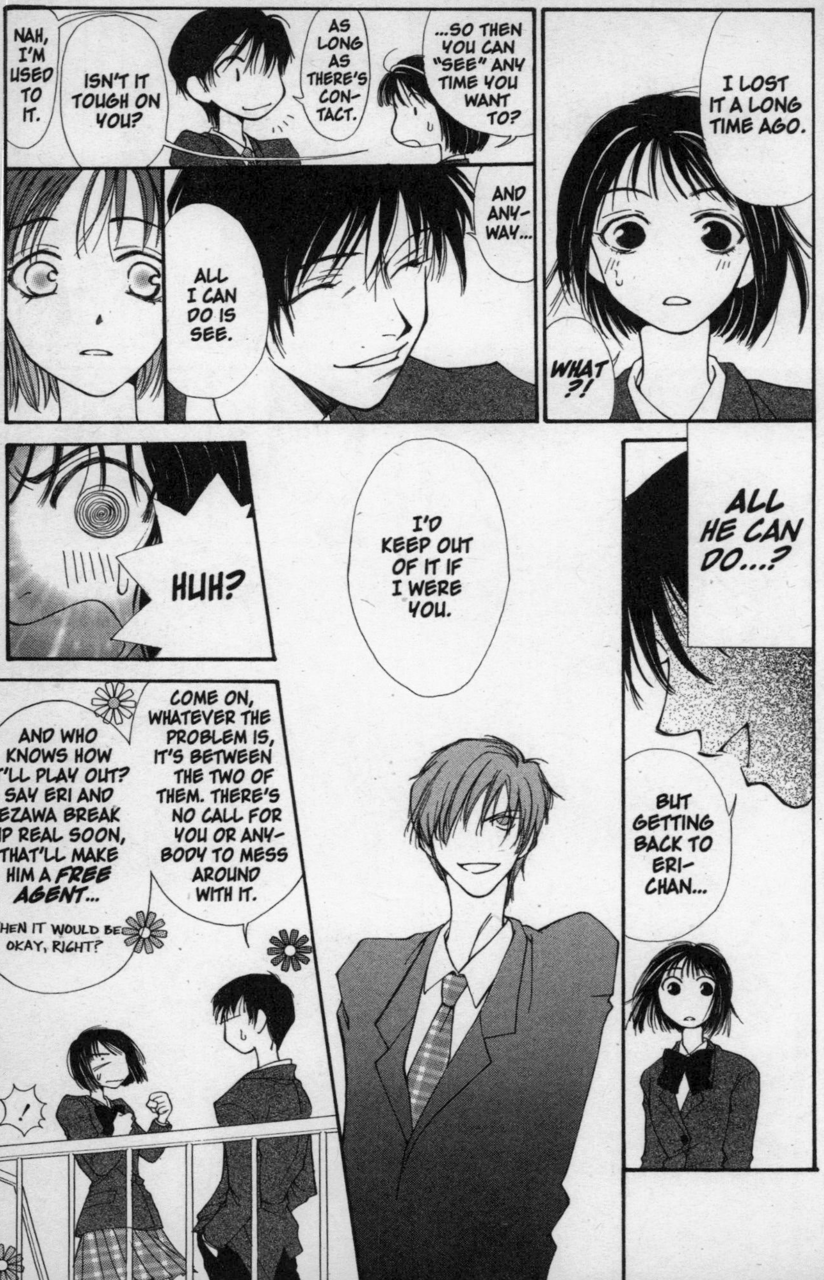
I LOST IT A LONG TIME AGO.
WHAT?!
...SO THEN YOU CAN "SEE" ANY TIME YOU WANT TO?
AS LONG AS THERE'S CONTACT.
ISN'T IT TOUGH ON YOU?
NAH, I'M USED TO IT.
AND ANYWAY...
ALL I CAN DO IS SEE.
ALL HE CAN DO...?
BUT GETTING BACK TO ERI-CHAN...
I'D KEEP OUT OF IT IF I WERE YOU.
HUH?
COME ON, WHATEVER THE PROBLEM IS, IT'S BETWEEN THE TWO OF THEM. THERE'S NO CALL FOR YOU OR ANYBODY TO MESS AROUND WITH IT.
AND WHO KNOWS HOW IT'LL PLAY OUT? SAY ERI AND EZAWA BREAK UP REAL SOON, THAT'LL MAKE HIM A *FREE AGENT*...
THEN IT WOULD BE OKAY, RIGHT?
!

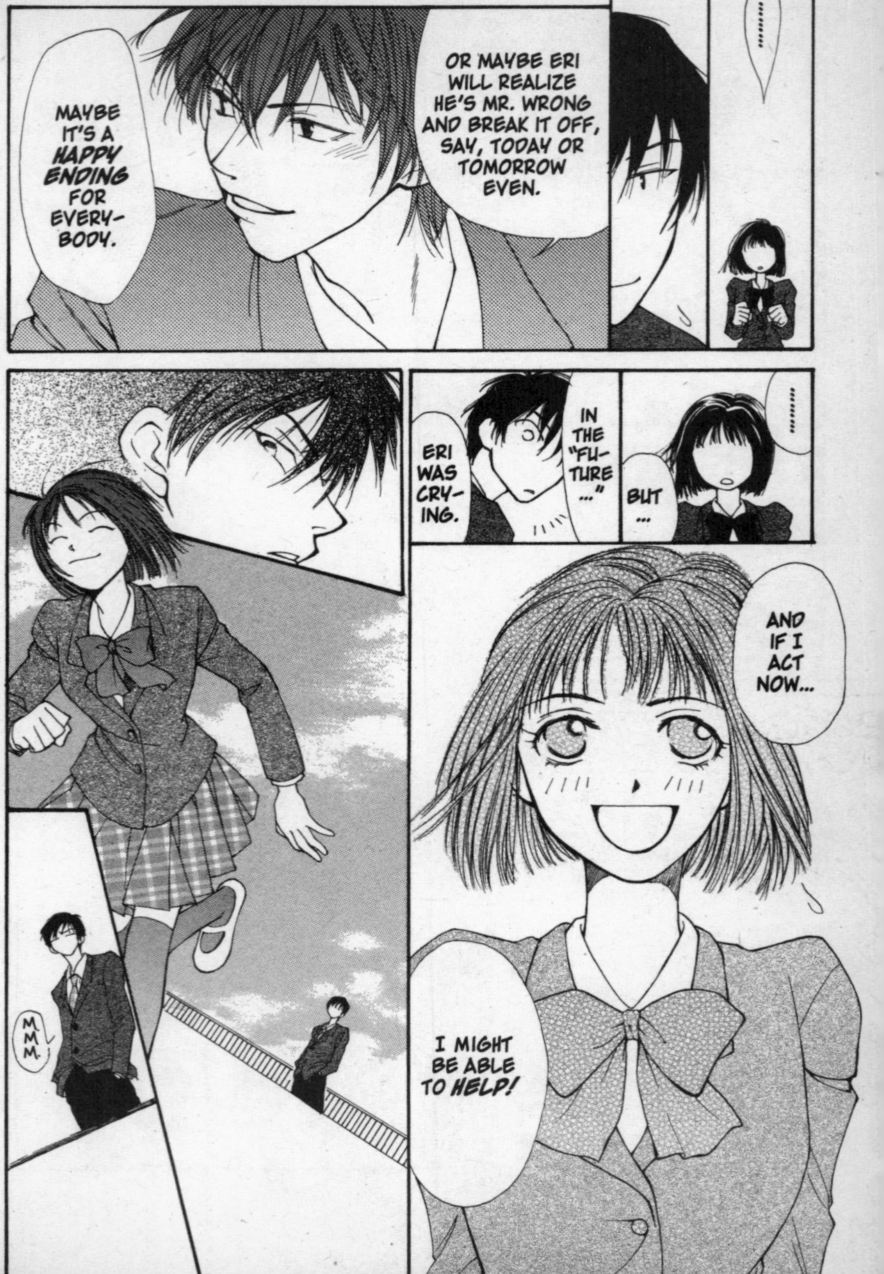
......
OR MAYBE ERI WILL REALIZE HE'S MR. WRONG AND BREAK IT OFF, SAY, TODAY OR TOMORROW EVEN.
MAYBE IT'S A ***HAPPY ENDING*** FOR EVERY-BODY.
......
BUT ...
IN THE "FU-TURE..."
ERI WAS CRY-ING.
AND IF I ACT NOW...
I MIGHT BE ABLE TO ***HELP!***
MMM.

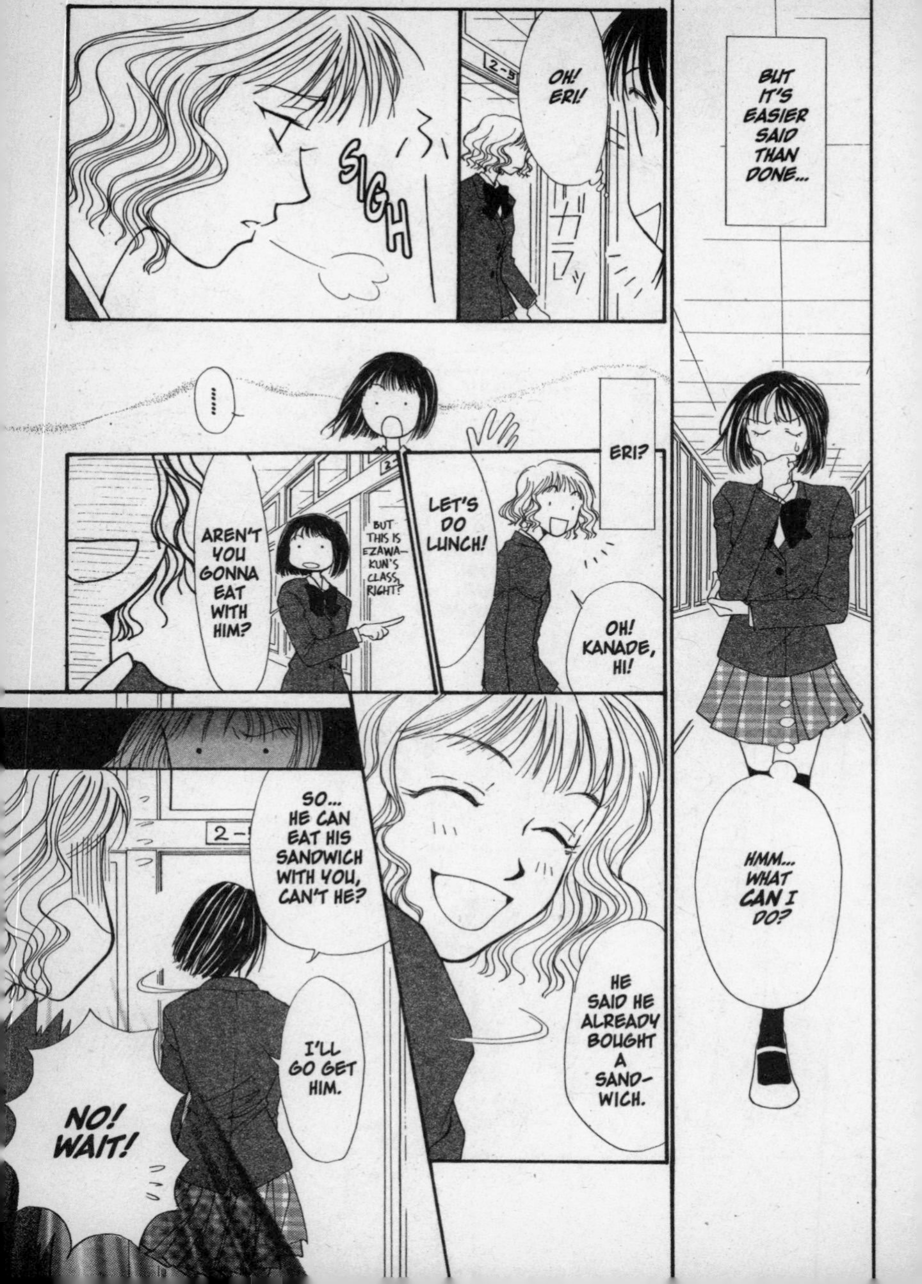
BUT IT'S EASIER SAID THAN DONE...
HMM... WHAT CAN I DO?
OH! ERI!
ガラッ
SIGH
......
ERI?
OH! KANADE, HI!
LET'S DO LUNCH!
BUT THIS IS EZAWA-KUN'S CLASS, RIGHT?
AREN'T YOU GONNA EAT WITH HIM?
HE SAID HE ALREADY BOUGHT A SANDWICH.
SO... HE CAN EAT HIS SANDWICH WITH YOU, CAN'T HE?
I'LL GO GET HIM.
NO! WAIT!

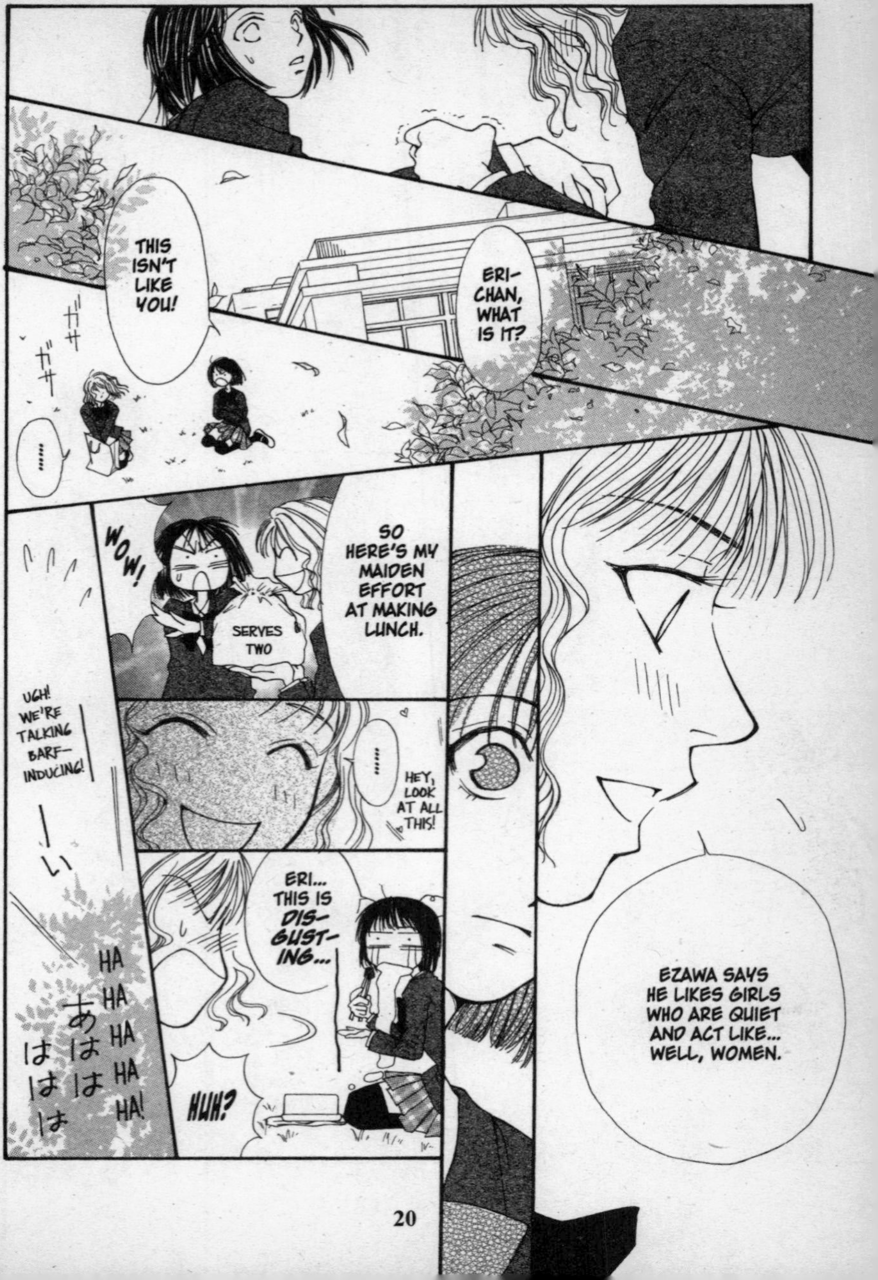
ERI-CHAN, WHAT IS IT?
THIS ISN'T LIKE YOU!
ガサ ガサ
……
EZAWA SAYS HE LIKES GIRLS WHO ARE QUIET AND ACT LIKE... WELL, WOMEN.
SO HERE'S MY MAIDEN EFFORT AT MAKING LUNCH.
SERVES TWO
WOW!
HEY, LOOK AT ALL THIS!
……
UGH! WE'RE TALKING BARF-INDUCING!
ーい
ERI... THIS IS DISGUSTING...
HUH?
HA HA HA HA HA!
あははは

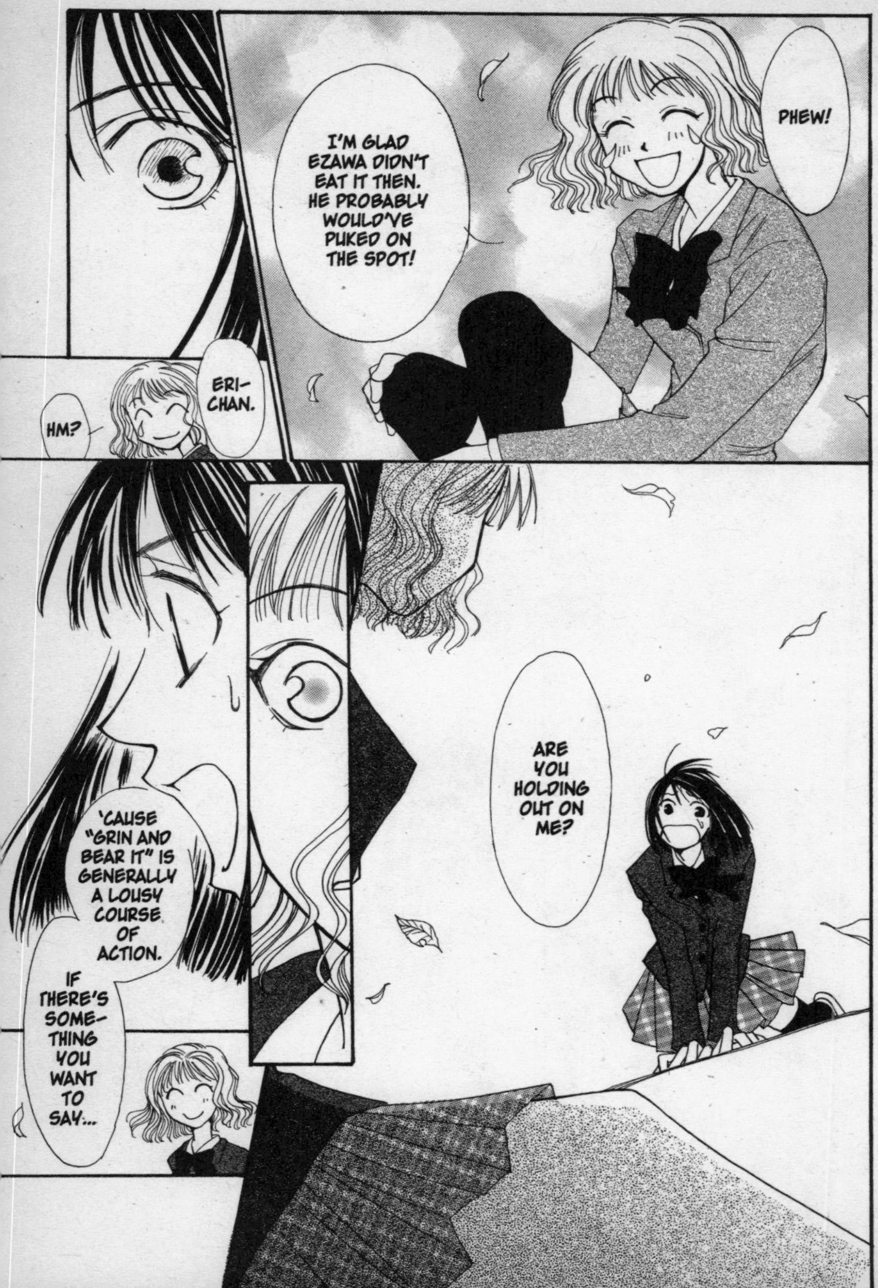
PHEW!
I'M GLAD EZAWA DIDN'T EAT IT THEN. HE PROBABLY WOULD'VE PUKED ON THE SPOT!
ERI-CHAN.
HM?
ARE YOU HOLDING OUT ON ME?
'CAUSE "GRIN AND BEAR IT" IS GENERALLY A LOUSY COURSE OF ACTION.
IF THERE'S SOME-THING YOU WANT TO SAY...

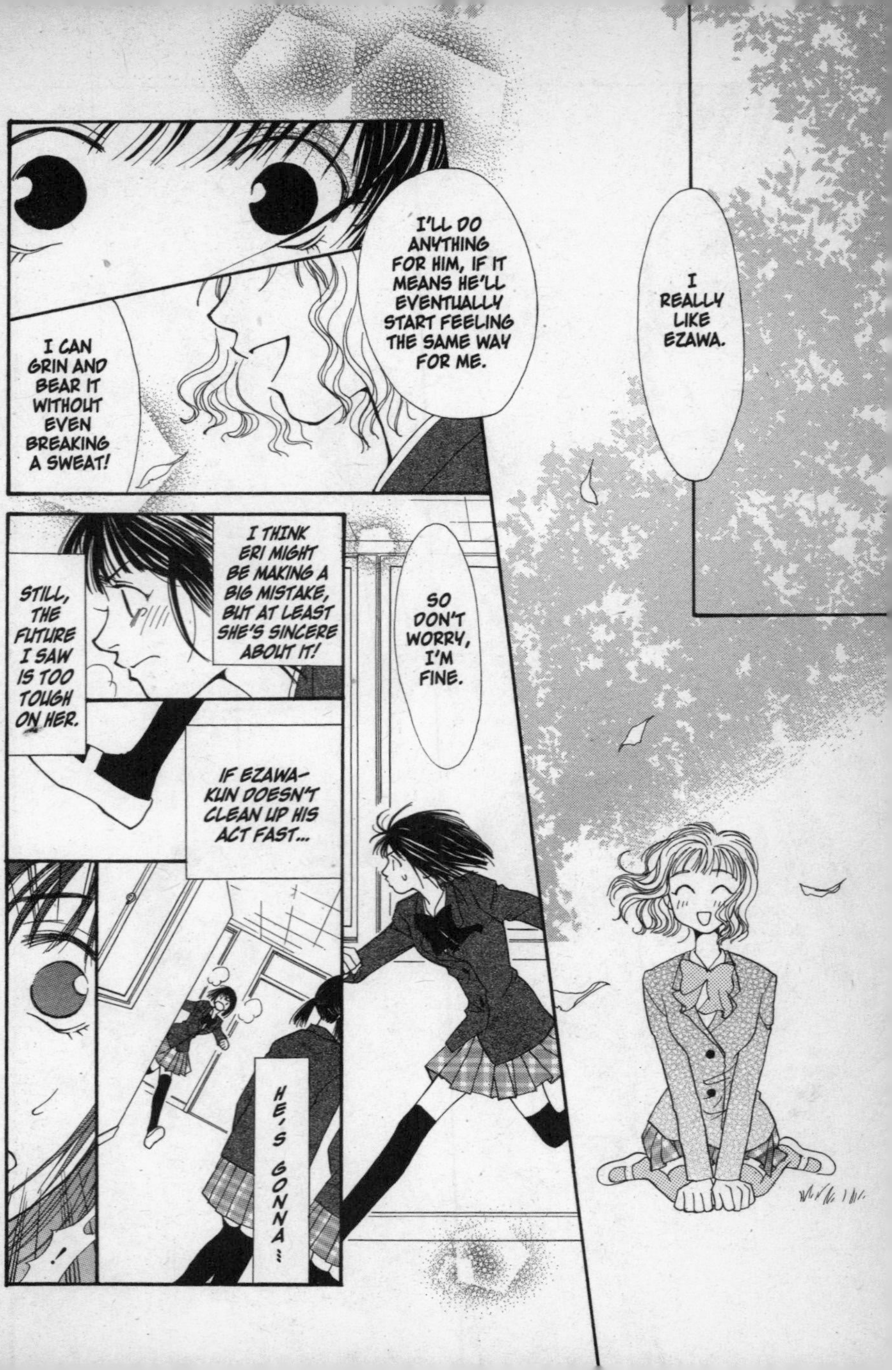
I REALLY LIKE EZAWA.
I'LL DO ANYTHING FOR HIM, IF IT MEANS HE'LL EVENTUALLY START FEELING THE SAME WAY FOR ME.
I CAN GRIN AND BEAR IT WITHOUT EVEN BREAKING A SWEAT!
SO DON'T WORRY, I'M FINE.
I THINK ERI MIGHT BE MAKING A BIG MISTAKE, BUT AT LEAST SHE'S SINCERE ABOUT IT!
STILL, THE FUTURE I SAW IS TOO TOUGH ON HER.
IF EZAWA-KUN DOESN'T CLEAN UP HIS ACT FAST...
HE'S GONNA..
!

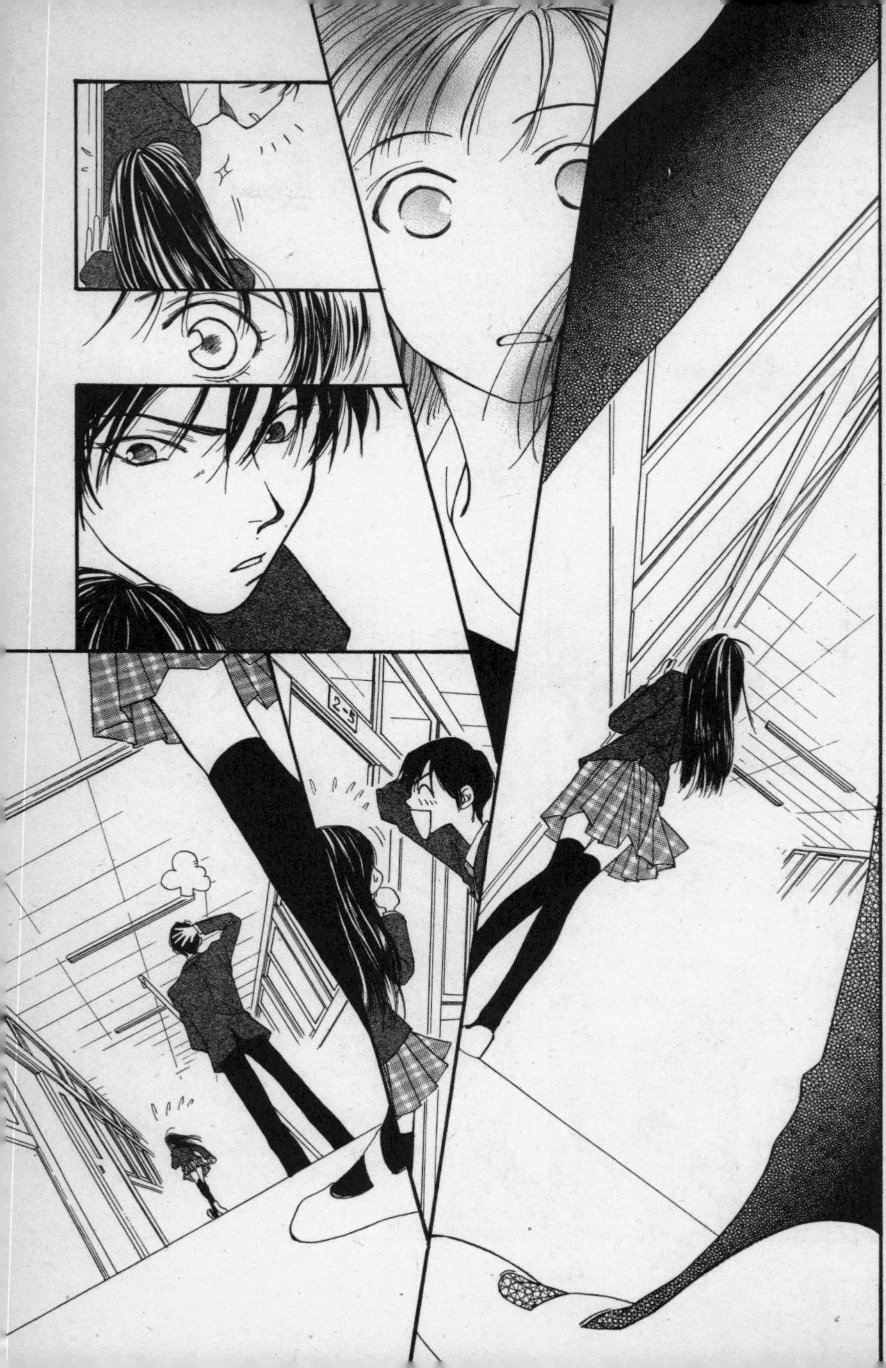
2-5

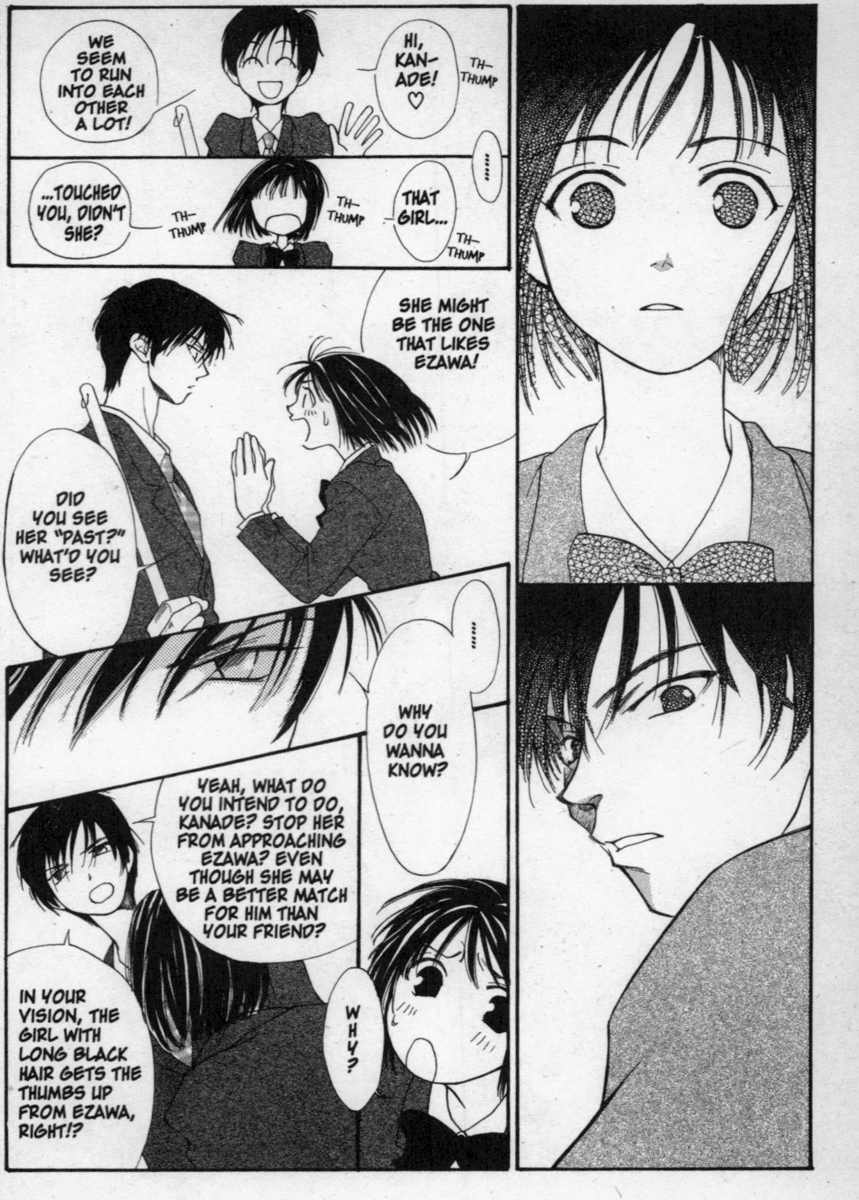
TH-THUMP
HI, KAN-ADE! ♡
WE SEEM TO RUN INTO EACH OTHER A LOT!
TH-THUMP
.....
THAT GIRL...
TH-THUMP
TH-THUMP
...TOUCHED YOU, DIDN'T SHE?
SHE MIGHT BE THE ONE THAT LIKES EZAWA!
DID YOU SEE HER "PAST?" WHAT'D YOU SEE?
.....
WHY DO YOU WANNA KNOW?
YEAH, WHAT DO YOU INTEND TO DO, KANADE? STOP HER FROM APPROACHING EZAWA? EVEN THOUGH SHE MAY BE A BETTER MATCH FOR HIM THAN YOUR FRIEND?
WHY?
IN YOUR VISION, THE GIRL WITH LONG BLACK HAIR GETS THE THUMBS UP FROM EZAWA, RIGHT!?

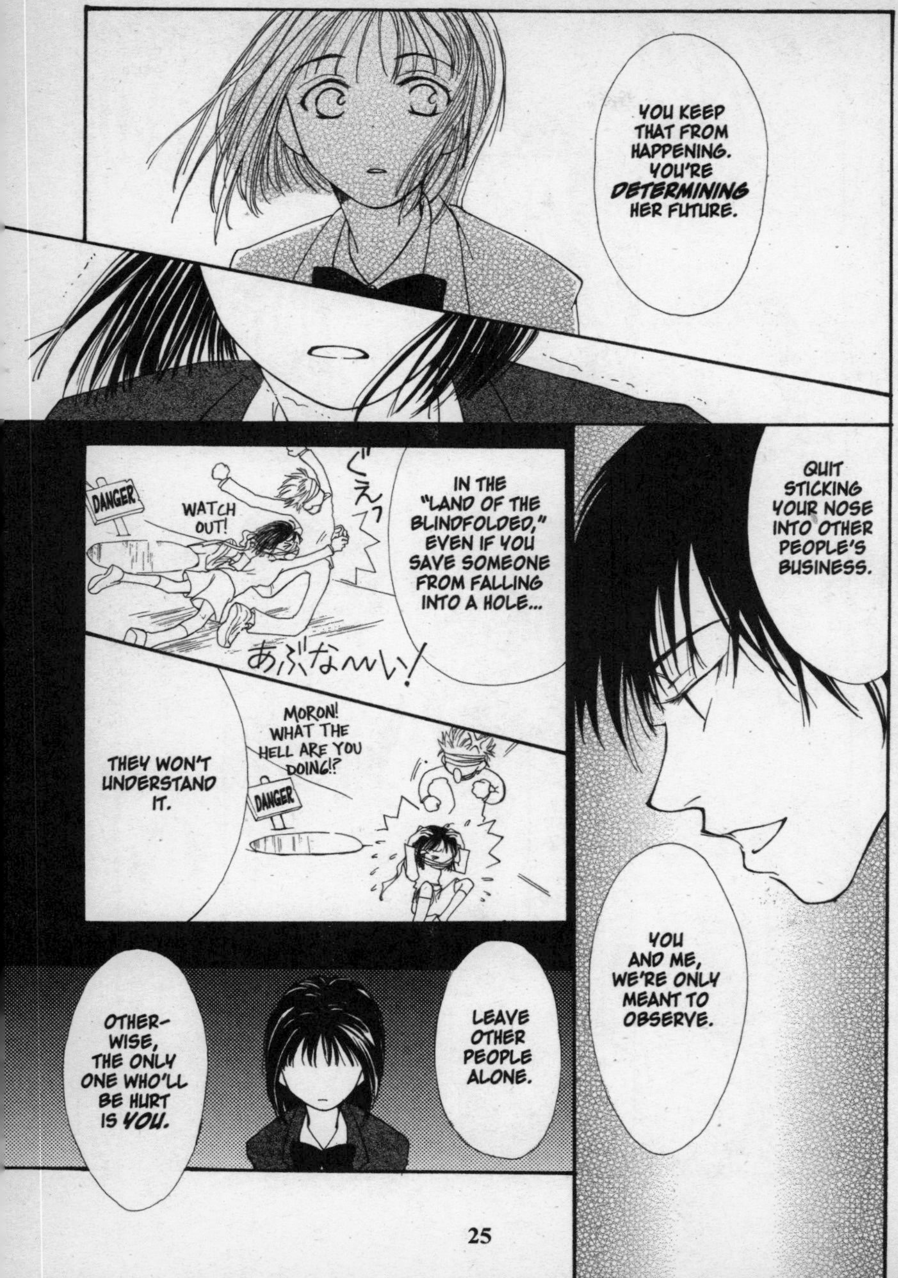

YOU KEEP THAT FROM HAPPENING. YOU'RE ***DETERMINING*** HER FUTURE.
QUIT STICKING YOUR NOSE INTO OTHER PEOPLE'S BUSINESS.
YOU AND ME, WE'RE ONLY MEANT TO OBSERVE.
IN THE "LAND OF THE BLINDFOLDED," EVEN IF YOU SAVE SOMEONE FROM FALLING INTO A HOLE...
ぐえっ
DANGER
WATCH OUT!
あぶな〜い!
MORON! WHAT THE HELL ARE YOU DOING!?
DANGER
THEY WON'T UNDERSTAND IT.
LEAVE OTHER PEOPLE ALONE.
OTHER-WISE, THE ONLY ONE WHO'LL BE HURT IS ***YOU.***

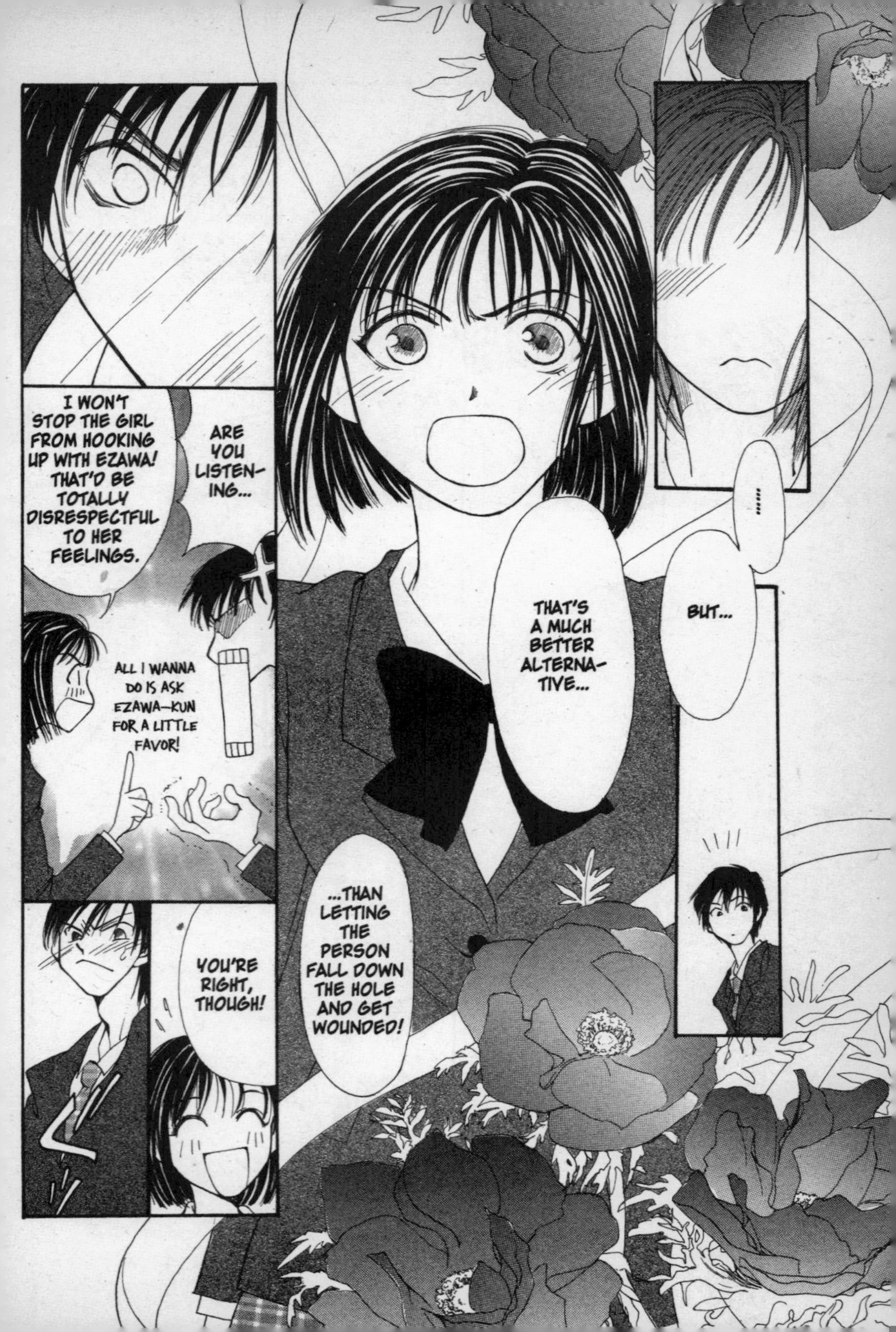
......
BUT...
THAT'S A MUCH BETTER ALTERNA-TIVE...
...THAN LETTING THE PERSON FALL DOWN THE HOLE AND GET WOUNDED!
ARE YOU LISTEN-ING...
I WON'T STOP THE GIRL FROM HOOKING UP WITH EZAWA! THAT'D BE TOTALLY DISRESPECTFUL TO HER FEELINGS.
ALL I WANNA DO IS ASK EZAWA-KUN FOR A LITTLE FAVOR!
YOU'RE RIGHT, THOUGH!

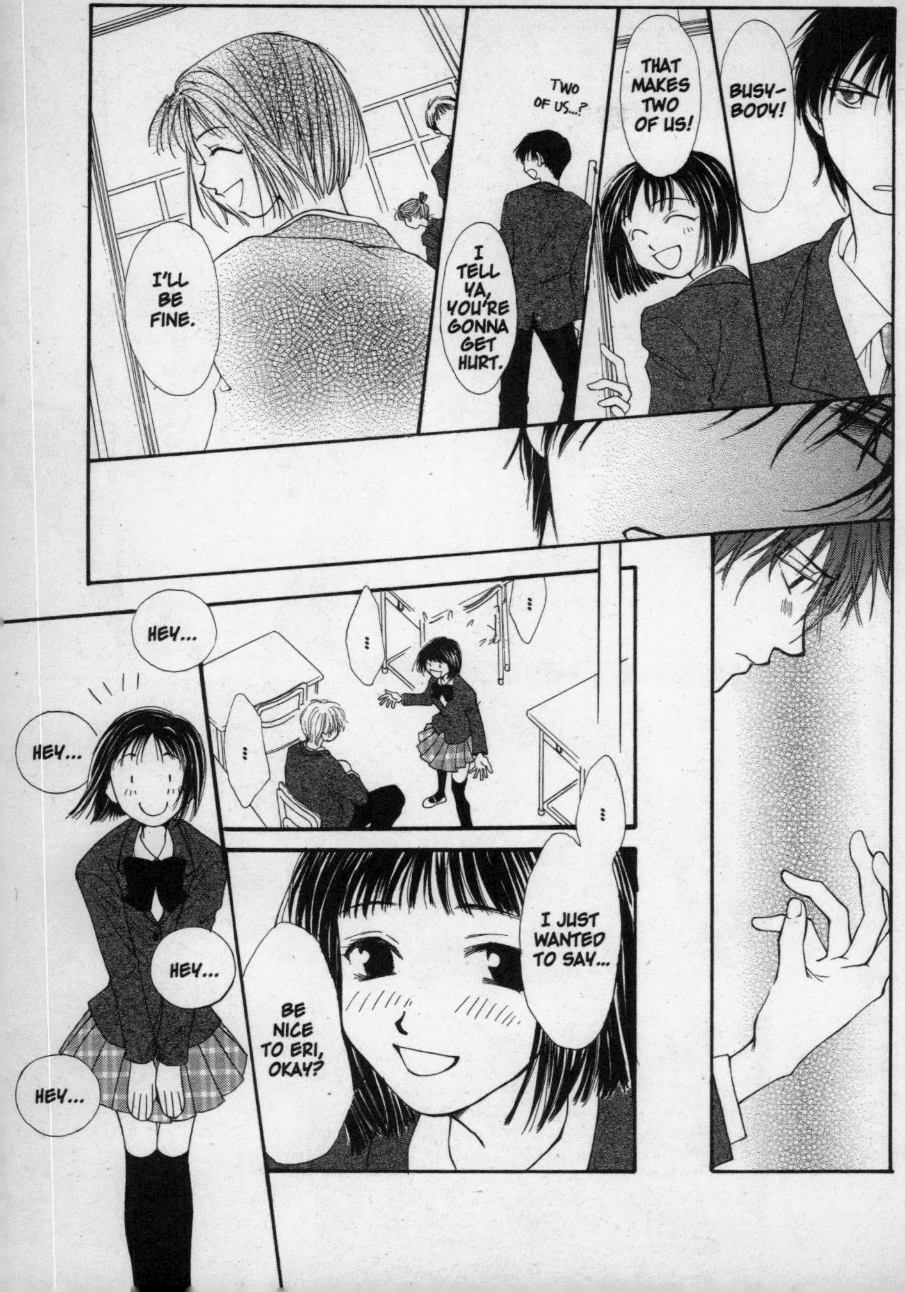
BUSY-BODY!
THAT MAKES TWO OF US!
TWO OF US...?
I TELL YA, YOU'RE GONNA GET HURT.
I'LL BE FINE.
...
...
...
HEY...
...
I JUST WANTED TO SAY...
BE NICE TO ERI, OKAY?
HEY...
HEY...
HEY...

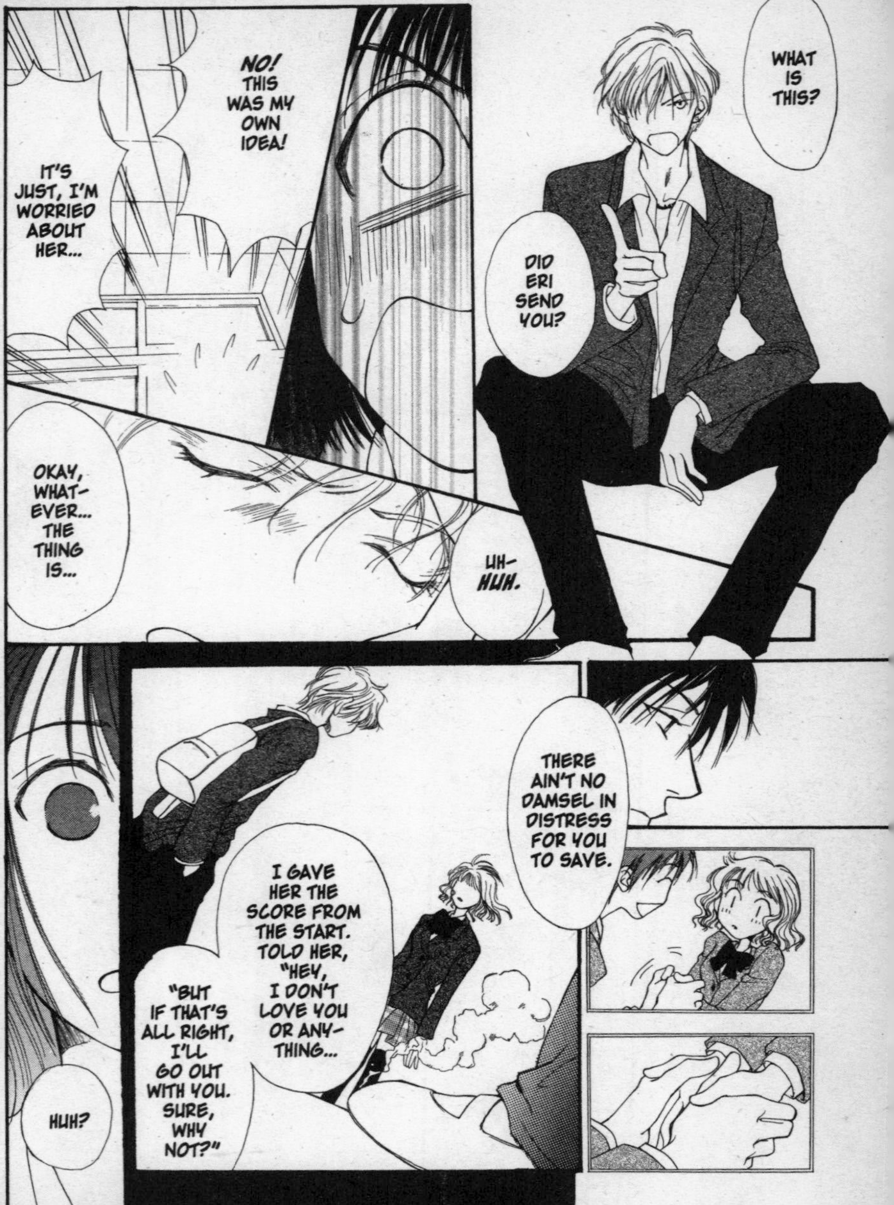
WHAT IS THIS?
DID ERI SEND YOU?
NO! THIS WAS MY OWN IDEA!
IT'S JUST, I'M WORRIED ABOUT HER...
UH-HUH.
OKAY, WHATEVER... THE THING IS...
THERE AIN'T NO DAMSEL IN DISTRESS FOR YOU TO SAVE.
I GAVE HER THE SCORE FROM THE START. TOLD HER, "HEY, I DON'T LOVE YOU OR ANYTHING...
"BUT IF THAT'S ALL RIGHT, I'LL GO OUT WITH YOU. SURE, WHY NOT?"
HUH?

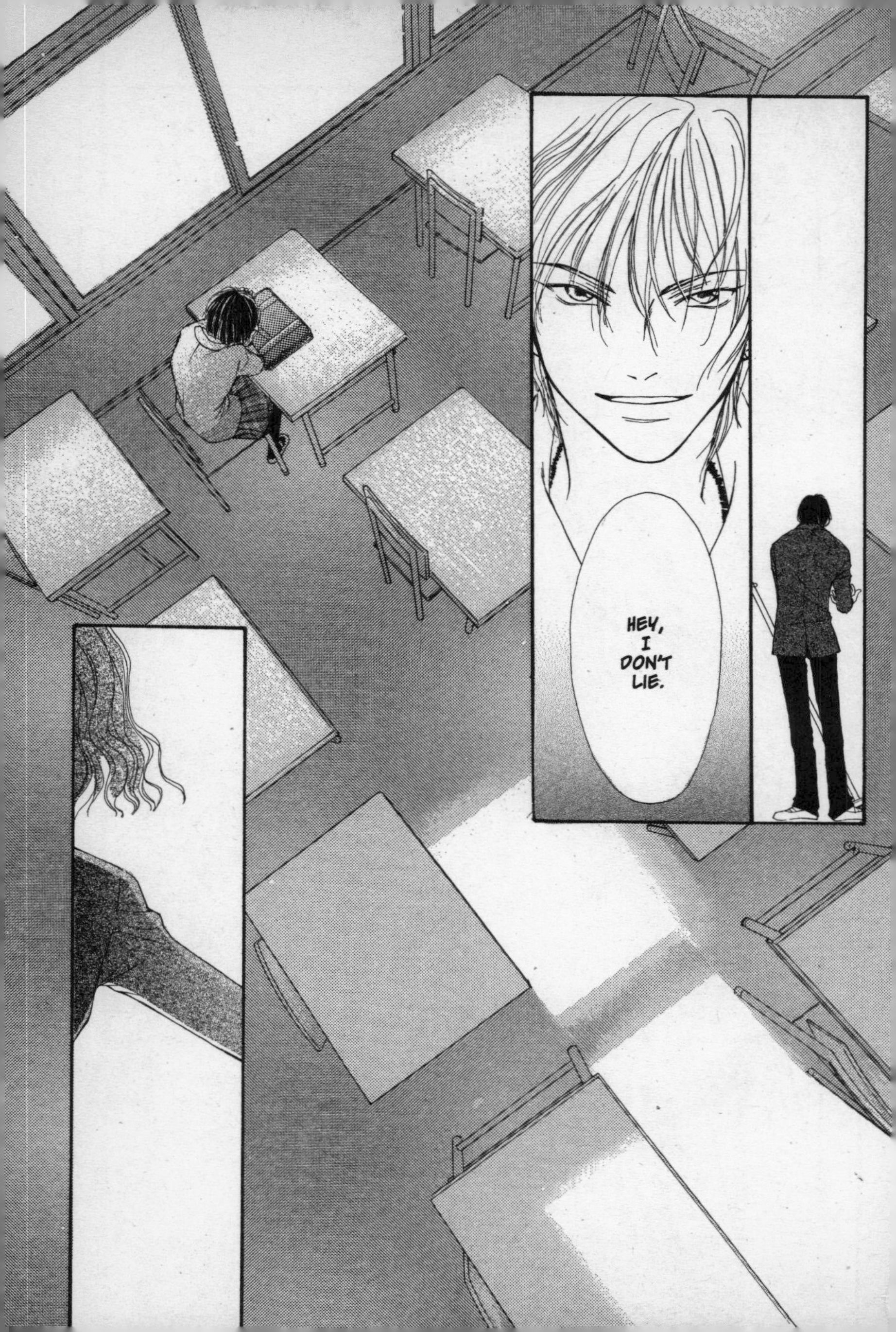
HEY, I DON'T LIE.

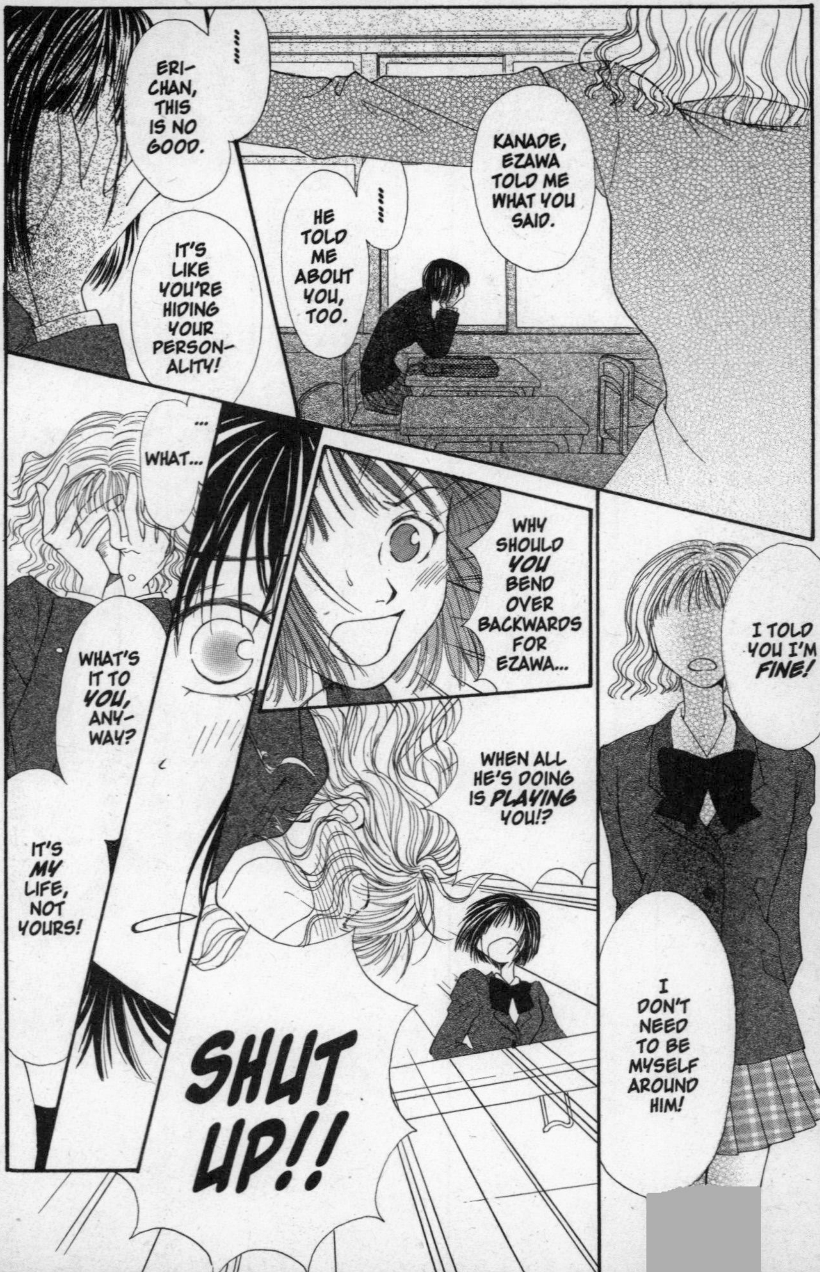

KANADE, EZAWA TOLD ME WHAT YOU SAID.
......
HE TOLD ME ABOUT YOU, TOO.
......
ERI-CHAN, THIS IS NO GOOD.
IT'S LIKE YOU'RE HIDING YOUR PERSON-ALITY!
I TOLD YOU I'M *FINE!*
I DON'T NEED TO BE MYSELF AROUND HIM!
WHY SHOULD *YOU* BEND OVER BACKWARDS FOR EZAWA...
WHEN ALL HE'S DOING IS *PLAYING* YOU!?
... WHAT...
WHAT'S IT TO *YOU,* ANY-WAY?
IT'S *MY* LIFE, NOT YOURS!
SHUT UP!!

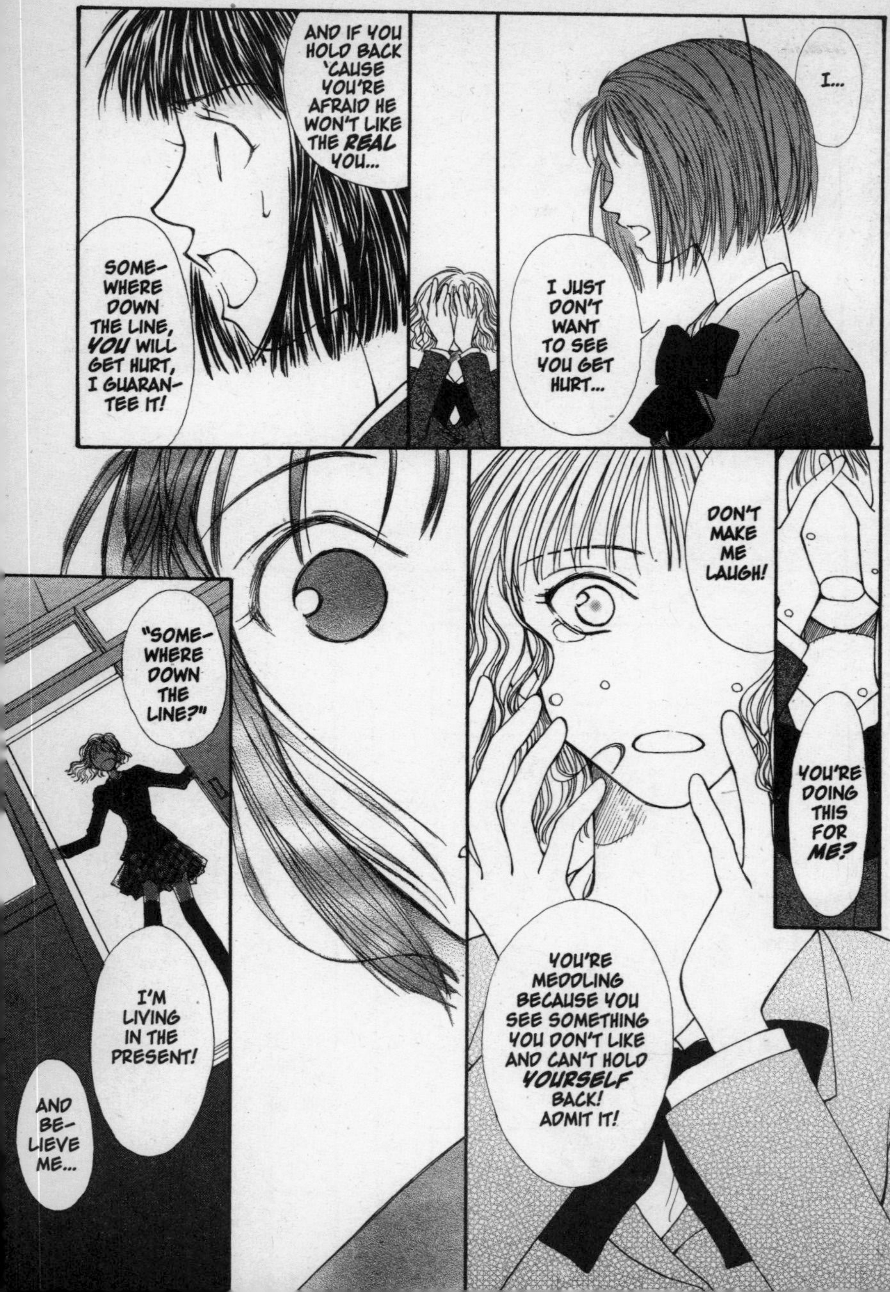
I...
I JUST DON'T WANT TO SEE YOU GET HURT...
AND IF YOU HOLD BACK 'CAUSE YOU'RE AFRAID HE WON'T LIKE THE *REAL* YOU...
SOMEWHERE DOWN THE LINE, *YOU* WILL GET HURT, I GUARANTEE IT!
DON'T MAKE ME LAUGH!
YOU'RE DOING THIS FOR *ME?*
YOU'RE MEDDLING BECAUSE YOU SEE SOMETHING YOU DON'T LIKE AND CAN'T HOLD *YOURSELF* BACK! ADMIT IT!
"SOMEWHERE DOWN THE LINE?"
I'M LIVING IN THE PRESENT!
AND BELIEVE ME...

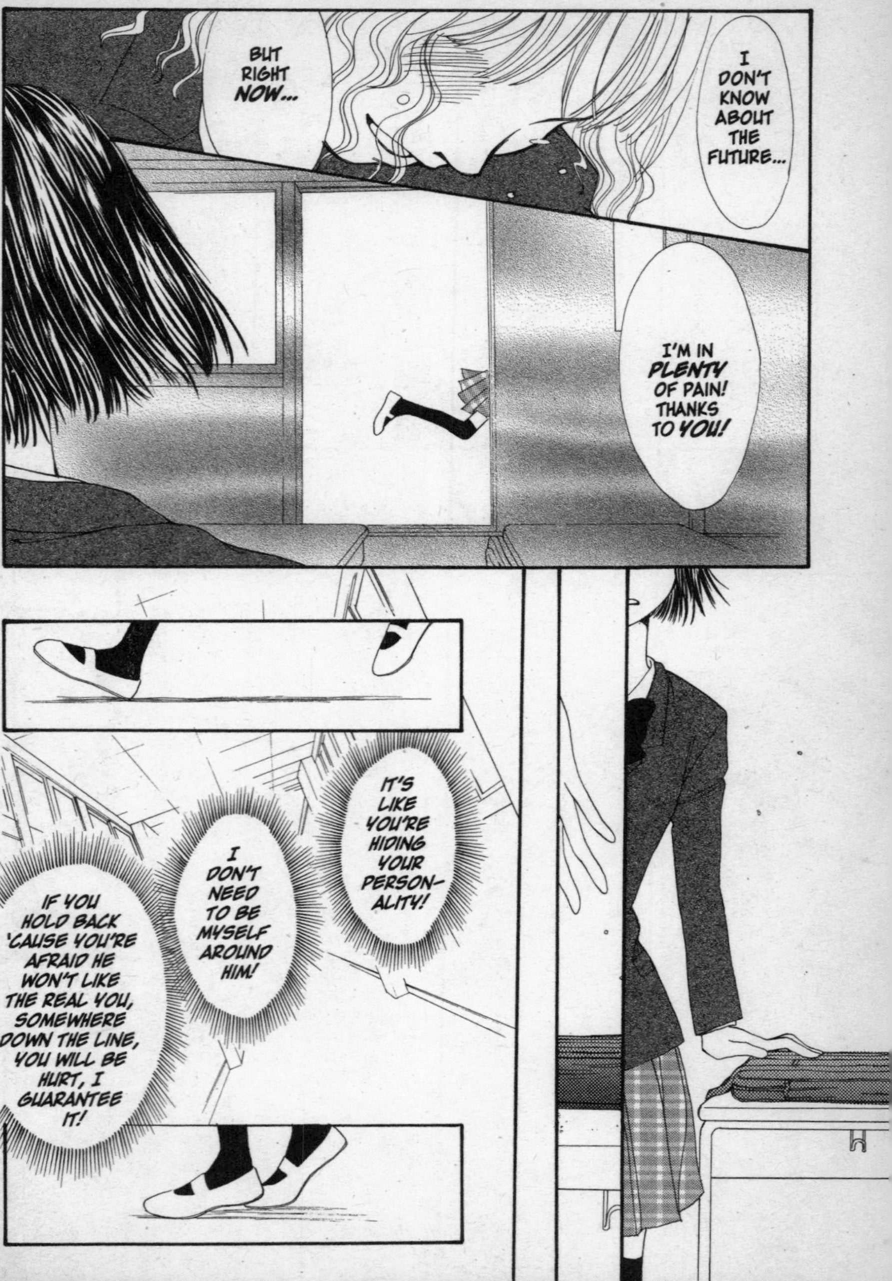

I DON'T KNOW ABOUT THE FUTURE...
BUT RIGHT NOW...
I'M IN PLENTY OF PAIN! THANKS TO YOU!
IT'S LIKE YOU'RE HIDING YOUR PERSON-ALITY!
I DON'T NEED TO BE MYSELF AROUND HIM!
IF YOU HOLD BACK 'CAUSE YOU'RE AFRAID HE WON'T LIKE THE REAL YOU, SOMEWHERE DOWN THE LINE, YOU WILL BE HURT, I GUARANTEE IT!

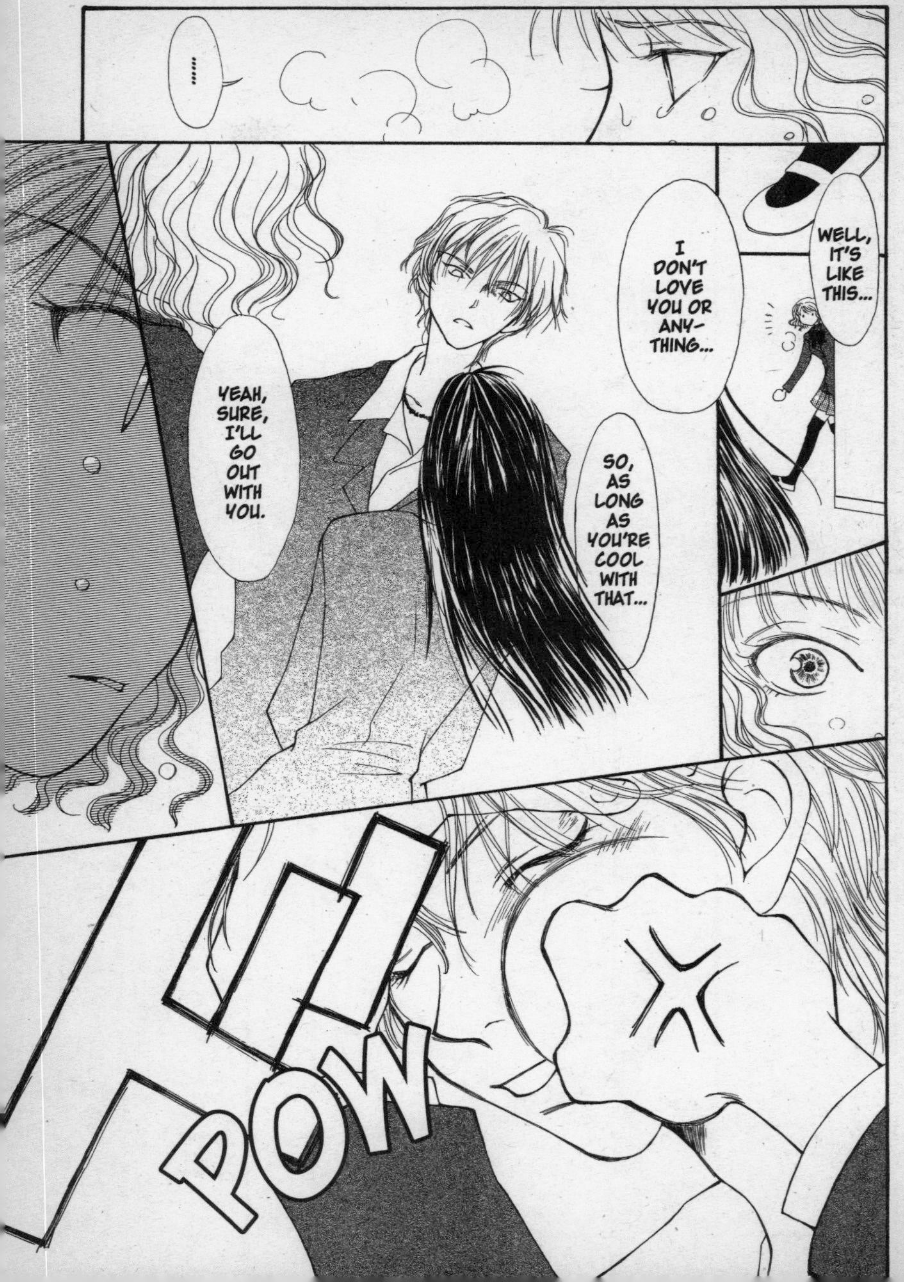
......
WELL, IT'S LIKE THIS...
I DON'T LOVE YOU OR ANYTHING...
SO, AS LONG AS YOU'RE COOL WITH THAT...
YEAH, SURE, I'LL GO OUT WITH YOU.
POW

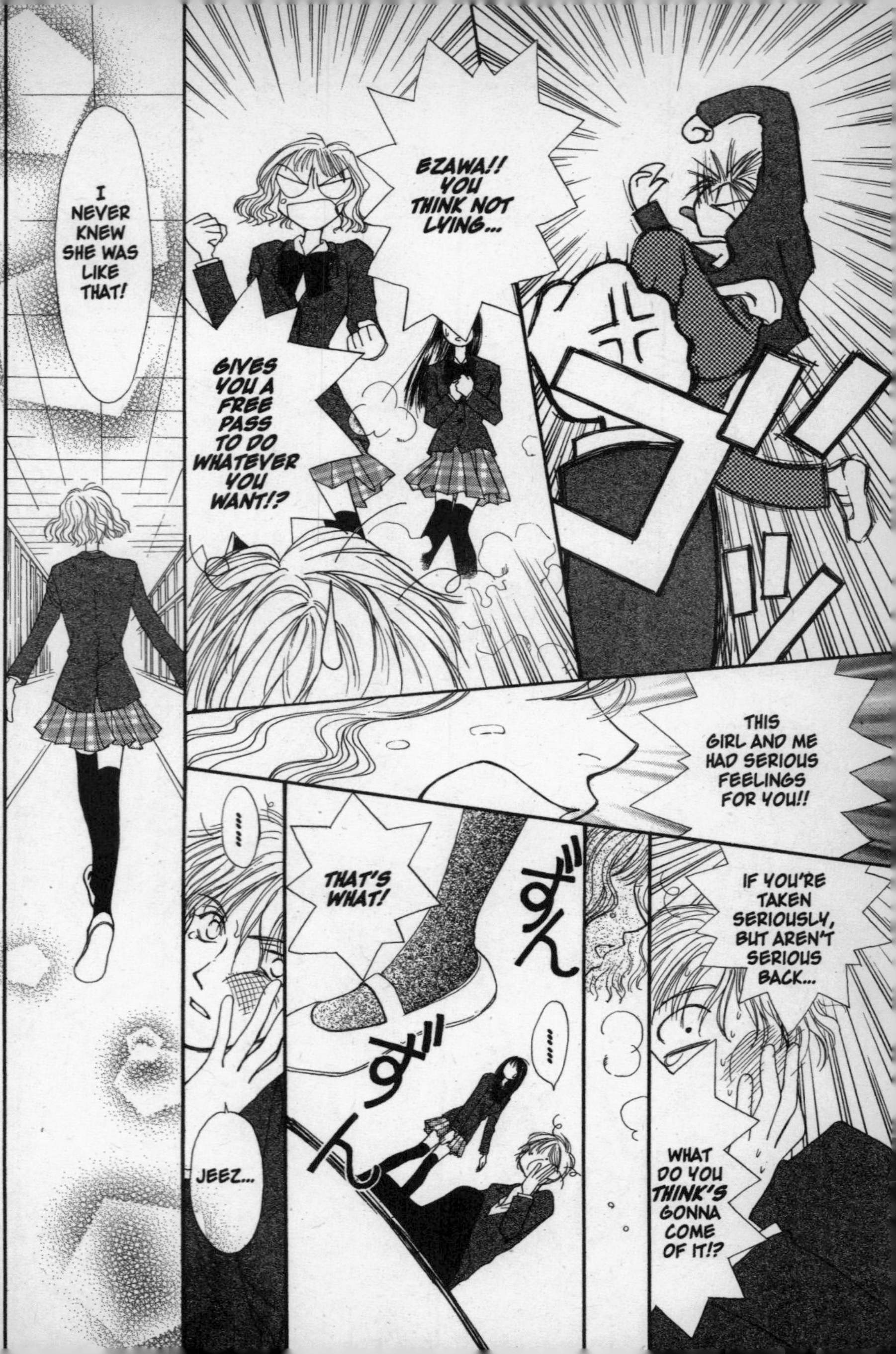
EZAWA!! YOU THINK NOT LYING...
GIVES YOU A FREE PASS TO DO WHATEVER YOU WANT!?
THIS GIRL AND ME HAD SERIOUS FEELINGS FOR YOU!!
IF YOU'RE TAKEN SERIOUSLY, BUT AREN'T SERIOUS BACK...
WHAT DO YOU THINK'S GONNA COME OF IT!?
THAT'S WHAT!
ずん
ずん
.....
.....
JEEZ...
I NEVER KNEW SHE WAS LIKE THAT!

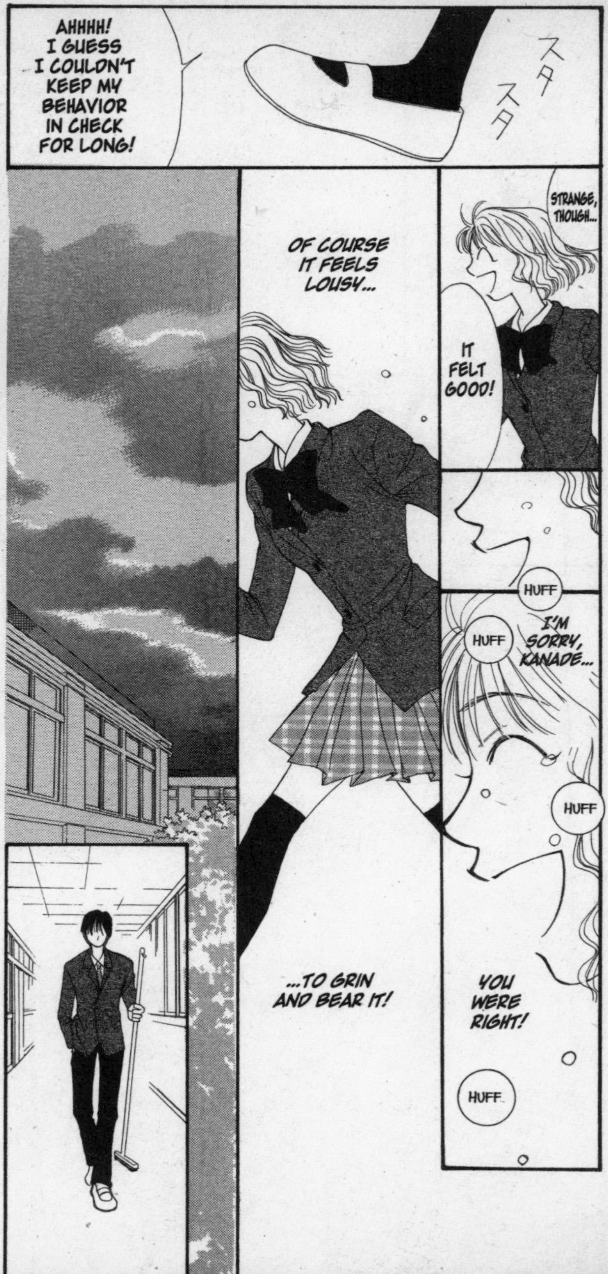
スタスタ
AHHHH! I GUESS I COULDN'T KEEP MY BEHAVIOR IN CHECK FOR LONG!
STRANGE, THOUGH...
IT FELT GOOD!
HUFF
HUFF
I'M SORRY, KANADE...
HUFF
YOU WERE RIGHT!
HUFF
OF COURSE IT FEELS LOUSY...
...TO GRIN AND BEAR IT!

Sakura Mail

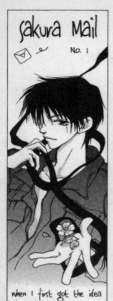

No. 1

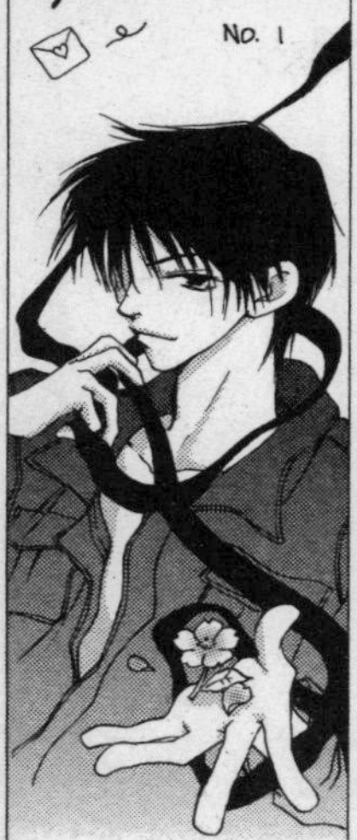

When I first got the idea for this story, Arou and Kanade's powers were reversed. (Kanade could see the past while Arou could see the future.) Not only that, the main setting and their ages were completely different. Then, as I began to twist and contort the story, the characters' personalities changed little by little, until finally, I started to fall in love with them. I had a blast drawing the story, which was originally intended to be a one-shot deal, but unexpectedly, I was encouraged and allowed to continue. And so continue I did, which accounts for this trade paperback.

(Which was only made possible by all of you! Thank youuuuu!)

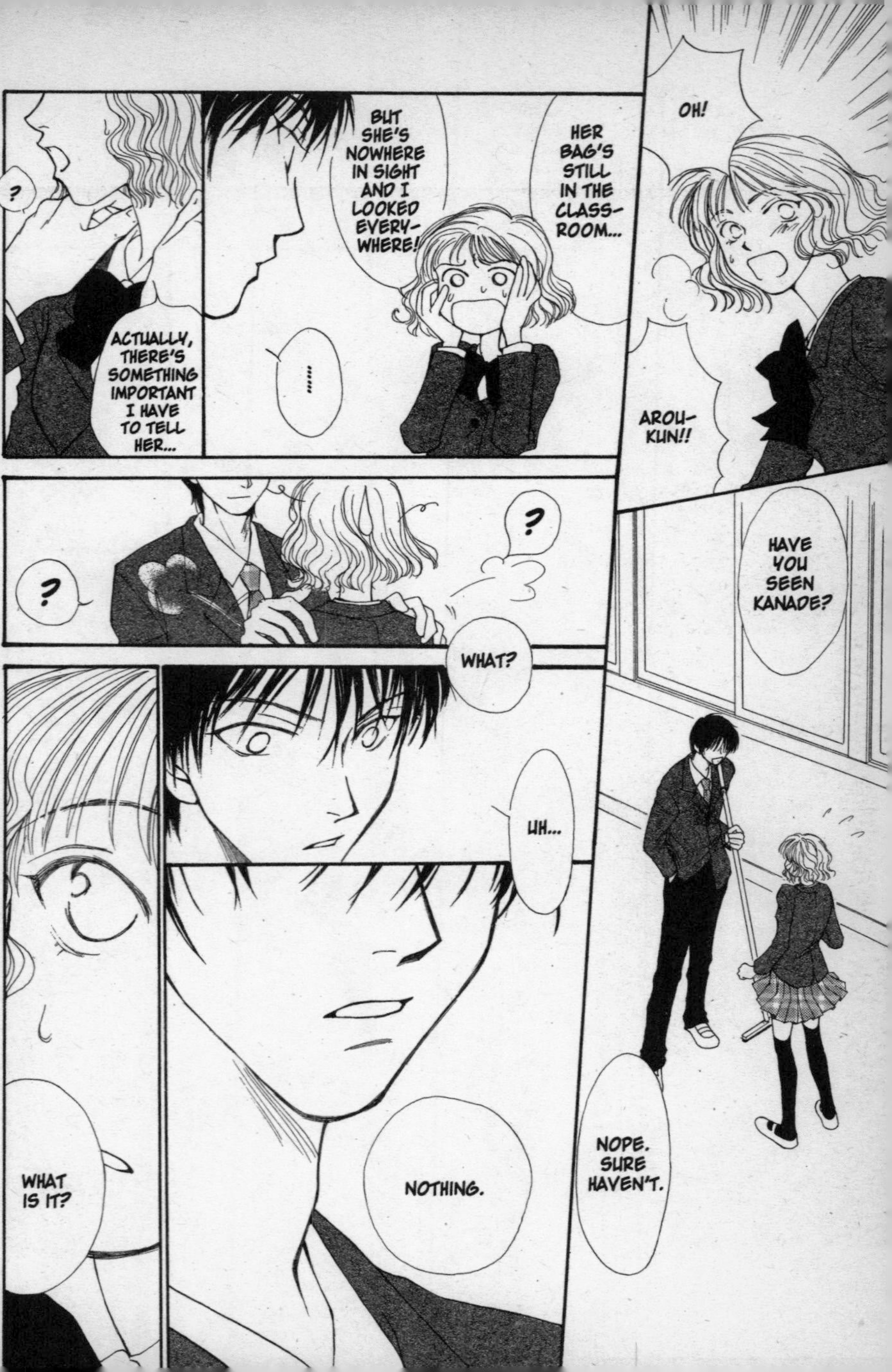
OH!
AROU-KUN!!
HAVE YOU SEEN KANADE?
NOPE. SURE HAVEN'T.
HER BAG'S STILL IN THE CLASSROOM...
BUT SHE'S NOWHERE IN SIGHT AND I LOOKED EVERYWHERE!
......
ACTUALLY, THERE'S SOMETHING IMPORTANT I HAVE TO TELL HER...
?
?
?
WHAT?
UH...
NOTHING.
WHAT IS IT?

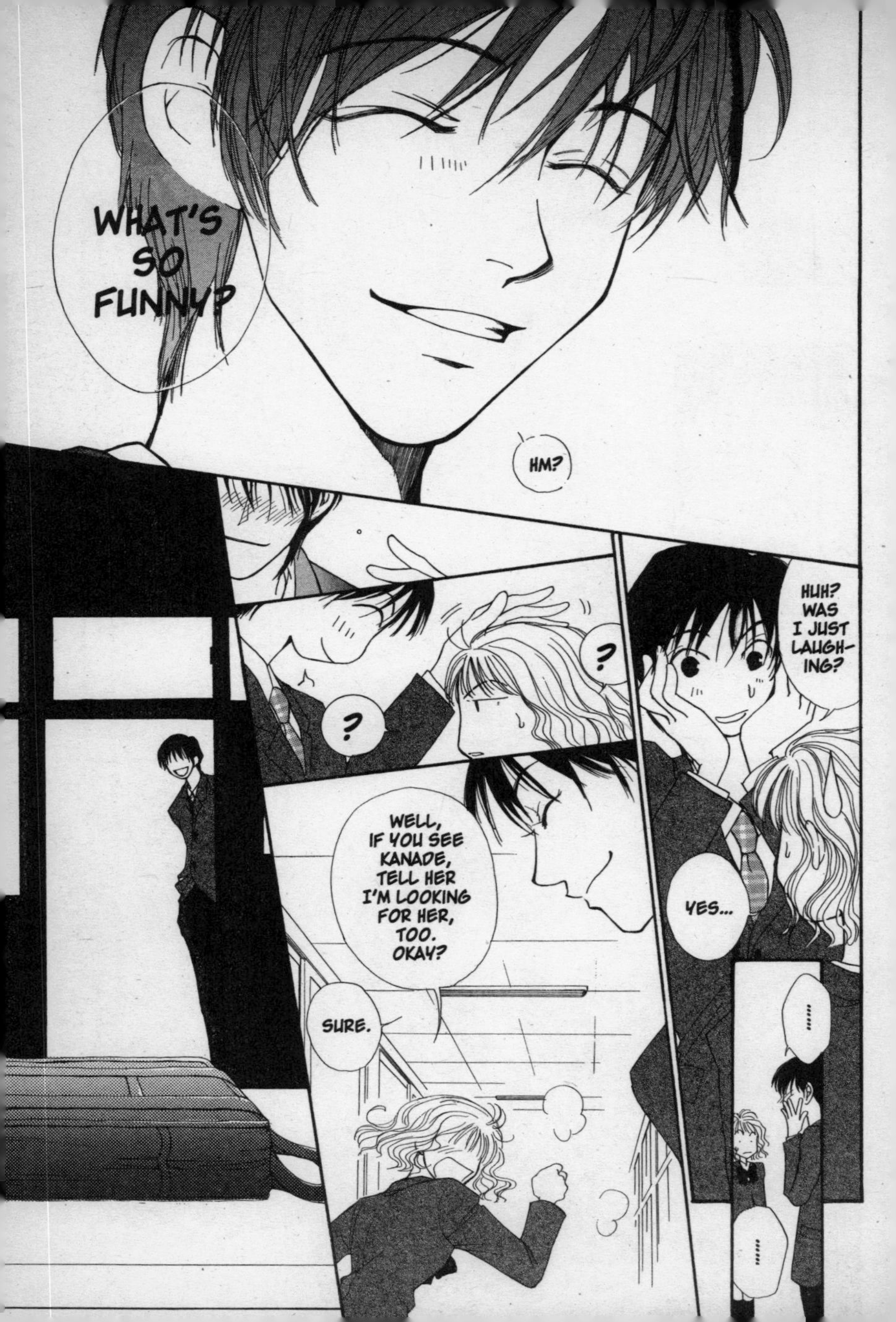
WHAT'S SO FUNNY?
HM?
HUH? WAS I JUST LAUGH-ING?
?
?
WELL, IF YOU SEE KANADE, TELL HER I'M LOOKING FOR HER, TOO. OKAY?
YES...
SURE.
......
......

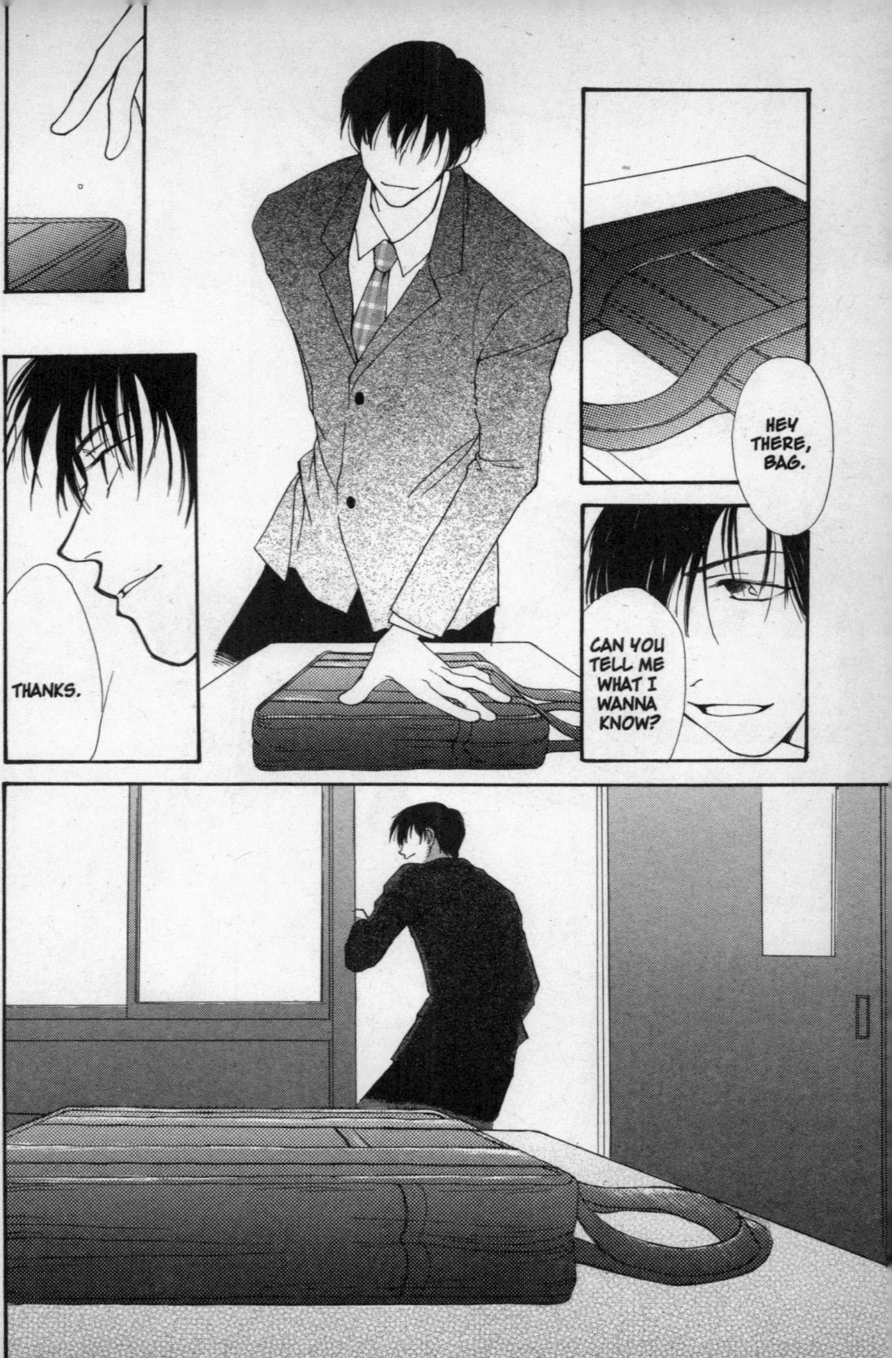
HEY THERE, BAG.
CAN YOU TELL ME WHAT I WANNA KNOW?
THANKS.

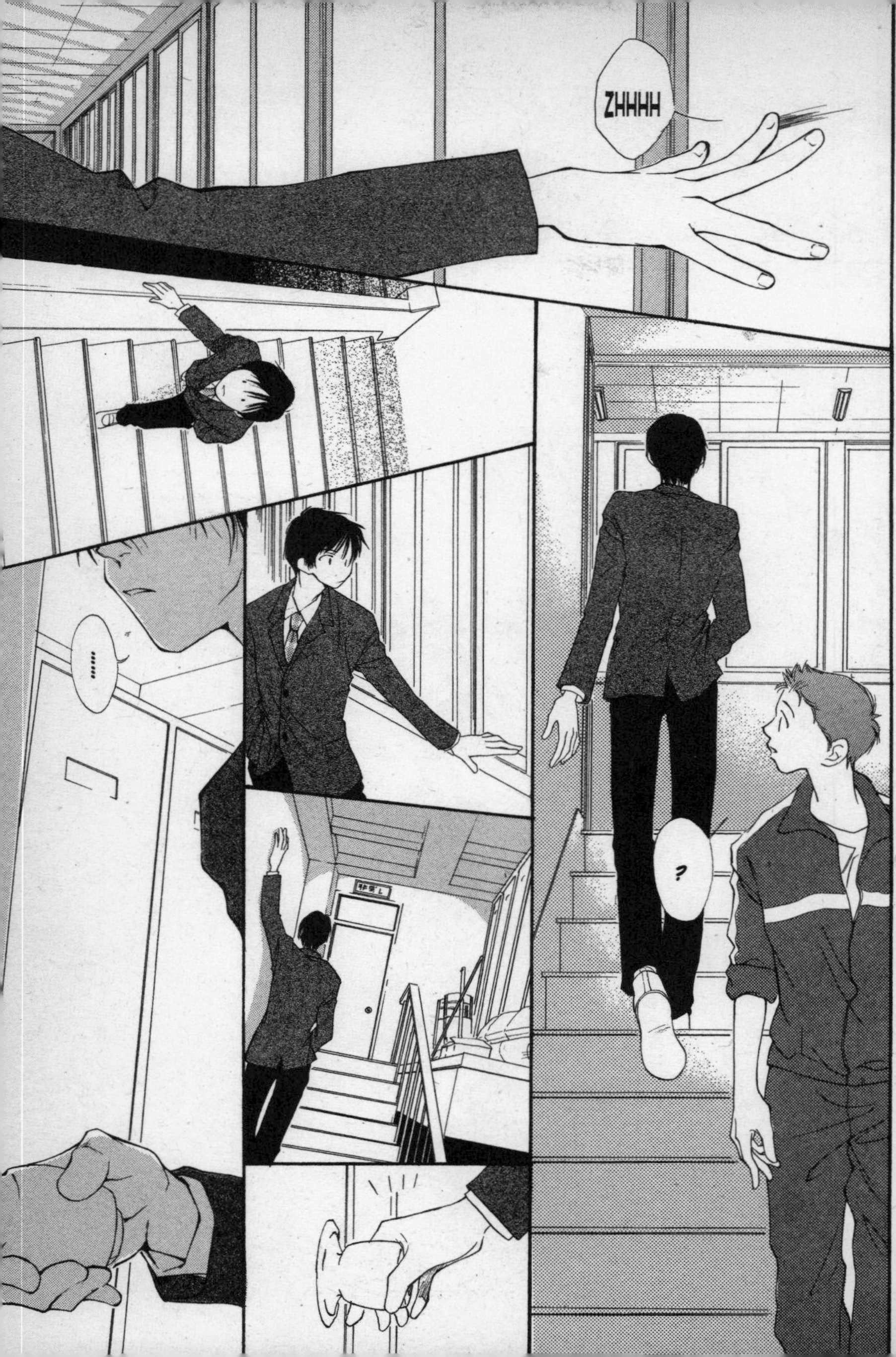
ZHHHH
......
?

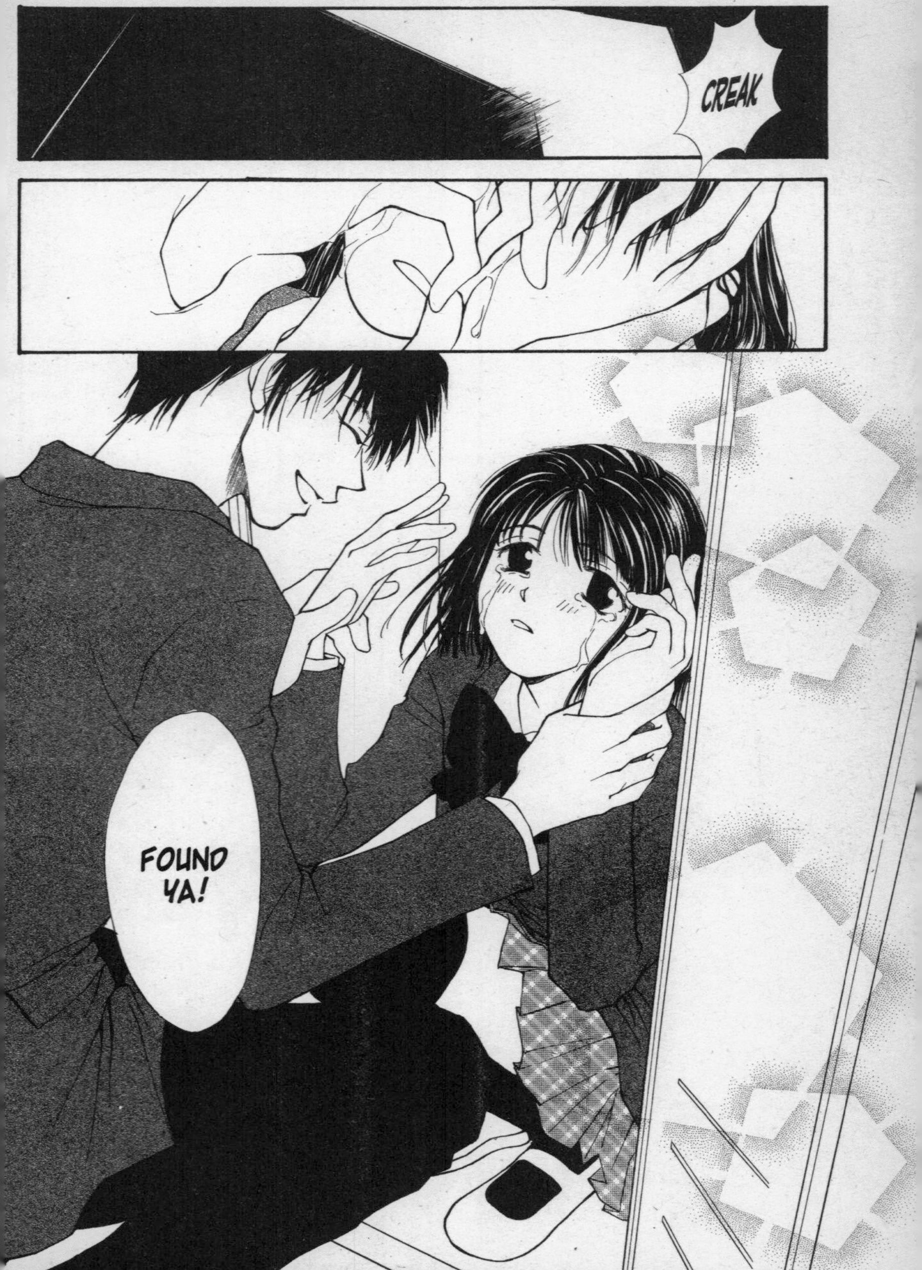
CREAK
FOUND YA!

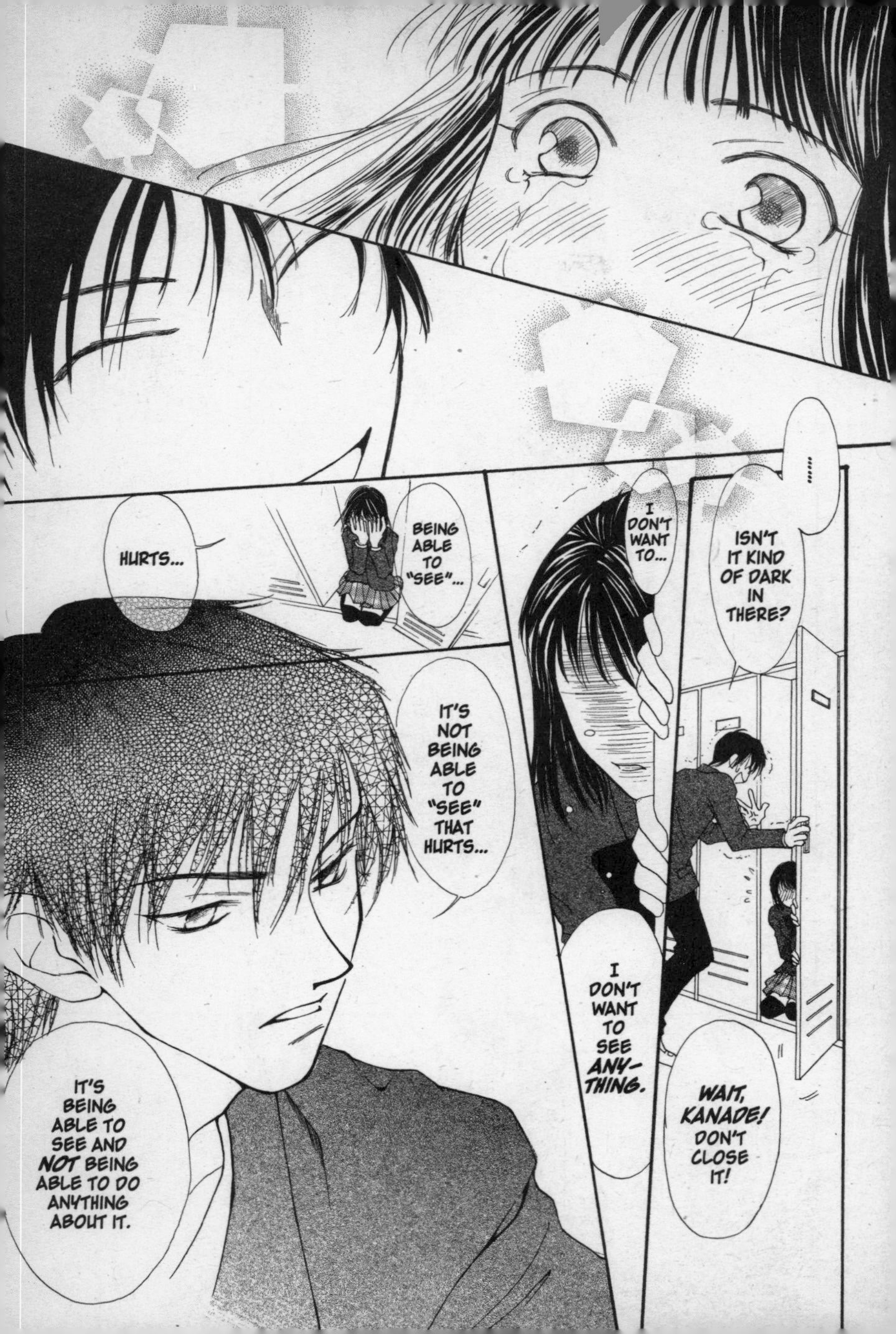
......
ISN'T IT KIND OF DARK IN THERE?
WAIT, KANADE! DON'T CLOSE IT!
I DON'T WANT TO...
I DON'T WANT TO SEE ANYTHING.
BEING ABLE TO "SEE"...
HURTS...
IT'S NOT BEING ABLE TO "SEE" THAT HURTS...
IT'S BEING ABLE TO SEE AND NOT BEING ABLE TO DO ANYTHING ABOUT IT.

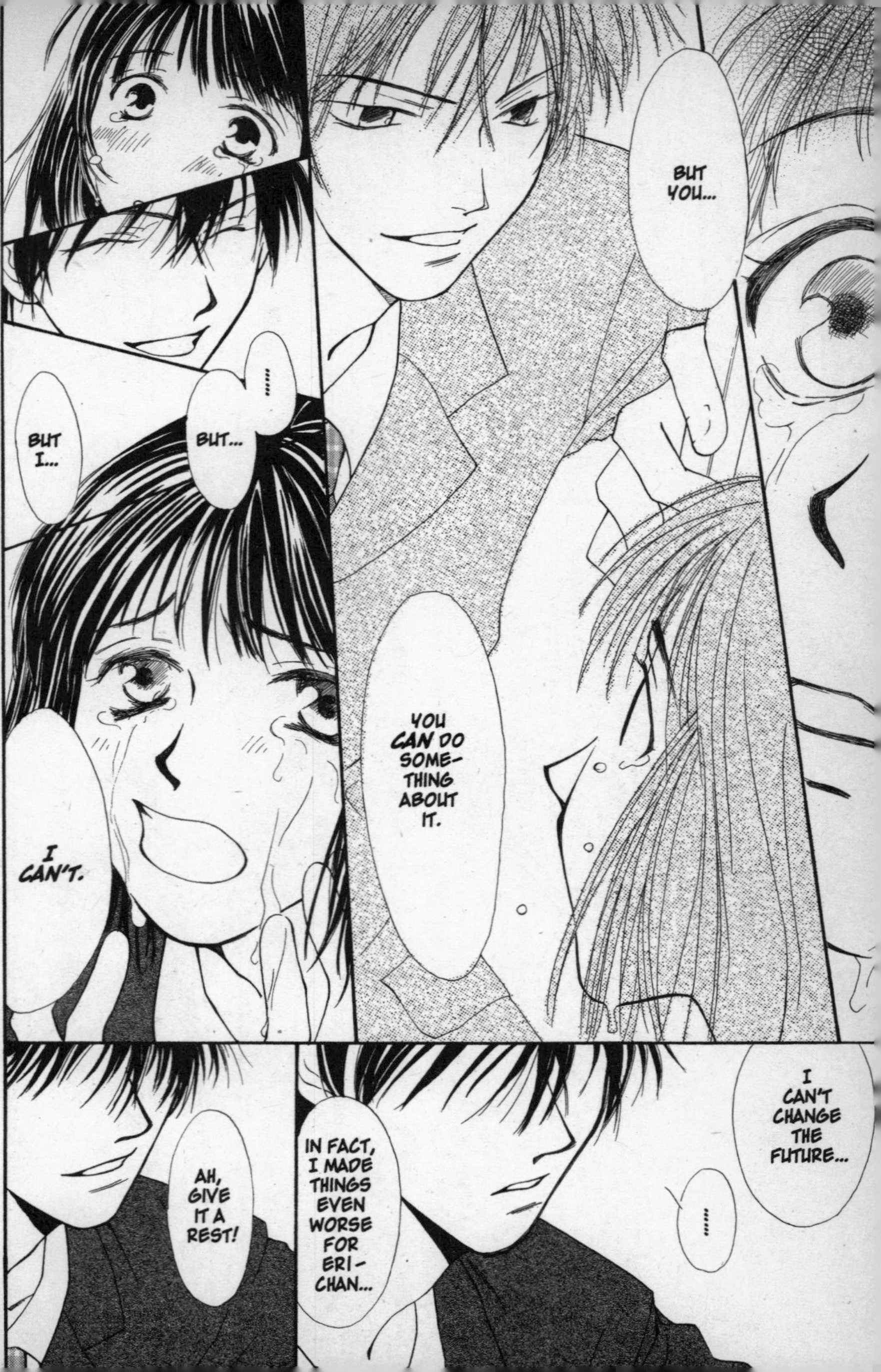
BUT YOU...
YOU CAN DO SOME-THING ABOUT IT.
...
BUT...
BUT I...
I CAN'T.
I CAN'T CHANGE THE FUTURE...
...
IN FACT, I MADE THINGS EVEN WORSE FOR ERI-CHAN...
AH, GIVE IT A REST!

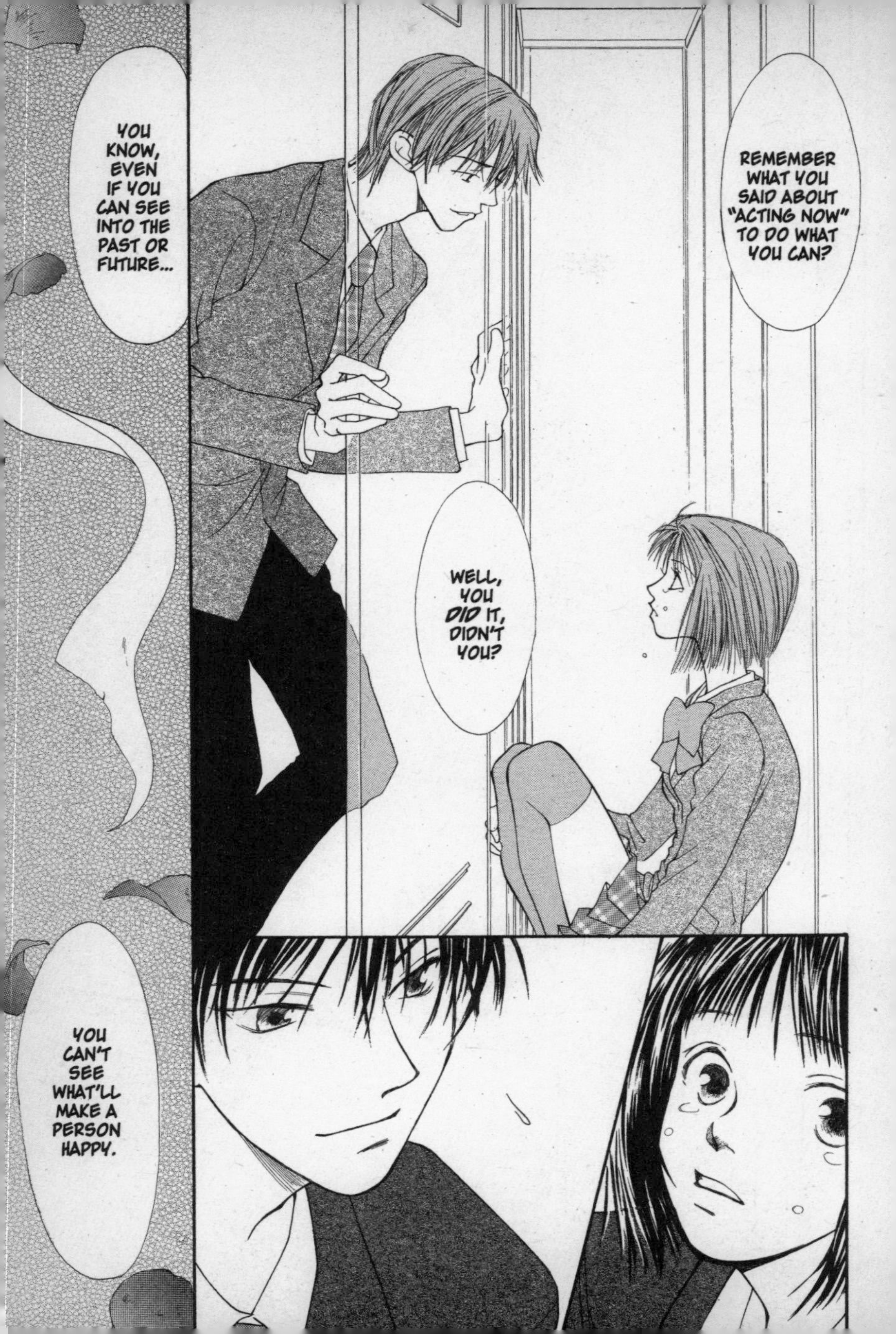
REMEMBER WHAT YOU SAID ABOUT "ACTING NOW" TO DO WHAT YOU CAN?
WELL, YOU *DID* IT, DIDN'T YOU?
YOU KNOW, EVEN IF YOU CAN SEE INTO THE PAST OR FUTURE...
YOU CAN'T SEE WHAT'LL MAKE A PERSON HAPPY.

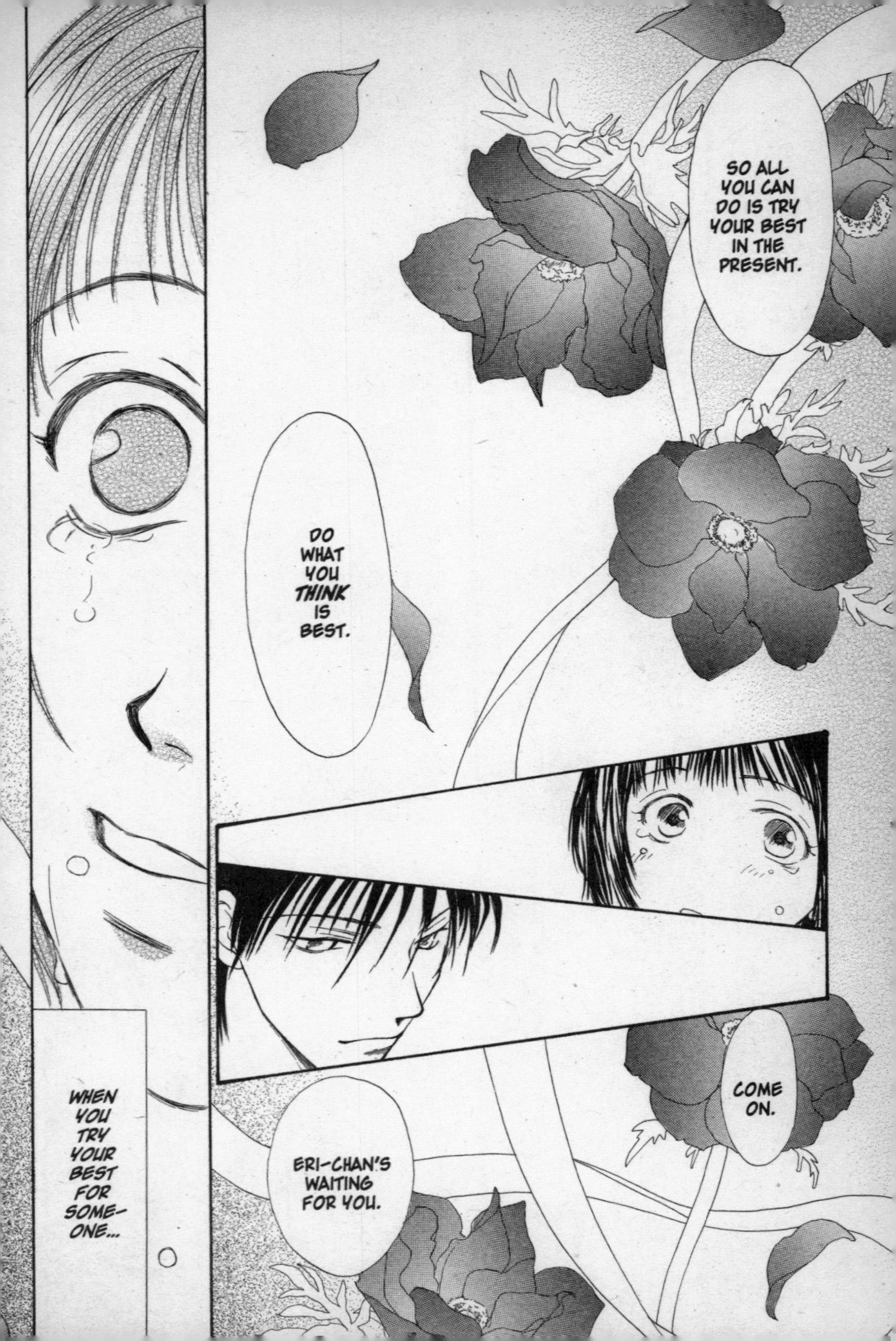
SO ALL YOU CAN DO IS TRY YOUR BEST IN THE PRESENT.
DO WHAT YOU *THINK* IS BEST.
COME ON.
ERI-CHAN'S WAITING FOR YOU.
WHEN YOU TRY YOUR BEST FOR SOME-ONE...

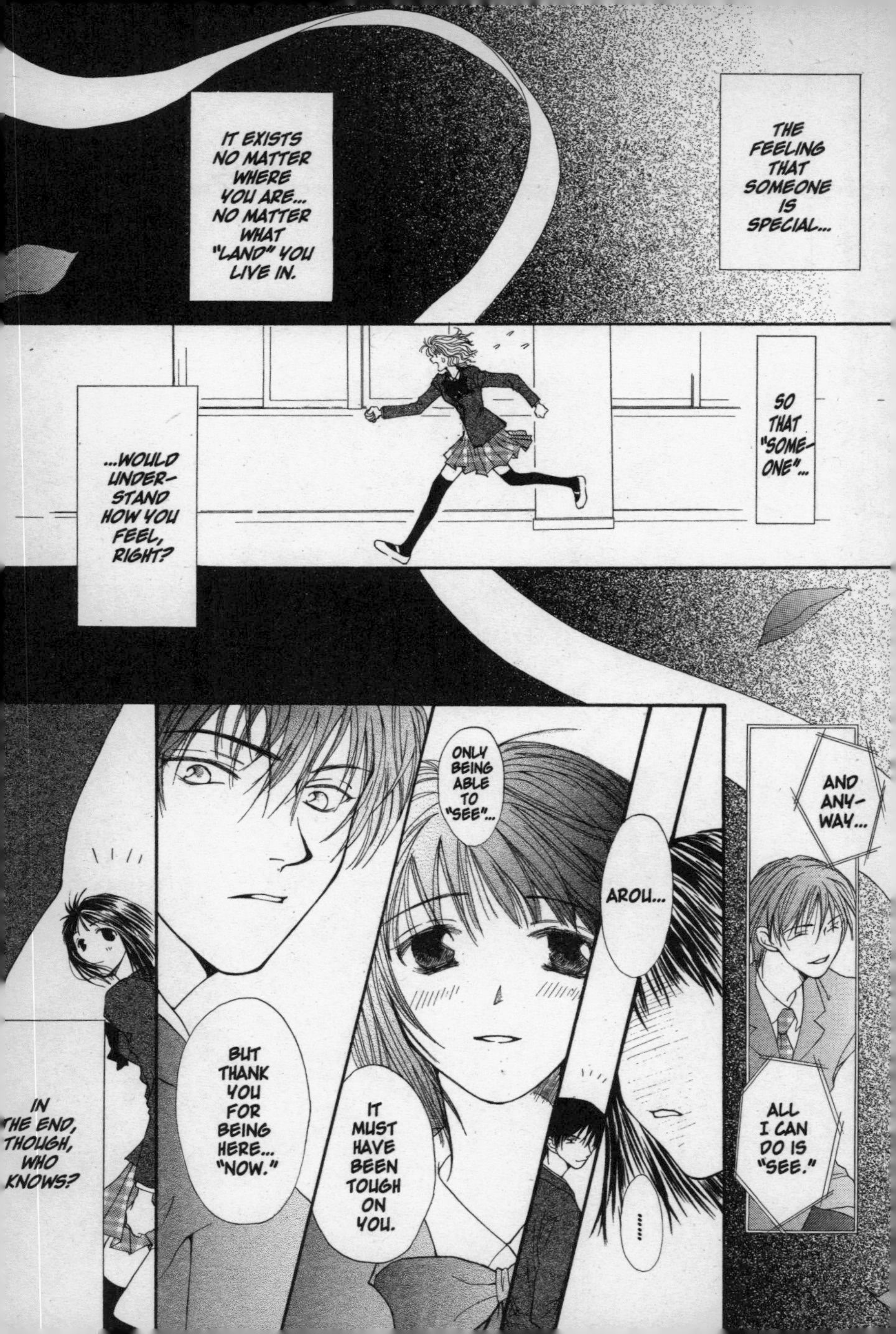
THE FEELING THAT SOMEONE IS SPECIAL...
IT EXISTS NO MATTER WHERE YOU ARE... NO MATTER WHAT "LAND" YOU LIVE IN.
SO THAT "SOMEONE"...
...WOULD UNDERSTAND HOW YOU FEEL, RIGHT?
AND ANYWAY...
ALL I CAN DO IS "SEE."
AROU...
......
ONLY BEING ABLE TO "SEE"...
IT MUST HAVE BEEN TOUGH ON YOU.
BUT THANK YOU FOR BEING HERE... "NOW."
IN THE END, THOUGH, WHO KNOWS?

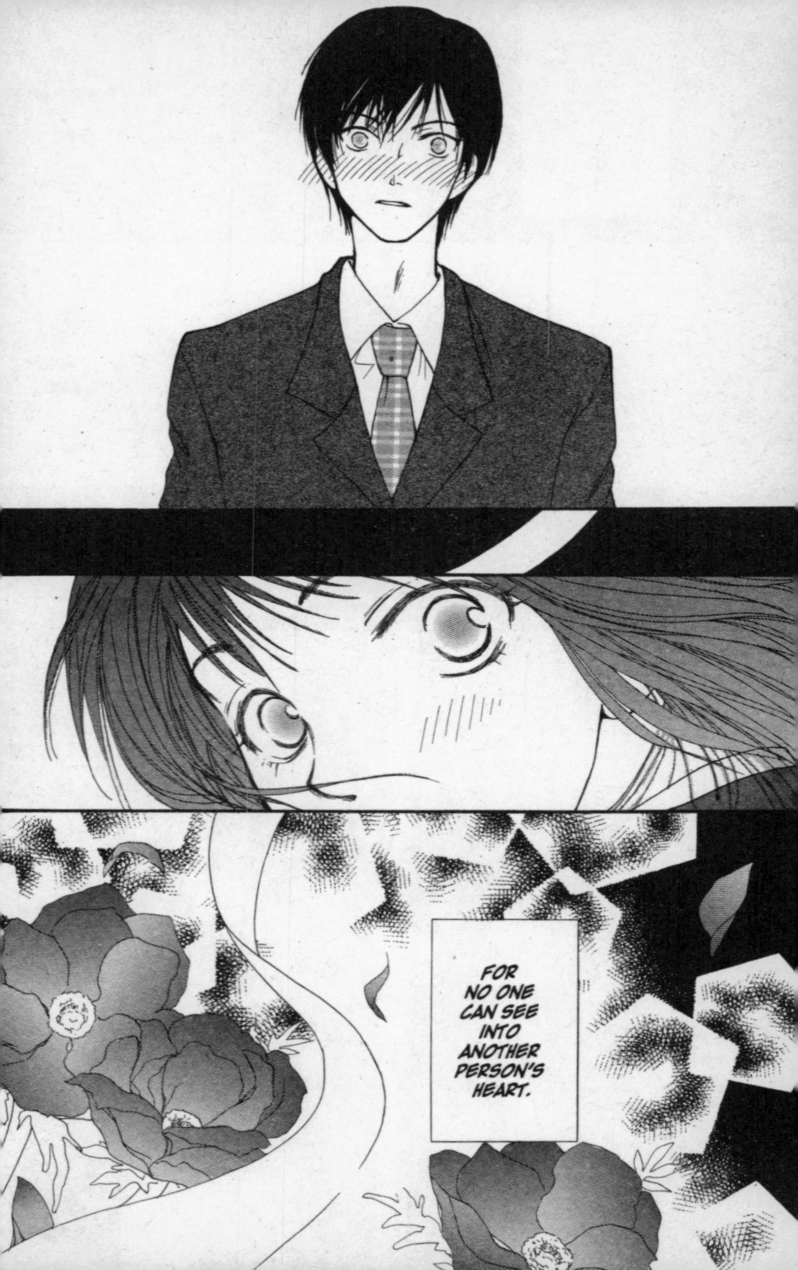
FOR NO ONE CAN SEE INTO ANOTHER PERSON'S HEART.

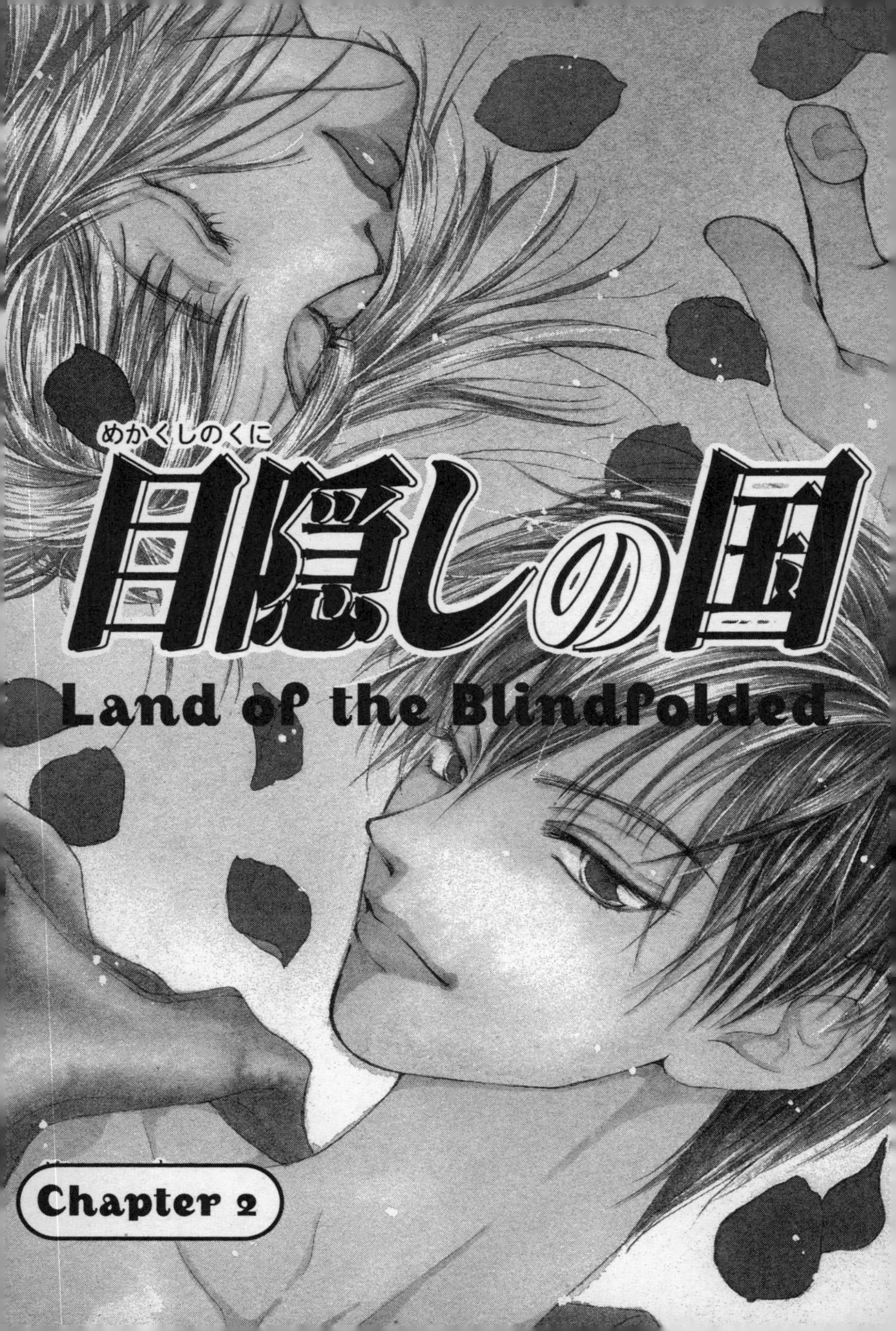
めかくしのくに
目隠しの国
Land of the Blindfolded
Chapter 2

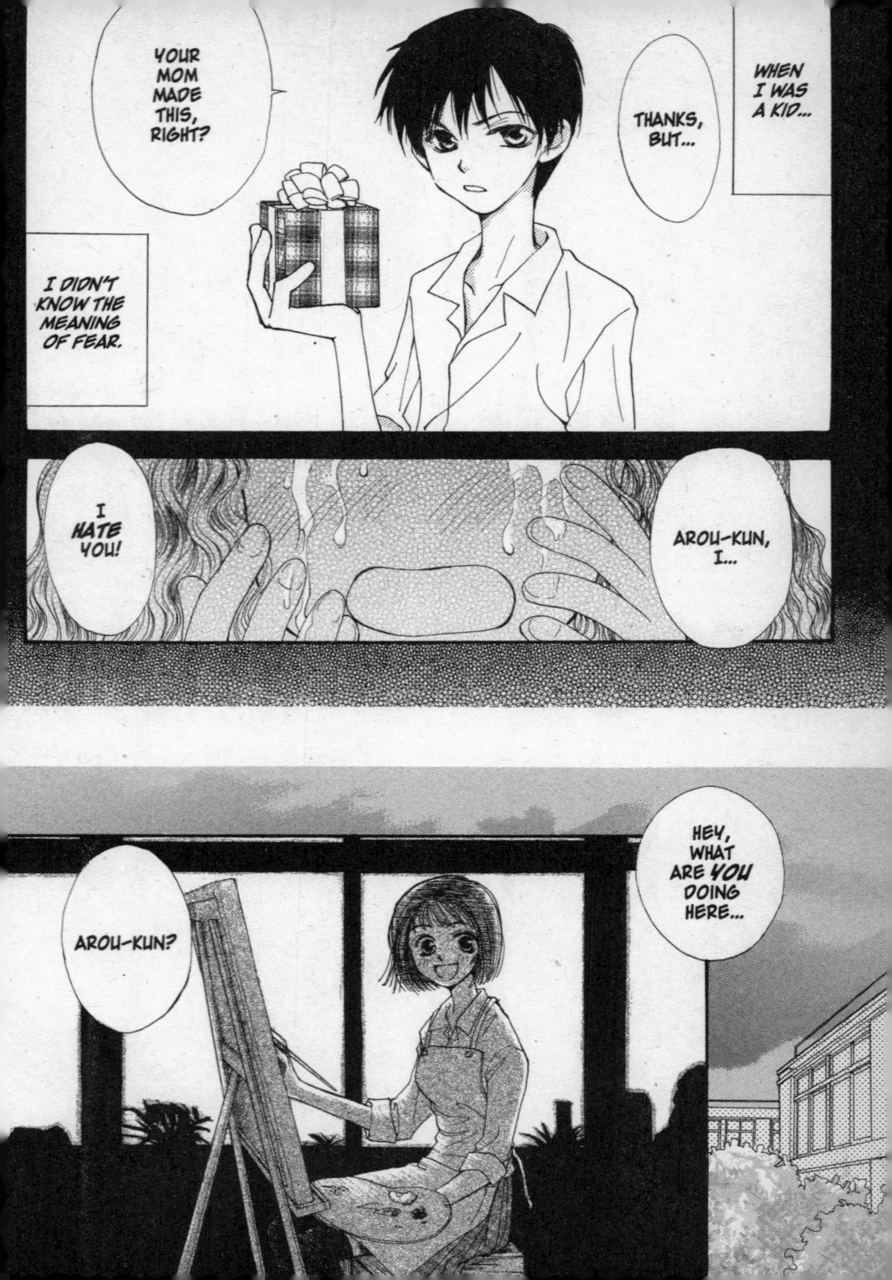
WHEN I WAS A KID...
THANKS, BUT...
YOUR MOM MADE THIS, RIGHT?
I DIDN'T KNOW THE MEANING OF FEAR.
AROU-KUN, I...
I HATE YOU!
HEY, WHAT ARE YOU DOING HERE...
AROU-KUN?

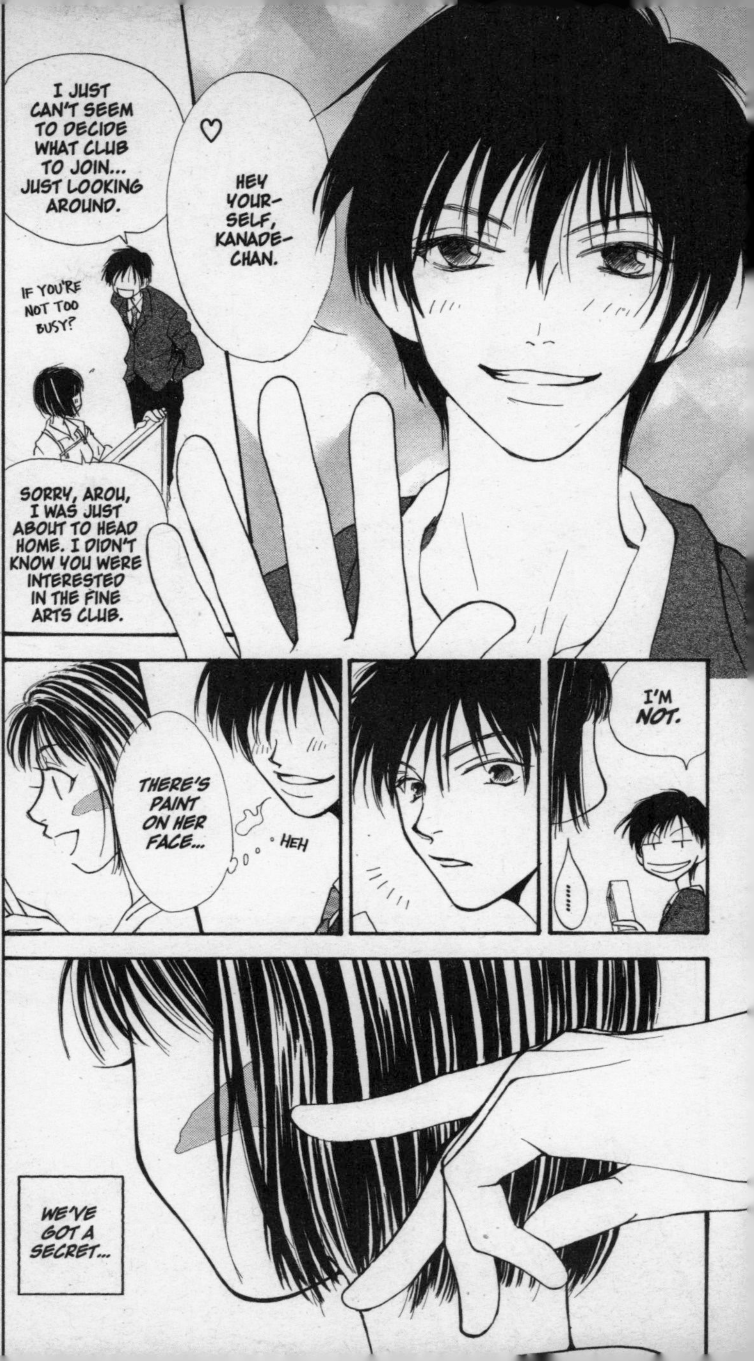
♡
HEY YOURSELF, KANADE-CHAN.
I JUST CAN'T SEEM TO DECIDE WHAT CLUB TO JOIN... JUST LOOKING AROUND.
IF YOU'RE NOT TOO BUSY?
SORRY, AROU, I WAS JUST ABOUT TO HEAD HOME. I DIDN'T KNOW YOU WERE INTERESTED IN THE FINE ARTS CLUB.
I'M NOT.
......
THERE'S PAINT ON HER FACE...
HEH
WE'VE GOT A SECRET...

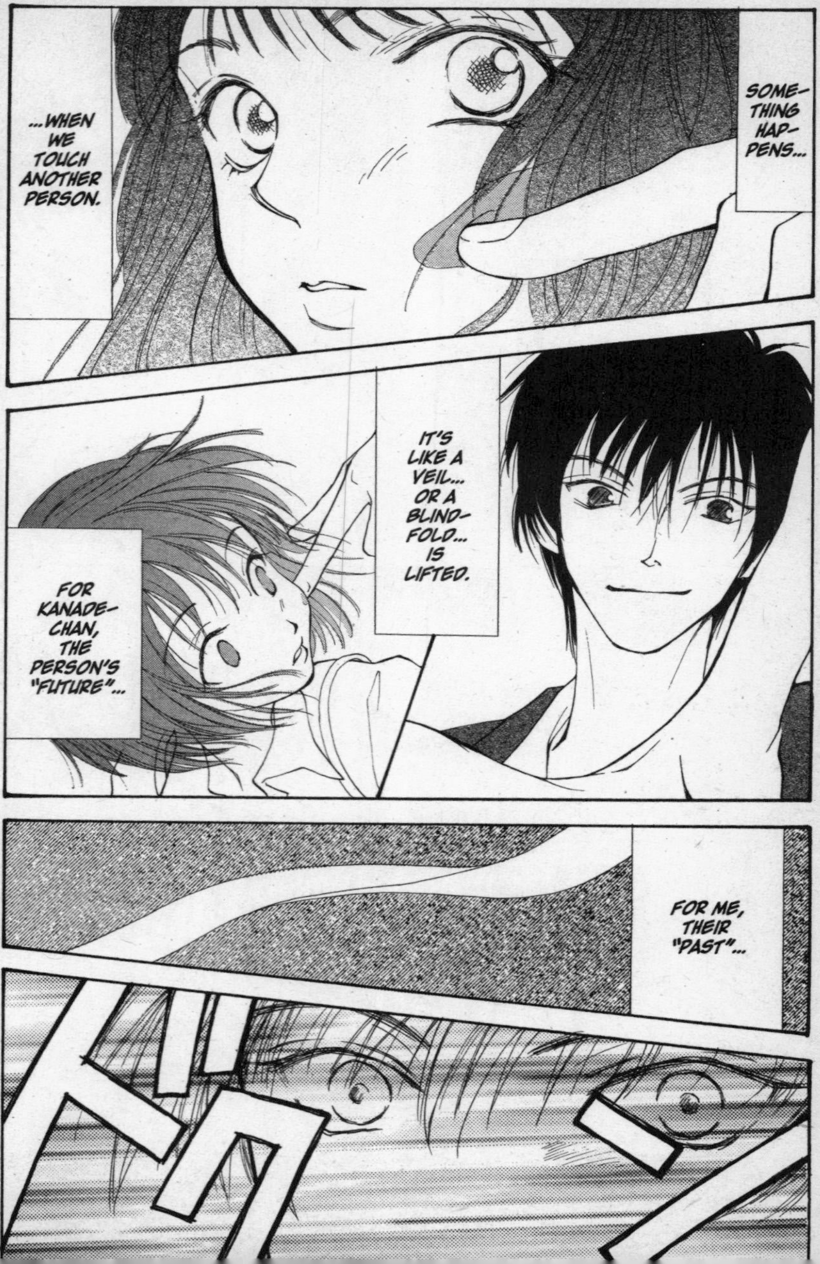
SOME-
THING
HAP-
PENS...
...WHEN
WE
TOUCH
ANOTHER
PERSON.
IT'S
LIKE A
VEIL...
OR A
BLIND-
FOLD...
IS
LIFTED.
FOR
KANADE-
CHAN,
THE
PERSON'S
"FUTURE"...
FOR ME,
THEIR
"PAST"...

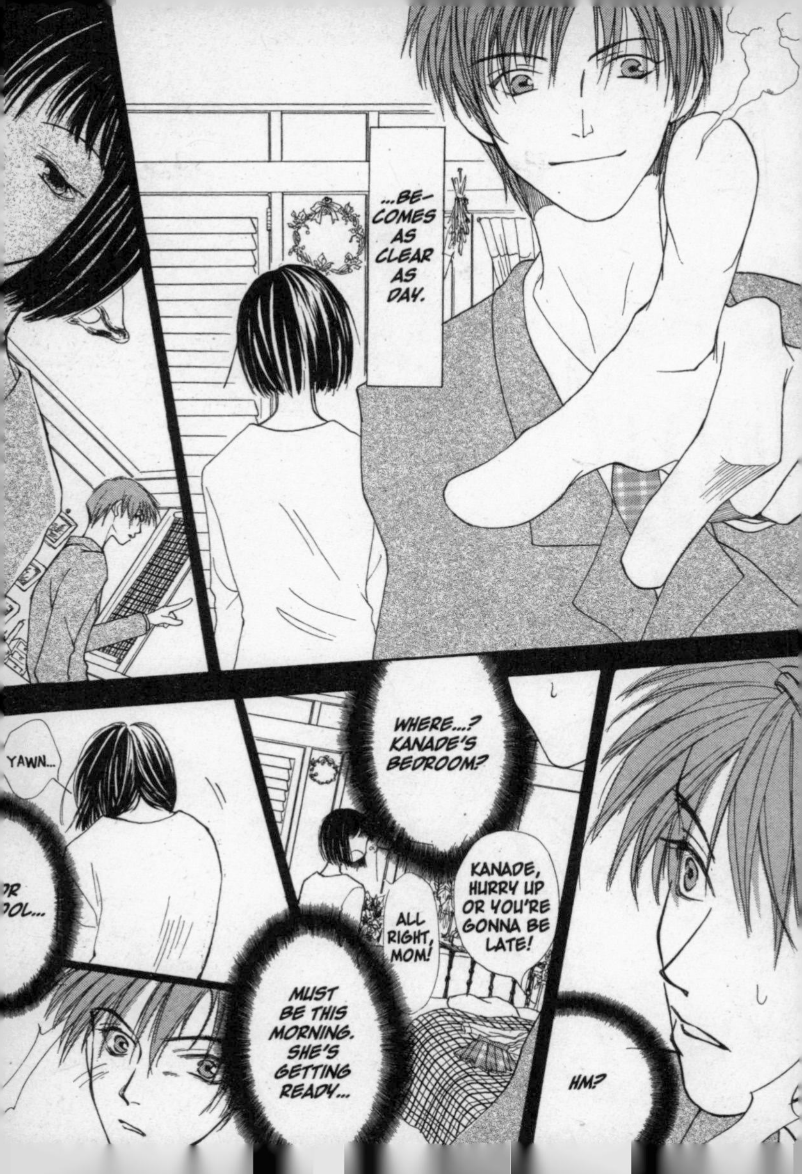
...BE-
COMES
AS
CLEAR
AS
DAY.
HM?
WHERE...?
KANADE'S
BEDROOM?
KANADE,
HURRY UP
OR YOU'RE
GONNA BE
LATE!
ALL
RIGHT,
MOM!
MUST
BE THIS
MORNING.
SHE'S
GETTING
READY...
YAWN...
OR
OOL...

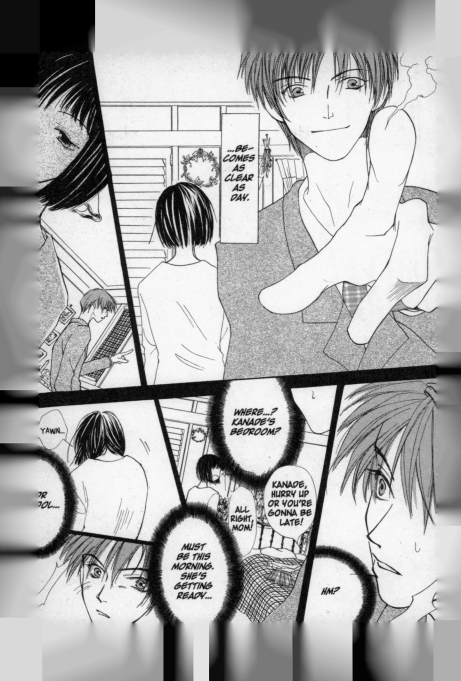

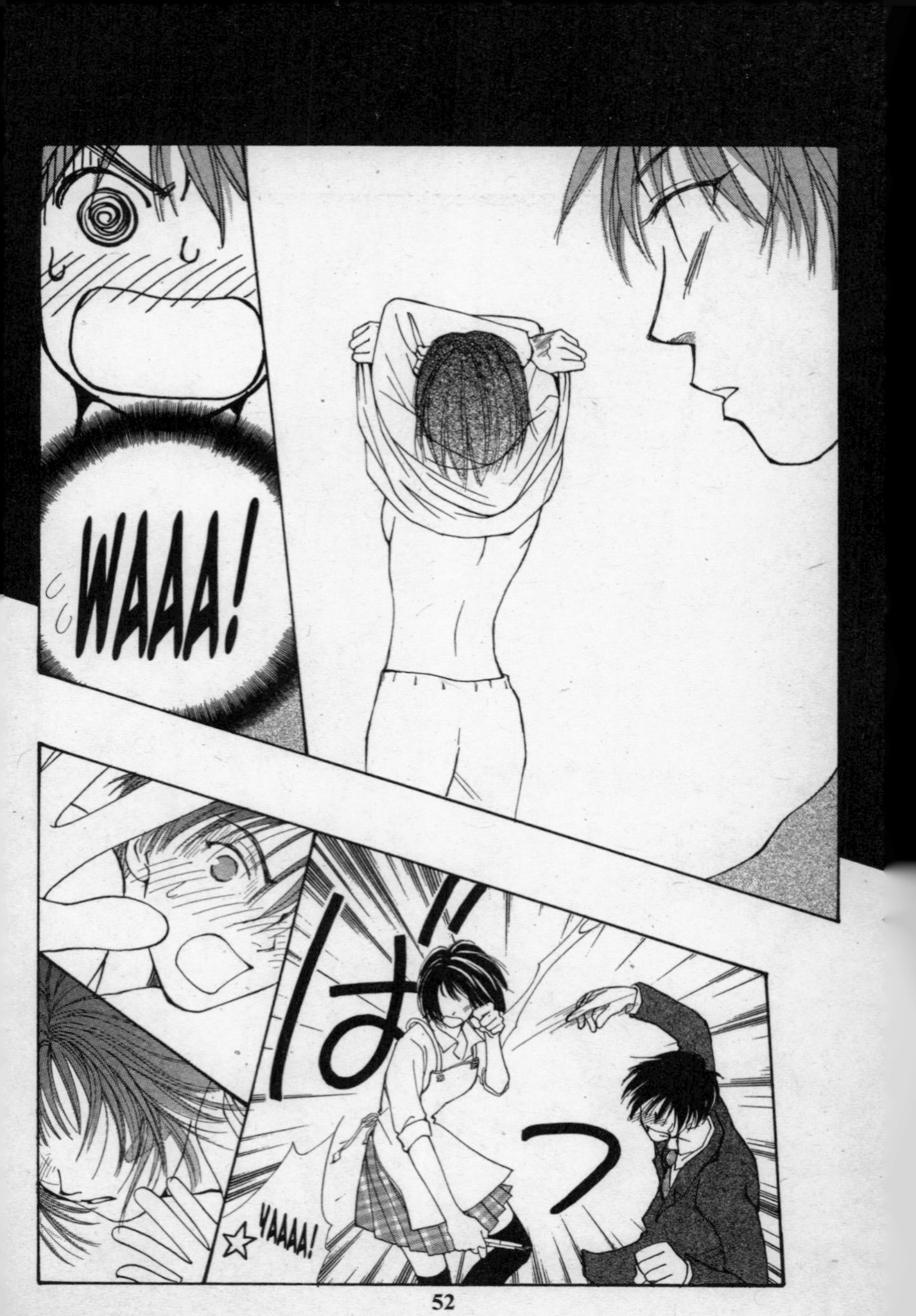
WAAA!
ばっ
YAAAA!

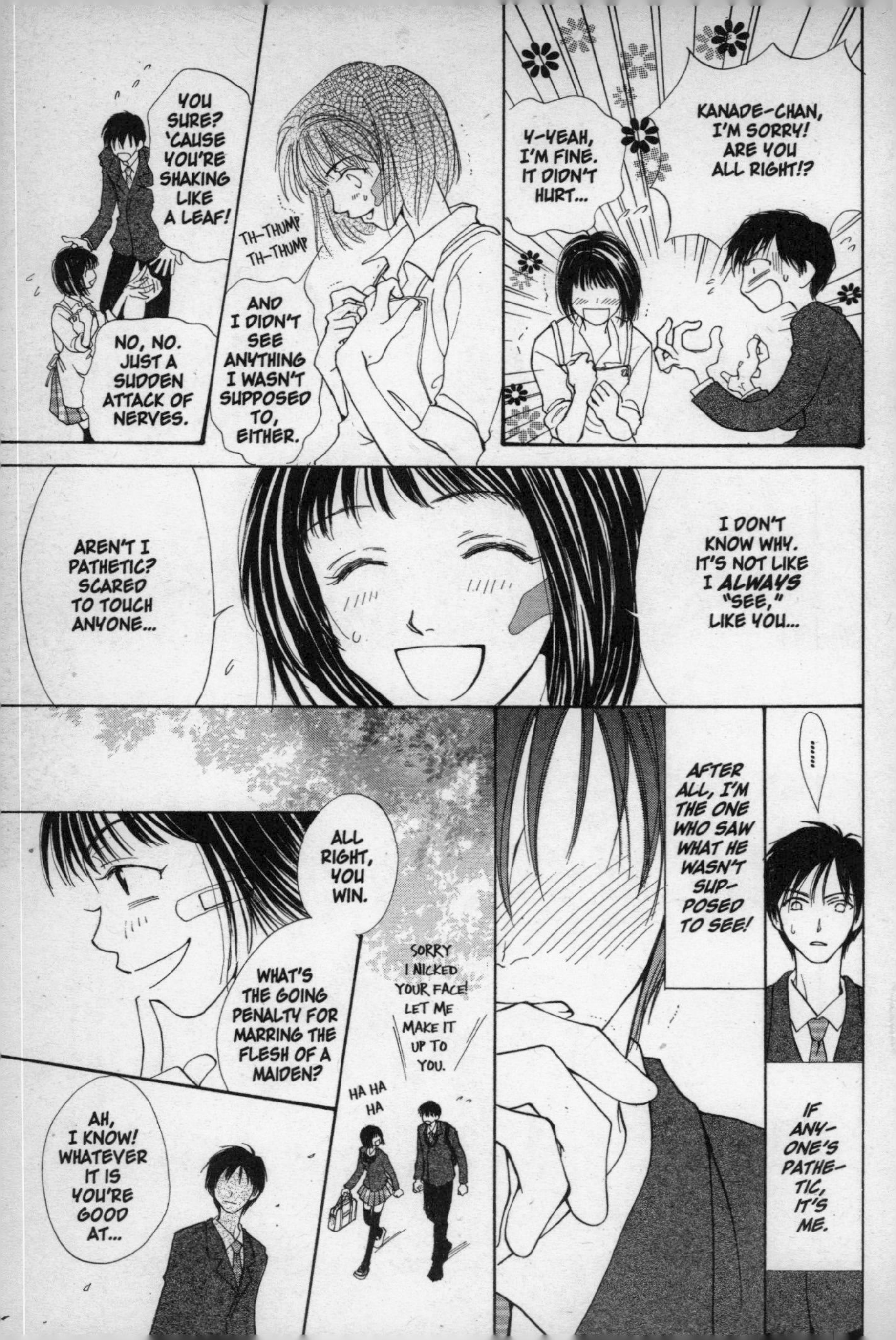
KANADE-CHAN, I'M SORRY! ARE YOU ALL RIGHT!?
Y-YEAH, I'M FINE. IT DIDN'T HURT...
TH-THUMP TH-THUMP
AND I DIDN'T SEE ANYTHING I WASN'T SUPPOSED TO, EITHER.
YOU SURE? 'CAUSE YOU'RE SHAKING LIKE A LEAF!
NO, NO. JUST A SUDDEN ATTACK OF NERVES.
I DON'T KNOW WHY. IT'S NOT LIKE I *ALWAYS* "SEE," LIKE YOU...
AREN'T I PATHETIC? SCARED TO TOUCH ANYONE...
......
AFTER ALL, I'M THE ONE WHO SAW WHAT HE WASN'T SUP-POSED TO SEE!
IF ANY-ONE'S PATHE-TIC, IT'S ME.
ALL RIGHT, YOU WIN.
WHAT'S THE GOING PENALTY FOR MARRING THE FLESH OF A MAIDEN?
SORRY I NICKED YOUR FACE! LET ME MAKE IT UP TO YOU.
HA HA HA
AH, I KNOW! WHATEVER IT IS YOU'RE GOOD AT...

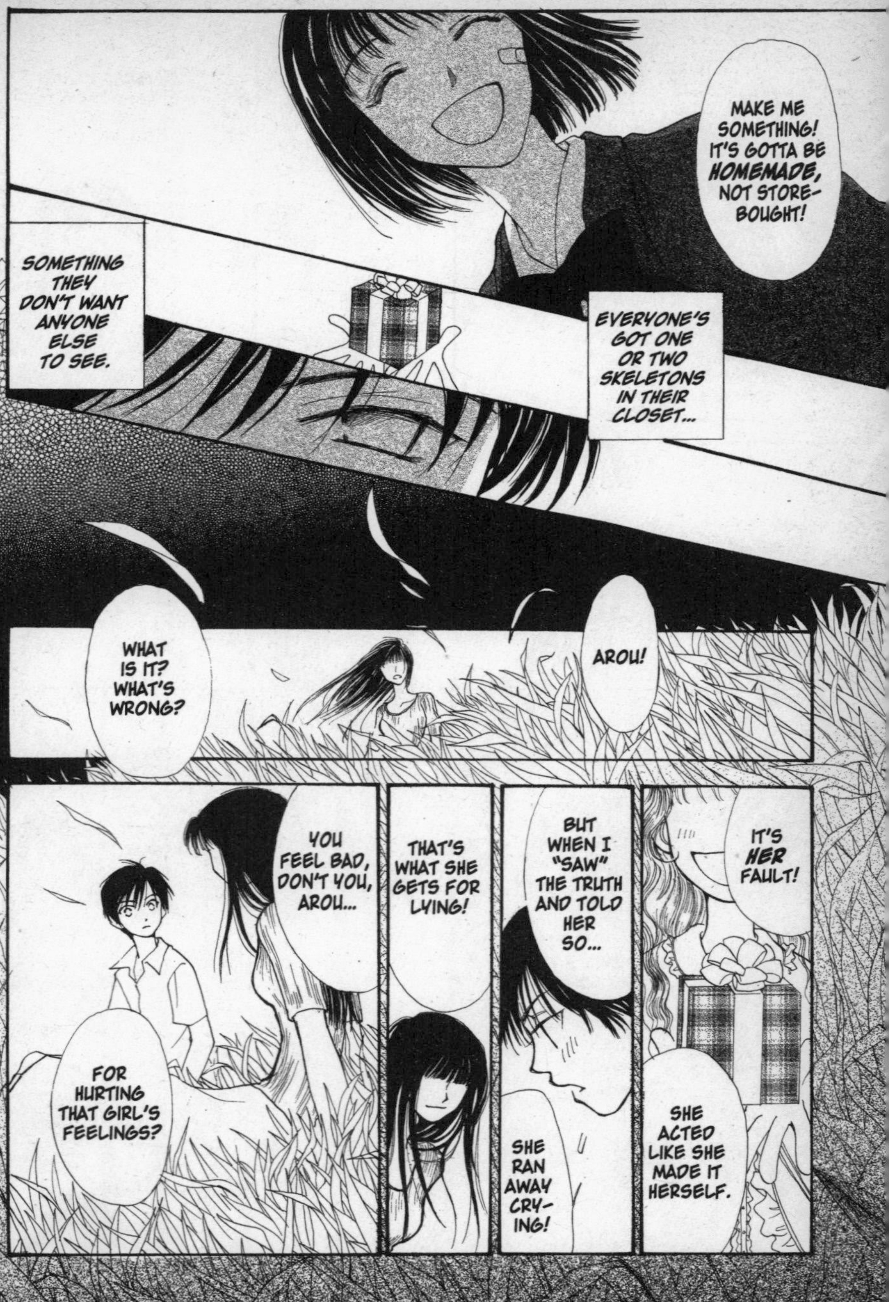
MAKE ME SOMETHING! IT'S GOTTA BE **HOMEMADE,** NOT STORE-BOUGHT!
EVERYONE'S GOT ONE OR TWO SKELETONS IN THEIR CLOSET...
SOMETHING THEY DON'T WANT ANYONE ELSE TO SEE.
AROU!
WHAT IS IT? WHAT'S WRONG?
IT'S **HER** FAULT!
SHE ACTED LIKE SHE MADE IT HERSELF.
BUT WHEN I "SAW" THE TRUTH AND TOLD HER SO...
SHE RAN AWAY CRY-ING!
THAT'S WHAT SHE GETS FOR LYING!
YOU FEEL BAD, DON'T YOU, AROU...
FOR HURTING THAT GIRL'S FEELINGS?

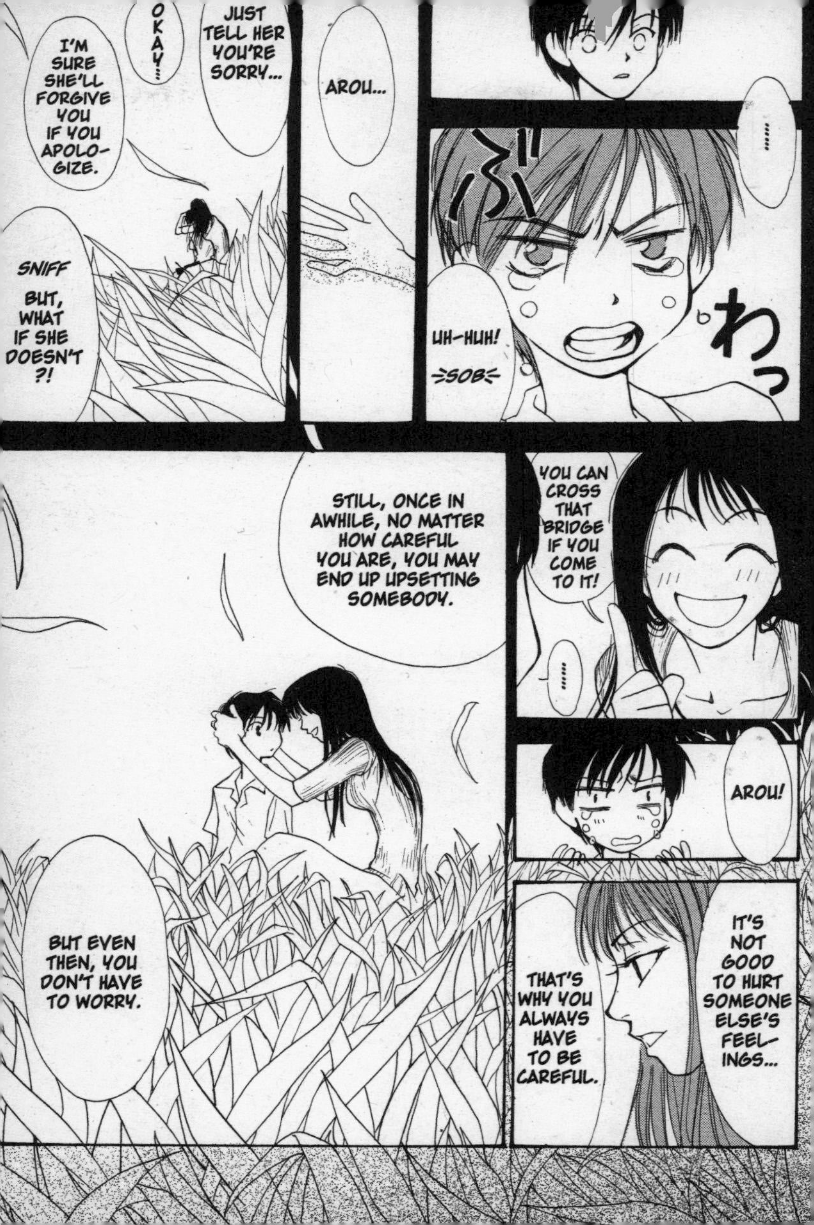
......
ぶ
UH-HUH!
≈SOB≈
わっ
AROU...
JUST TELL HER YOU'RE SORRY...
OKAY...
I'M SURE SHE'LL FORGIVE YOU IF YOU APOLOGIZE.
SNIFF
BUT, WHAT IF SHE DOESN'T ?!
YOU CAN CROSS THAT BRIDGE IF YOU COME TO IT!
......
AROU!
IT'S NOT GOOD TO HURT SOMEONE ELSE'S FEELINGS...
THAT'S WHY YOU ALWAYS HAVE TO BE CAREFUL.
STILL, ONCE IN AWHILE, NO MATTER HOW CAREFUL YOU ARE, YOU MAY END UP UPSETTING SOMEBODY.
BUT EVEN THEN, YOU DON'T HAVE TO WORRY.

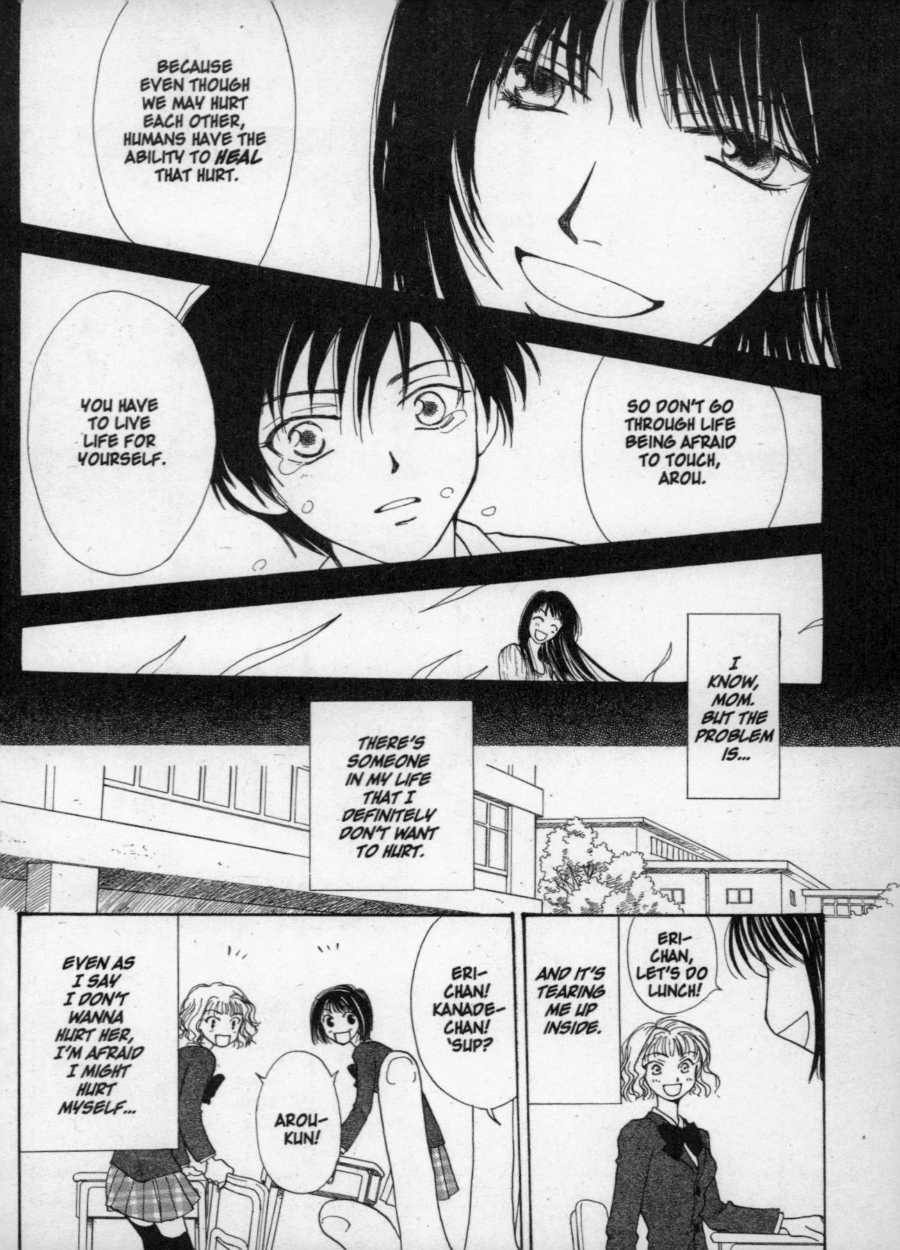
BECAUSE EVEN THOUGH WE MAY HURT EACH OTHER, HUMANS HAVE THE ABILITY TO HEAL THAT HURT.
SO DON'T GO THROUGH LIFE BEING AFRAID TO TOUCH, AROU.
YOU HAVE TO LIVE LIFE FOR YOURSELF.
I KNOW, MOM. BUT THE PROBLEM IS...
THERE'S SOMEONE IN MY LIFE THAT I DEFINITELY DON'T WANT TO HURT.
ERI-CHAN, LET'S DO LUNCH!
AND IT'S TEARING ME UP INSIDE.
ERI-CHAN! KANADE-CHAN! 'SUP?
EVEN AS I SAY I DON'T WANNA HURT HER, I'M AFRAID I MIGHT HURT MYSELF...
AROU-KUN!

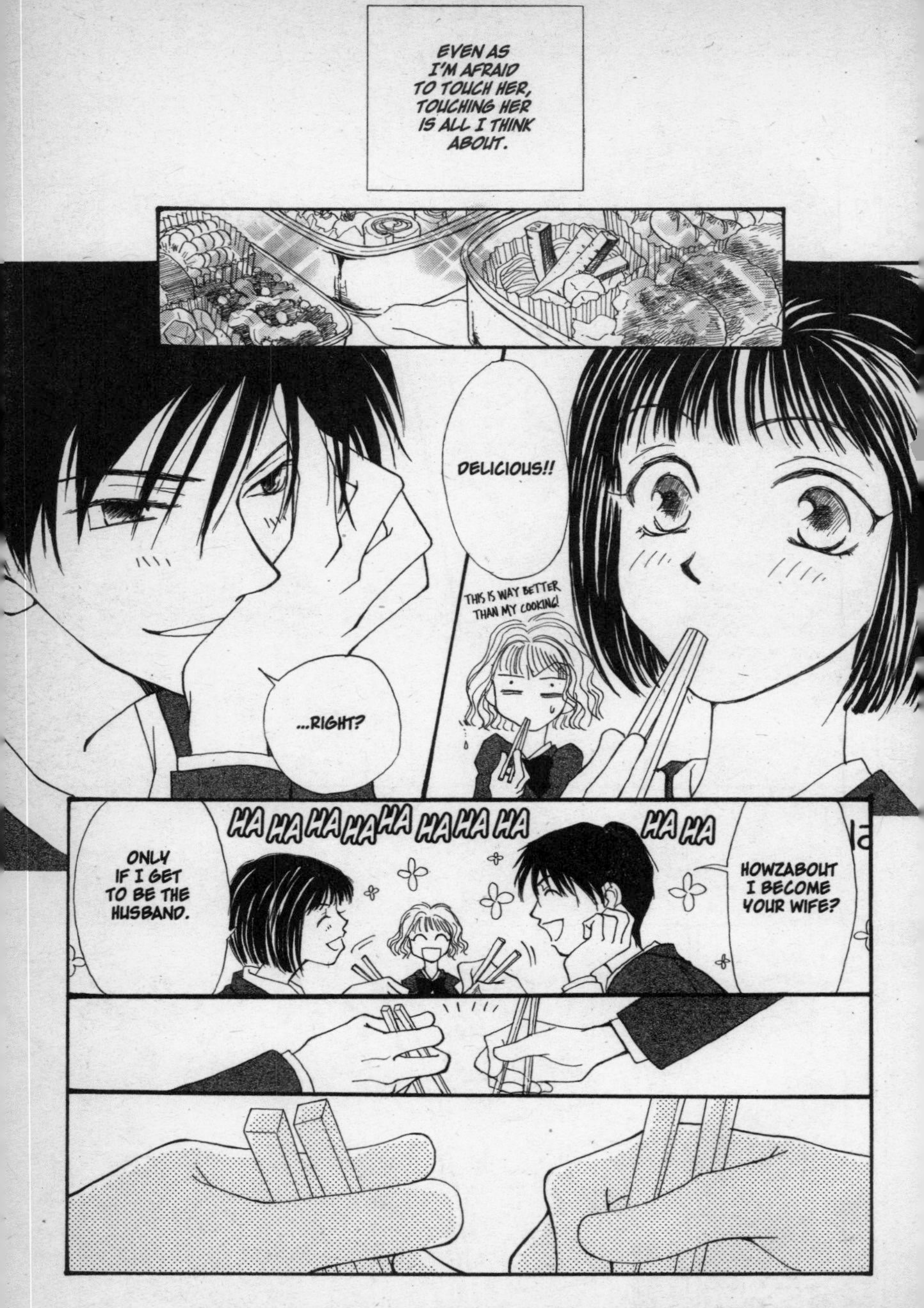
EVEN AS I'M AFRAID TO TOUCH HER, TOUCHING HER IS ALL I THINK ABOUT.
DELICIOUS!!
THIS IS WAY BETTER THAN MY COOKING!
...RIGHT?
HOWZABOUT I BECOME YOUR WIFE?
HA HA HA HA HA HA HA HA HA HA HA HA
ONLY IF I GET TO BE THE HUSBAND.

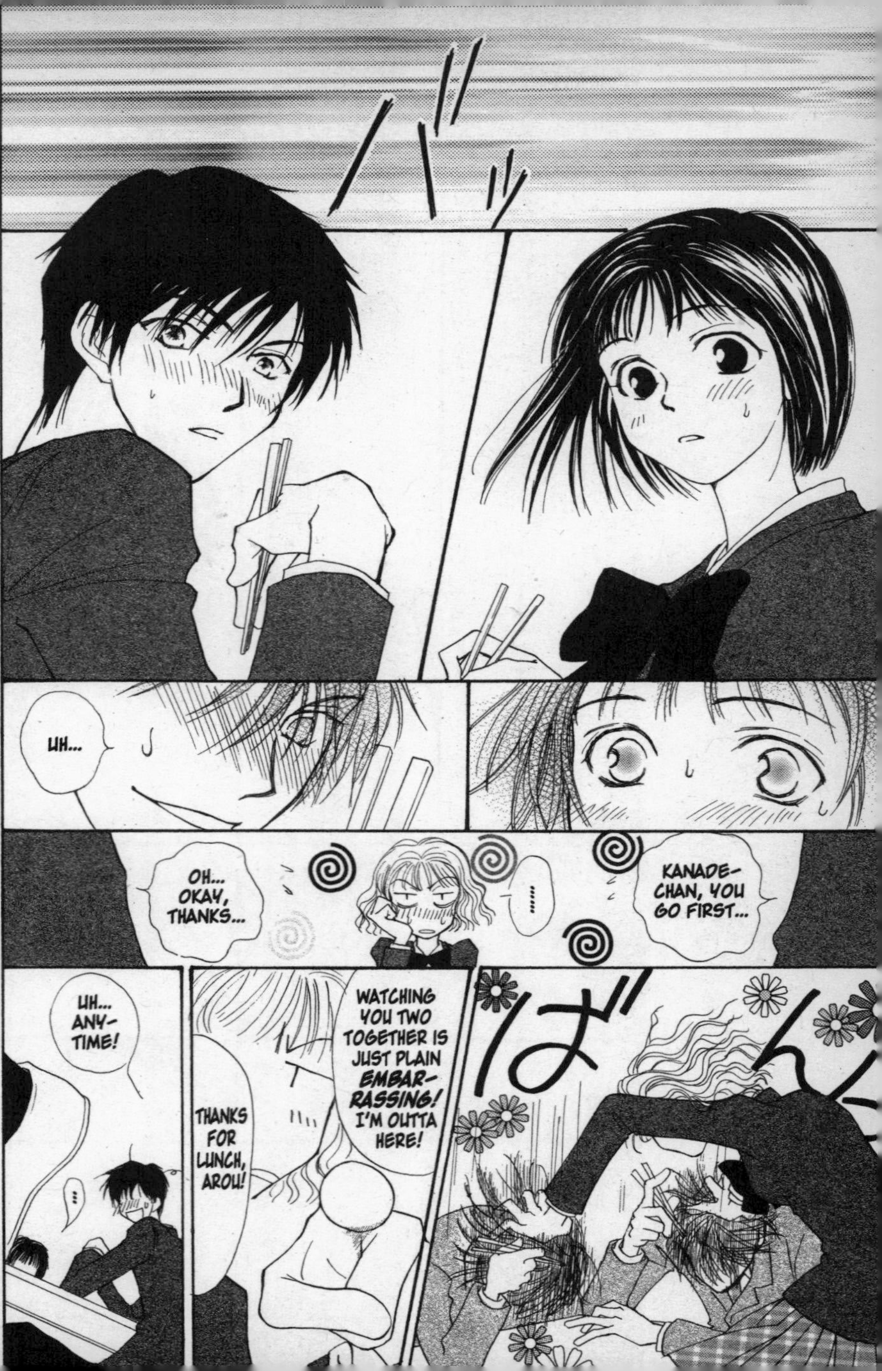
バッ
UH...
KANADE-CHAN, YOU GO FIRST...
......
OH... OKAY, THANKS...
ばん
WATCHING YOU TWO TOGETHER IS JUST PLAIN EMBARRASSING! I'M OUTTA HERE!
THANKS FOR LUNCH, AROU!
UH... ANY-TIME!
...

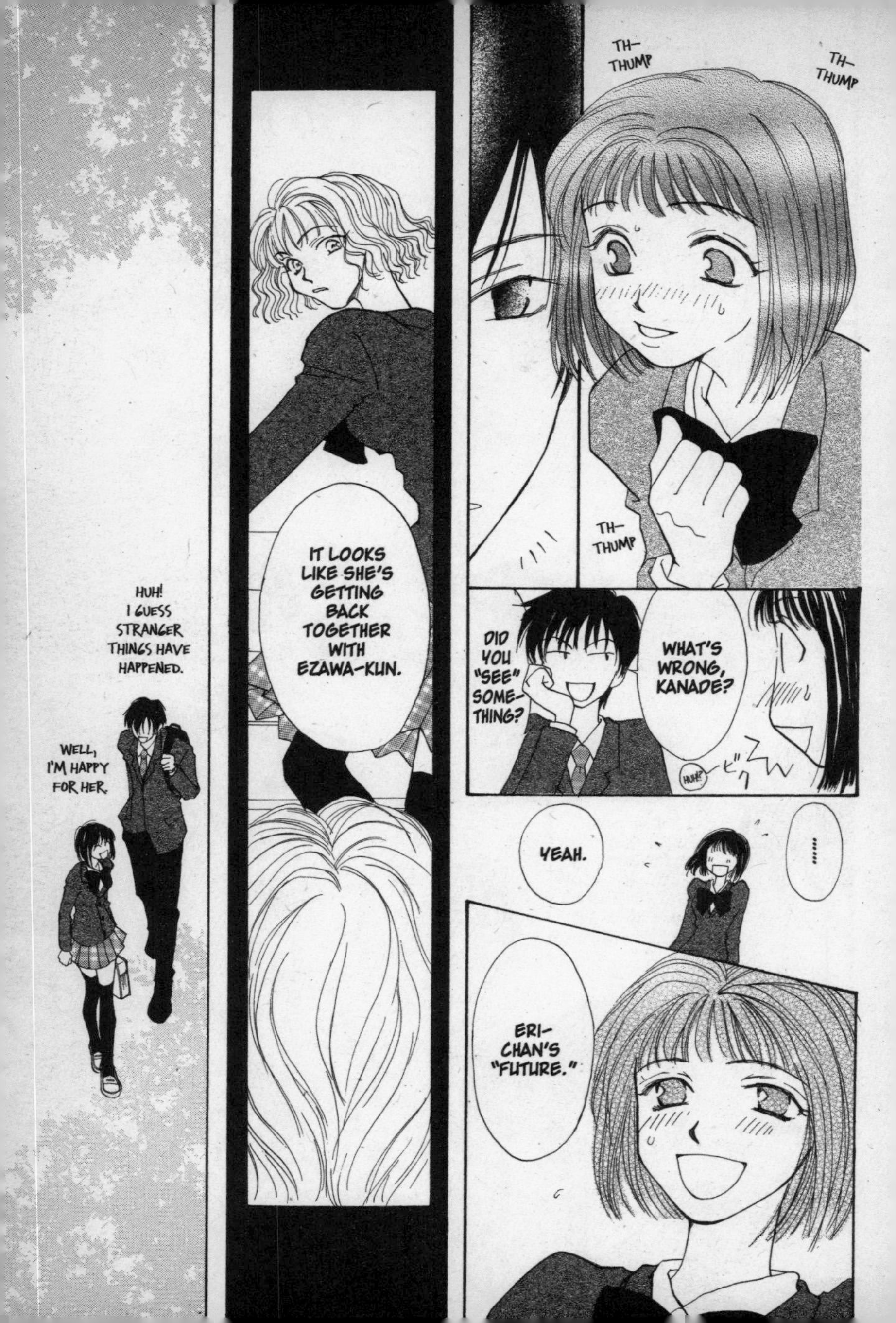
TH-THUMP
TH-THUMP
TH-THUMP
WHAT'S WRONG, KANADE?
HUH!?
ビク
DID YOU "SEE" SOMETHING?
......
YEAH.
ERI-CHAN'S "FUTURE."
IT LOOKS LIKE SHE'S GETTING BACK TOGETHER WITH EZAWA-KUN.
HUH! I GUESS STRANGER THINGS HAVE HAPPENED.
WELL, I'M HAPPY FOR HER.

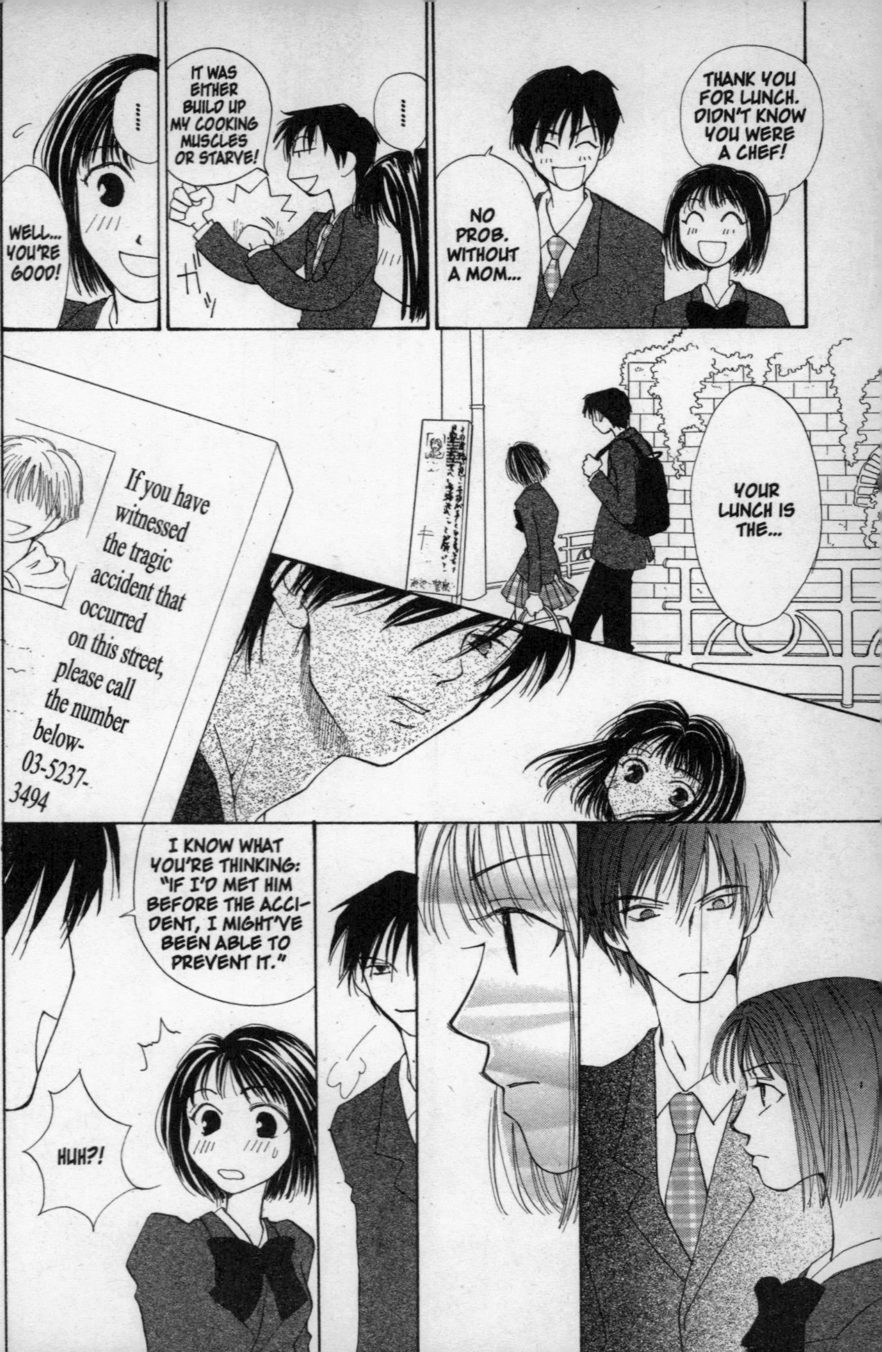
THANK YOU FOR LUNCH. DIDN'T KNOW YOU WERE A CHEF!
NO PROB. WITHOUT A MOM...
......
IT WAS EITHER BUILD UP MY COOKING MUSCLES OR STARVE!
......
WELL... YOU'RE GOOD!
YOUR LUNCH IS THE...
If you have witnessed the tragic accident that occurred on this street, please call the number below- 03-5237-3494
I KNOW WHAT YOU'RE THINKING: "IF I'D MET HIM BEFORE THE ACCI-DENT, I MIGHT'VE BEEN ABLE TO PREVENT IT."
HUH?!

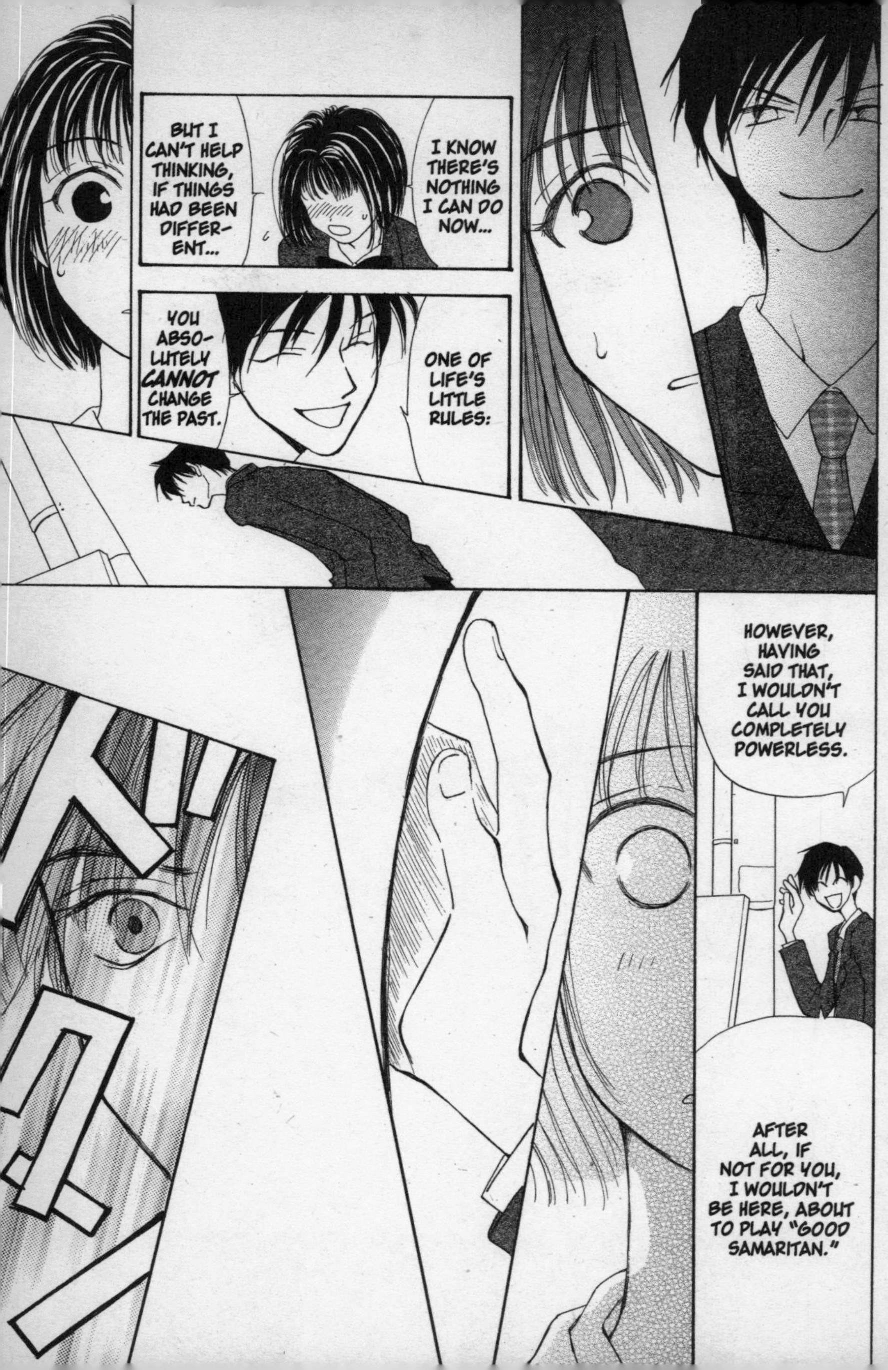

I KNOW THERE'S NOTHING I CAN DO NOW...
BUT I CAN'T HELP THINKING, IF THINGS HAD BEEN DIFFERENT...
ONE OF LIFE'S LITTLE RULES:
YOU ABSOLUTELY ***CANNOT*** CHANGE THE PAST.
HOWEVER, HAVING SAID THAT, I WOULDN'T CALL YOU COMPLETELY POWERLESS.
AFTER ALL, IF NOT FOR YOU, I WOULDN'T BE HERE, ABOUT TO PLAY "GOOD SAMARITAN."

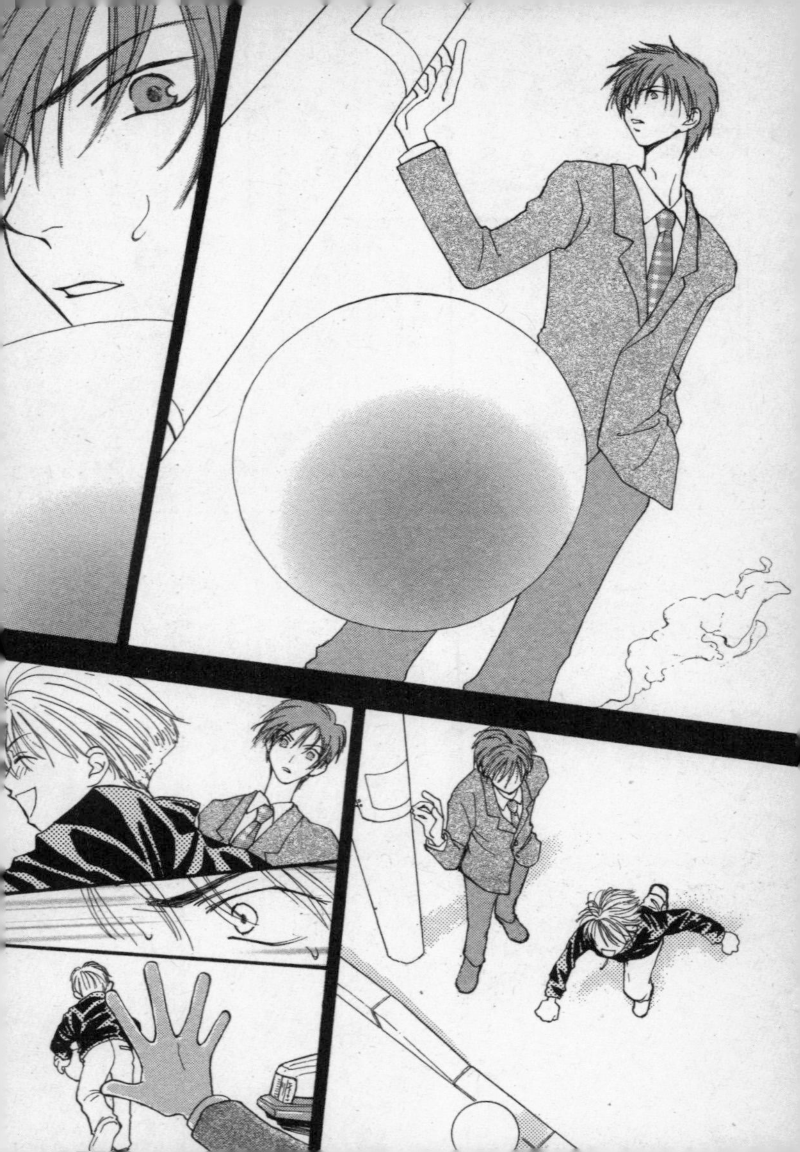

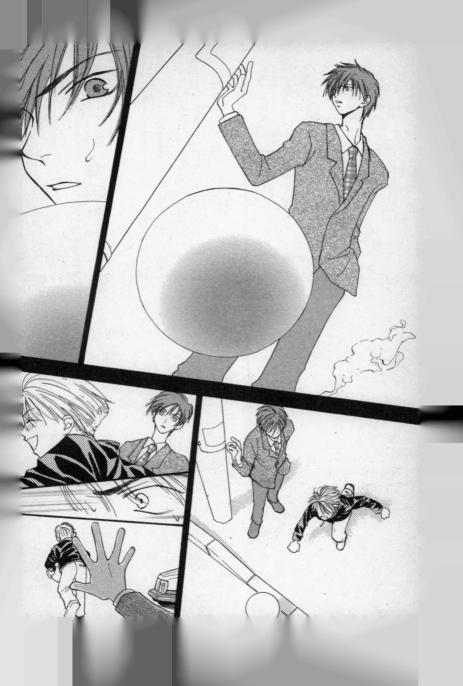

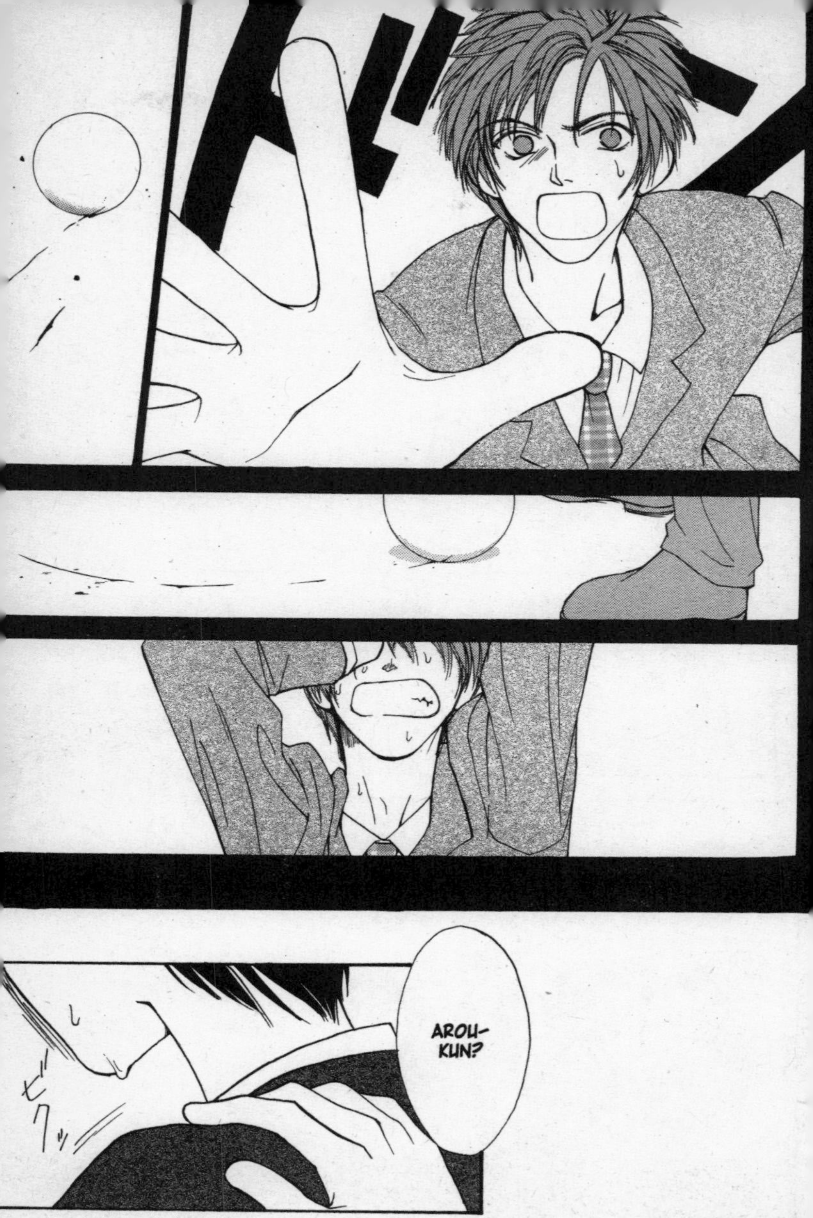
AROU-KUN?

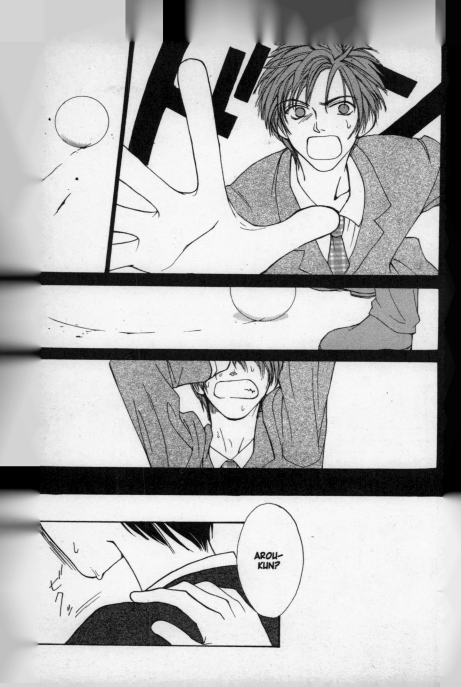

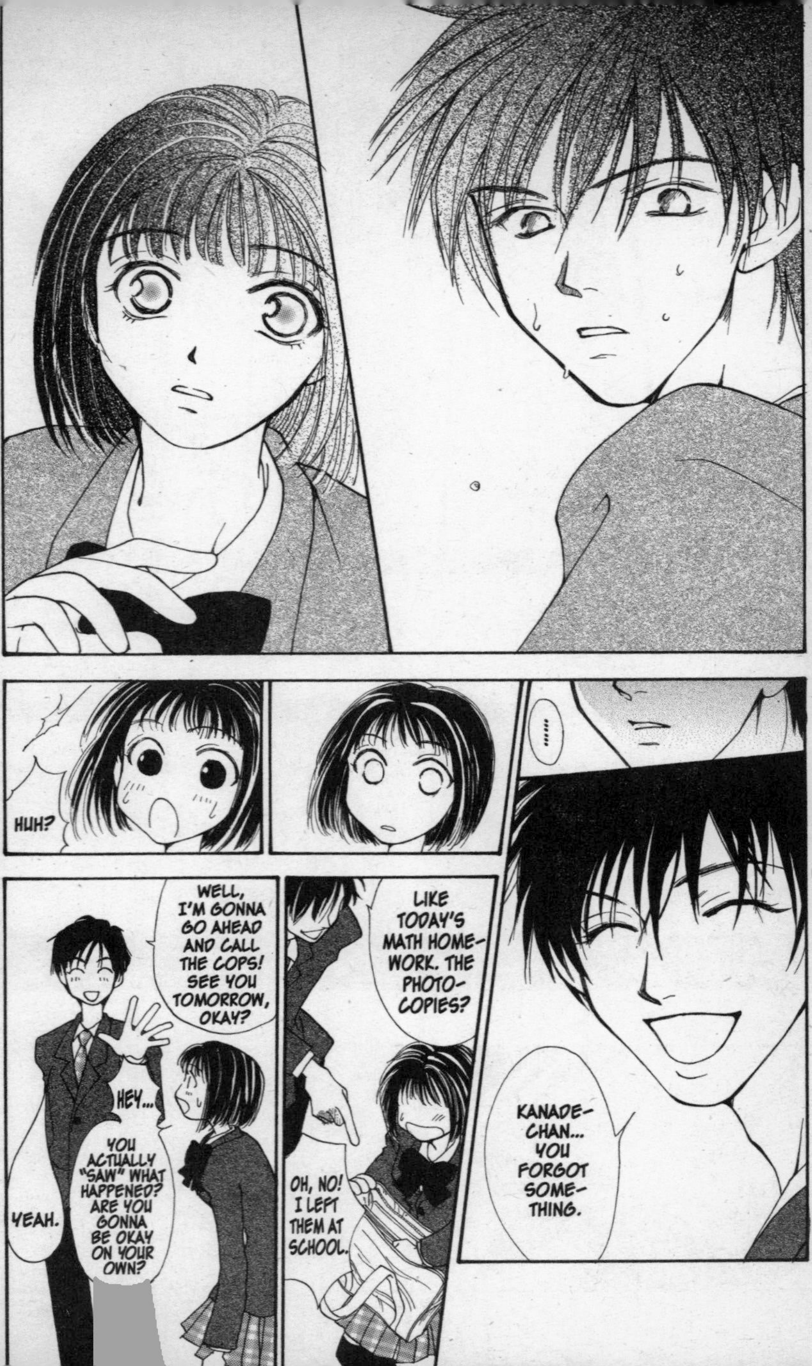
......
KANADE-CHAN... YOU FORGOT SOME-THING.
HUH?
LIKE TODAY'S MATH HOME-WORK. THE PHOTO-COPIES?
OH, NO! I LEFT THEM AT SCHOOL.
WELL, I'M GONNA GO AHEAD AND CALL THE COPS! SEE YOU TOMORROW, OKAY?
HEY...
YOU ACTUALLY "SAW" WHAT HAPPENED? ARE YOU GONNA BE OKAY ON YOUR OWN?
YEAH.

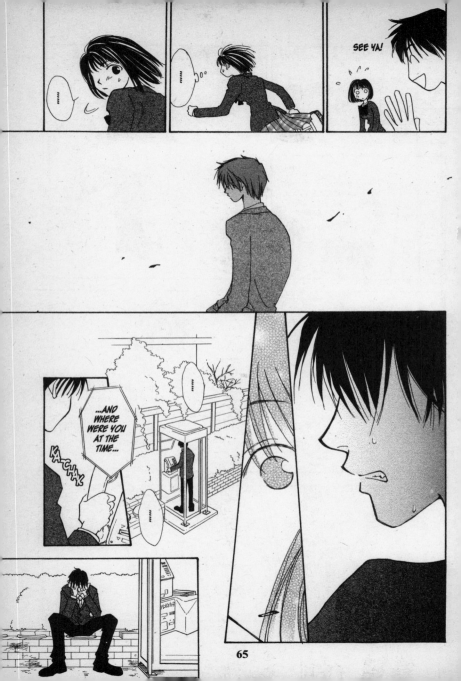

SEE YA!

...AND WHERE WERE YOU AT THE TIME...

KA-CHAK

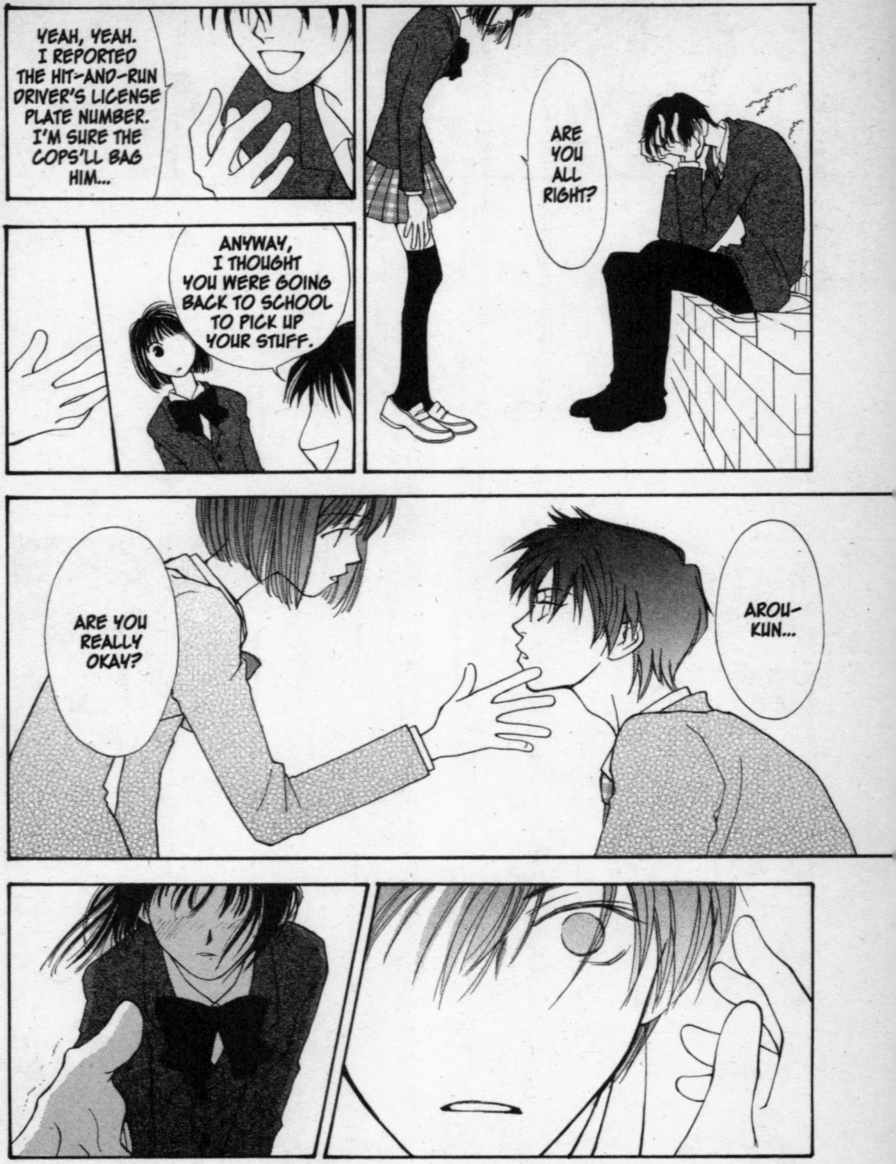
ARE YOU ALL RIGHT?
YEAH, YEAH. I REPORTED THE HIT-AND-RUN DRIVER'S LICENSE PLATE NUMBER. I'M SURE THE COPS'LL BAG HIM...
ANYWAY, I THOUGHT YOU WERE GOING BACK TO SCHOOL TO PICK UP YOUR STUFF.
AROU-KUN...
ARE YOU REALLY OKAY?

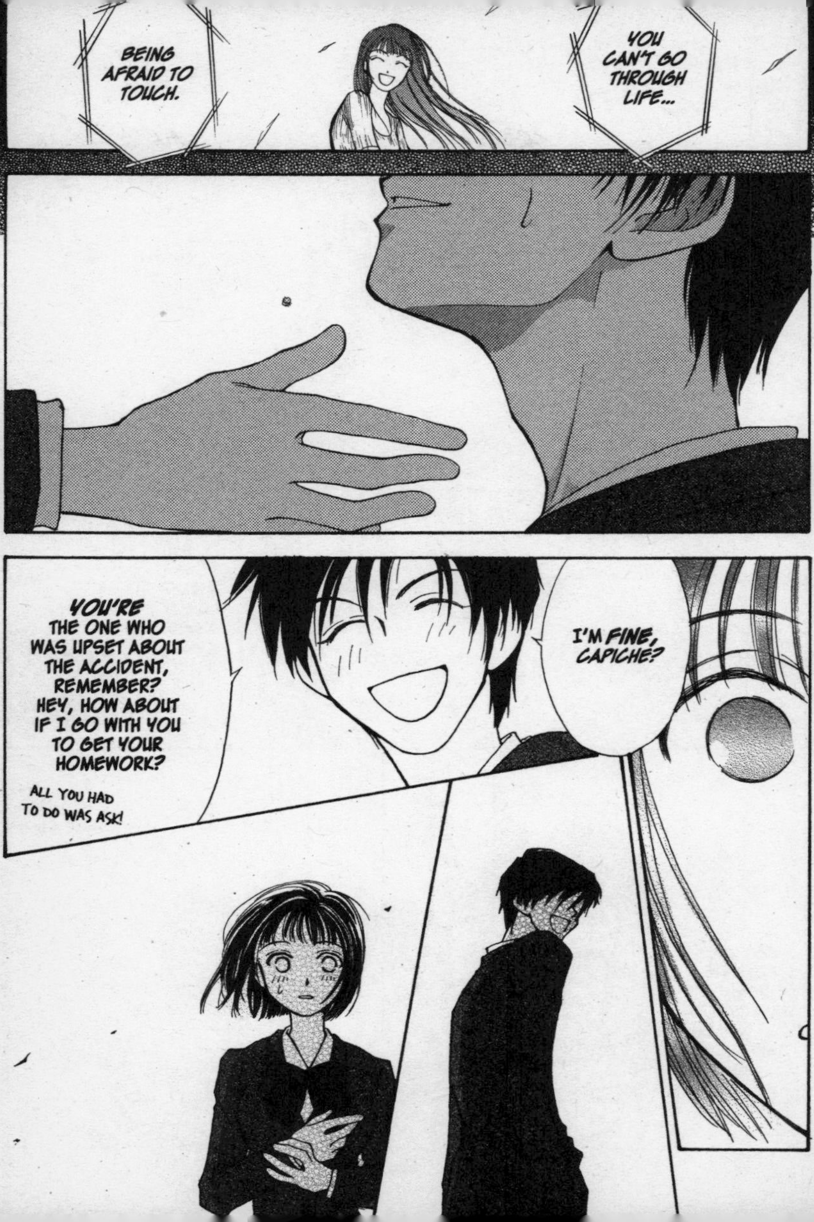
YOU CAN'T GO THROUGH LIFE...
BEING AFRAID TO TOUCH.
I'M *FINE*, CAPICHE?
YOU'RE THE ONE WHO WAS UPSET ABOUT THE ACCIDENT, REMEMBER? HEY, HOW ABOUT IF I GO WITH YOU TO GET YOUR HOMEWORK?
ALL YOU HAD TO DO WAS ASK!

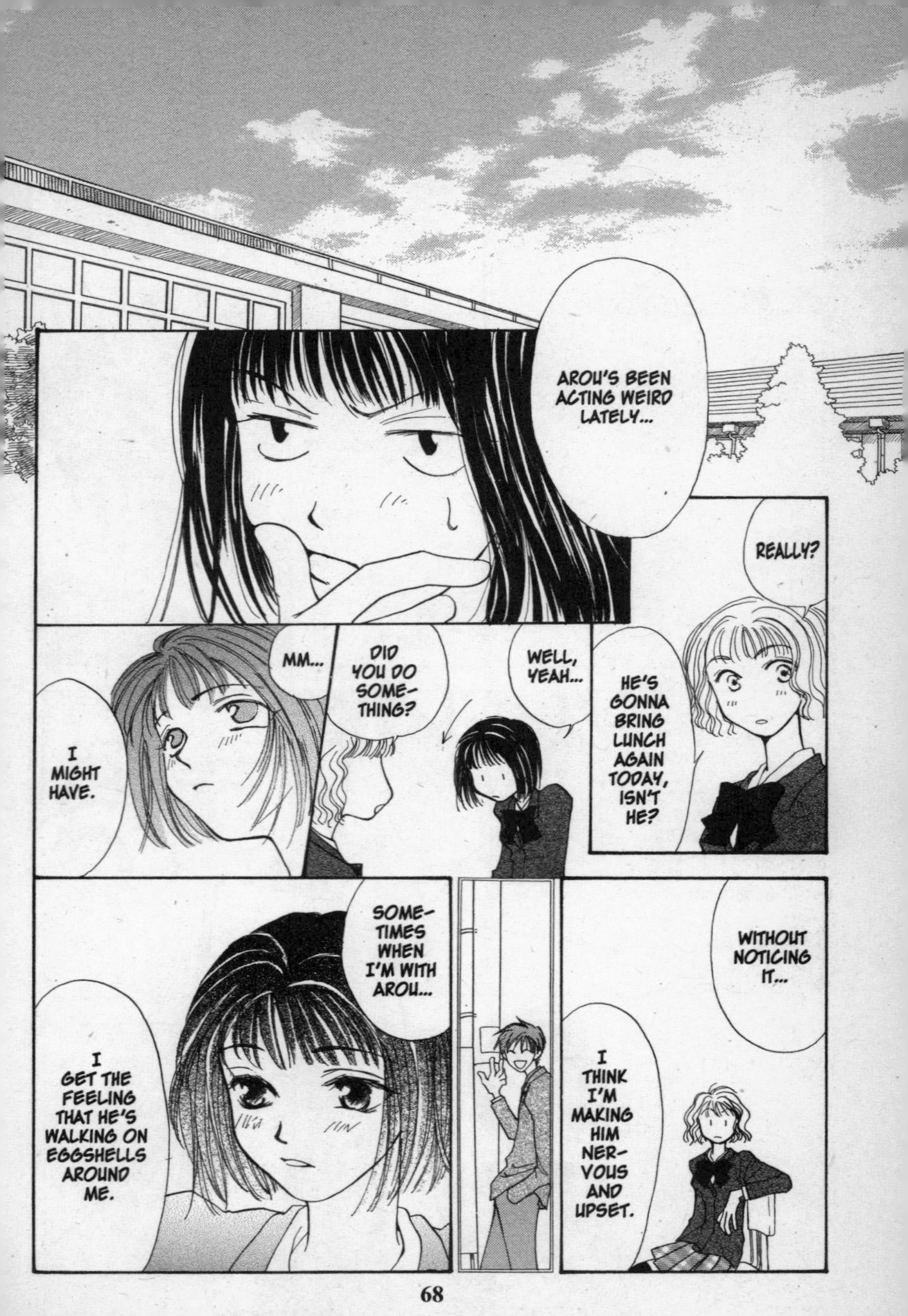
AROU'S BEEN ACTING WEIRD LATELY...
REALLY?
HE'S GONNA BRING LUNCH AGAIN TODAY, ISN'T HE?
WELL, YEAH...
DID YOU DO SOME-THING?
MM...
I MIGHT HAVE.
WITHOUT NOTICING IT...
I THINK I'M MAKING HIM NER-VOUS AND UPSET.
SOME-TIMES WHEN I'M WITH AROU...
I GET THE FEELING THAT HE'S WALKING ON EGGSHELLS AROUND ME.

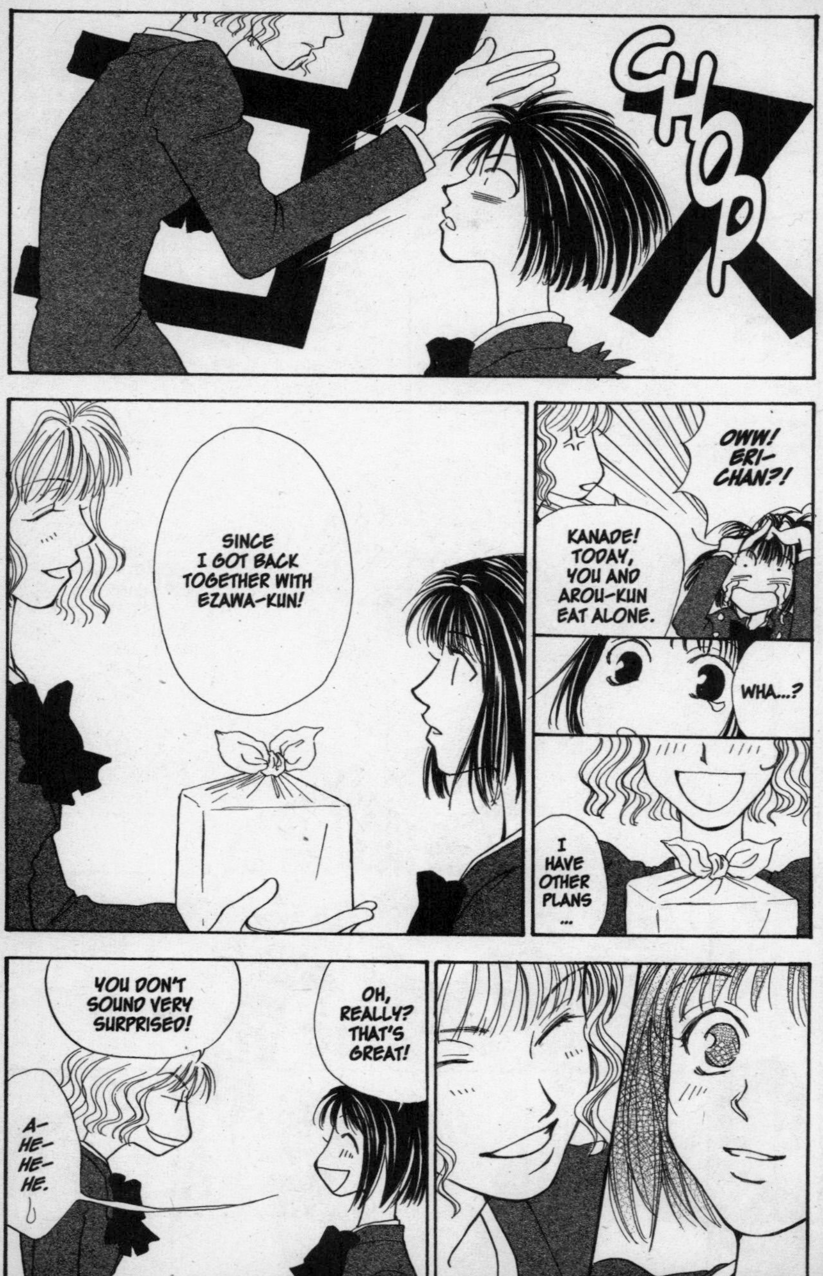
CHOP
OWW! ERI-CHAN?!
KANADE! TODAY, YOU AND AROU-KUN EAT ALONE.
WHA...?
I HAVE OTHER PLANS ...
SINCE I GOT BACK TOGETHER WITH EZAWA-KUN!
OH, REALLY? THAT'S GREAT!
YOU DON'T SOUND VERY SURPRISED!
A-HE-HE-HE.

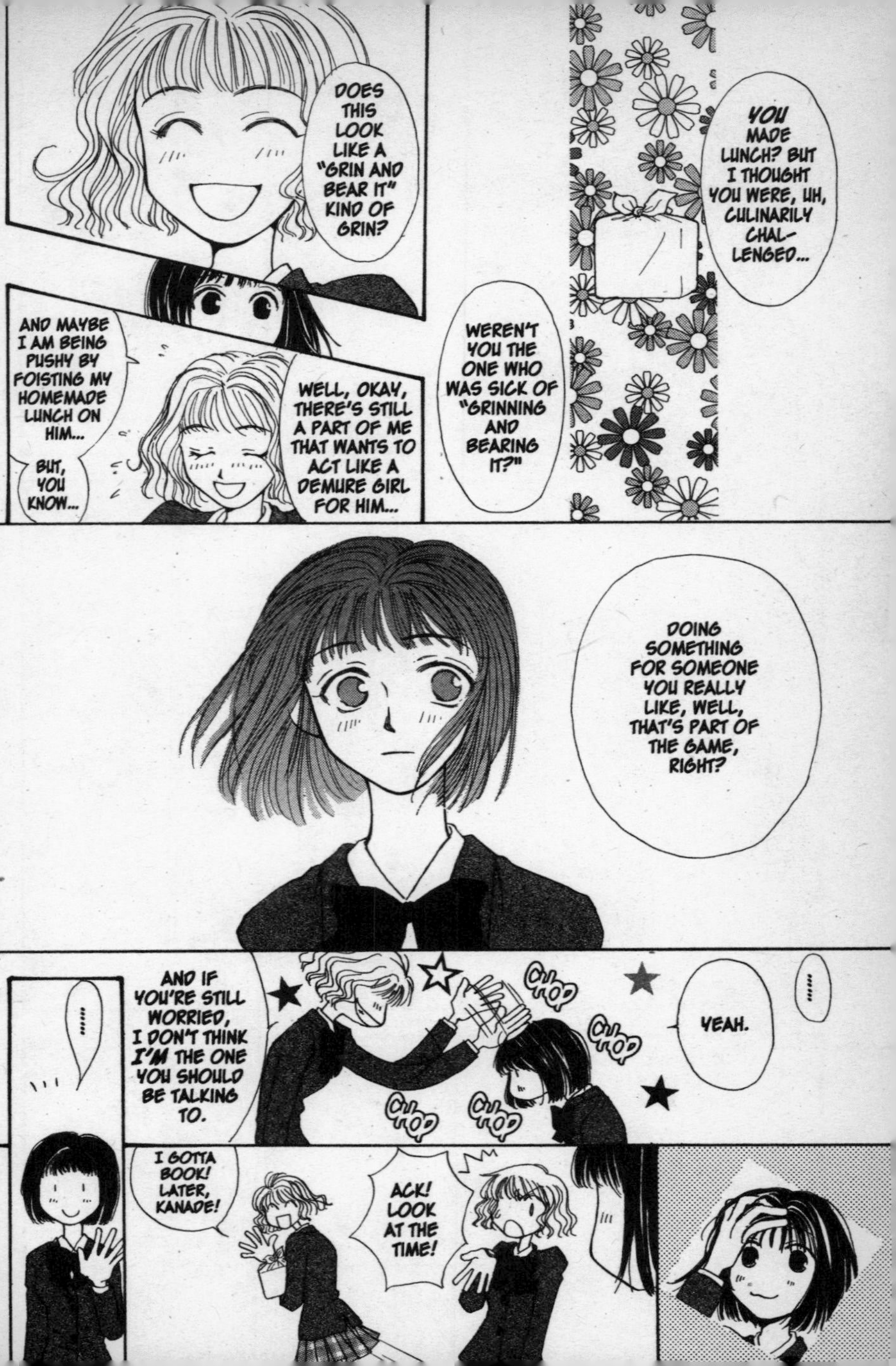
YOU MADE LUNCH? BUT I THOUGHT YOU WERE, UH, CULINARILY CHAL-LENGED...
WEREN'T YOU THE ONE WHO WAS SICK OF "GRINNING AND BEARING IT?"
DOES THIS LOOK LIKE A "GRIN AND BEAR IT" KIND OF GRIN?
WELL, OKAY, THERE'S STILL A PART OF ME THAT WANTS TO ACT LIKE A DEMURE GIRL FOR HIM...
AND MAYBE I AM BEING PUSHY BY FOISTING MY HOMEMADE LUNCH ON HIM...
BUT, YOU KNOW...
DOING SOMETHING FOR SOMEONE YOU REALLY LIKE, WELL, THAT'S PART OF THE GAME, RIGHT?
......
YEAH.
CHOP
CHOP
CHOP
CHOP
AND IF YOU'RE STILL WORRIED, I DON'T THINK I'M THE ONE YOU SHOULD BE TALKING TO.
......
ACK! LOOK AT THE TIME!
I GOTTA BOOK! LATER, KANADE!

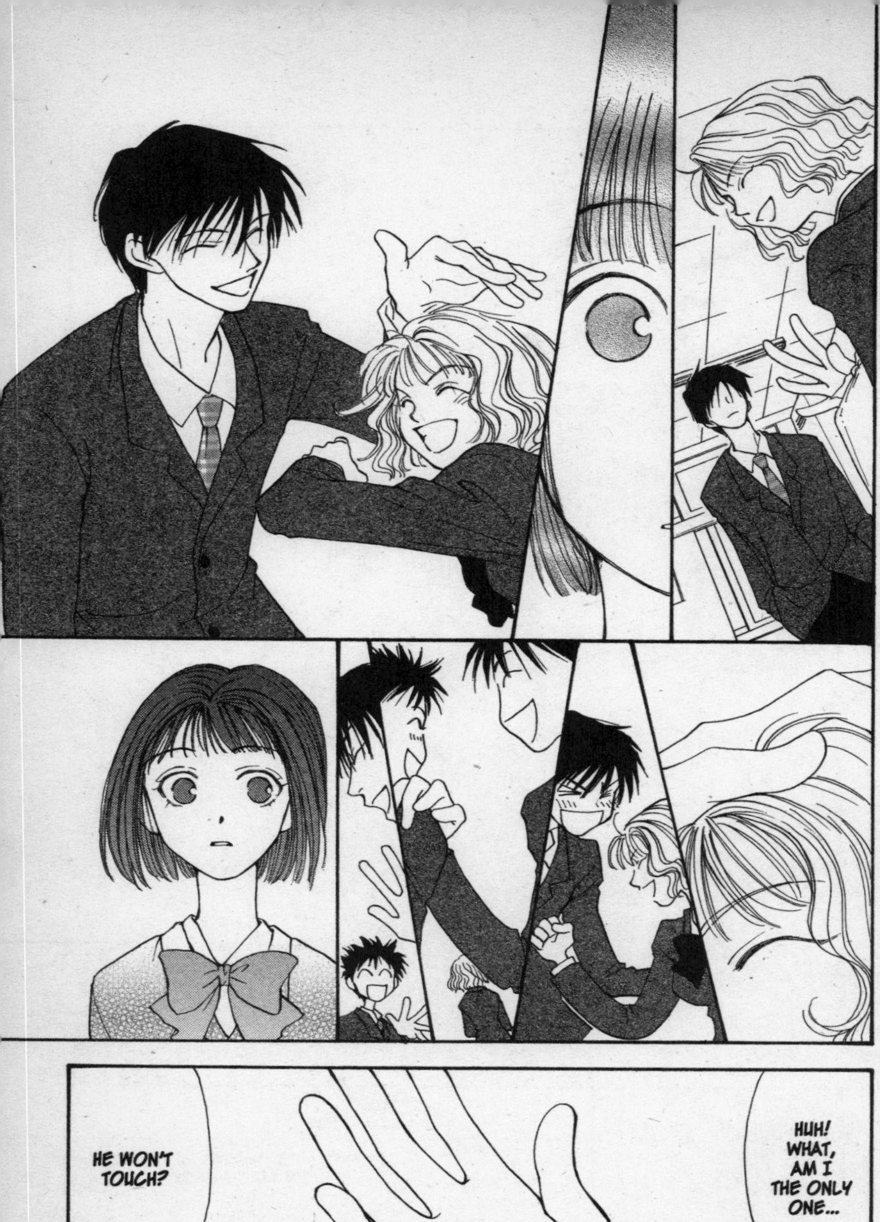
HUH! WHAT, AM I THE ONLY ONE...
HE WON'T TOUCH?

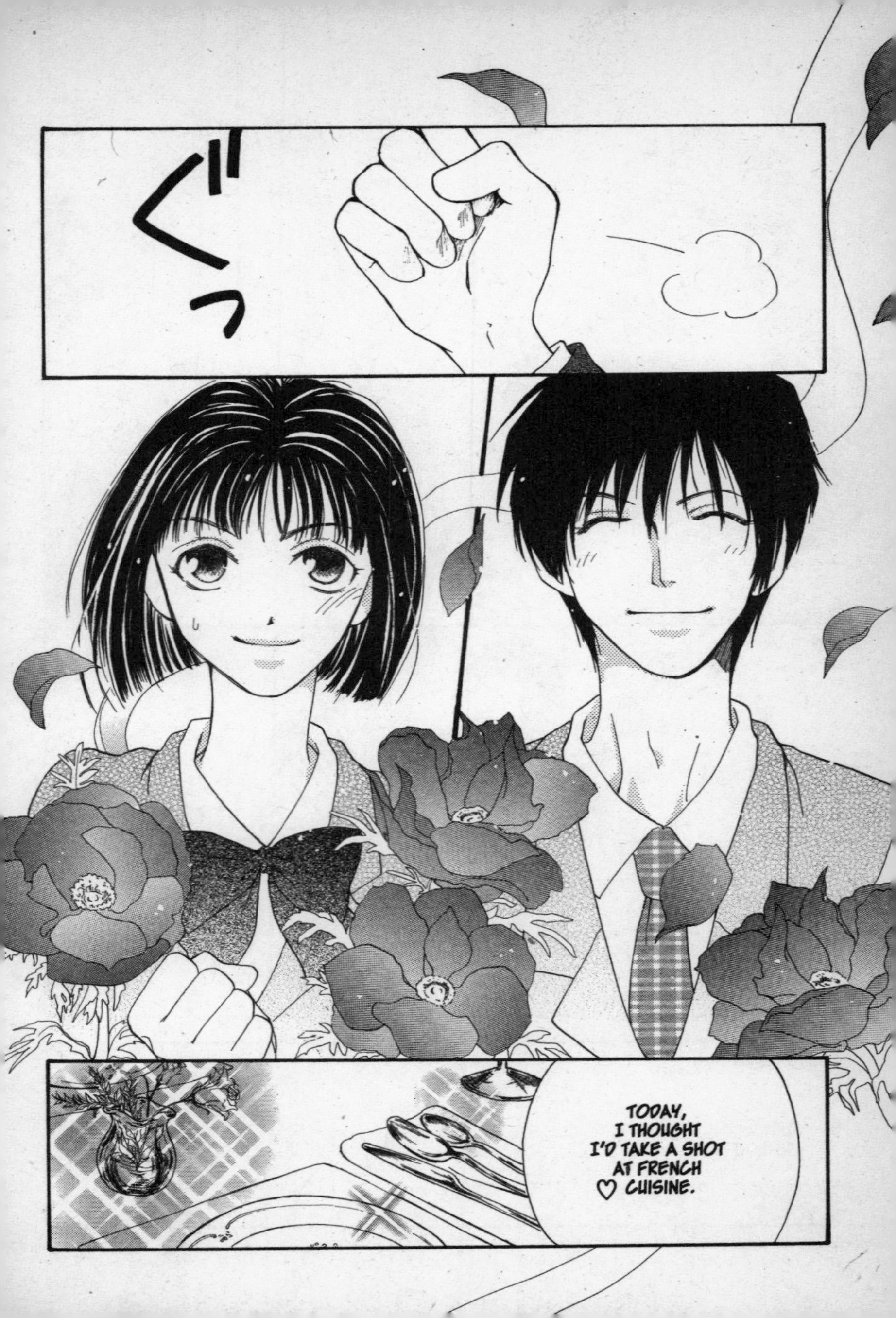
ぐっ
TODAY, I THOUGHT I'D TAKE A SHOT AT FRENCH ♡ CUISINE.

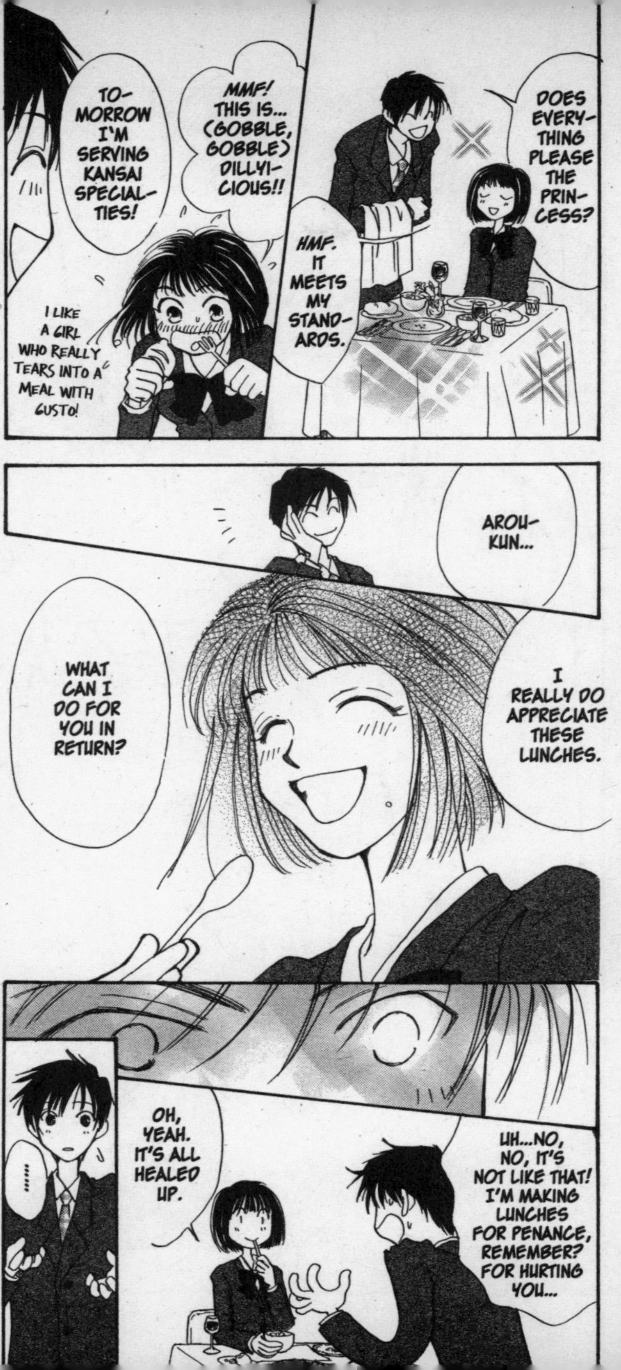
DOES EVERY-THING PLEASE THE PRIN-CESS?
HMF. IT MEETS MY STAND-ARDS.
MMF! THIS IS... (GOBBLE, GOBBLE) DILLYI-CIOUS!!
TO-MORROW I'M SERVING KANSAI SPECIAL-TIES!
I LIKE A GIRL WHO REALLY TEARS INTO A MEAL WITH GUSTO!
AROU-KUN...
I REALLY DO APPRECIATE THESE LUNCHES.
WHAT CAN I DO FOR YOU IN RETURN?
UH...NO, NO, IT'S NOT LIKE THAT! I'M MAKING LUNCHES FOR PENANCE, REMEMBER? FOR HURTING YOU...
OH, YEAH. IT'S ALL HEALED UP.
......

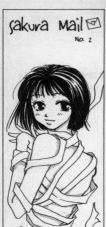

Sakura Mail

No. 2

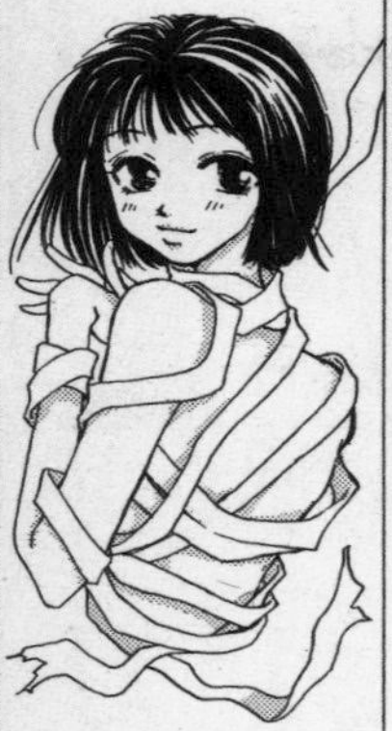

For the second story, I got to do a color cover, which took a long time at the drawing board to get right. This Kanade-chan was my first unsuccessful crack at it. "Land of the Blindfolded" was my first continuing series and because of that, creating this second story was hard. I had no idea where the story should go or even be about. Though I had the drive to do it, I spent a lot of time just sitting around, spinning my wheels. But finally, my editor, my family, friends, people around me, and the readers' letters of support lent me enough strength to complete this second story.

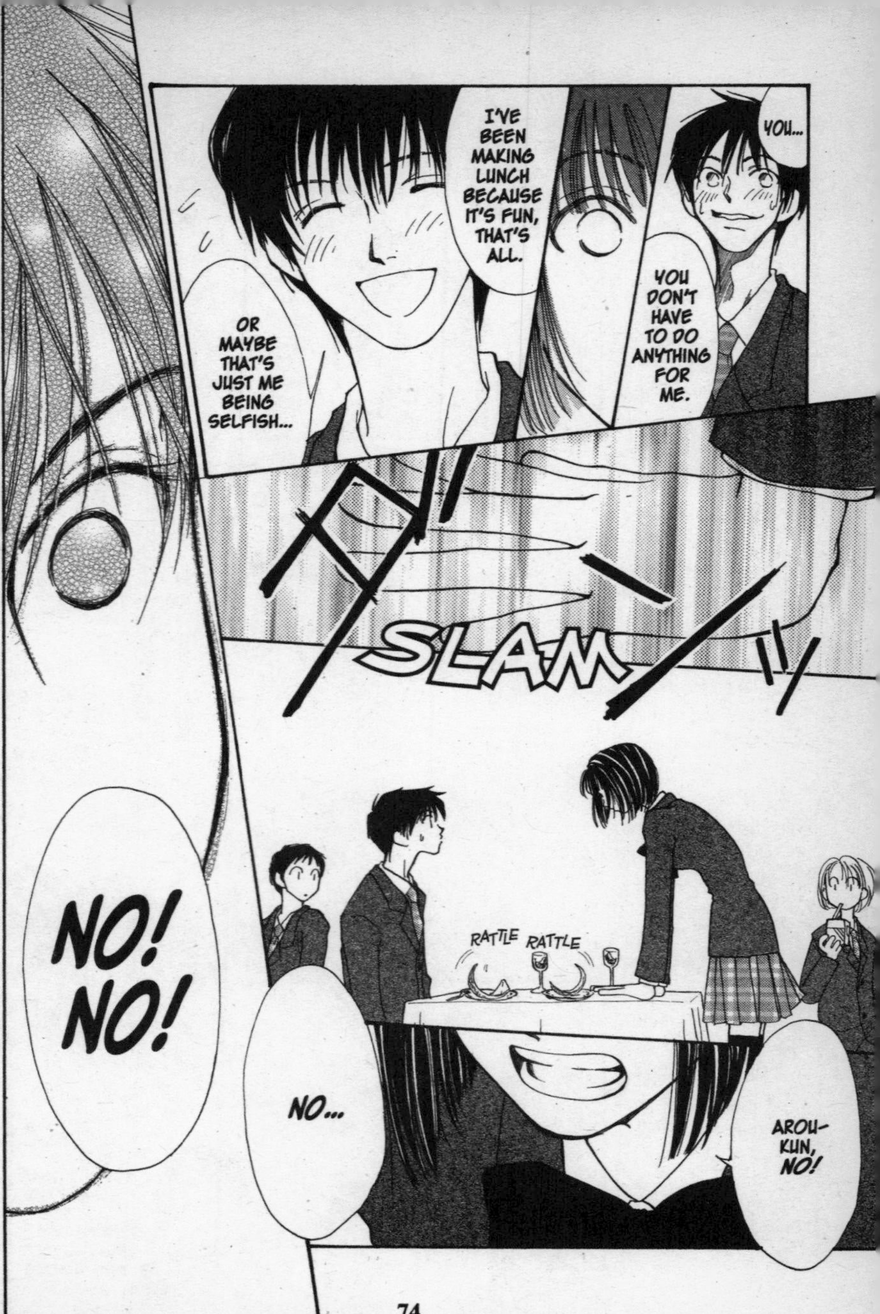
YOU...
YOU DON'T HAVE TO DO ANYTHING FOR ME.
I'VE BEEN MAKING LUNCH BECAUSE IT'S FUN, THAT'S ALL.
OR MAYBE THAT'S JUST ME BEING SELFISH...
SLAM
RATTLE RATTLE
AROU-KUN, NO!
NO...
NO! NO!

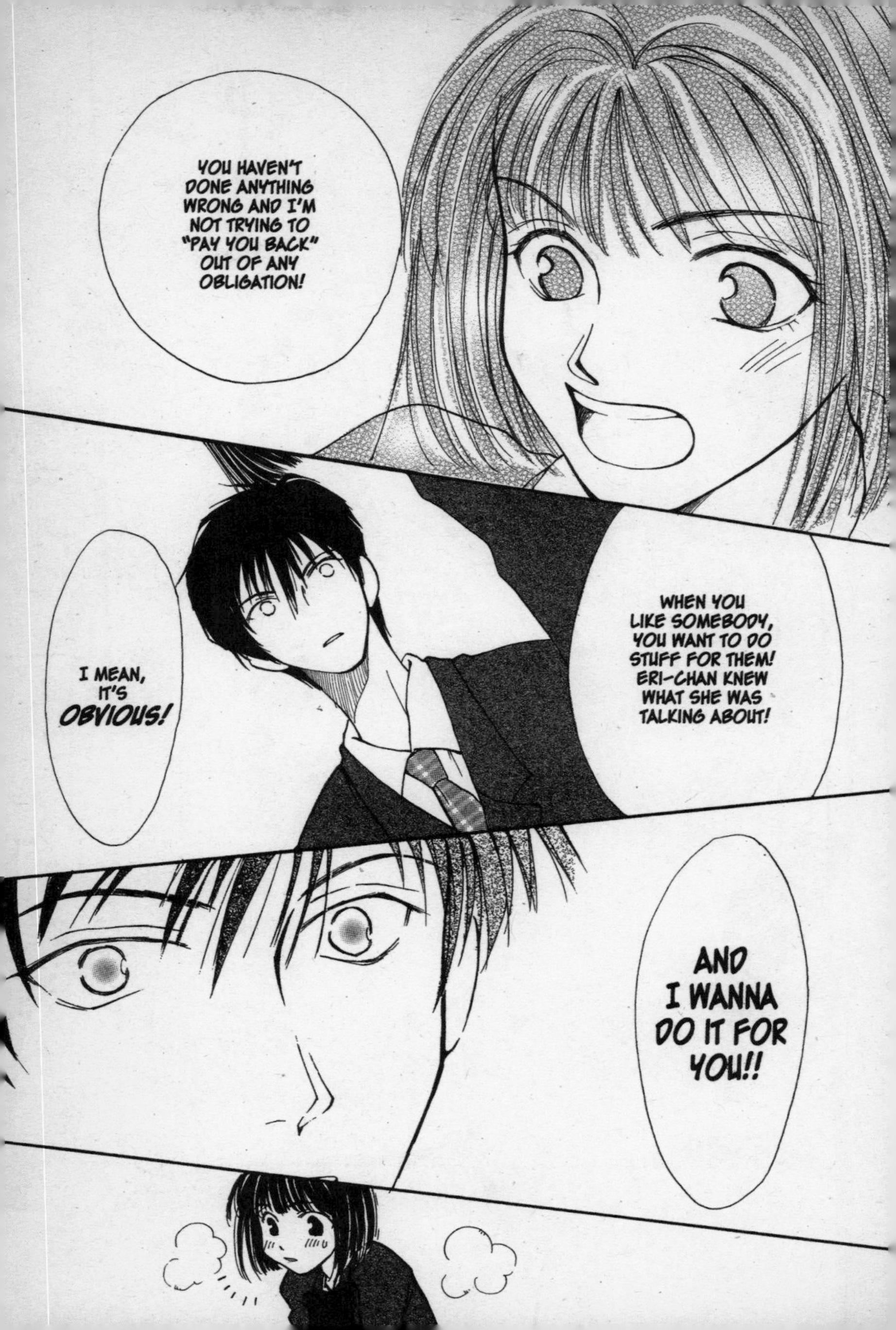
YOU HAVEN'T DONE ANYTHING WRONG AND I'M NOT TRYING TO "PAY YOU BACK" OUT OF ANY OBLIGATION!
WHEN YOU LIKE SOMEBODY, YOU WANT TO DO STUFF FOR THEM! ERI-CHAN KNEW WHAT SHE WAS TALKING ABOUT!
I MEAN, IT'S OBVIOUS!
AND I WANNA DO IT FOR YOU!!

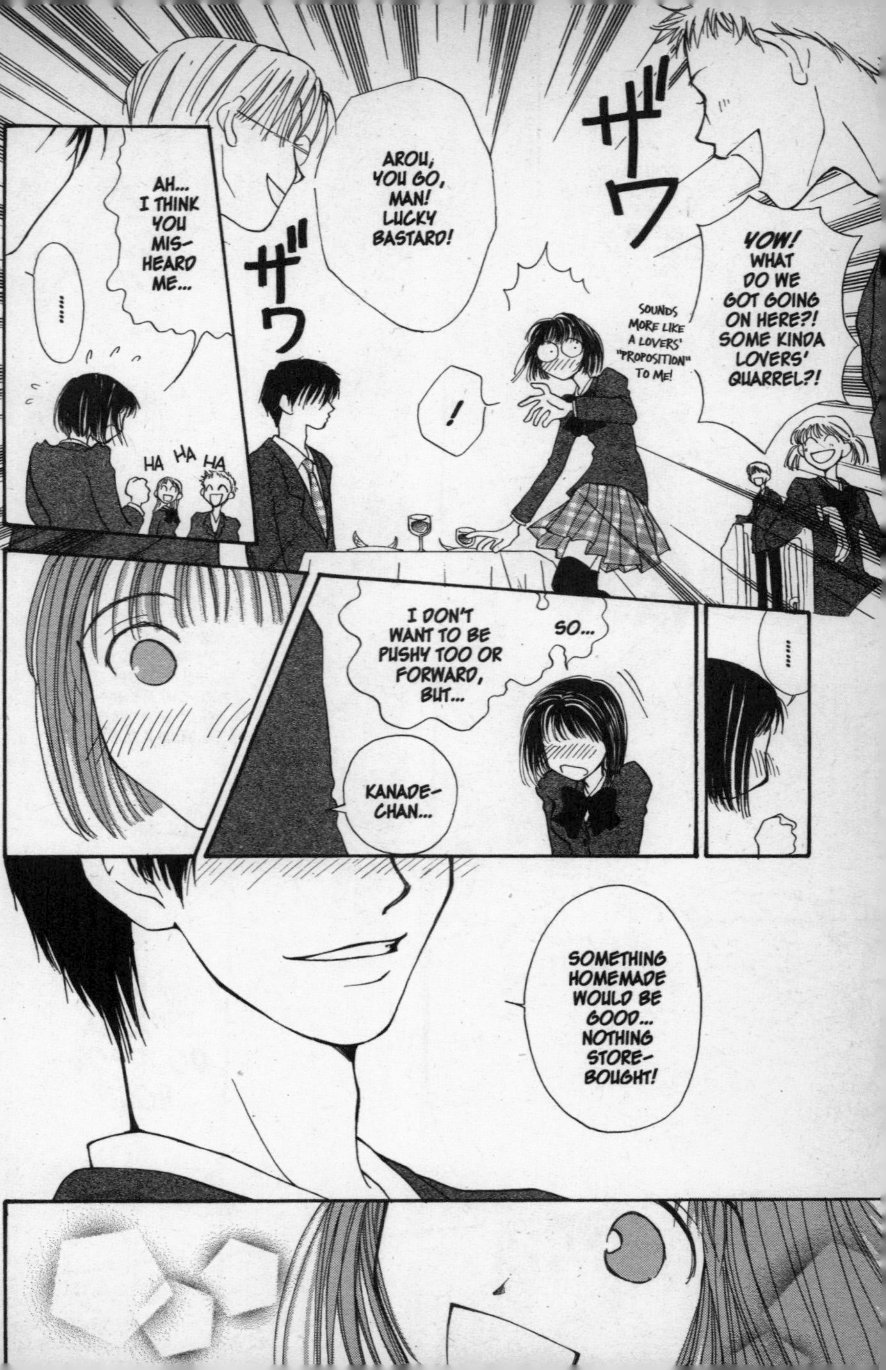
ザワ
YOW! WHAT DO WE GOT GOING ON HERE?! SOME KINDA LOVERS' QUARREL?!
SOUNDS MORE LIKE A LOVERS' "PROPOSITION" TO ME!
AROU, YOU GO, MAN! LUCKY BASTARD!
ザワ
!
AH... I THINK YOU MIS-HEARD ME...
HA HA HA
......
......
SO...
I DON'T WANT TO BE PUSHY TOO OR FORWARD, BUT...
KANADE-CHAN...
SOMETHING HOMEMADE WOULD BE GOOD... NOTHING STORE-BOUGHT!

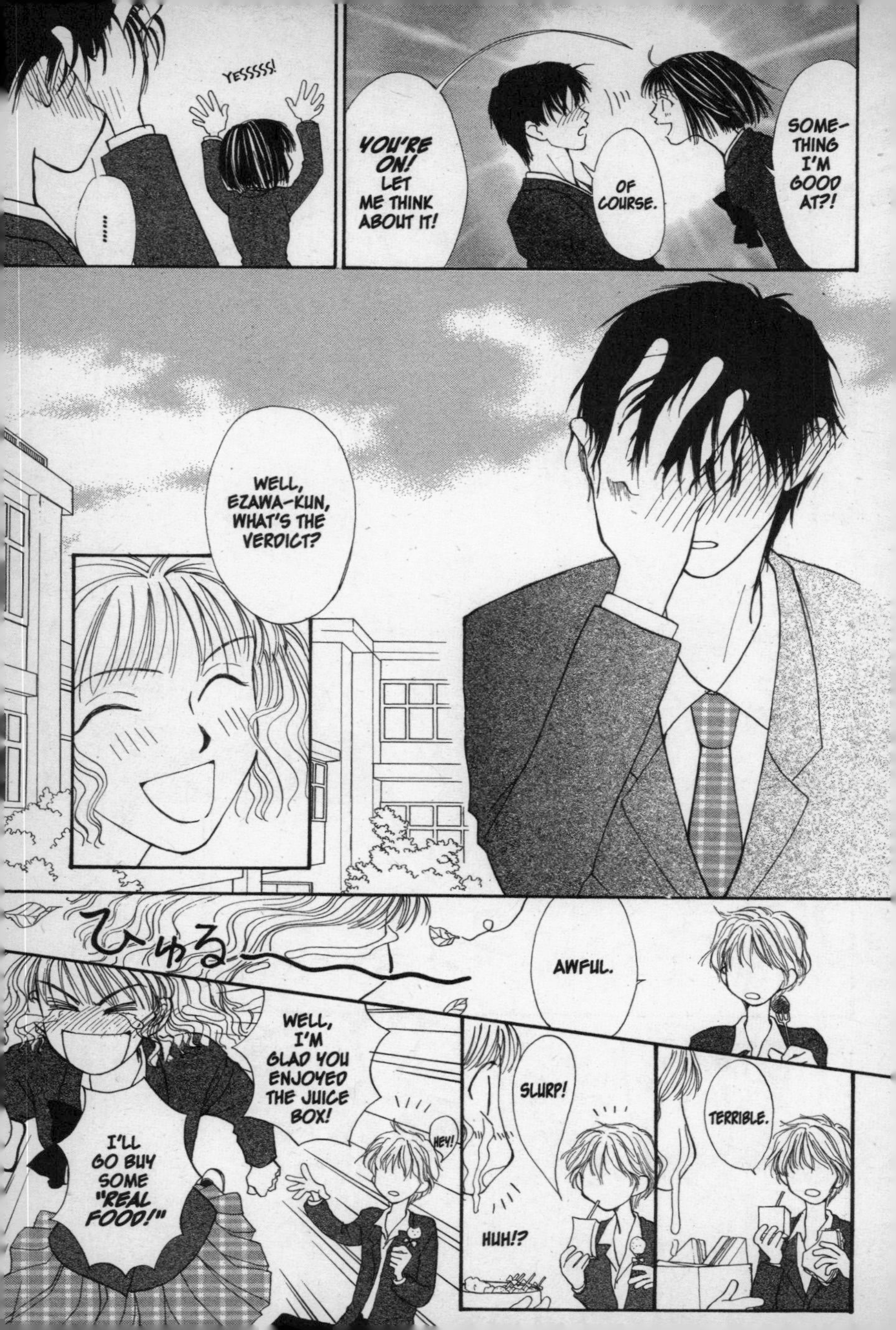
SOMETHING I'M GOOD AT?!
OF COURSE.
YOU'RE ON! LET ME THINK ABOUT IT!
YESSSSS!
......
WELL, EZAWA-KUN, WHAT'S THE VERDICT?
AWFUL.
TERRIBLE.
SLURP!
HUH!?
ひゅるー
WELL, I'M GLAD YOU ENJOYED THE JUICE BOX!
HEY!
I'LL GO BUY SOME "REAL FOOD!"

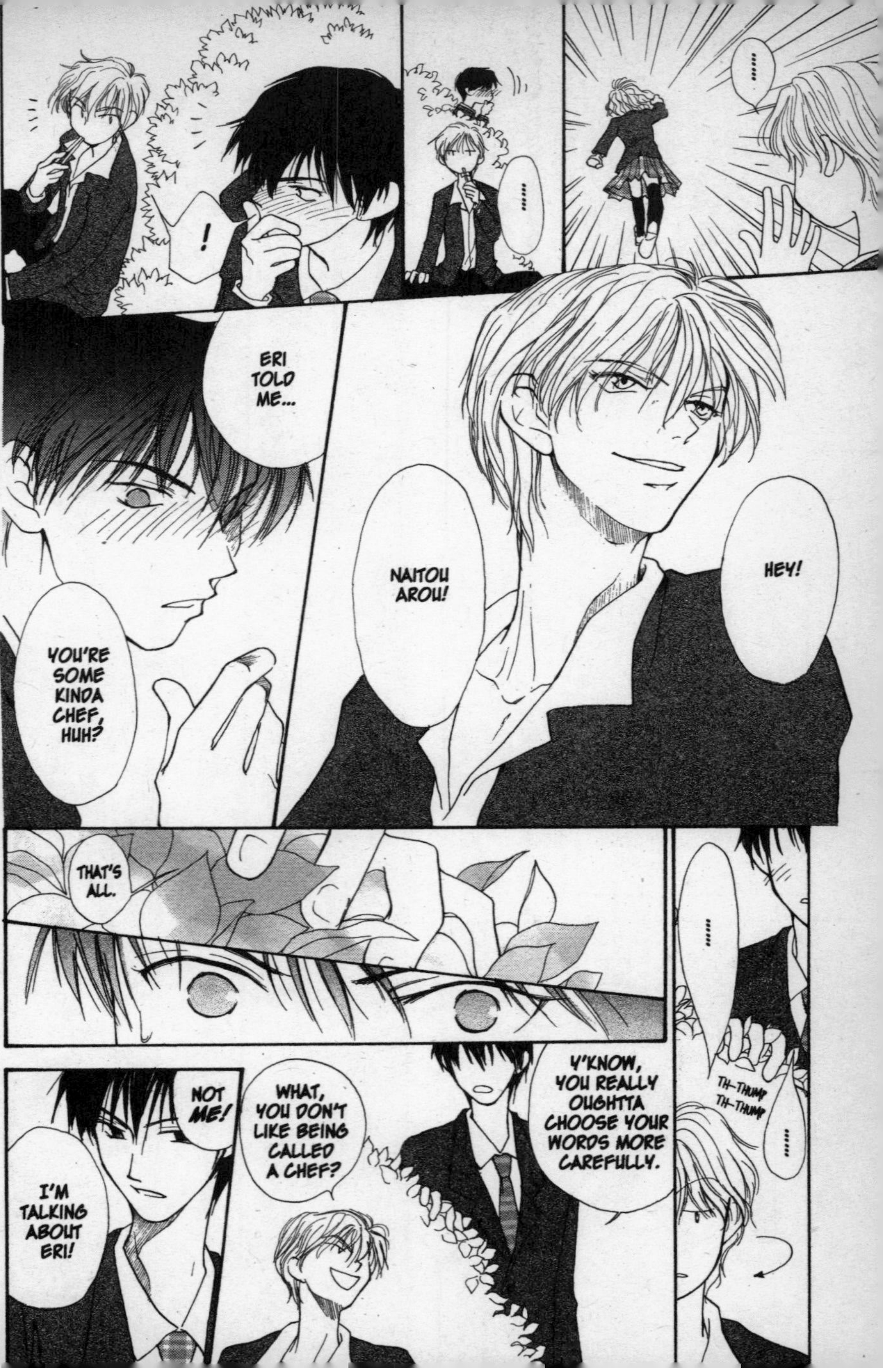
......
......
!
HEY!
NAITOU AROU!
ERI TOLD ME...
YOU'RE SOME KINDA CHEF, HUH?
......
TH-THUMP TH-THUMP
......
THAT'S ALL.
Y'KNOW, YOU REALLY OUGHTTA CHOOSE YOUR WORDS MORE CAREFULLY.
WHAT, YOU DON'T LIKE BEING CALLED A CHEF?
NOT ME!
I'M TALKING ABOUT ERI!

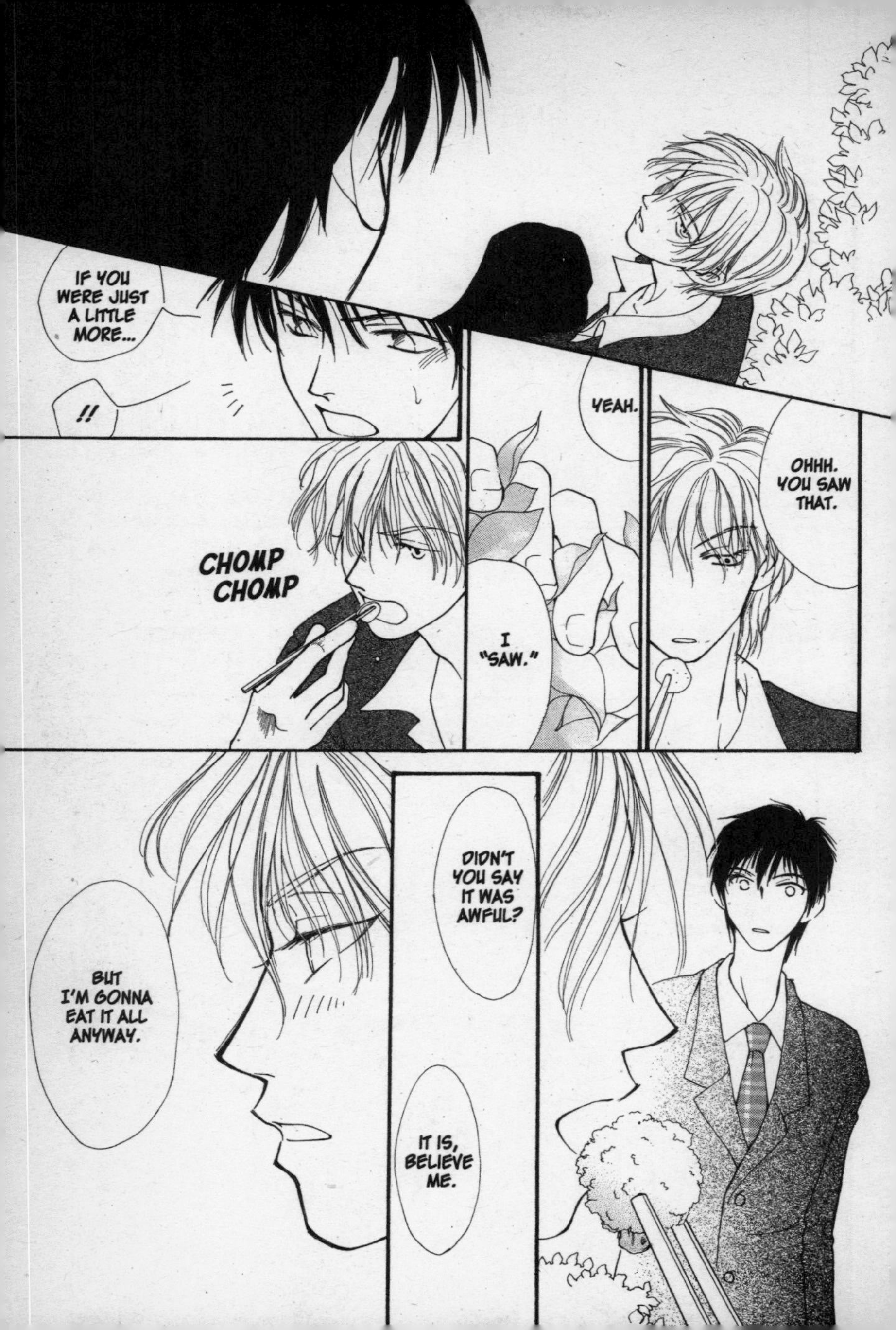
IF YOU WERE JUST A LITTLE MORE...
!!
OHHH. YOU SAW THAT.
YEAH.
I "SAW."
CHOMP CHOMP
DIDN'T YOU SAY IT WAS AWFUL?
BUT I'M GONNA EAT IT ALL ANYWAY.
IT IS, BELIEVE ME.

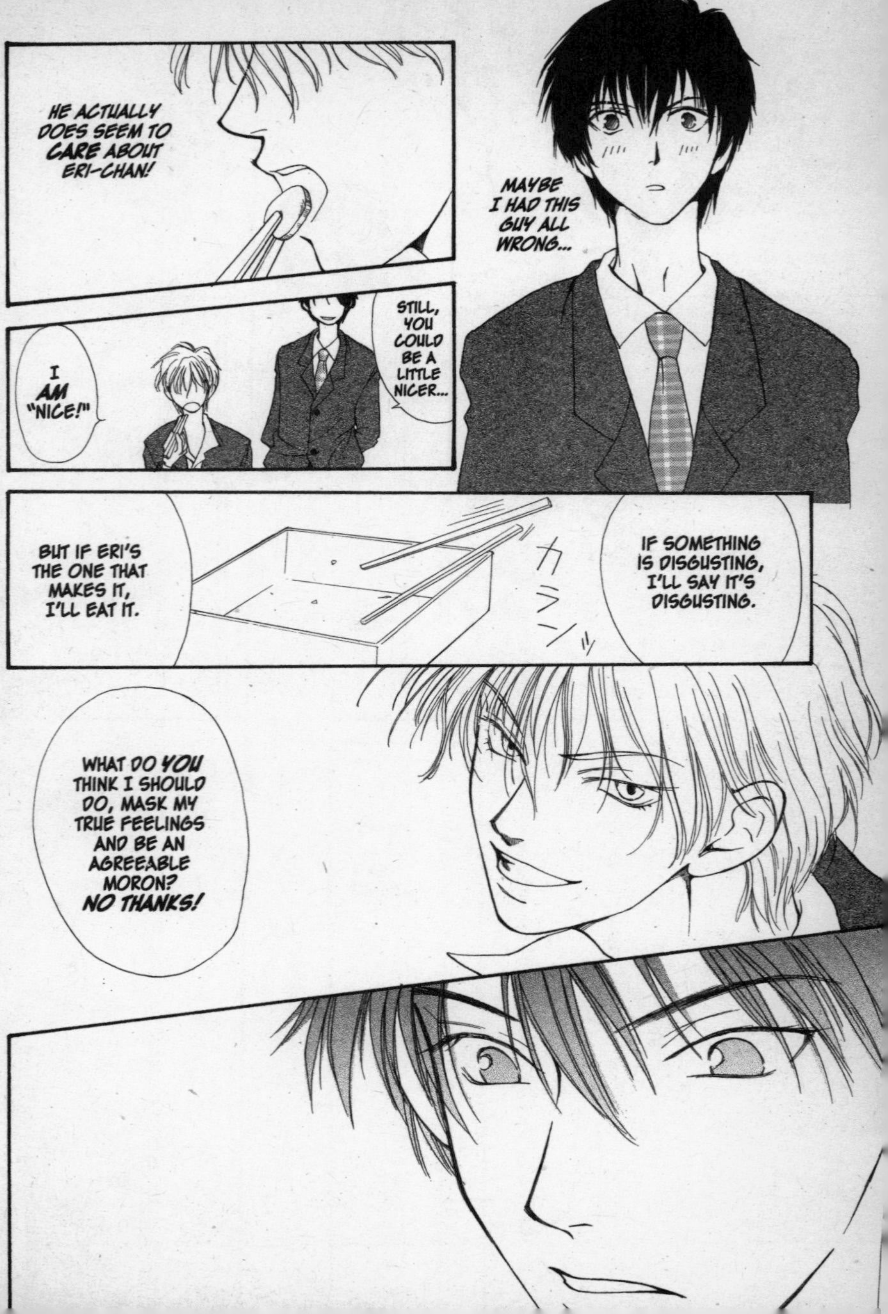
MAYBE I HAD THIS GUY ALL WRONG...
HE ACTUALLY DOES SEEM TO CARE ABOUT ERI-CHAN!
STILL, YOU COULD BE A LITTLE NICER...
I AM "NICE!"
IF SOMETHING IS DISGUSTING, I'LL SAY IT'S DISGUSTING.
カランッ
BUT IF ERI'S THE ONE THAT MAKES IT, I'LL EAT IT.
WHAT DO YOU THINK I SHOULD DO, MASK MY TRUE FEELINGS AND BE AN AGREEABLE MORON? NO THANKS!

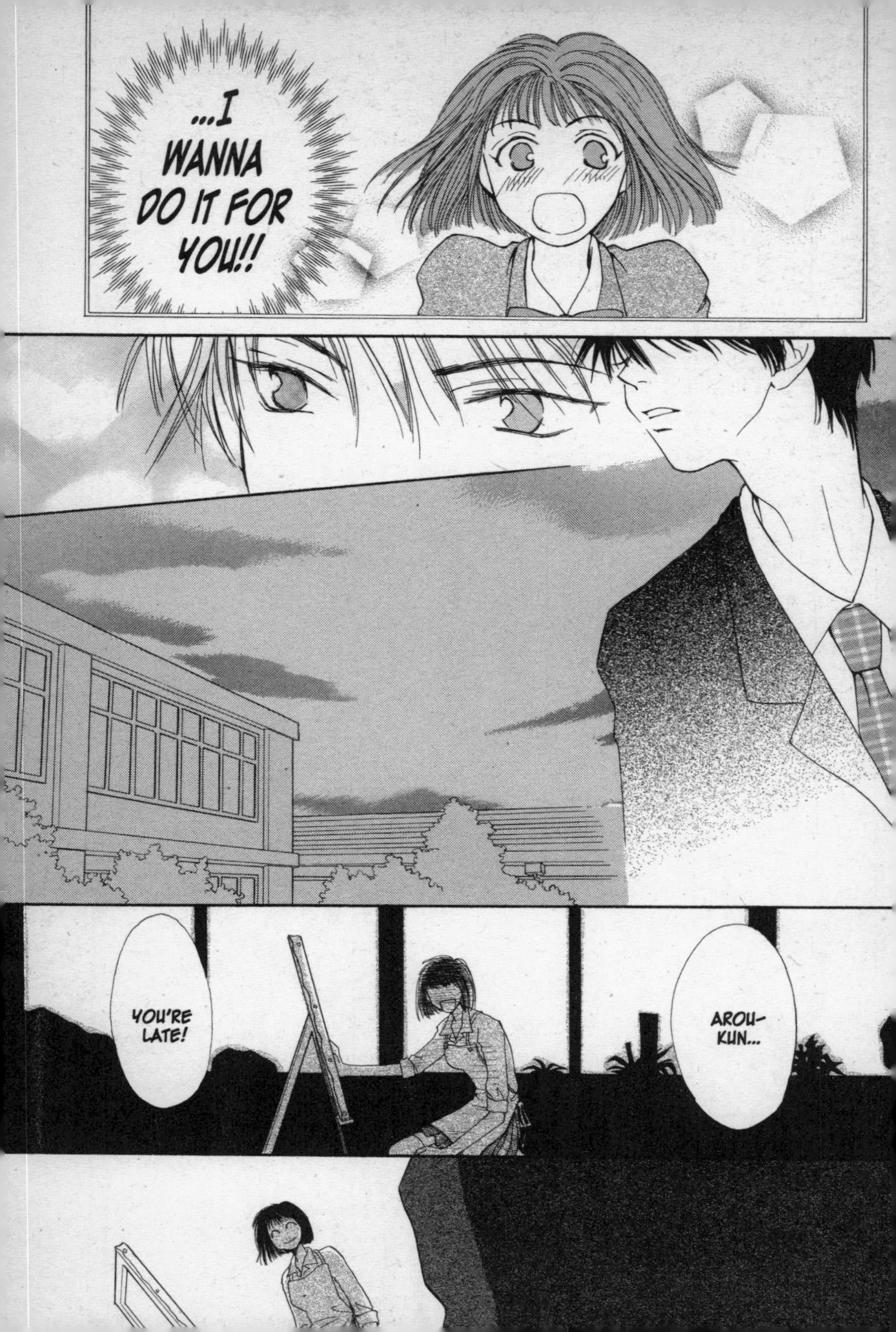
...I WANNA DO IT FOR YOU!!
AROU-KUN...
YOU'RE LATE!

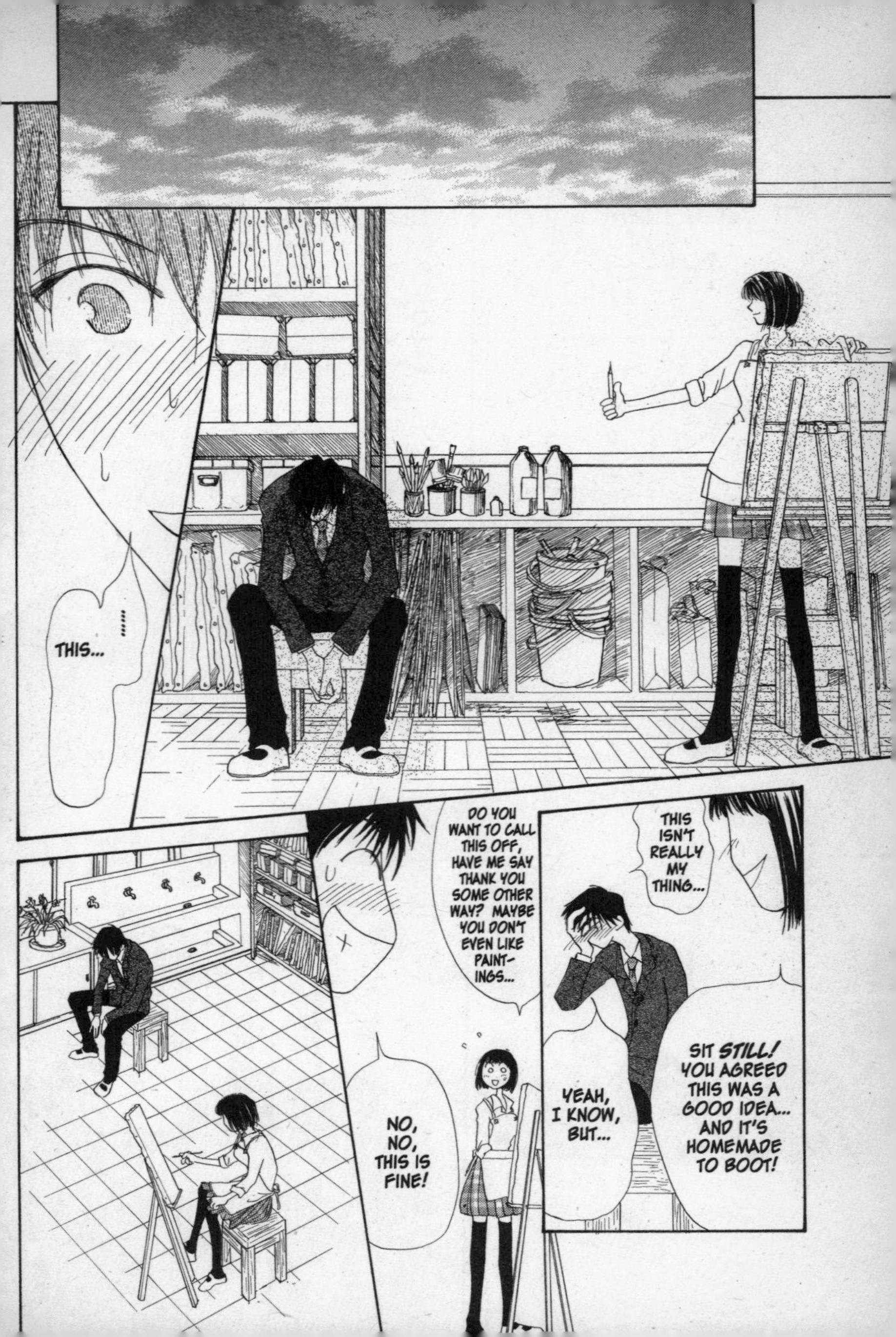
......
THIS...
THIS ISN'T REALLY MY THING...
SIT STILL! YOU AGREED THIS WAS A GOOD IDEA... AND IT'S HOMEMADE TO BOOT!
YEAH, I KNOW, BUT...
DO YOU WANT TO CALL THIS OFF, HAVE ME SAY THANK YOU SOME OTHER WAY? MAYBE YOU DON'T EVEN LIKE PAINT-INGS...
NO, NO, THIS IS FINE!

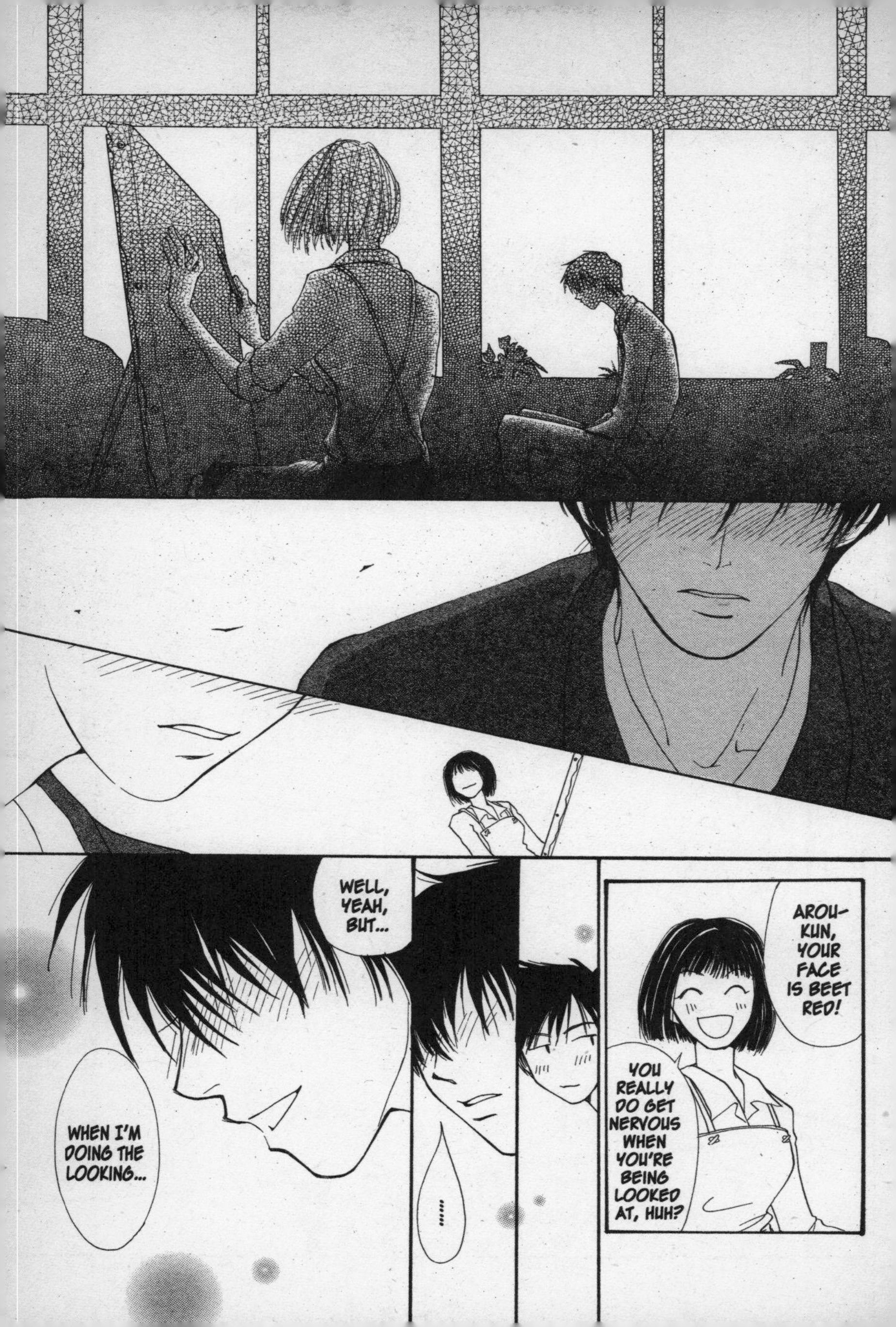
AROU-KUN, YOUR FACE IS BEET RED!
YOU REALLY DO GET NERVOUS WHEN YOU'RE BEING LOOKED AT, HUH?
......
WELL, YEAH, BUT...
WHEN I'M DOING THE LOOKING...

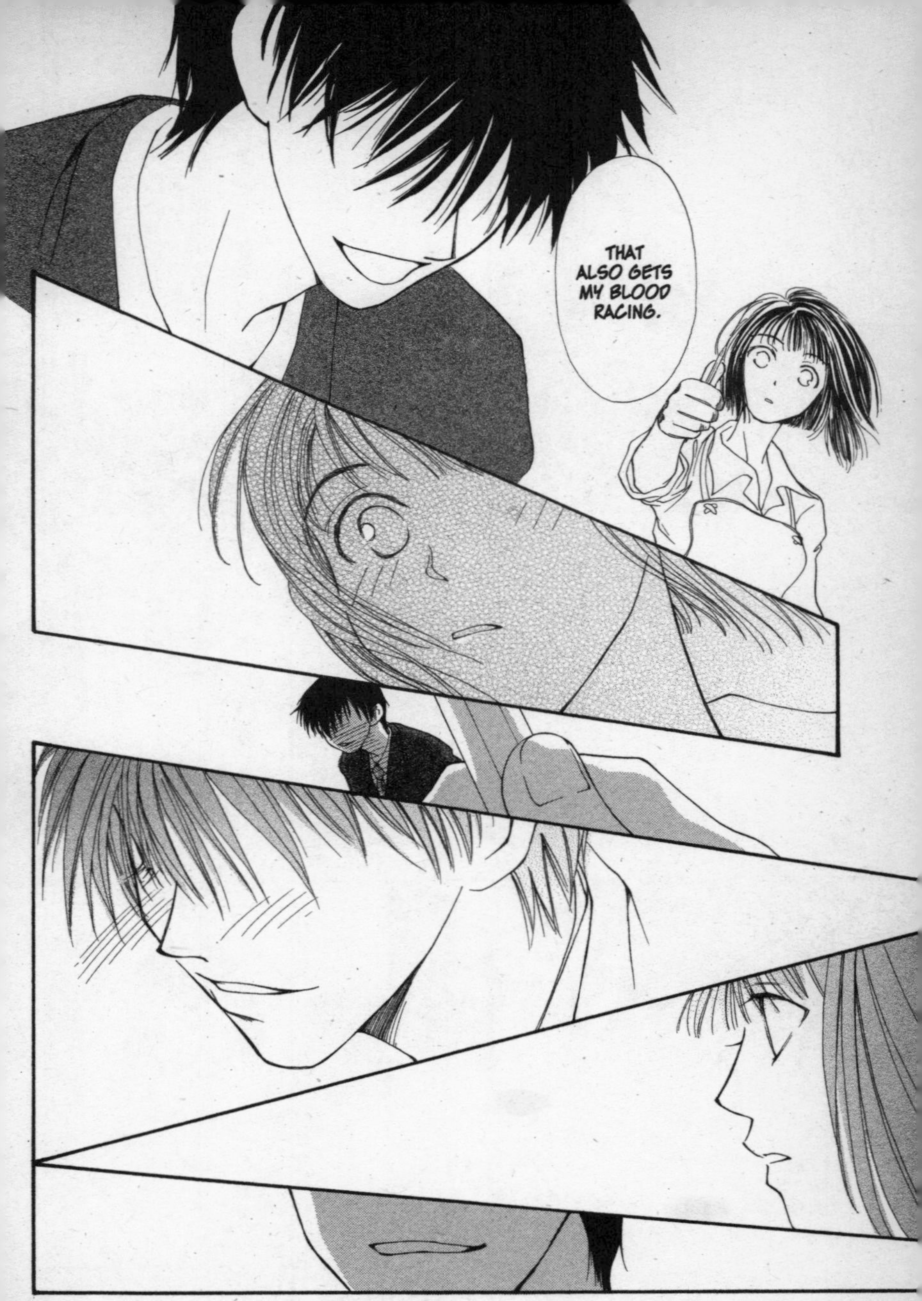
THAT ALSO GETS MY BLOOD RACING.

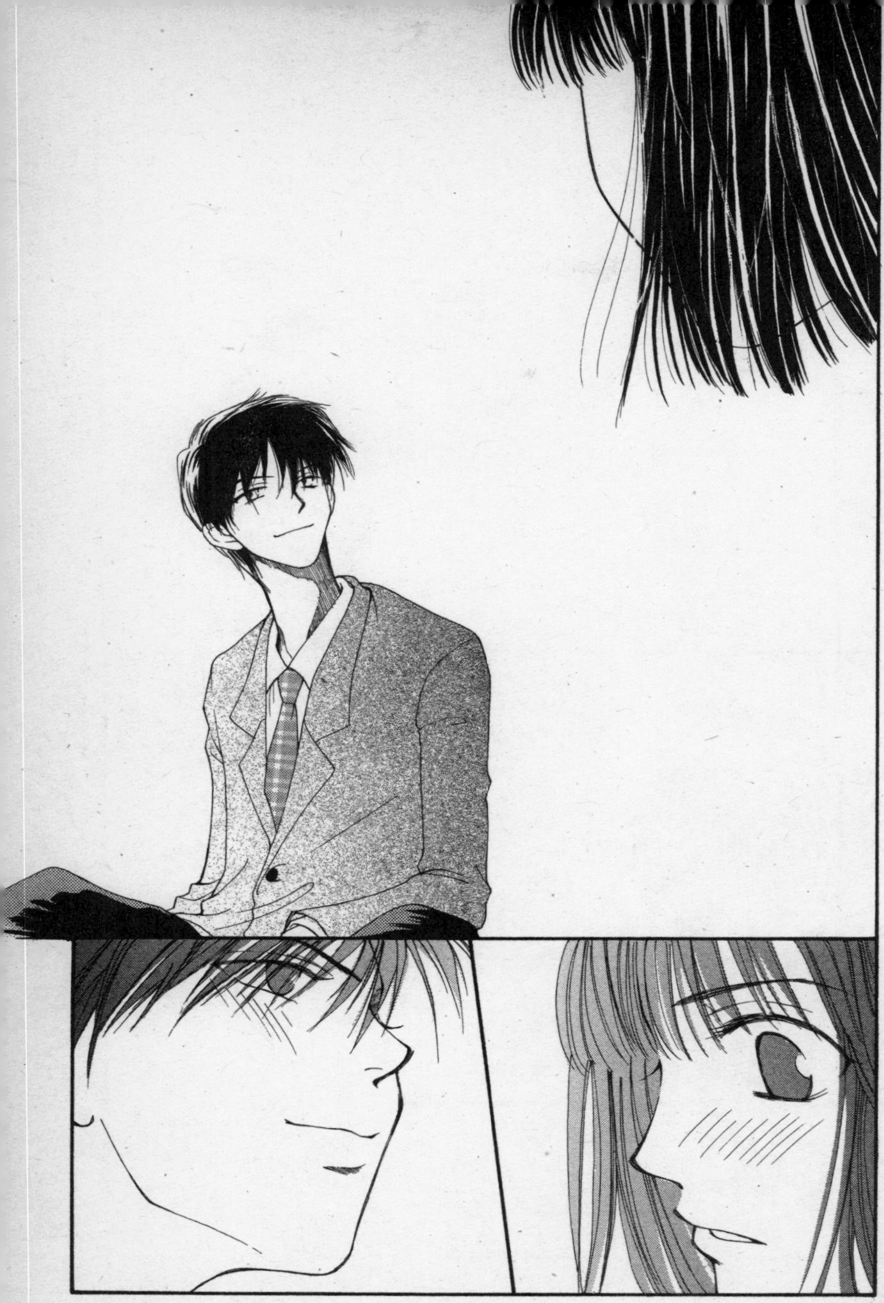

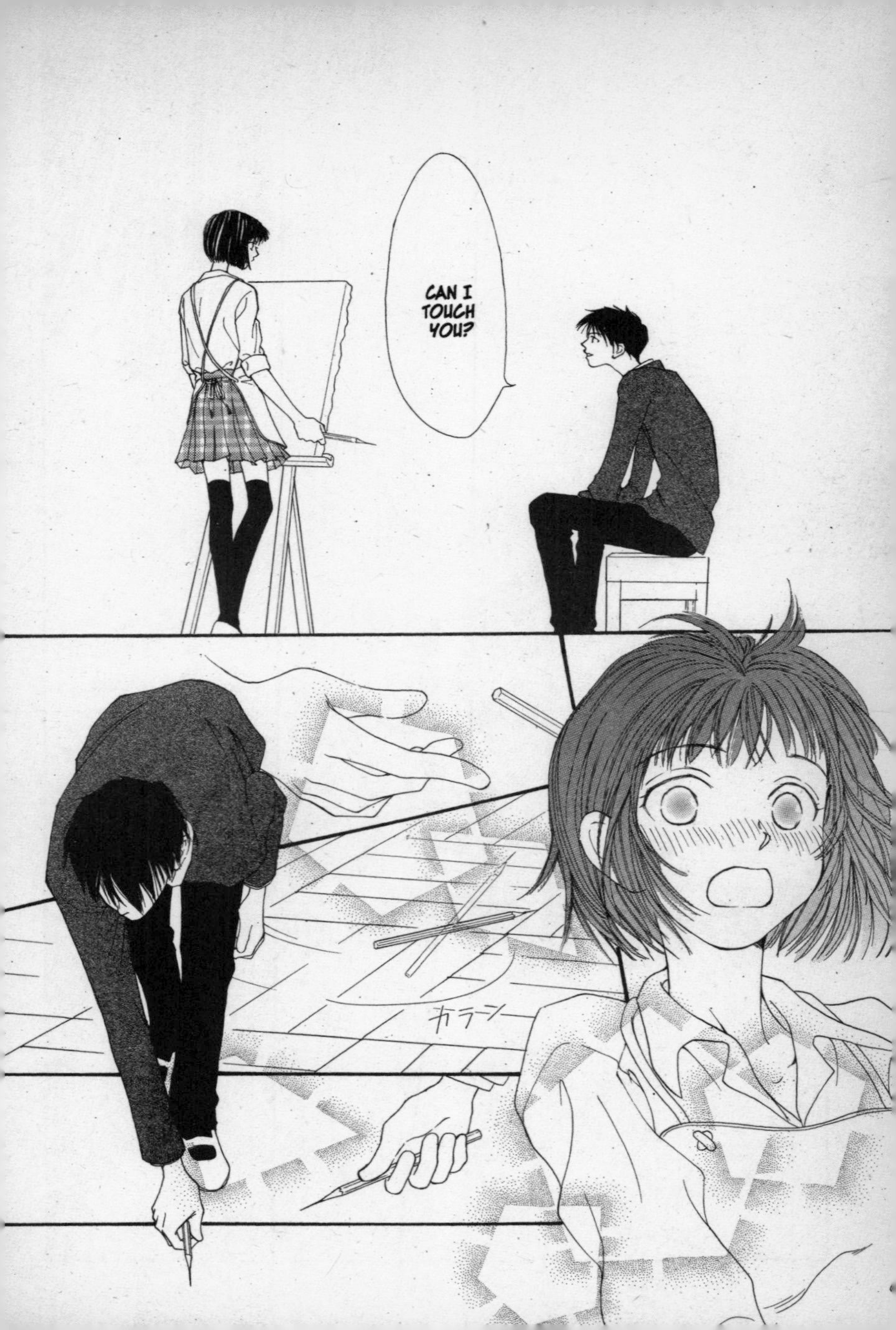
CAN I TOUCH YOU?
カラーン

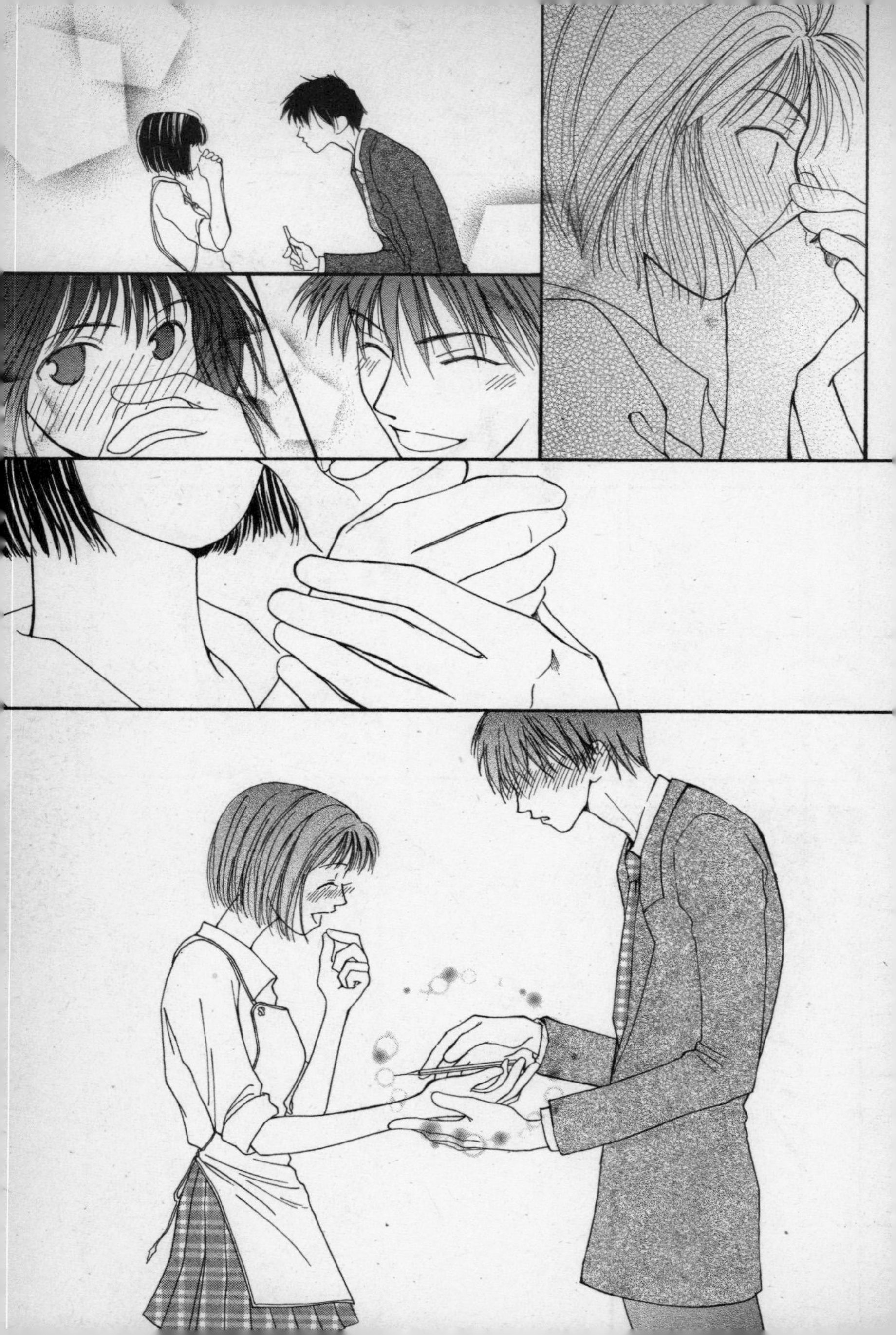

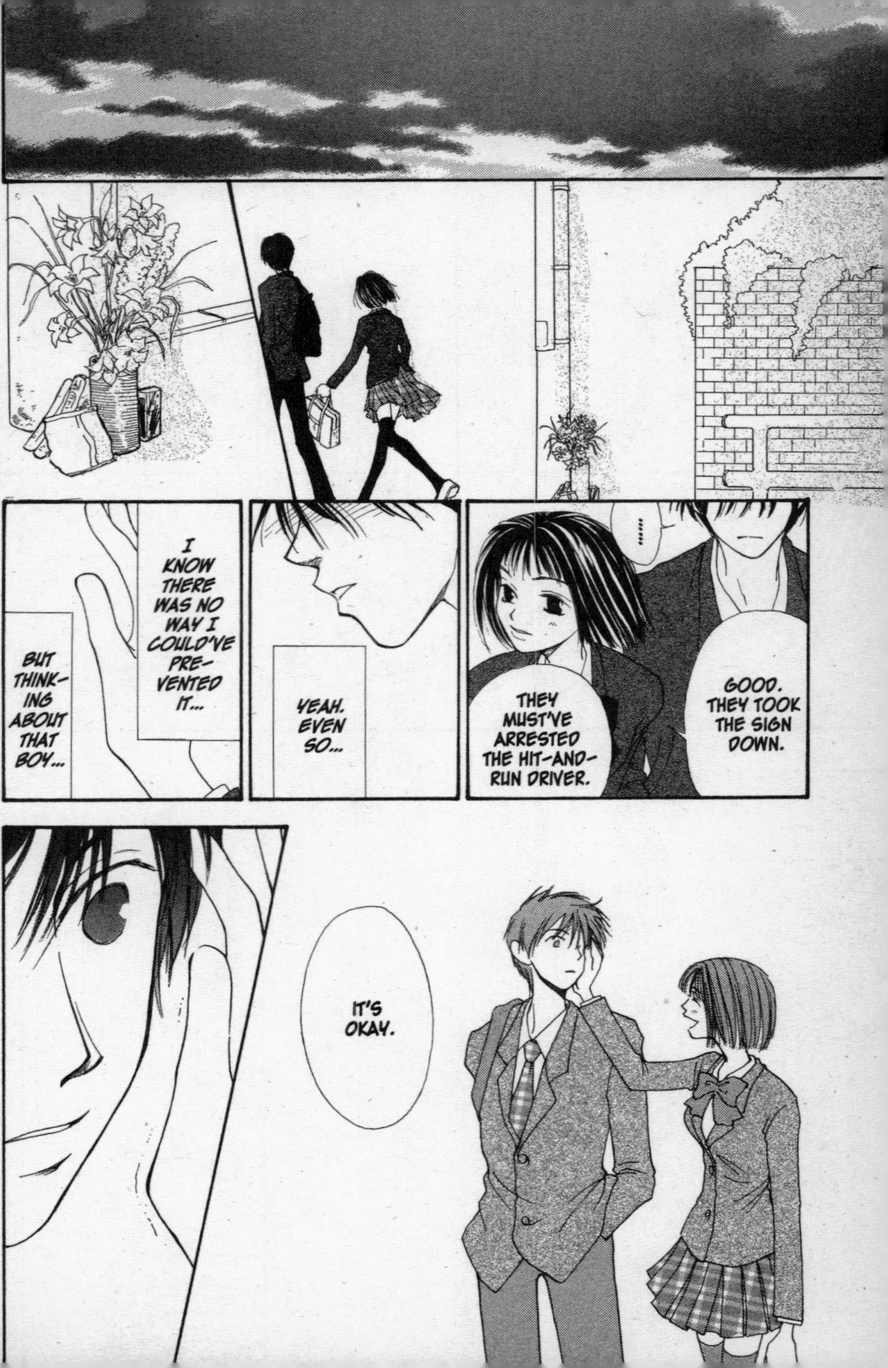
......
GOOD. THEY TOOK THE SIGN DOWN.
THEY MUST'VE ARRESTED THE HIT-AND-RUN DRIVER.
YEAH. EVEN SO...
I KNOW THERE WAS NO WAY I COULD'VE PREVENTED IT...
BUT THINKING ABOUT THAT BOY...
IT'S OKAY.

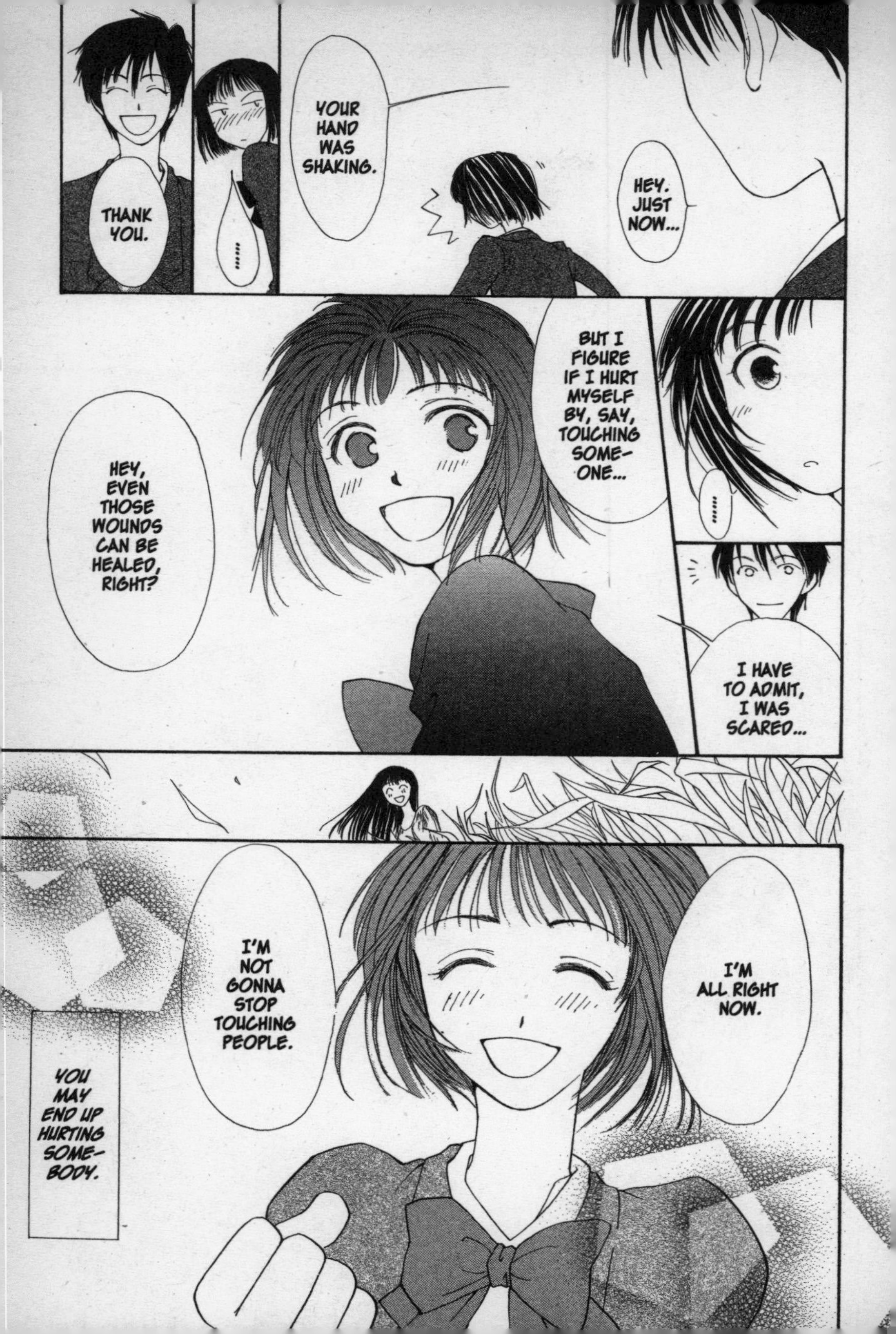
HEY. JUST NOW...
YOUR HAND WAS SHAKING.
......
THANK YOU.
......
I HAVE TO ADMIT, I WAS SCARED...
BUT I FIGURE IF I HURT MYSELF BY, SAY, TOUCHING SOME-ONE...
HEY, EVEN THOSE WOUNDS CAN BE HEALED, RIGHT?
I'M ALL RIGHT NOW.
I'M NOT GONNA STOP TOUCHING PEOPLE.
YOU MAY END UP HURTING SOME-BODY.

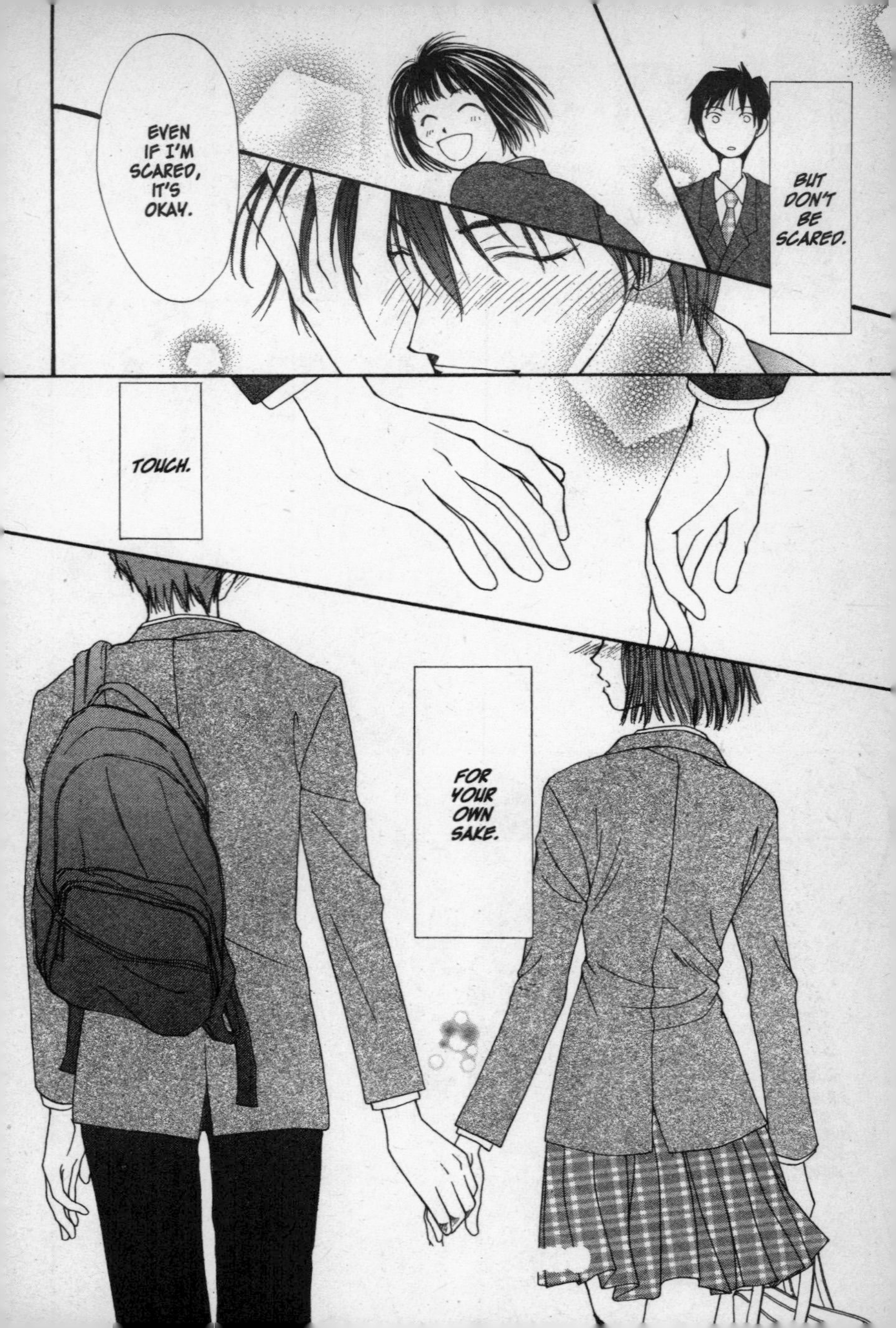

BUT DON'T BE SCARED.
EVEN IF I'M SCARED, IT'S OKAY.
TOUCH.
FOR YOUR OWN SAKE.

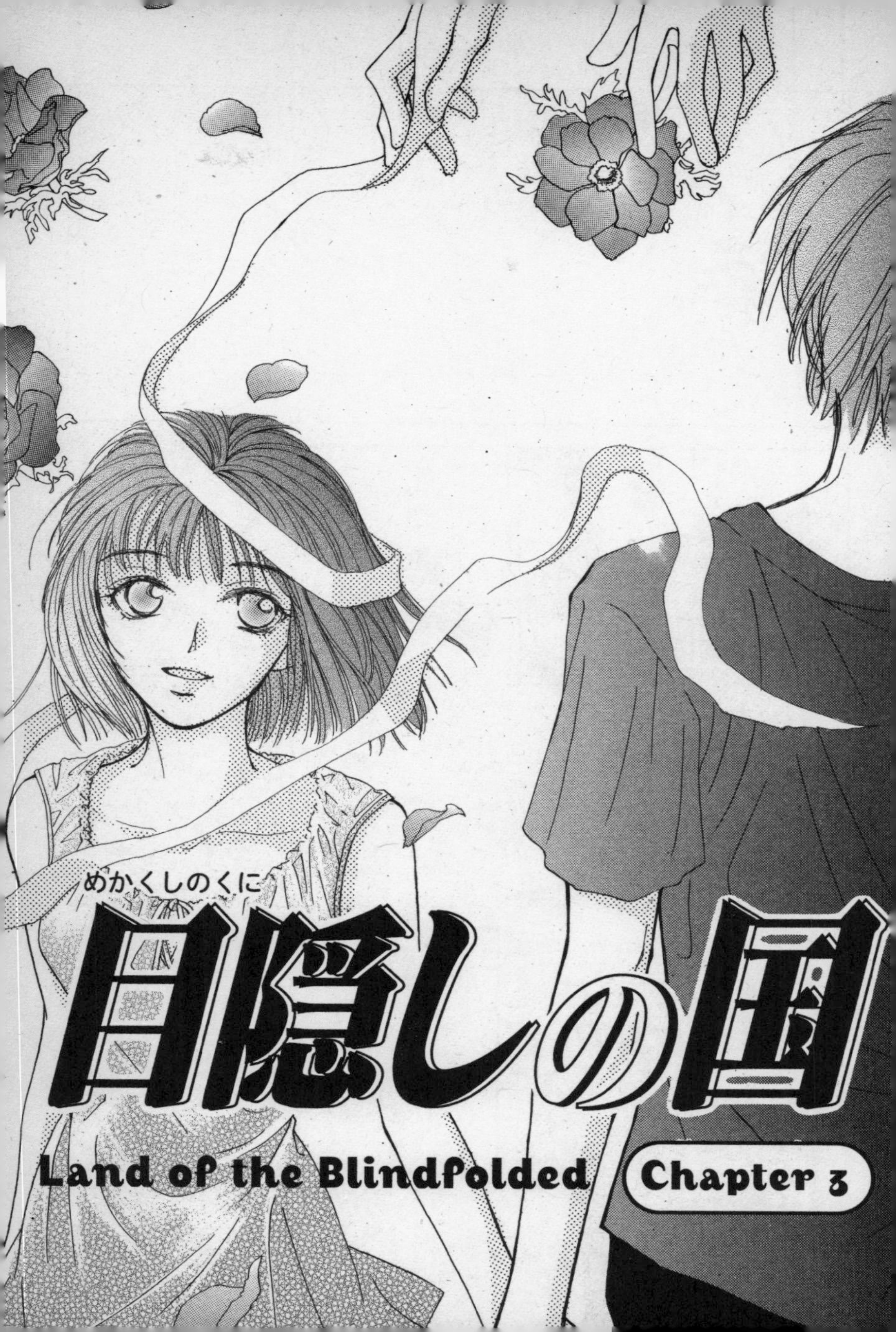
めかくしのくに
目隠しの国
Land of the Blindfolded
Chapter 3

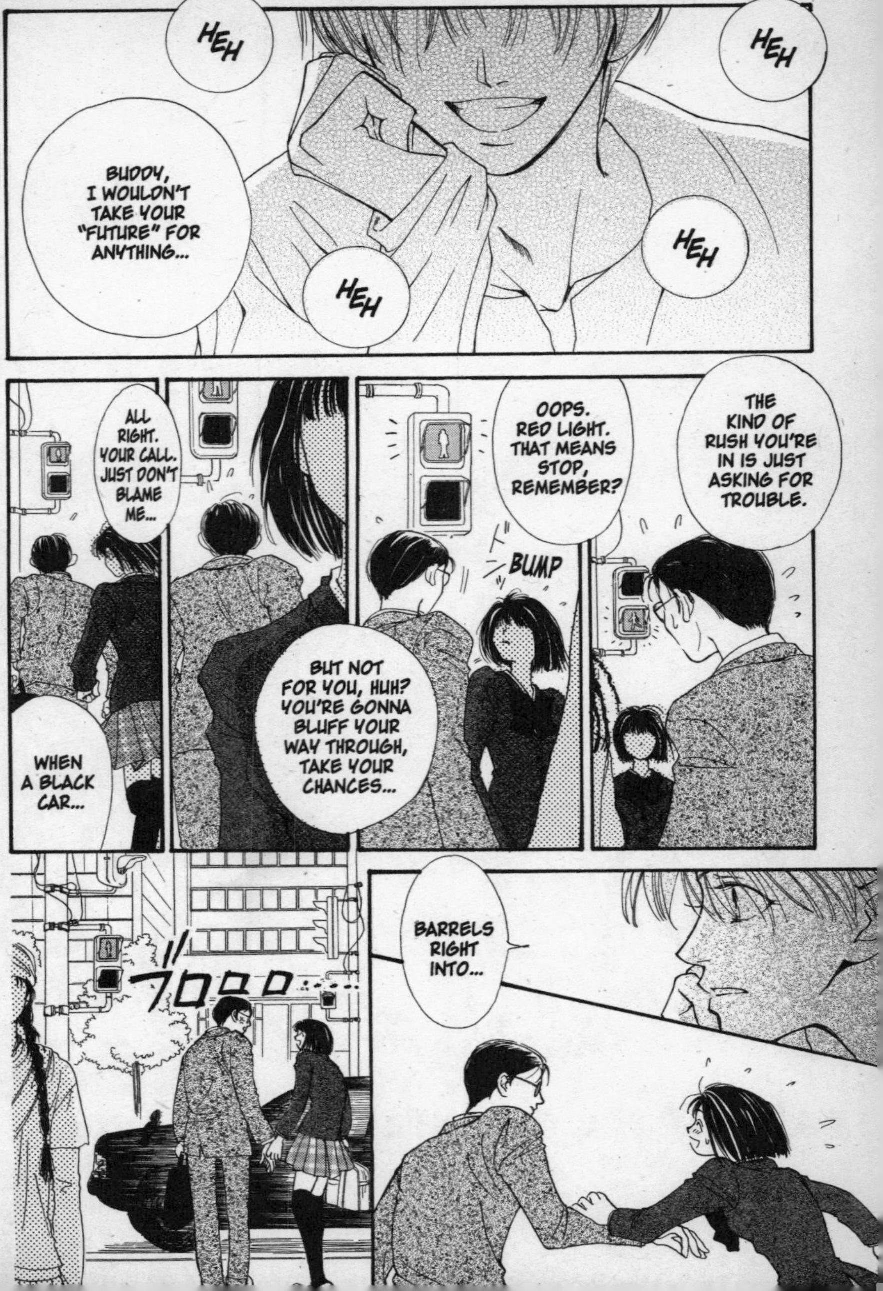
HEH
HEH
BUDDY, I WOULDN'T TAKE YOUR "FUTURE" FOR ANYTHING...
HEH
HEH
THE KIND OF RUSH YOU'RE IN IS JUST ASKING FOR TROUBLE.
OOPS. RED LIGHT. THAT MEANS STOP, REMEMBER?
ド
BUMP
BUT NOT FOR YOU, HUH? YOU'RE GONNA BLUFF YOUR WAY THROUGH, TAKE YOUR CHANCES...
ALL RIGHT. YOUR CALL. JUST DON'T BLAME ME...
WHEN A BLACK CAR...
BARRELS RIGHT INTO...
ブロロロ

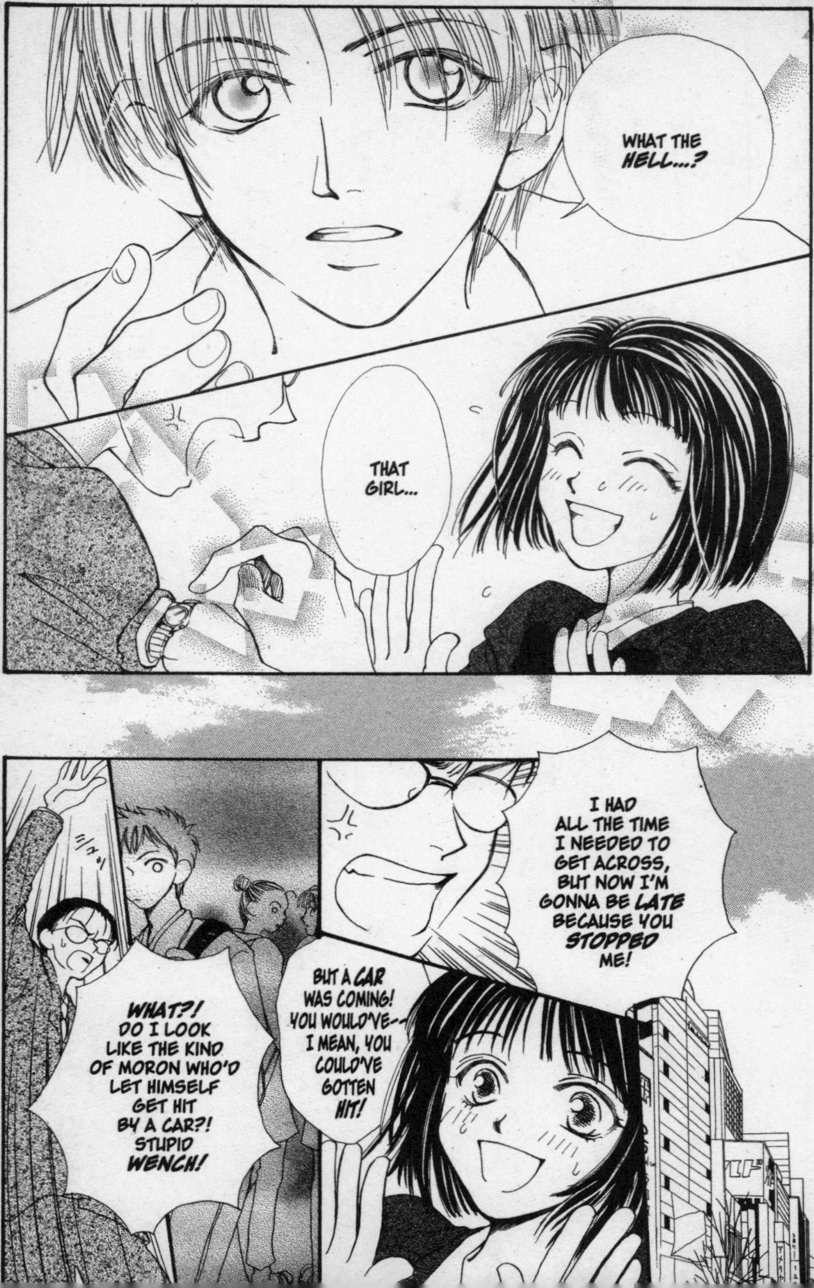
WHAT THE HELL...?
THAT GIRL...
I HAD ALL THE TIME I NEEDED TO GET ACROSS, BUT NOW I'M GONNA BE LATE BECAUSE YOU STOPPED ME!
BUT A CAR WAS COMING! YOU WOULD'VE-- I MEAN, YOU COULD'VE GOTTEN HIT!
WHAT?! DO I LOOK LIKE THE KIND OF MORON WHO'D LET HIMSELF GET HIT BY A CAR?! STUPID WENCH!

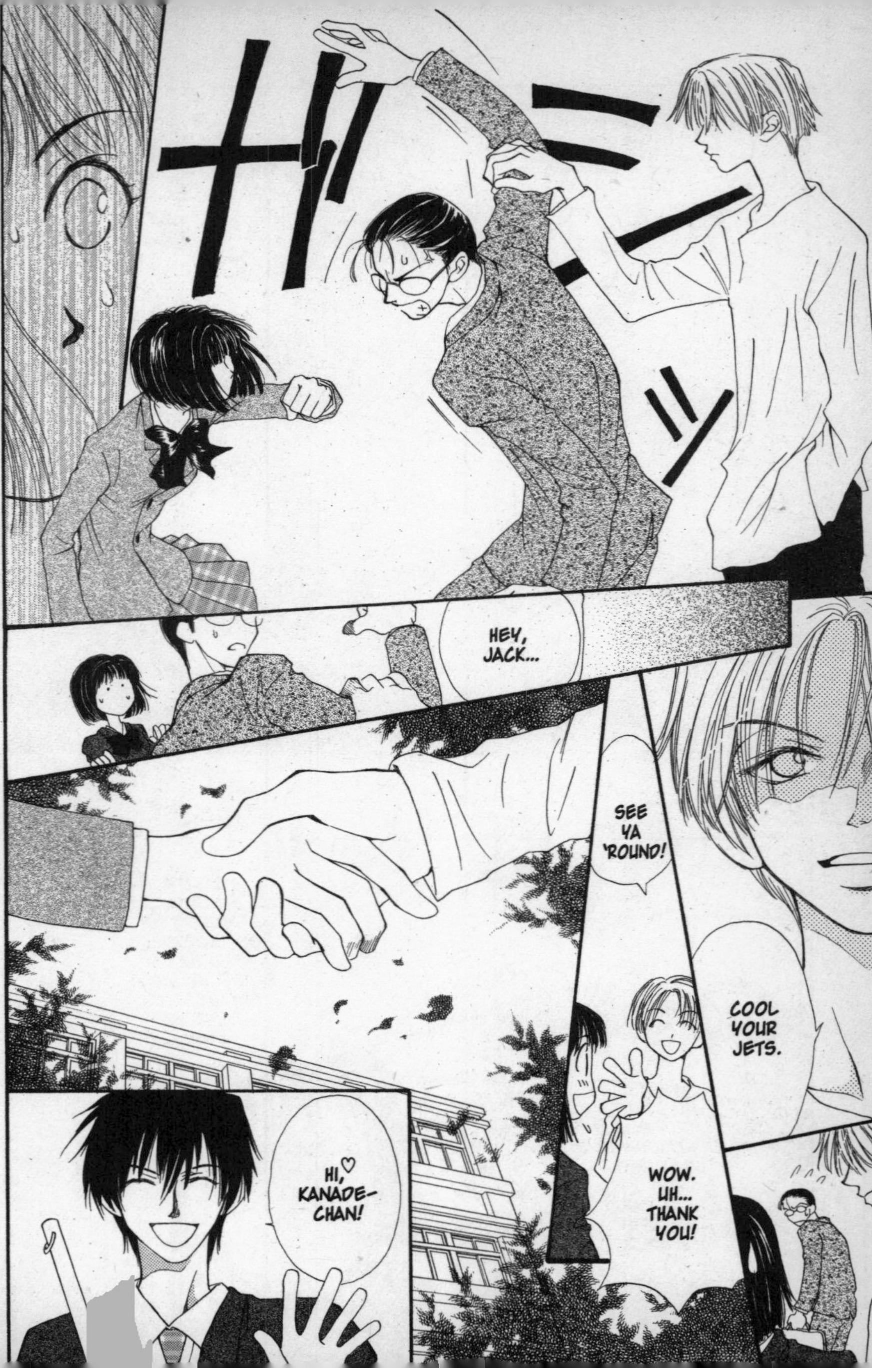
HEY, JACK...
COOL YOUR JETS.
SEE YA 'ROUND!
WOW. UH... THANK YOU!
HI, KANADE-CHAN!

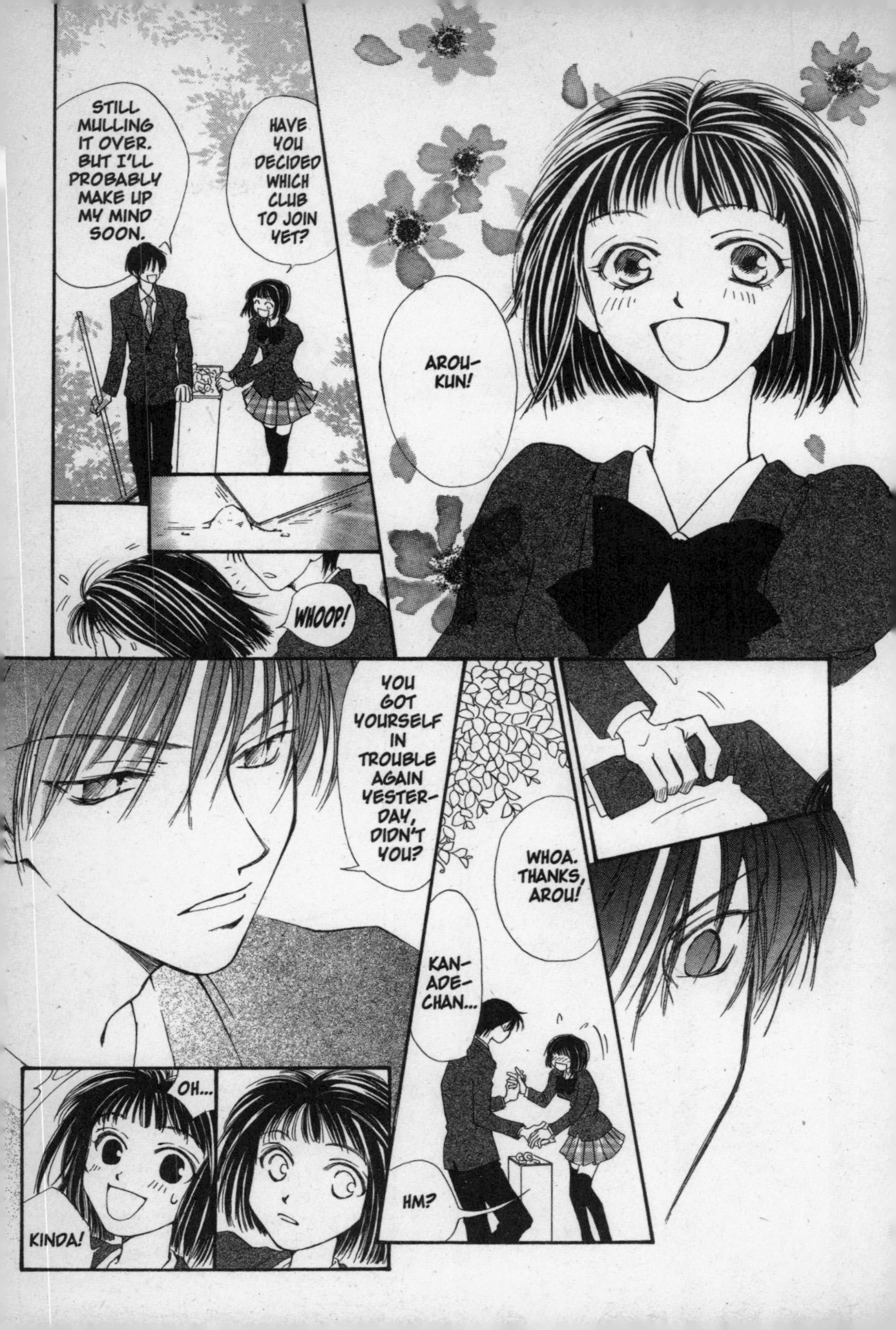
AROU-KUN!
HAVE YOU DECIDED WHICH CLUB TO JOIN YET?
STILL MULLING IT OVER. BUT I'LL PROBABLY MAKE UP MY MIND SOON.
WHOOP!
WHOA. THANKS, AROU!
KAN-ADE-CHAN...
HM?
YOU GOT YOURSELF IN TROUBLE AGAIN YESTER-DAY, DIDN'T YOU?
OH...
KINDA!

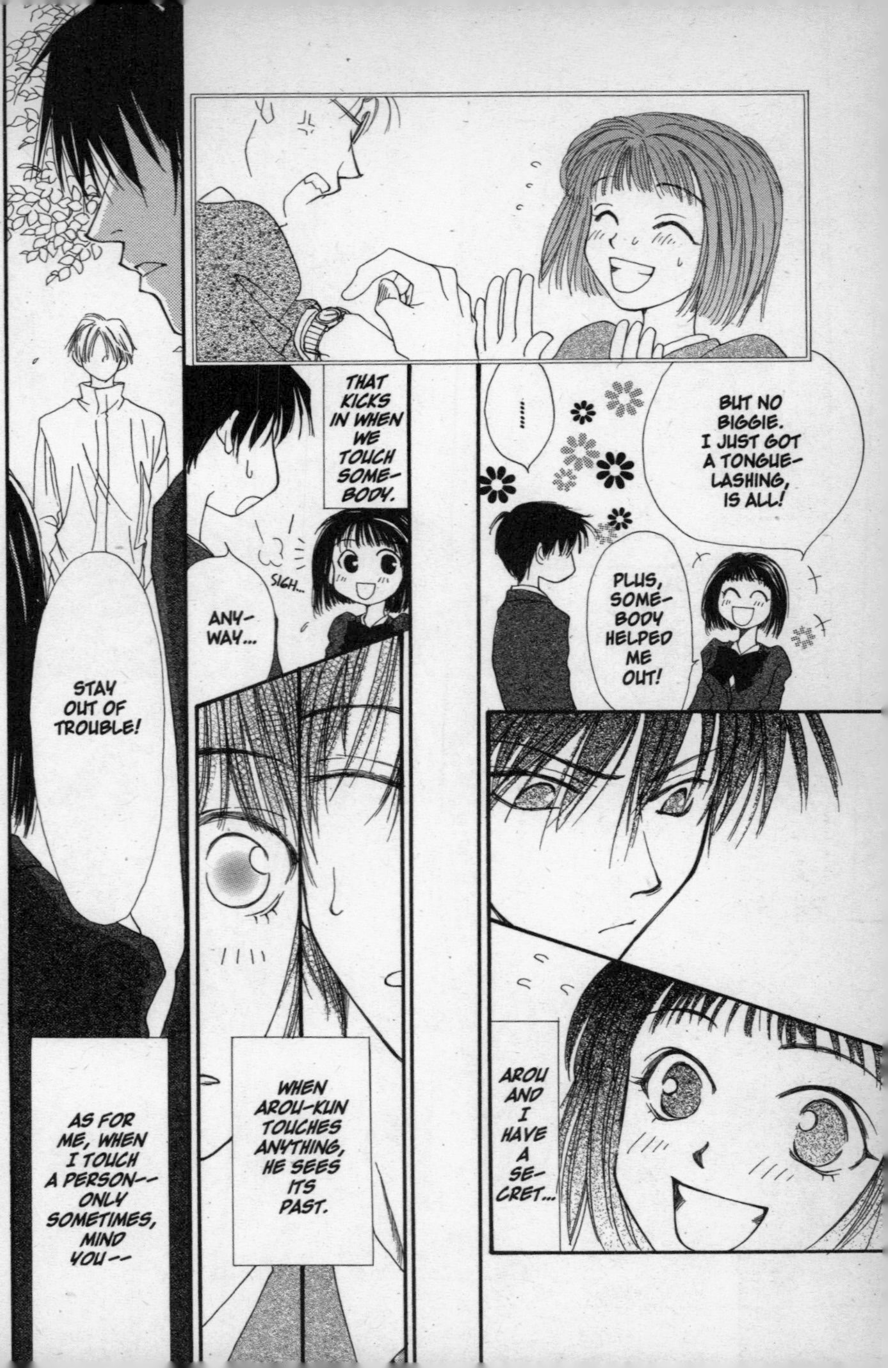
...
BUT NO BIGGIE. I JUST GOT A TONGUE-LASHING, IS ALL!
PLUS, SOMEBODY HELPED ME OUT!
THAT KICKS IN WHEN WE TOUCH SOMEBODY.
SIGH...
ANY-WAY...
AROU AND I HAVE A SE-CRET...
WHEN AROU-KUN TOUCHES ANYTHING, HE SEES ITS PAST.
STAY OUT OF TROUBLE!
AS FOR ME, WHEN I TOUCH A PERSON--ONLY SOMETIMES, MIND YOU--

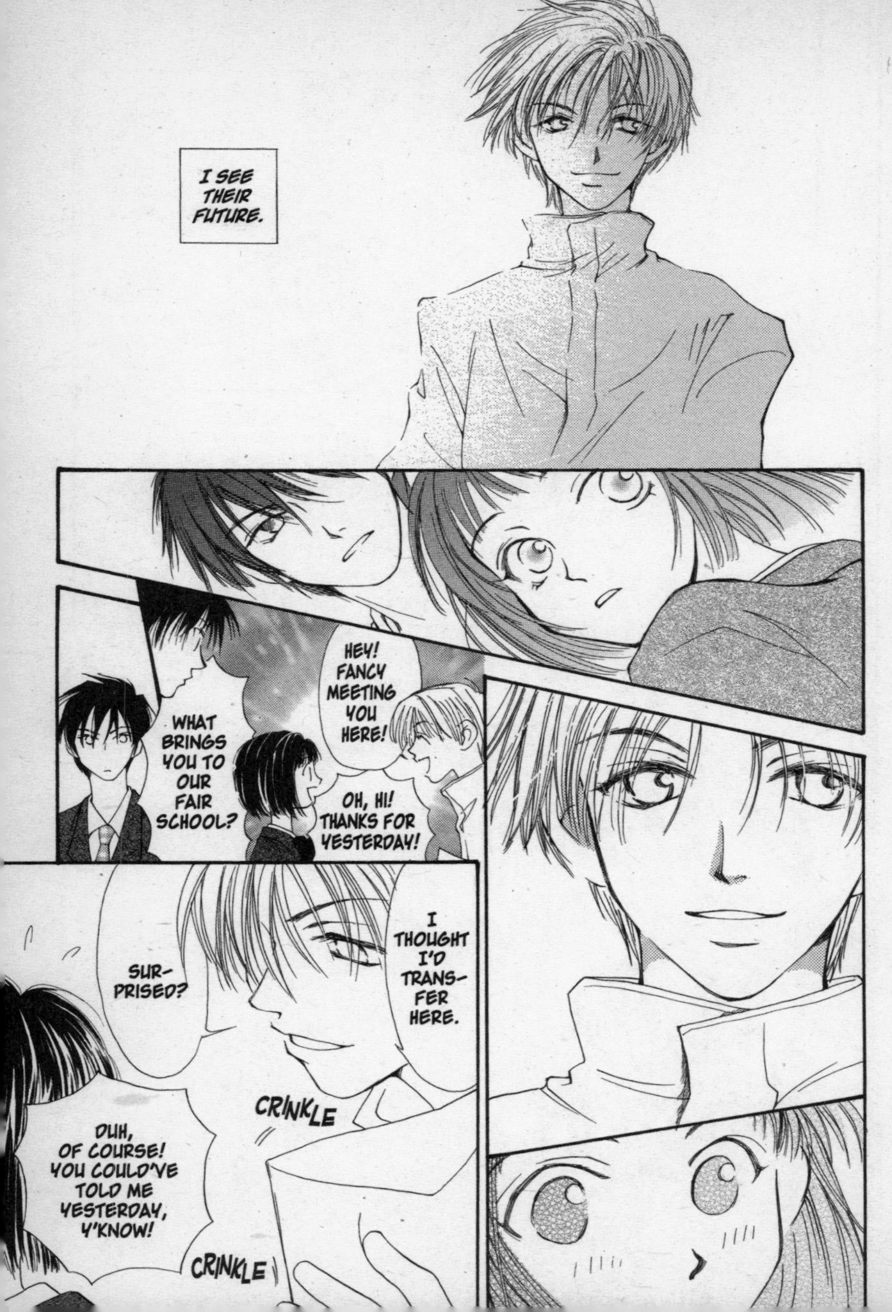
I SEE THEIR FUTURE.
HEY! FANCY MEETING YOU HERE!
OH, HI! THANKS FOR YESTERDAY!
WHAT BRINGS YOU TO OUR FAIR SCHOOL?
I THOUGHT I'D TRANS-FER HERE.
SUR-PRISED?
CRINKLE
DUH, OF COURSE! YOU COULD'VE TOLD ME YESTERDAY, Y'KNOW!
CRINKLE

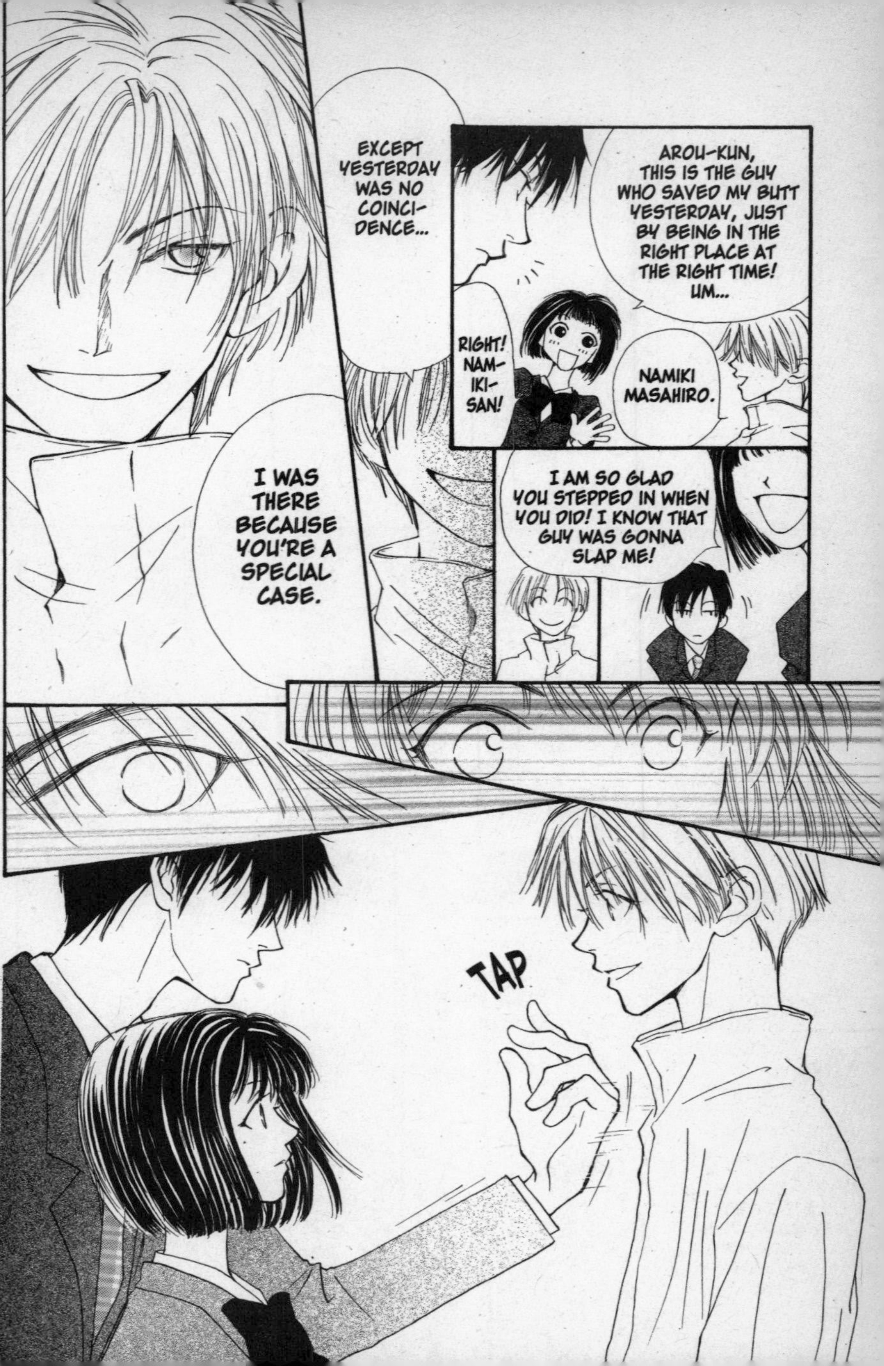

AROU-KUN, THIS IS THE GUY WHO SAVED MY BUTT YESTERDAY, JUST BY BEING IN THE RIGHT PLACE AT THE RIGHT TIME! UM...
NAMIKI MASAHIRO.
RIGHT! NAM-IKI-SAN!
I AM SO GLAD YOU STEPPED IN WHEN YOU DID! I KNOW THAT GUY WAS GONNA SLAP ME!
EXCEPT YESTERDAY WAS NO COINCI-DENCE...
I WAS THERE BECAUSE YOU'RE A SPECIAL CASE.
TAP

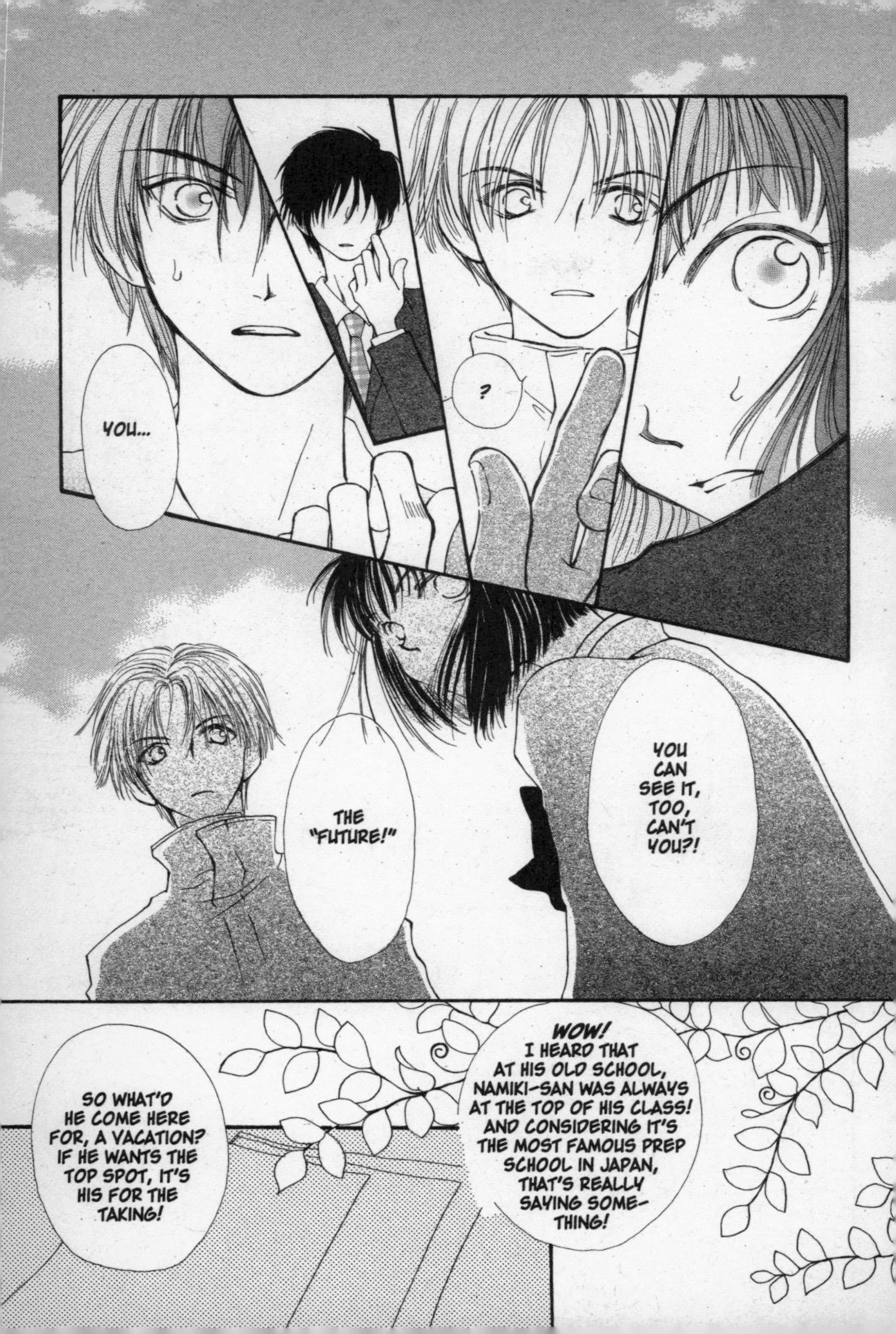
?
YOU...
YOU CAN SEE IT, TOO, CAN'T YOU?!
THE "FUTURE!"
WOW! I HEARD THAT AT HIS OLD SCHOOL, NAMIKI-SAN WAS ALWAYS AT THE TOP OF HIS CLASS! AND CONSIDERING IT'S THE MOST FAMOUS PREP SCHOOL IN JAPAN, THAT'S REALLY SAYING SOME-THING!
SO WHAT'D HE COME HERE FOR, A VACATION? IF HE WANTS THE TOP SPOT, IT'S HIS FOR THE TAKING!

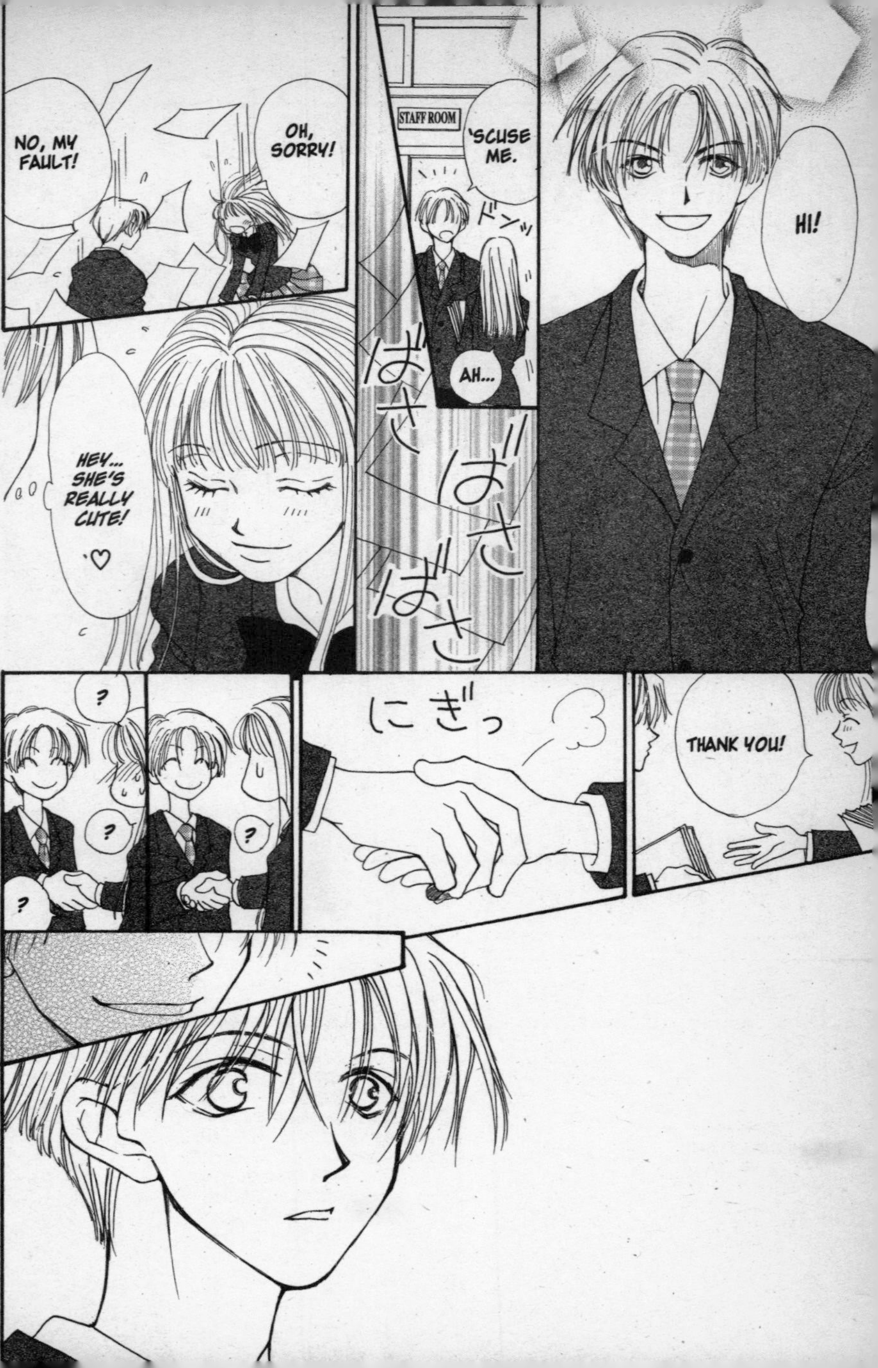
HI!
'SCUSE ME.
ドンッ
AH...
ばさ
ばさ
ばさ
ばさ
OH, SORRY!
NO, MY FAULT!
HEY... SHE'S REALLY CUTE! ♡
THANK YOU!
にぎっ
?
?
?
?

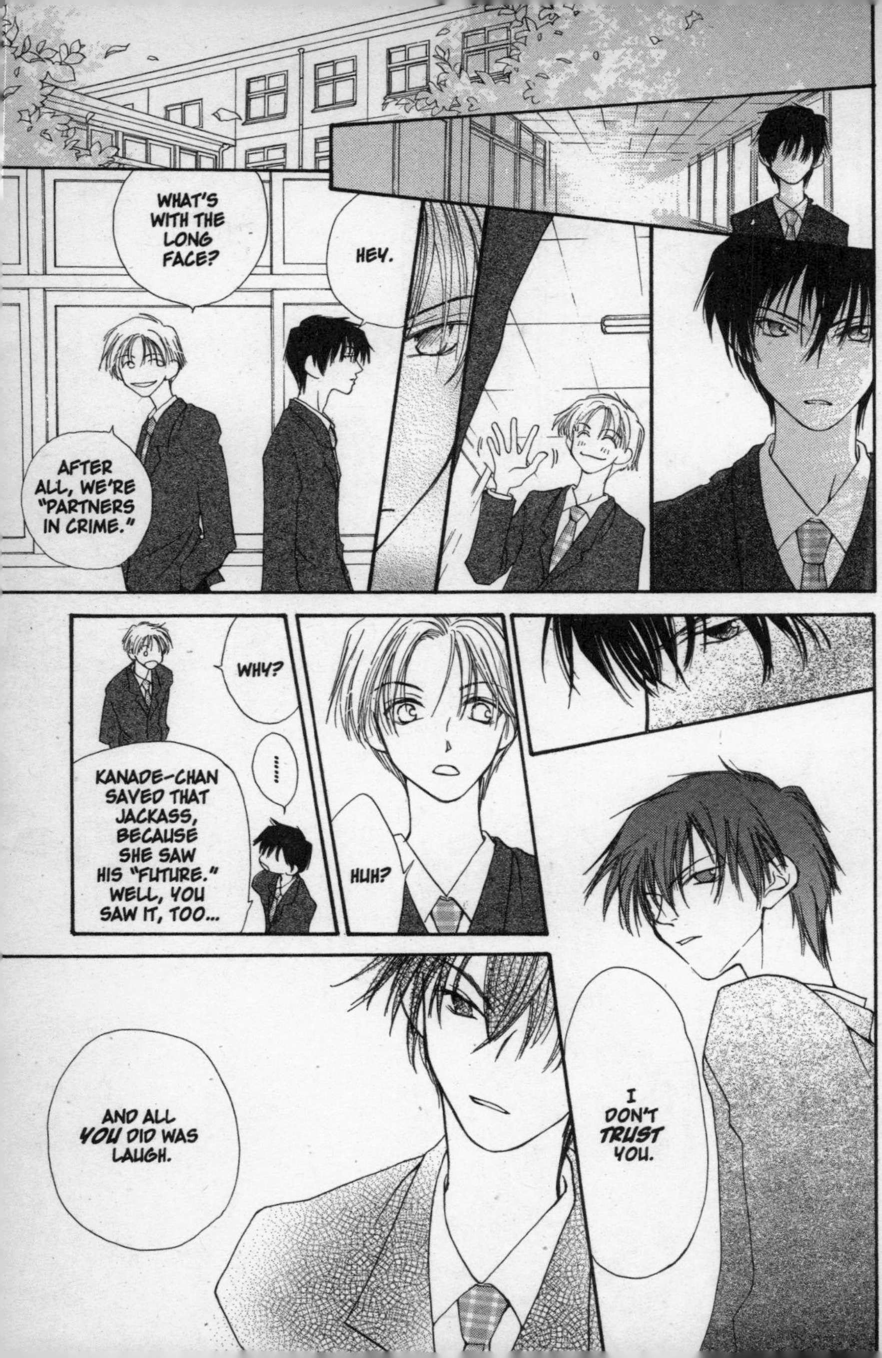

HEY.
WHAT'S WITH THE LONG FACE?
AFTER ALL, WE'RE "PARTNERS IN CRIME."
HUH?
WHY?
......
KANADE-CHAN SAVED THAT JACKASS, BECAUSE SHE SAW HIS "FUTURE." WELL, YOU SAW IT, TOO...
I DON'T *TRUST* YOU.
AND ALL *YOU* DID WAS LAUGH.

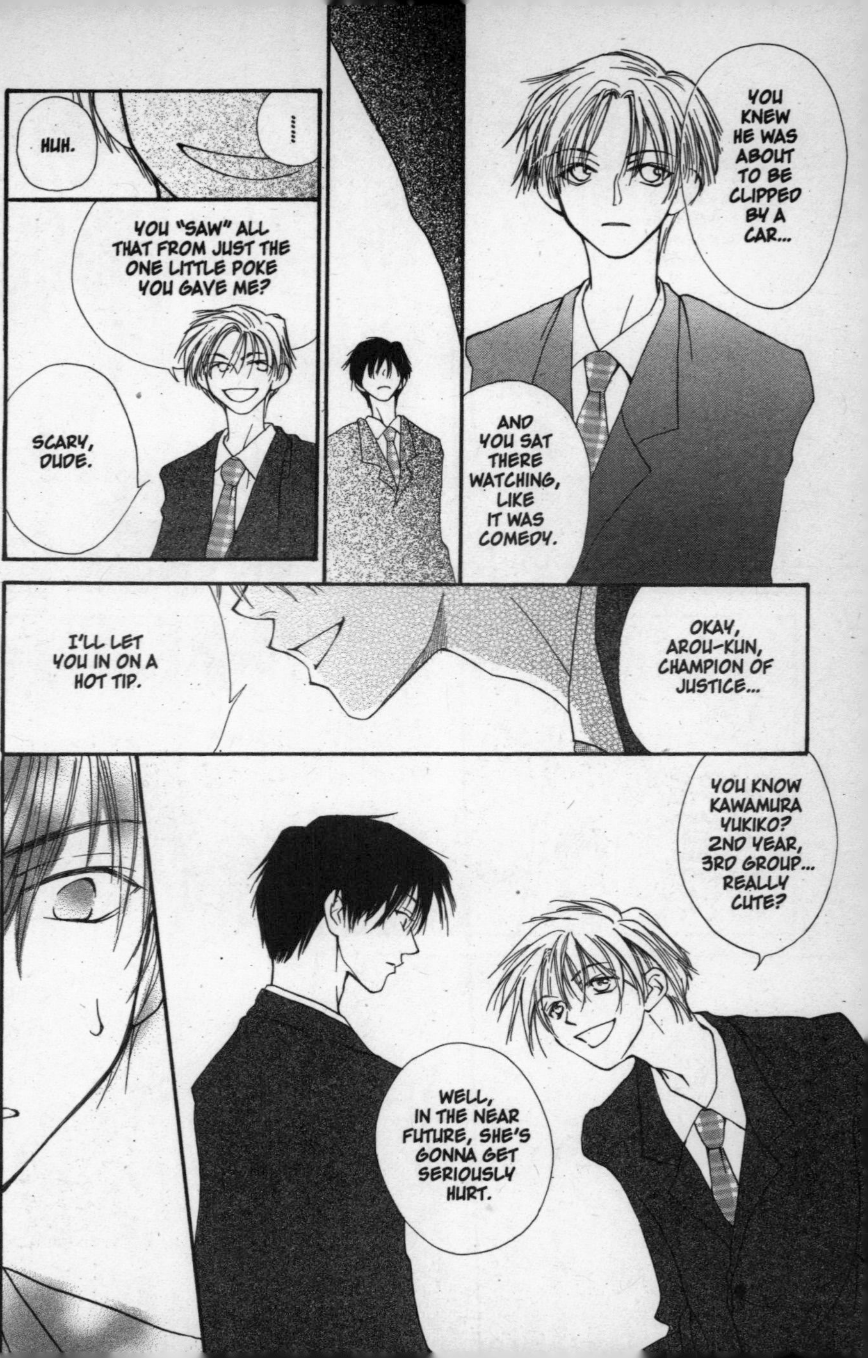
YOU KNEW HE WAS ABOUT TO BE CLIPPED BY A CAR...
AND YOU SAT THERE WATCHING, LIKE IT WAS COMEDY.
......
HUH.
YOU "SAW" ALL THAT FROM JUST THE ONE LITTLE POKE YOU GAVE ME?
SCARY, DUDE.
OKAY, AROU-KUN, CHAMPION OF JUSTICE...
I'LL LET YOU IN ON A HOT TIP.
YOU KNOW KAWAMURA YUKIKO? 2ND YEAR, 3RD GROUP... REALLY CUTE?
WELL, IN THE NEAR FUTURE, SHE'S GONNA GET SERIOUSLY HURT.

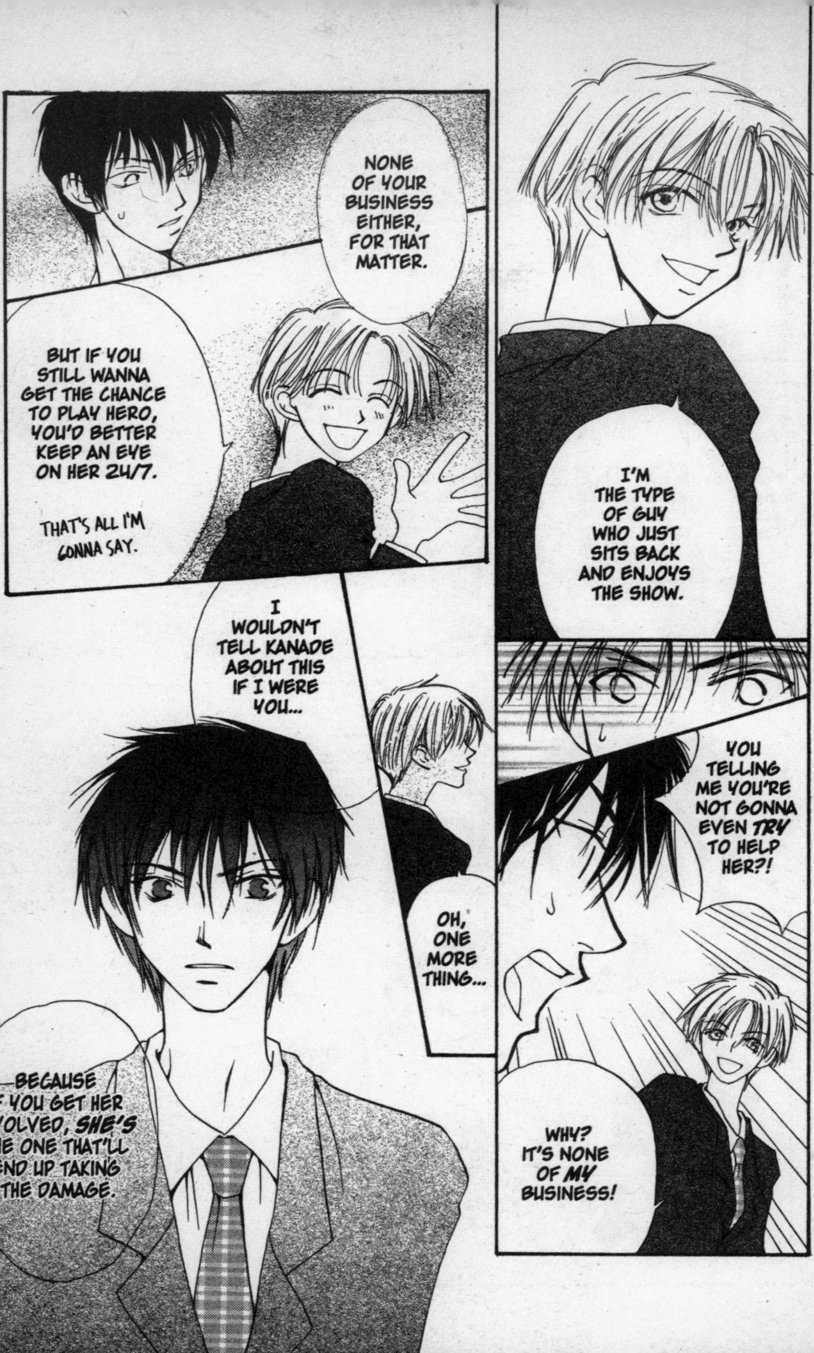
I'M THE TYPE OF GUY WHO JUST SITS BACK AND ENJOYS THE SHOW.
NONE OF YOUR BUSINESS EITHER, FOR THAT MATTER.
BUT IF YOU STILL WANNA GET THE CHANCE TO PLAY HERO, YOU'D BETTER KEEP AN EYE ON HER 24/7.
THAT'S ALL I'M GONNA SAY.
YOU TELLING ME YOU'RE NOT GONNA EVEN TRY TO HELP HER?!
WHY? IT'S NONE OF MY BUSINESS!
OH, ONE MORE THING...
I WOULDN'T TELL KANADE ABOUT THIS IF I WERE YOU...
BECAUSE IF YOU GET HER INVOLVED, SHE'S THE ONE THAT'LL END UP TAKING THE DAMAGE.

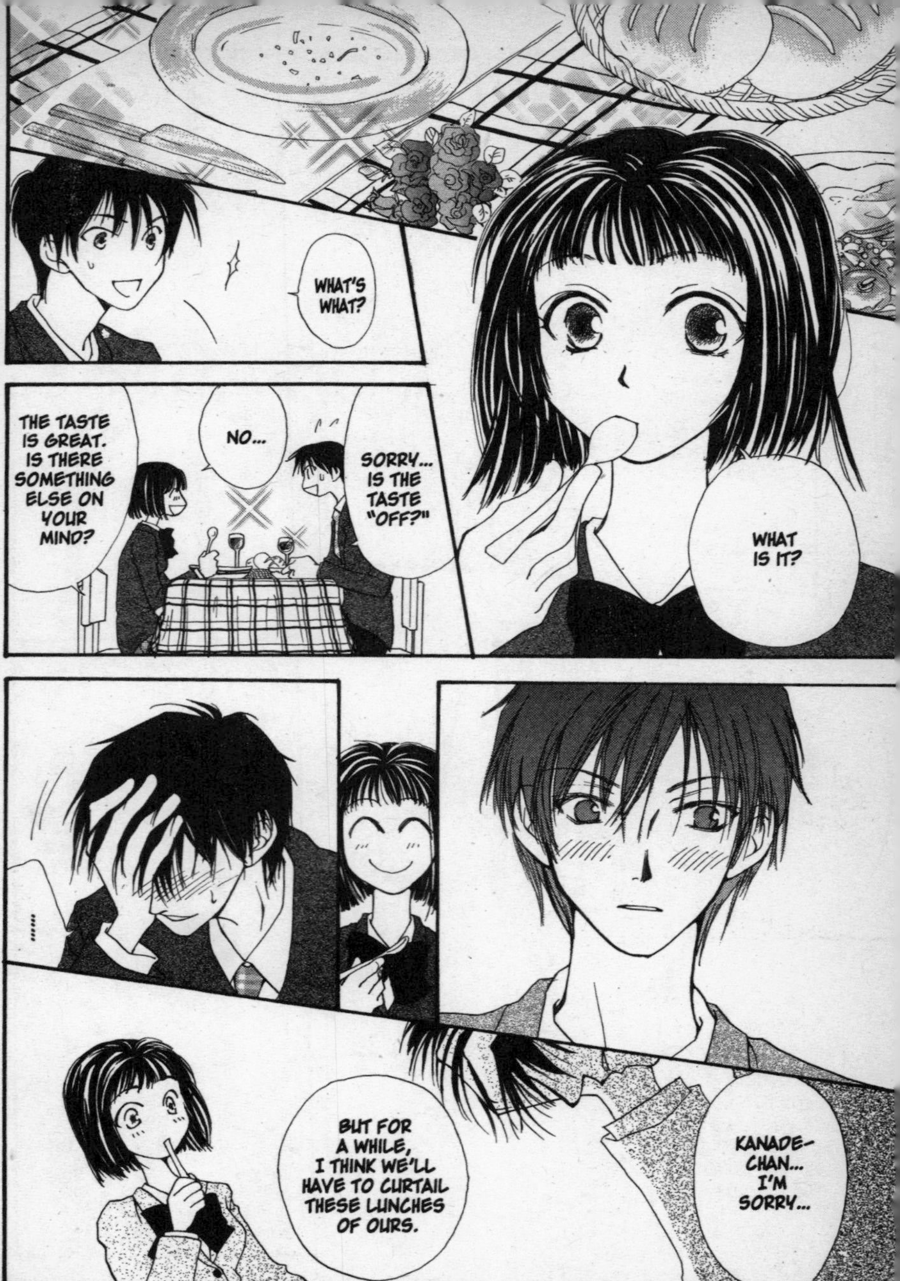
WHAT IS IT?
WHAT'S WHAT?
SORRY... IS THE TASTE "OFF?"
NO...
THE TASTE IS GREAT. IS THERE SOMETHING ELSE ON YOUR MIND?
......
KANADE-CHAN... I'M SORRY...
BUT FOR A WHILE, I THINK WE'LL HAVE TO CURTAIL THESE LUNCHES OF OURS.

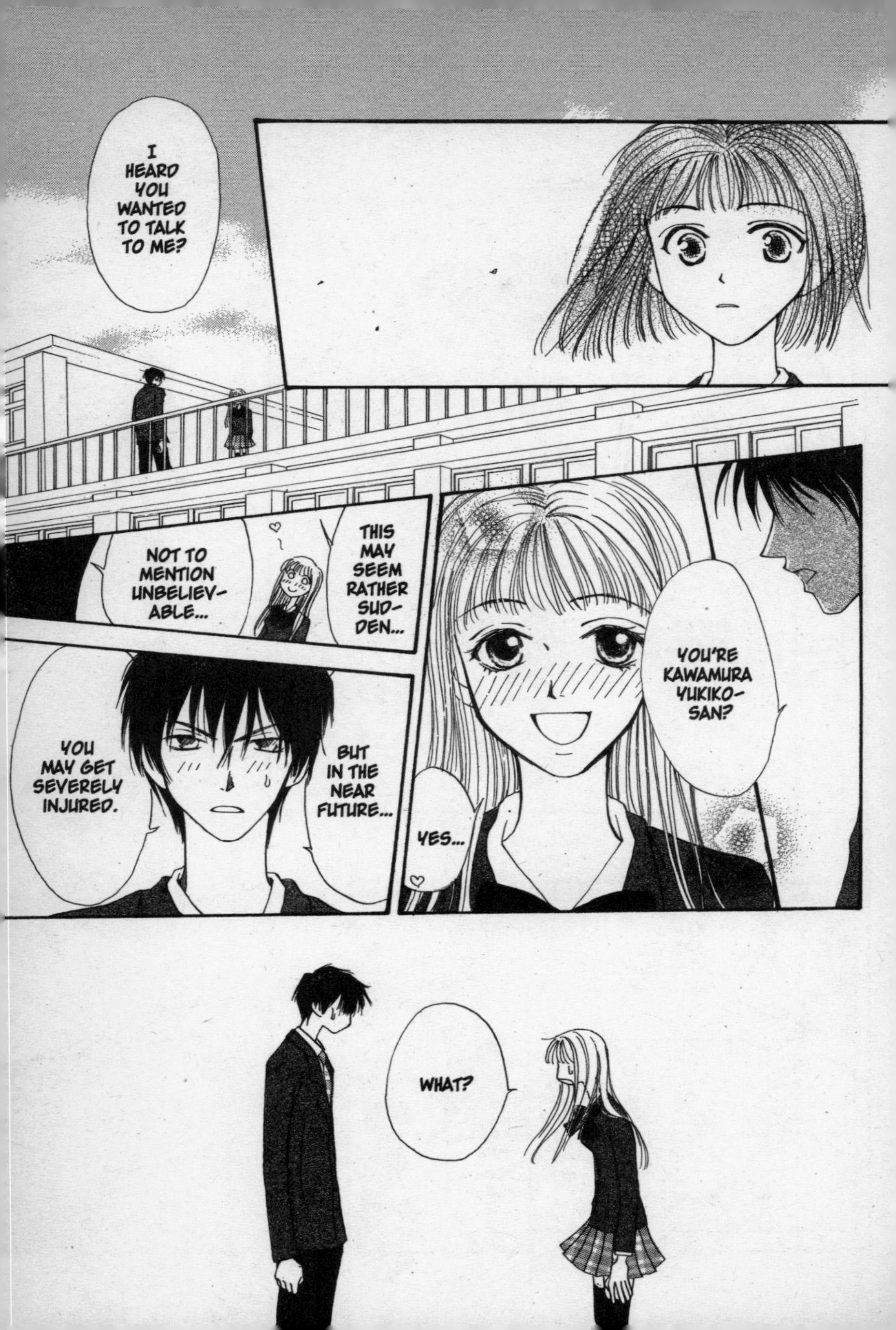
I HEARD YOU WANTED TO TALK TO ME?
YOU'RE KAWAMURA YUKIKO-SAN?
YES...
THIS MAY SEEM RATHER SUD-DEN...
NOT TO MENTION UNBELIEV-ABLE...
BUT IN THE NEAR FUTURE...
YOU MAY GET SEVERELY INJURED.
WHAT?

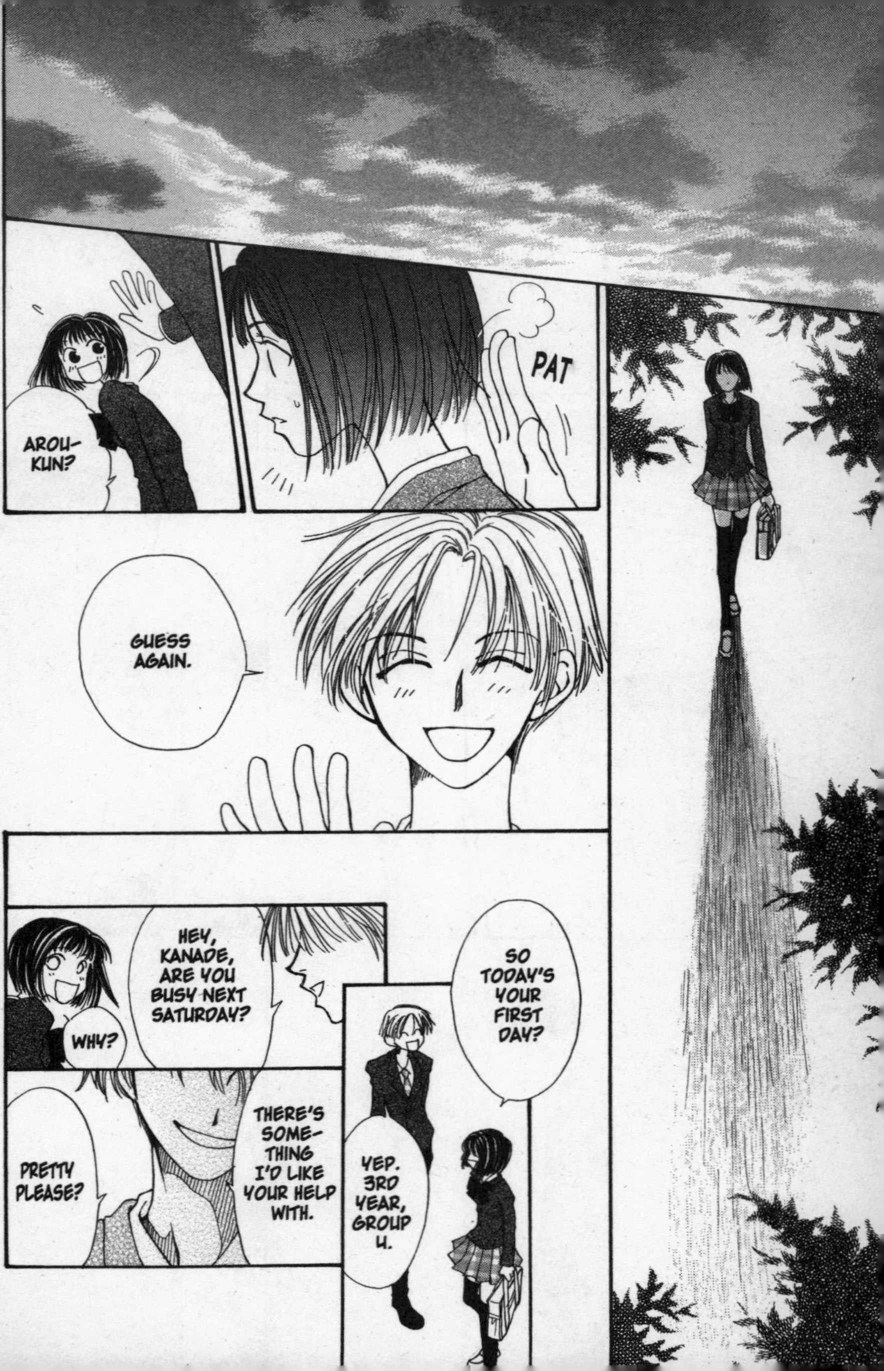
PAT
AROU-KUN?
GUESS AGAIN.
SO TODAY'S YOUR FIRST DAY?
YEP. 3RD YEAR, GROUP 4.
HEY, KANADE, ARE YOU BUSY NEXT SATURDAY?
WHY?
THERE'S SOME-THING I'D LIKE YOUR HELP WITH.
PRETTY PLEASE?

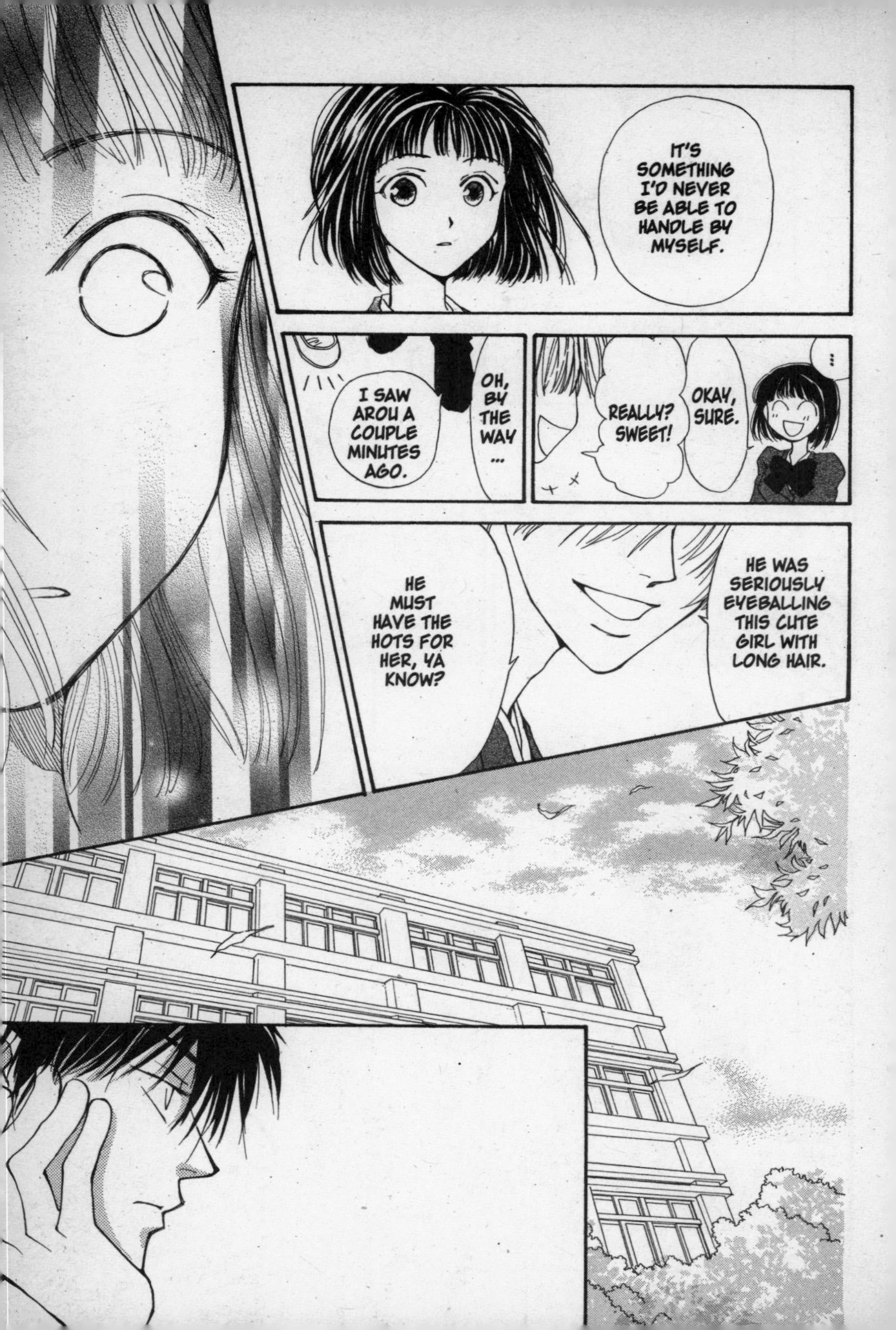
IT'S SOMETHING I'D NEVER BE ABLE TO HANDLE BY MYSELF.
...
OKAY, SURE.
REALLY? SWEET!
OH, BY THE WAY...
I SAW AROU A COUPLE MINUTES AGO.
HE WAS SERIOUSLY EYEBALLING THIS CUTE GIRL WITH LONG HAIR.
HE MUST HAVE THE HOTS FOR HER, YA KNOW?

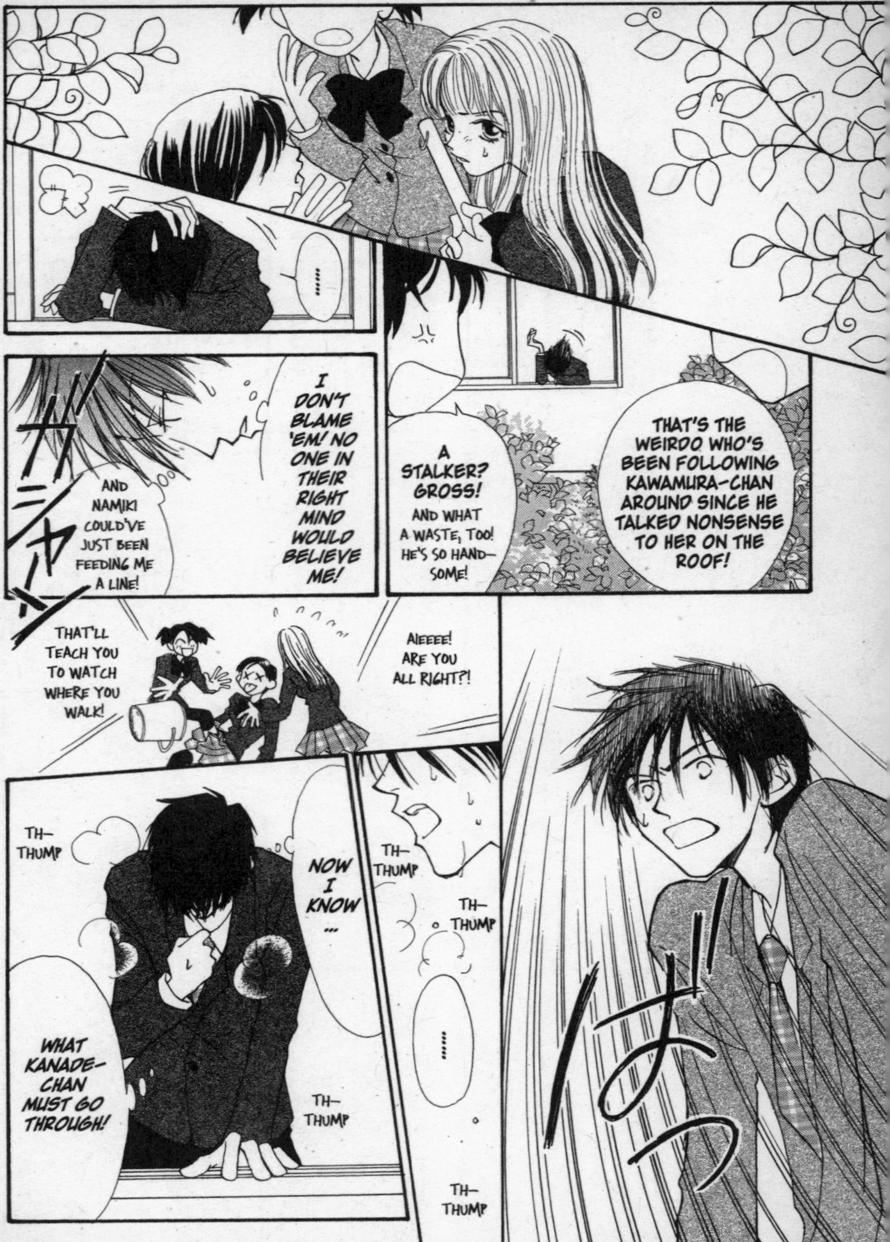
......
THAT'S THE WEIRDO WHO'S BEEN FOLLOWING KAWAMURA-CHAN AROUND SINCE HE TALKED NONSENSE TO HER ON THE ROOF!
A STALKER? GROSS!
AND WHAT A WASTE, TOO! HE'S SO HAND-SOME!
I DON'T BLAME 'EM! NO ONE IN THEIR RIGHT MIND WOULD BELIEVE ME!
AND NAMIKI COULD'VE JUST BEEN FEEDING ME A LINE!
ガシャーン
AIEEEE! ARE YOU ALL RIGHT?!
THAT'LL TEACH YOU TO WATCH WHERE YOU WALK!
はっ
TH-THUMP
TH-THUMP
......
TH-THUMP
TH-THUMP
NOW I KNOW...
WHAT KANADE-CHAN MUST GO THROUGH!
TH-THUMP

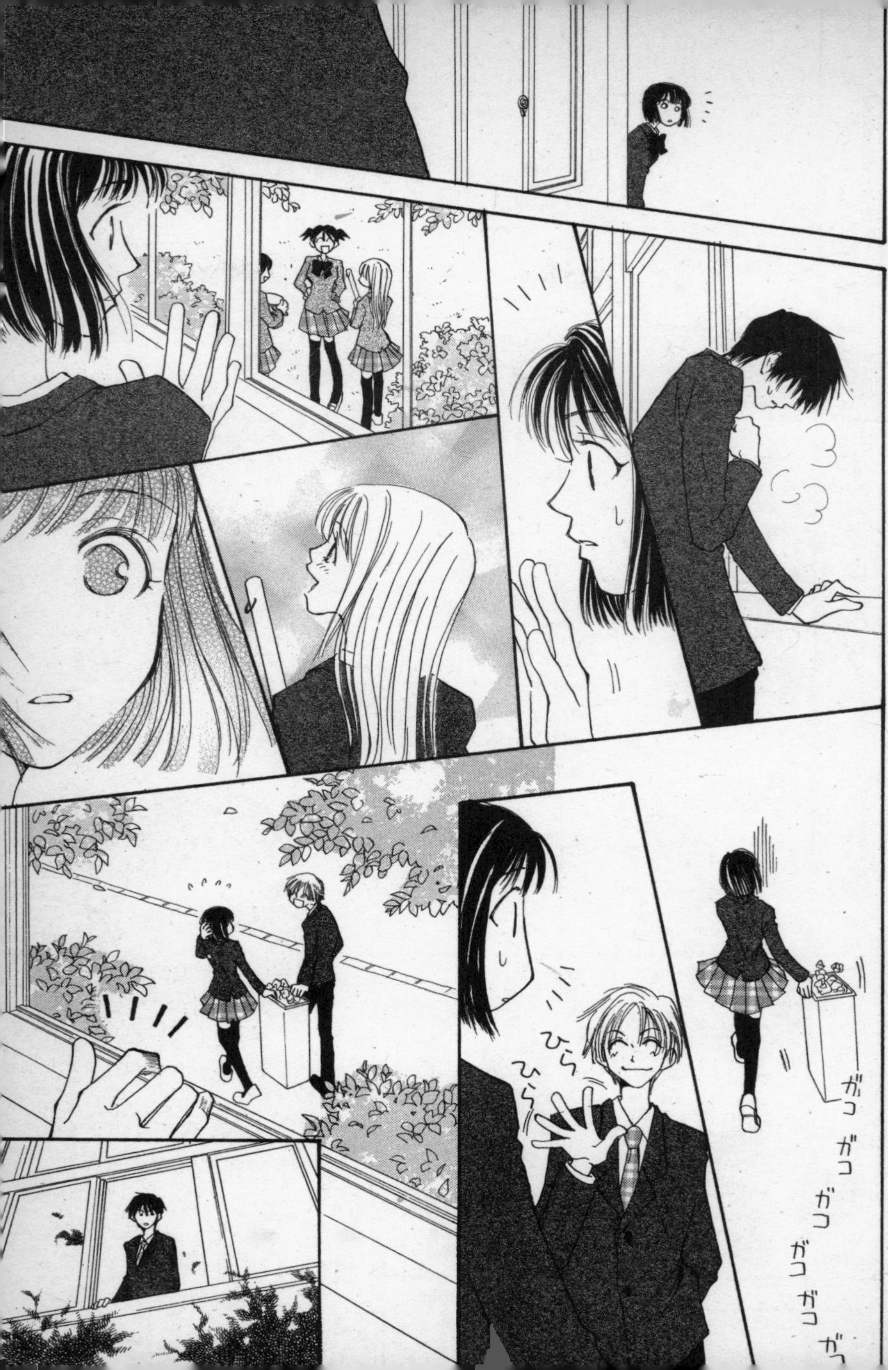
ガコ ガコ ガコ ガコ ガコ ガッ
ひら ひら

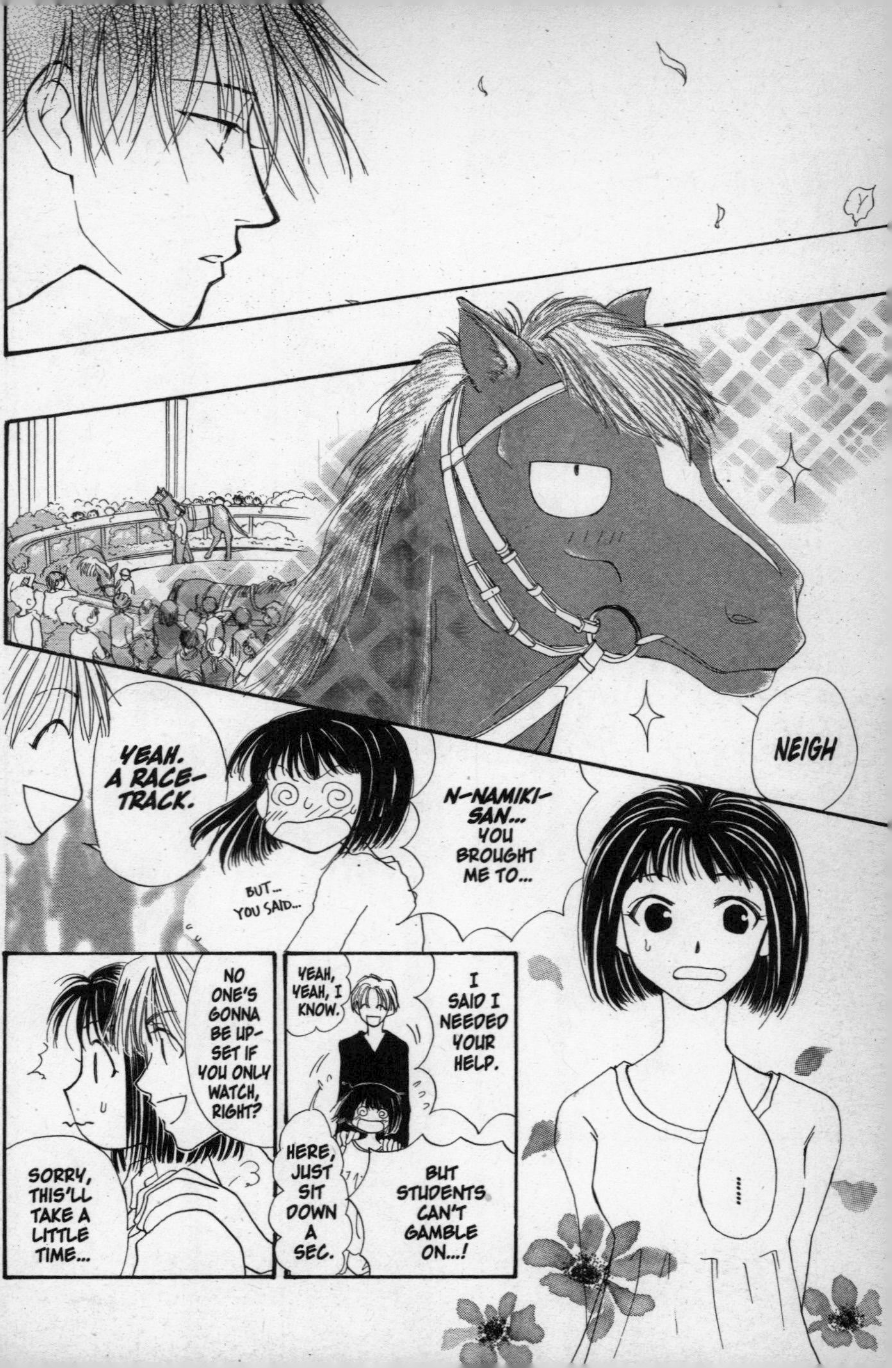
NEIGH
N-NAMIKI-SAN... YOU BROUGHT ME TO...
YEAH. A RACE-TRACK.
BUT... YOU SAID...
......
I SAID I NEEDED YOUR HELP.
YEAH, YEAH, I KNOW.
BUT STUDENTS CAN'T GAMBLE ON...!
HERE, JUST SIT DOWN A SEC.
NO ONE'S GONNA BE UP-SET IF YOU ONLY WATCH, RIGHT?
SORRY, THIS'LL TAKE A LITTLE TIME...

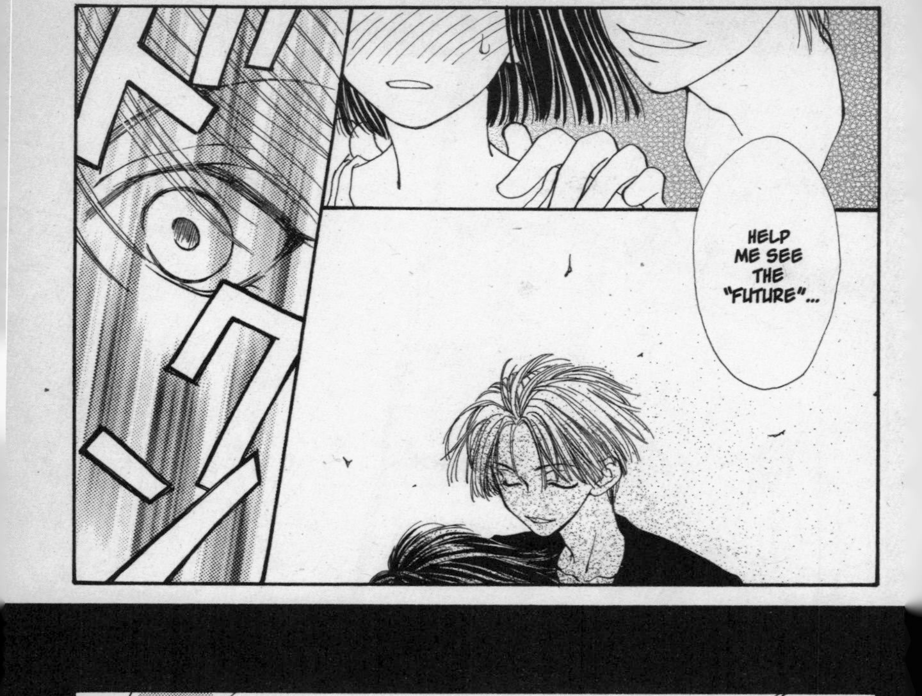
HELP ME SEE THE "FUTURE"...
ドクン

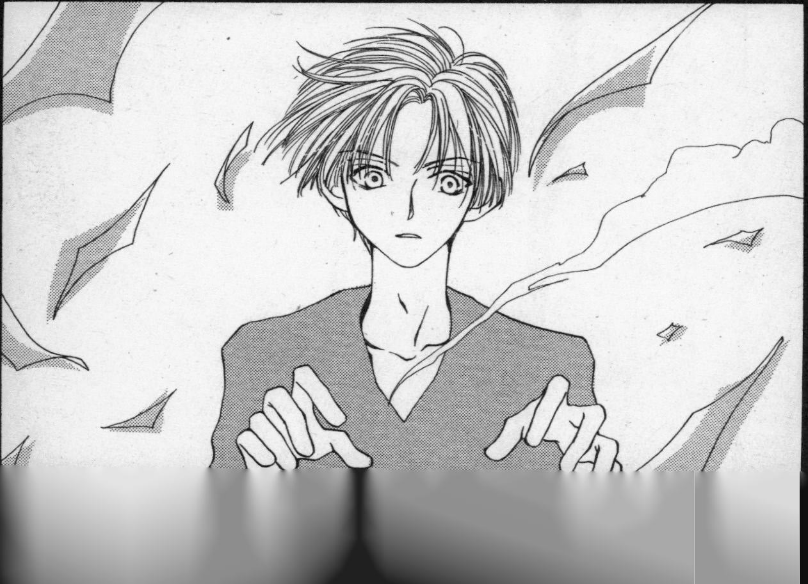

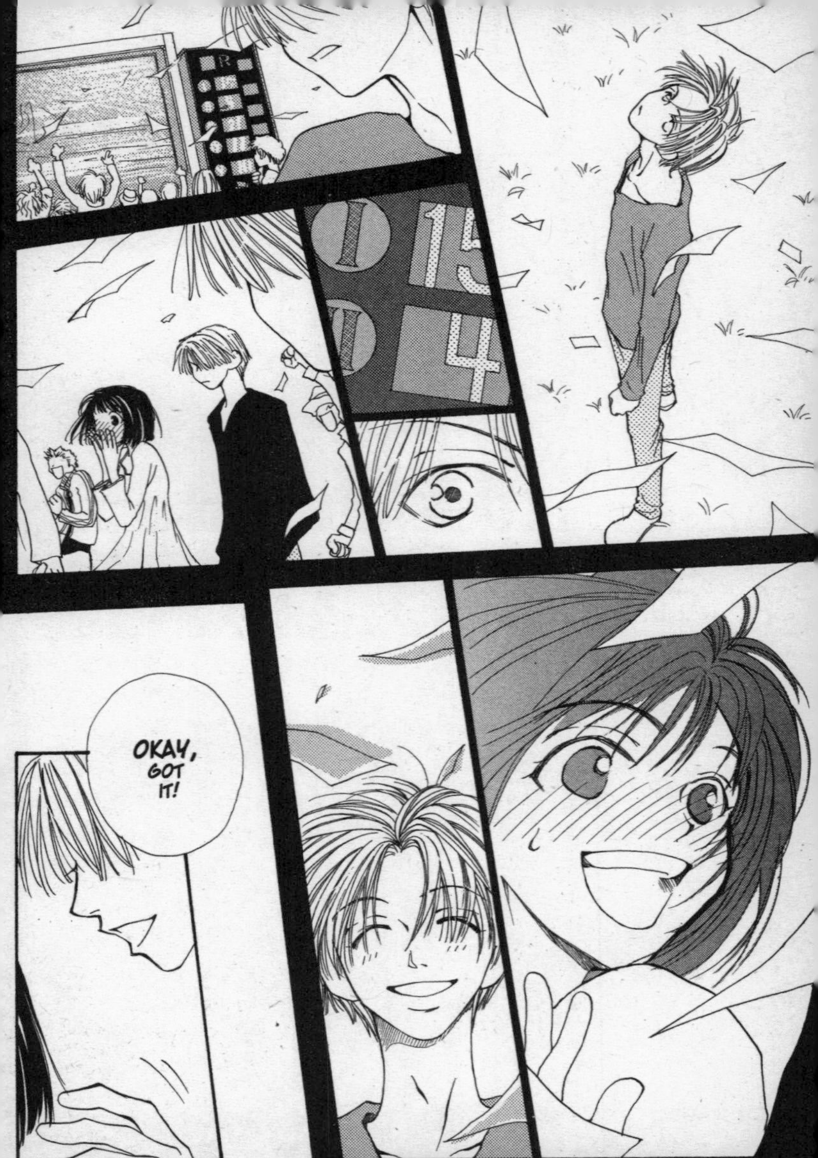
OKAY, GOT IT!

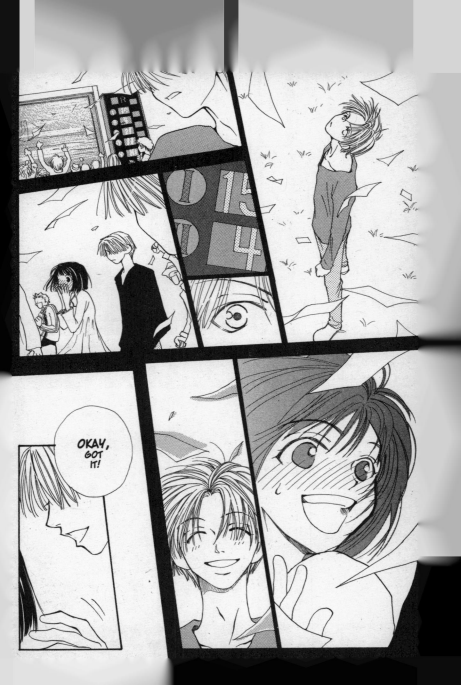

Sakura Mail

No. 3

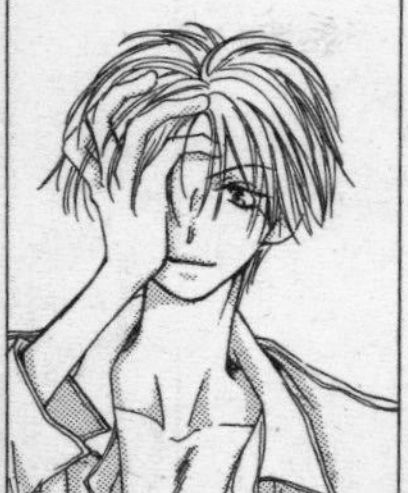

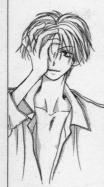

Namiki-kun makes his debut in the third story. "Your stories never have bad guys in them. Humans aren't nearly as goody-goody as you make them out to be." After my mother, who scorns as well as praises, so cannily pointed this out to me, I took great delight in creating Namiki. While I wouldn't go so far as to call him a "bad guy," he does have his imperfections, which makes it a lot of fun to write! I do tend to think that within every good person is at least a little piece of "darkness" that the person carries around, ashamed to let the rest of the world see. Come to think of it, that's not a bad idea for a story.

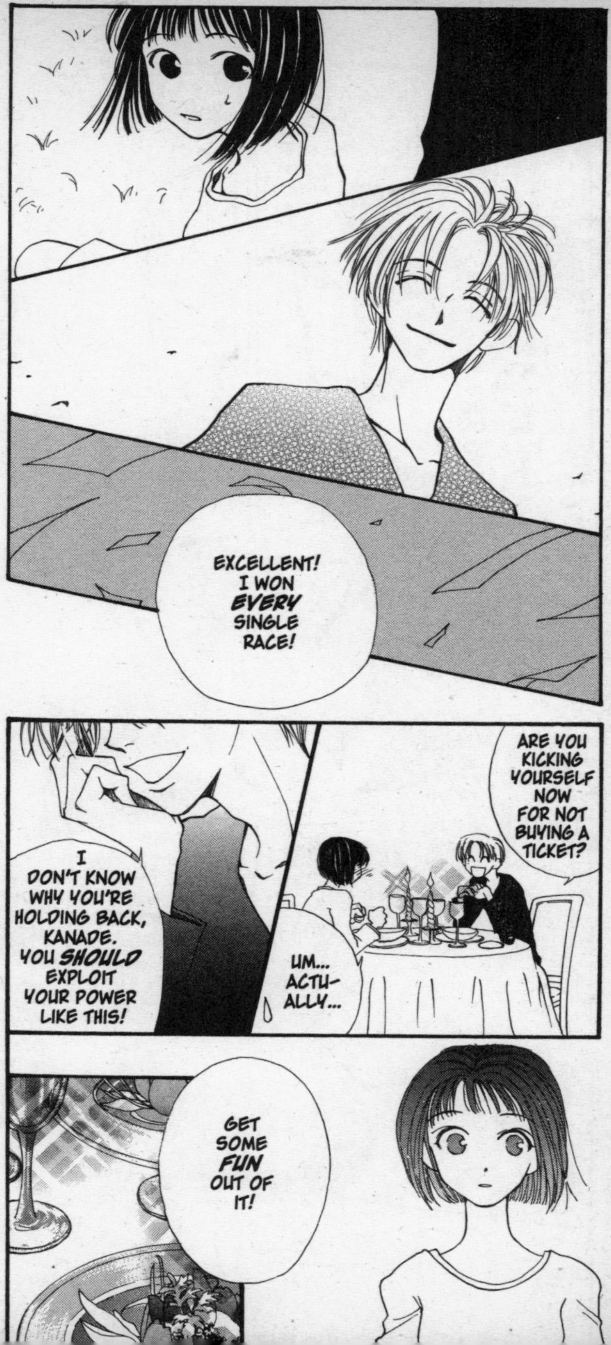
EXCELLENT! I WON EVERY SINGLE RACE!
ARE YOU KICKING YOURSELF NOW FOR NOT BUYING A TICKET?
UM... ACTU-ALLY...
I DON'T KNOW WHY YOU'RE HOLDING BACK, KANADE. YOU SHOULD EXPLOIT YOUR POWER LIKE THIS!
GET SOME FUN OUT OF IT!

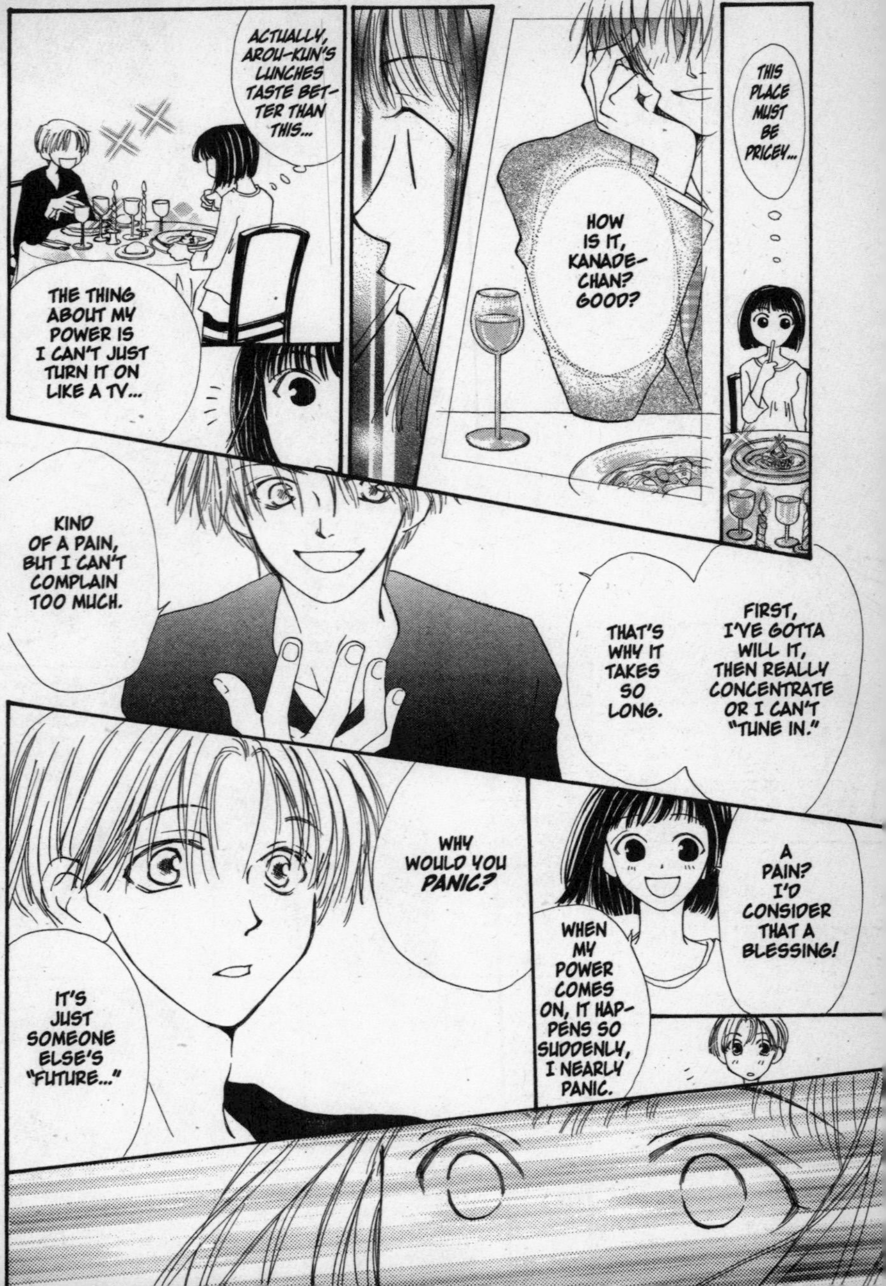
THIS PLACE MUST BE PRICEY...
HOW IS IT, KANADE-CHAN? GOOD?
ACTUALLY, AROU-KUN'S LUNCHES TASTE BET-TER THAN THIS...
THE THING ABOUT MY POWER IS I CAN'T JUST TURN IT ON LIKE A TV...
FIRST, I'VE GOTTA WILL IT, THEN REALLY CONCENTRATE OR I CAN'T "TUNE IN."
THAT'S WHY IT TAKES SO LONG.
KIND OF A PAIN, BUT I CAN'T COMPLAIN TOO MUCH.
A PAIN? I'D CONSIDER THAT A BLESSING!
WHEN MY POWER COMES ON, IT HAP-PENS SO SUDDENLY, I NEARLY PANIC.
WHY WOULD YOU *PANIC?*
IT'S JUST SOMEONE ELSE'S "FUTURE..."

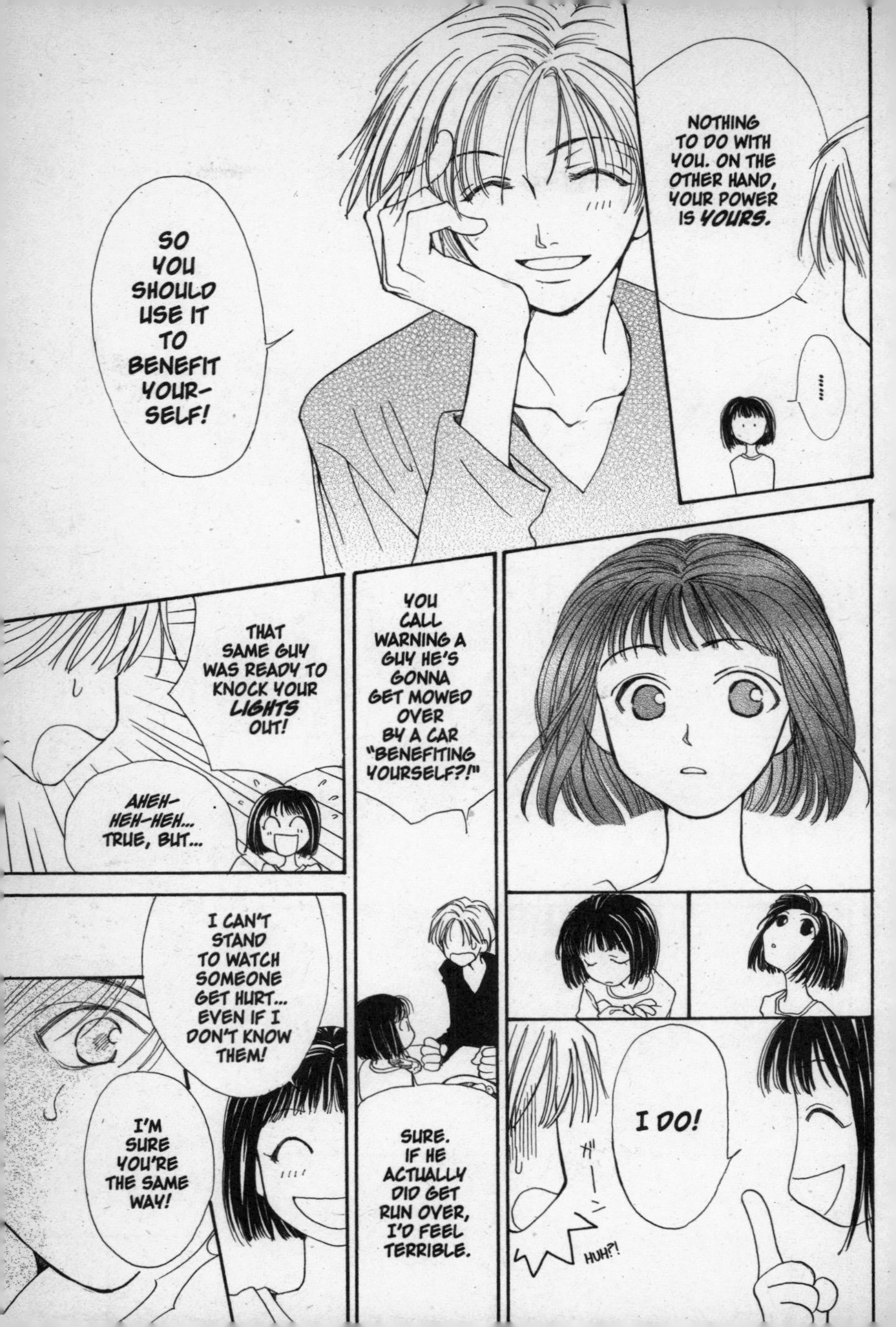
NOTHING TO DO WITH YOU. ON THE OTHER HAND, YOUR POWER IS YOURS.
......
SO YOU SHOULD USE IT TO BENEFIT YOURSELF!
YOU CALL WARNING A GUY HE'S GONNA GET MOWED OVER BY A CAR "BENEFITING YOURSELF?!"
THAT SAME GUY WAS READY TO KNOCK YOUR LIGHTS OUT!
AHEH-HEH-HEH... TRUE, BUT...
I CAN'T STAND TO WATCH SOMEONE GET HURT... EVEN IF I DON'T KNOW THEM!
I'M SURE YOU'RE THE SAME WAY!
SURE. IF HE ACTUALLY DID GET RUN OVER, I'D FEEL TERRIBLE.
I DO!
HUH?!

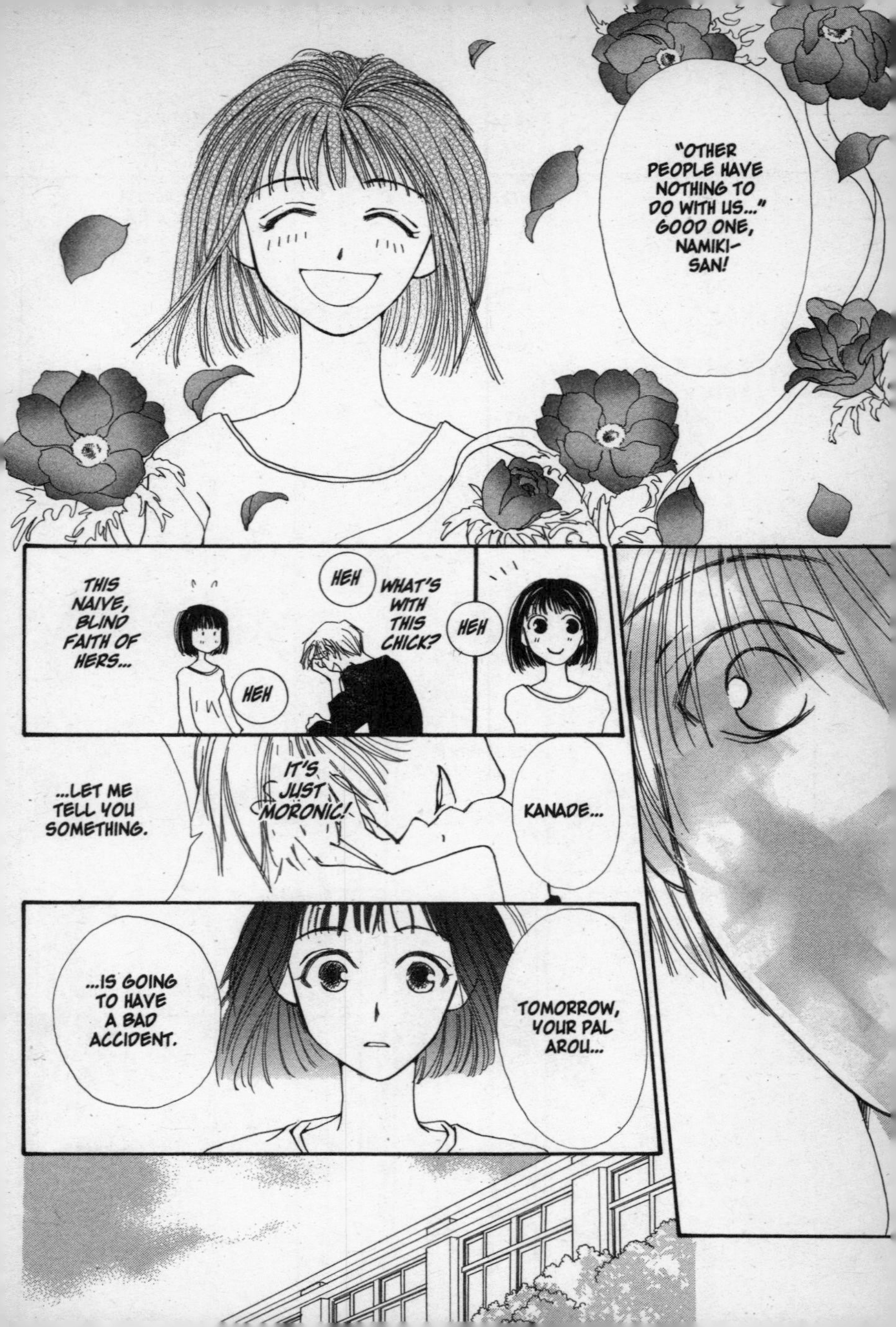
"OTHER PEOPLE HAVE NOTHING TO DO WITH US..." GOOD ONE, NAMIKI-SAN!
HEH
WHAT'S WITH THIS CHICK?
HEH
THIS NAIVE, BLIND FAITH OF HERS...
HEH
KANADE...
IT'S JUST MORONIC!
...LET ME TELL YOU SOMETHING.
TOMORROW, YOUR PAL AROU...
...IS GOING TO HAVE A BAD ACCIDENT.

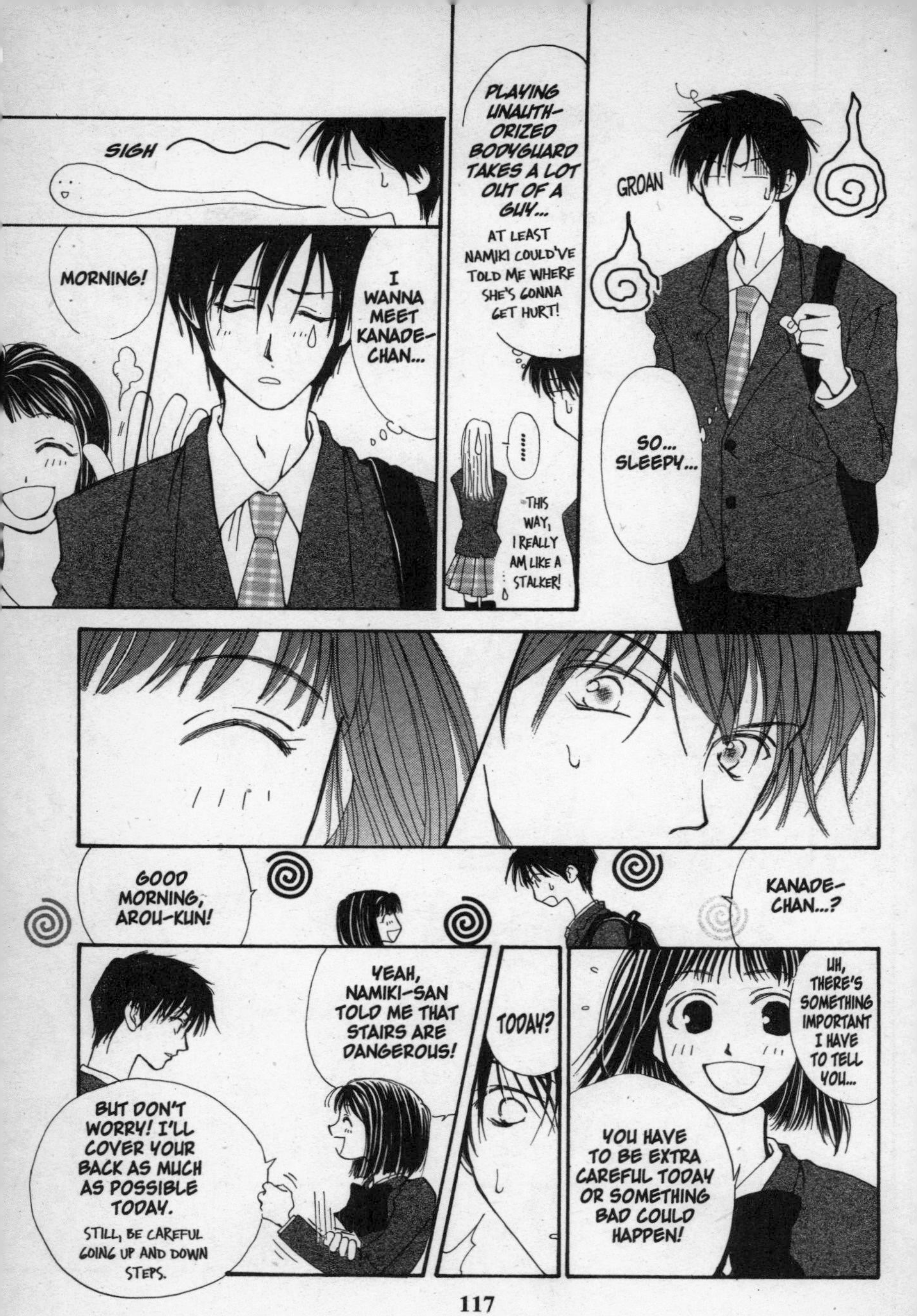
GROAN
SO... SLEEPY...
PLAYING UNAUTHORIZED BODYGUARD TAKES A LOT OUT OF A GUY...
AT LEAST NAMIKI COULD'VE TOLD ME WHERE SHE'S GONNA GET HURT!
......
THIS WAY, I REALLY AM LIKE A STALKER!
SIGH
I WANNA MEET KANADE-CHAN...
MORNING!
KANADE-CHAN...?
GOOD MORNING, AROU-KUN!
UH, THERE'S SOMETHING IMPORTANT I HAVE TO TELL YOU...
YOU HAVE TO BE EXTRA CAREFUL TODAY OR SOMETHING BAD COULD HAPPEN!
TODAY?
YEAH, NAMIKI-SAN TOLD ME THAT STAIRS ARE DANGEROUS!
BUT DON'T WORRY! I'LL COVER YOUR BACK AS MUCH AS POSSIBLE TODAY.
STILL, BE CAREFUL GOING UP AND DOWN STEPS.

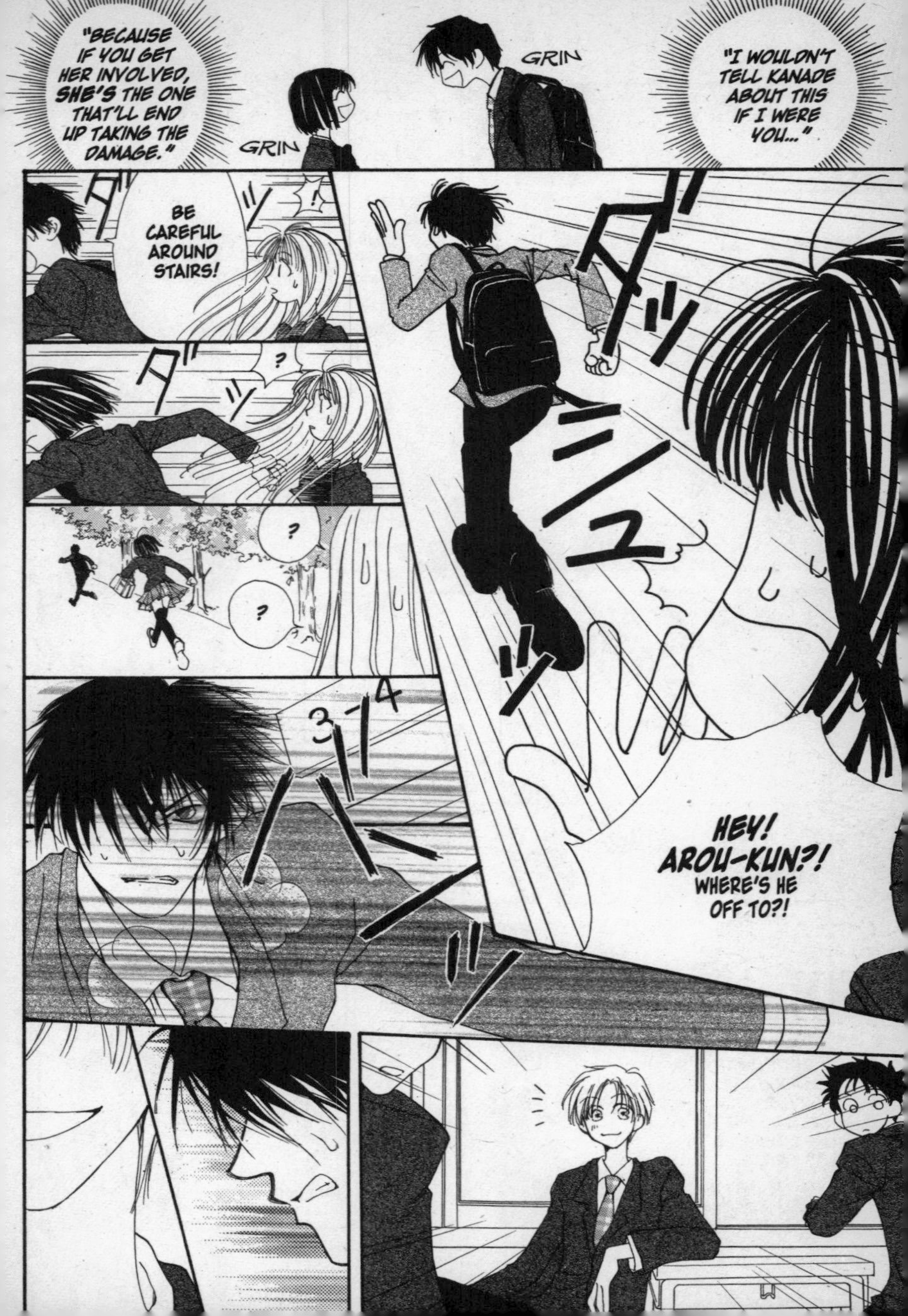
"I WOULDN'T TELL KANADE ABOUT THIS IF I WERE YOU..."
GRIN
GRIN
"BECAUSE IF YOU GET HER INVOLVED, SHE'S THE ONE THAT'LL END UP TAKING THE DAMAGE."
HEY! AROU-KUN?! WHERE'S HE OFF TO?!
!
BE CAREFUL AROUND STAIRS!
?
?
?
3-4

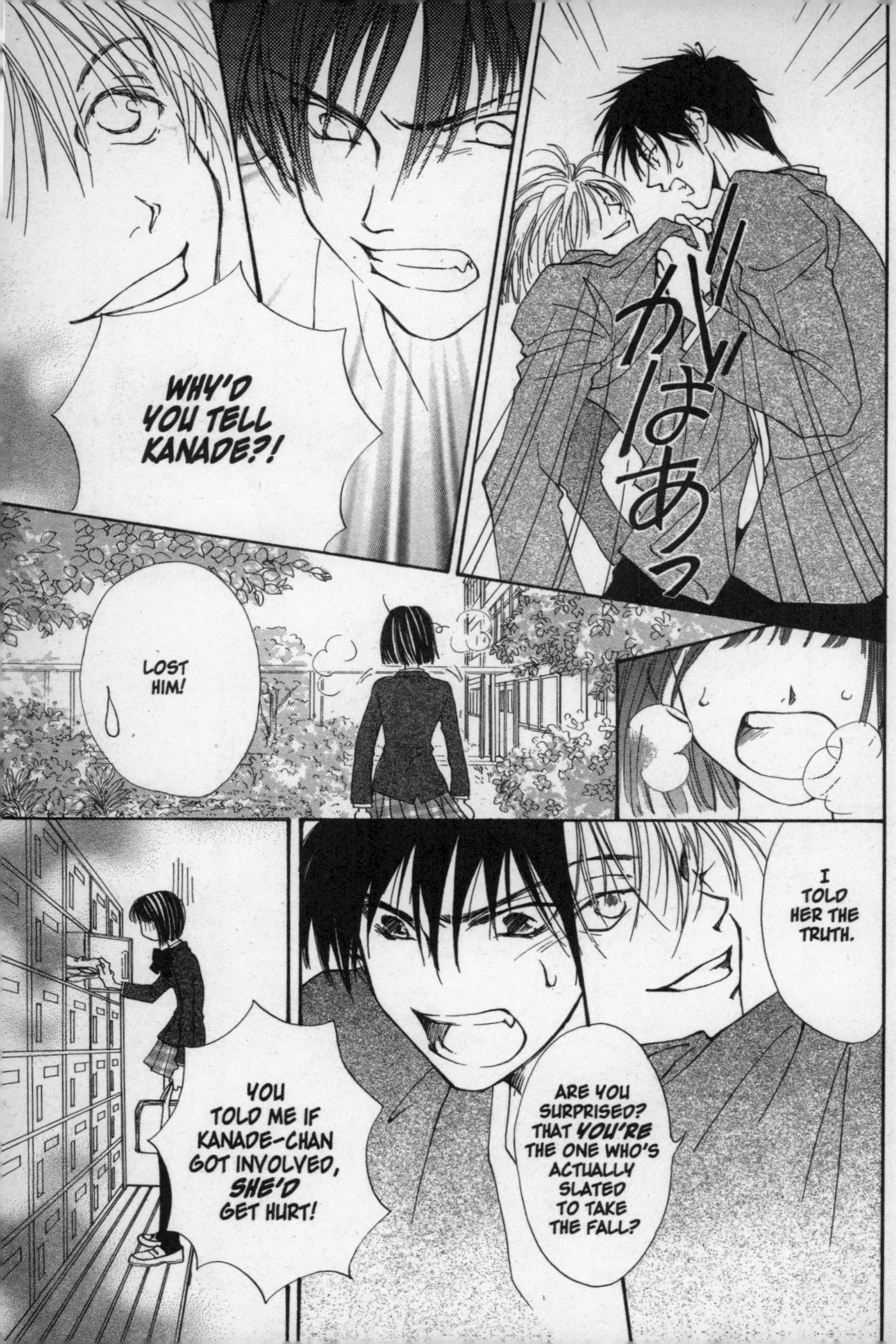
がばあっ
WHY'D YOU TELL KANADE?!
LOST HIM!
I TOLD HER THE TRUTH.
ARE YOU SURPRISED? THAT YOU'RE THE ONE WHO'S ACTUALLY SLATED TO TAKE THE FALL?
YOU TOLD ME IF KANADE-CHAN GOT INVOLVED, SHE'D GET HURT!

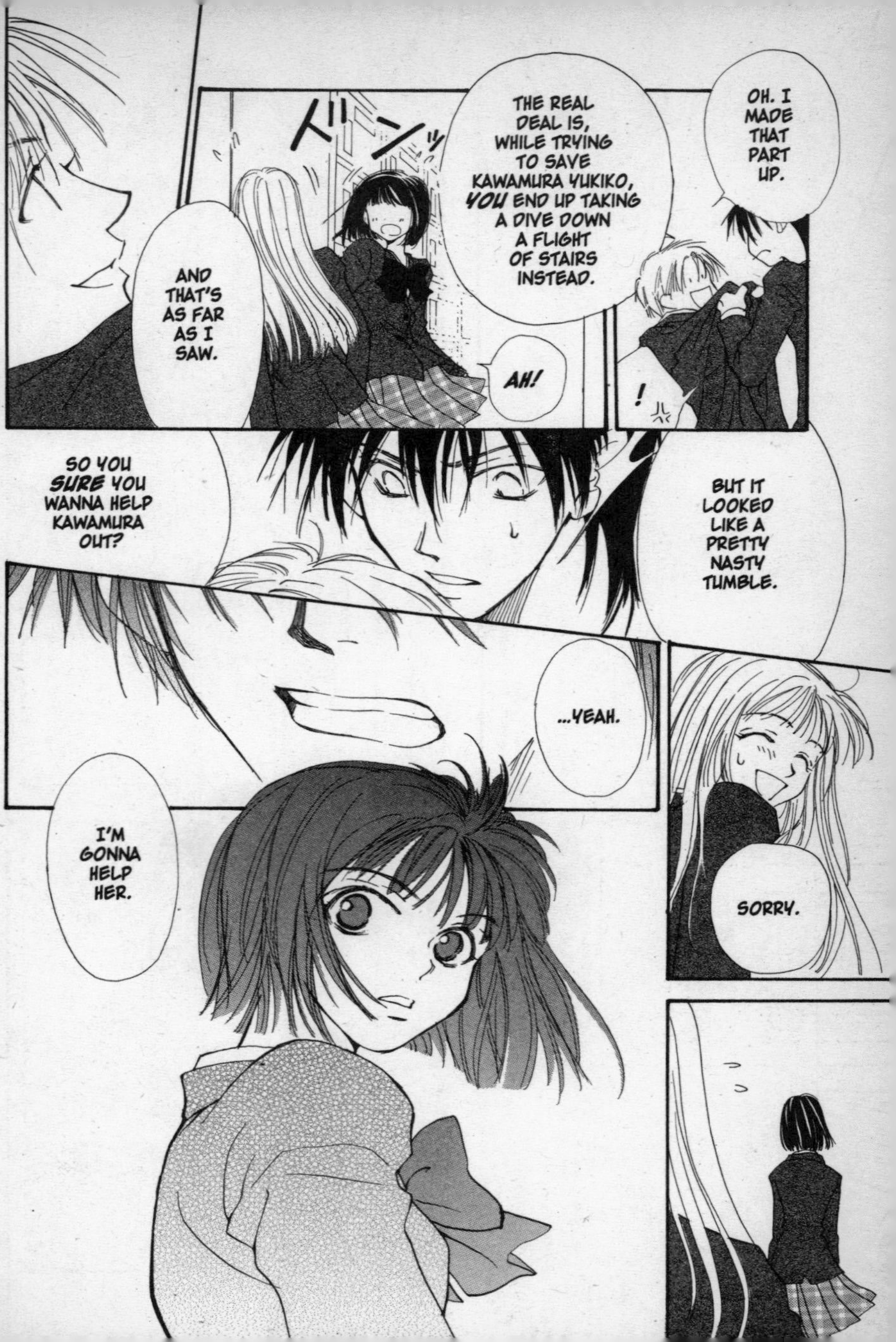
OH. I MADE THAT PART UP.
!
THE REAL DEAL IS, WHILE TRYING TO SAVE KAWAMURA YUKIKO, YOU END UP TAKING A DIVE DOWN A FLIGHT OF STAIRS INSTEAD.
ドンッ
AH!
AND THAT'S AS FAR AS I SAW.
BUT IT LOOKED LIKE A PRETTY NASTY TUMBLE.
SO YOU SURE YOU WANNA HELP KAWAMURA OUT?
SORRY.
...YEAH.
I'M GONNA HELP HER.

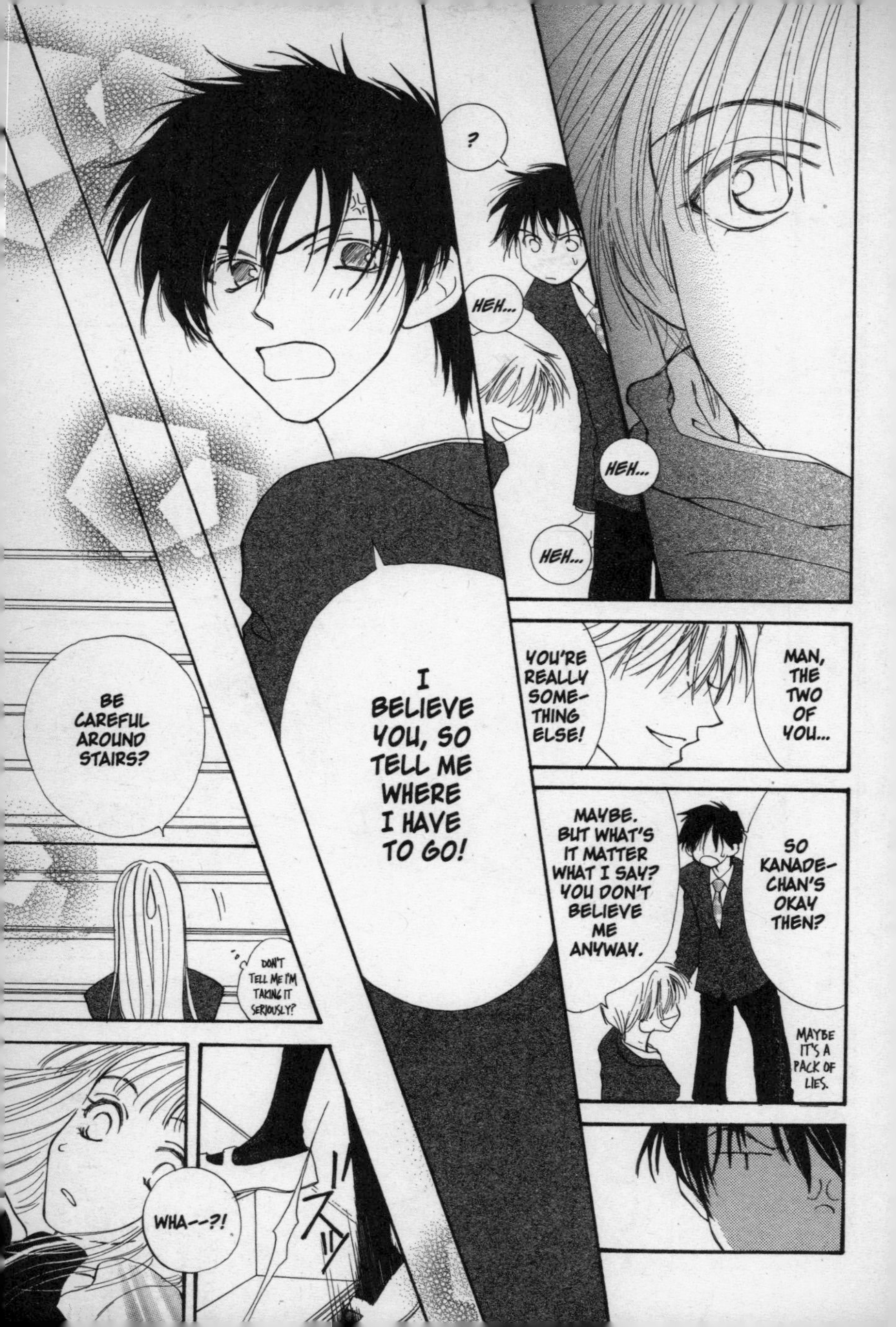
?
HEH...
HEH...
HEH...
MAN, THE TWO OF YOU...
YOU'RE REALLY SOMETHING ELSE!
SO KANADE-CHAN'S OKAY THEN?
MAYBE. BUT WHAT'S IT MATTER WHAT I SAY? YOU DON'T BELIEVE ME ANYWAY.
MAYBE IT'S A PACK OF LIES.
I BELIEVE YOU, SO TELL ME WHERE I HAVE TO GO!
BE CAREFUL AROUND STAIRS?
DON'T TELL ME I'M TAKING IT SERIOUSLY?
WHA--?!

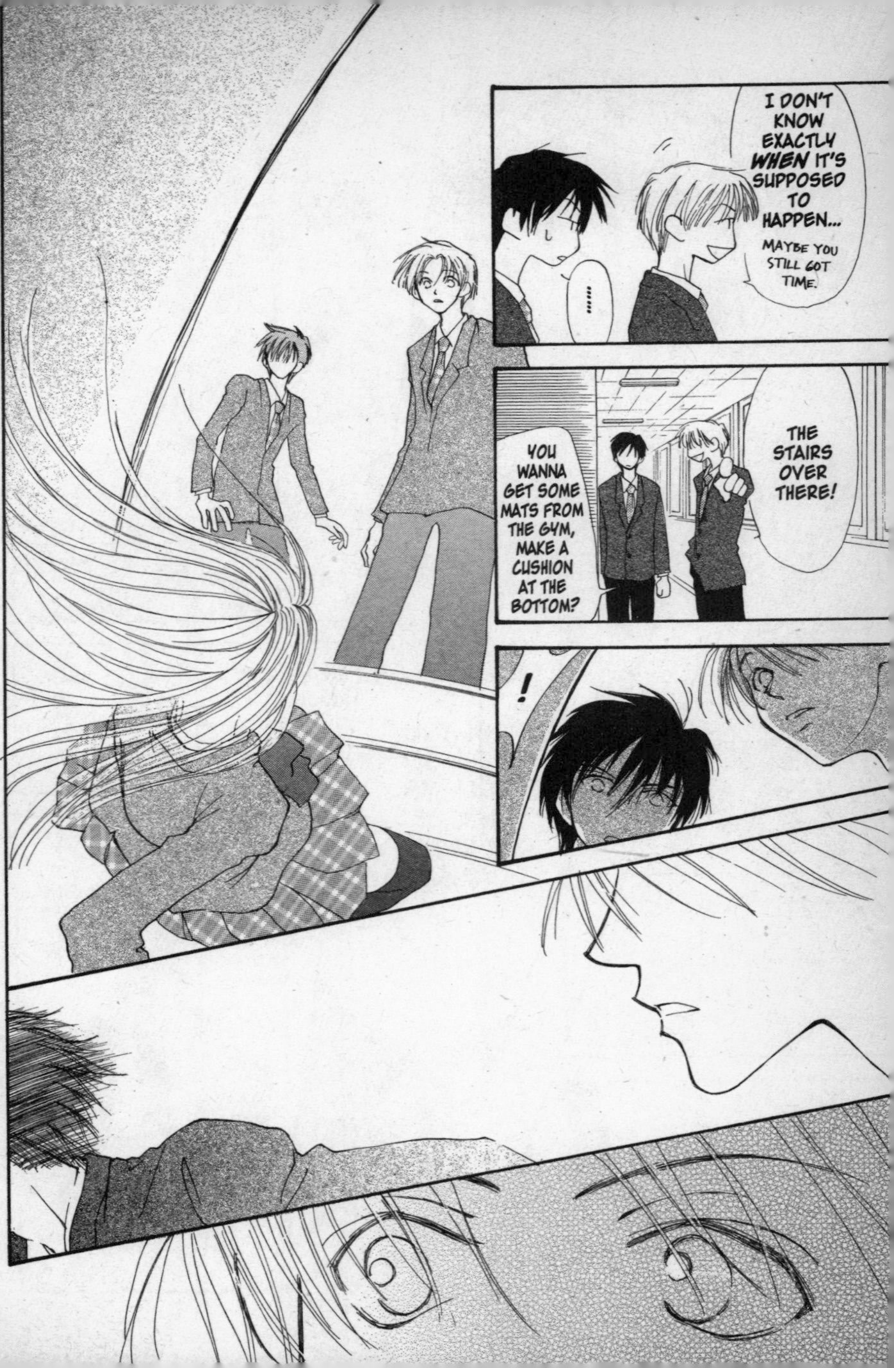
I DON'T KNOW EXACTLY WHEN IT'S SUPPOSED TO HAPPEN...
MAYBE YOU STILL GOT TIME.
......
THE STAIRS OVER THERE!
YOU WANNA GET SOME MATS FROM THE GYM, MAKE A CUSHION AT THE BOTTOM?
!

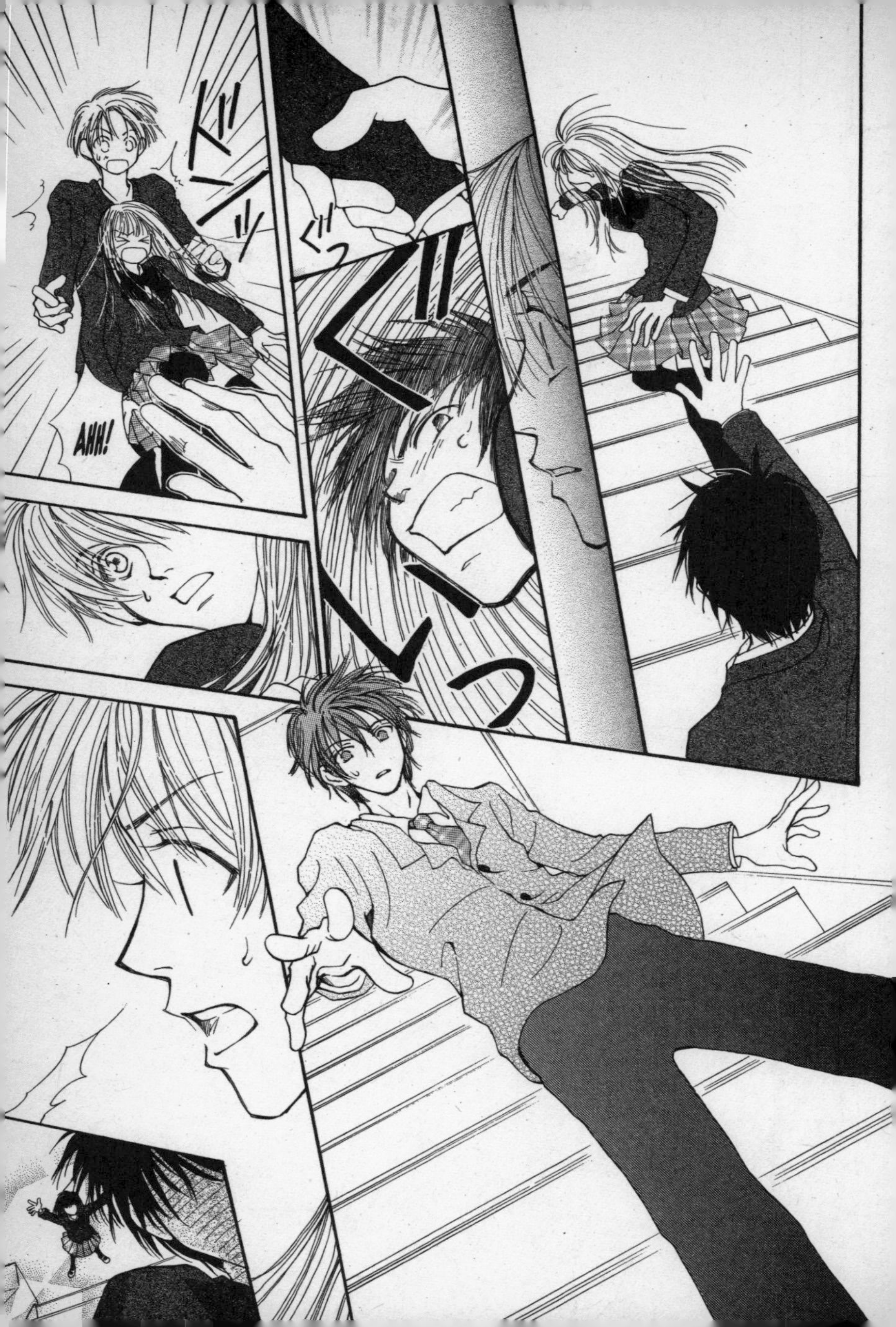
ぐっ
ぐいっ
ドンッ
AHH!

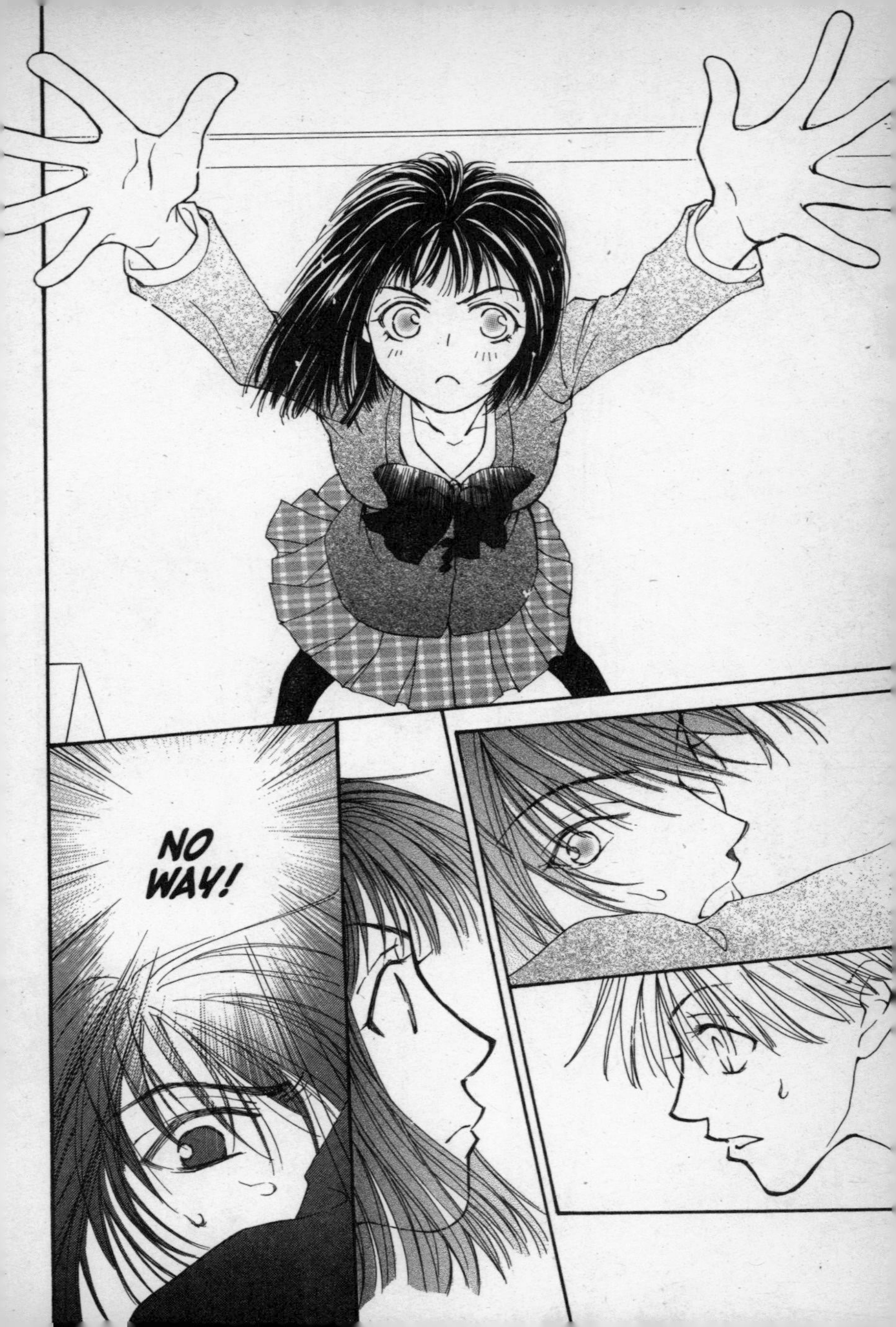
NO WAY!

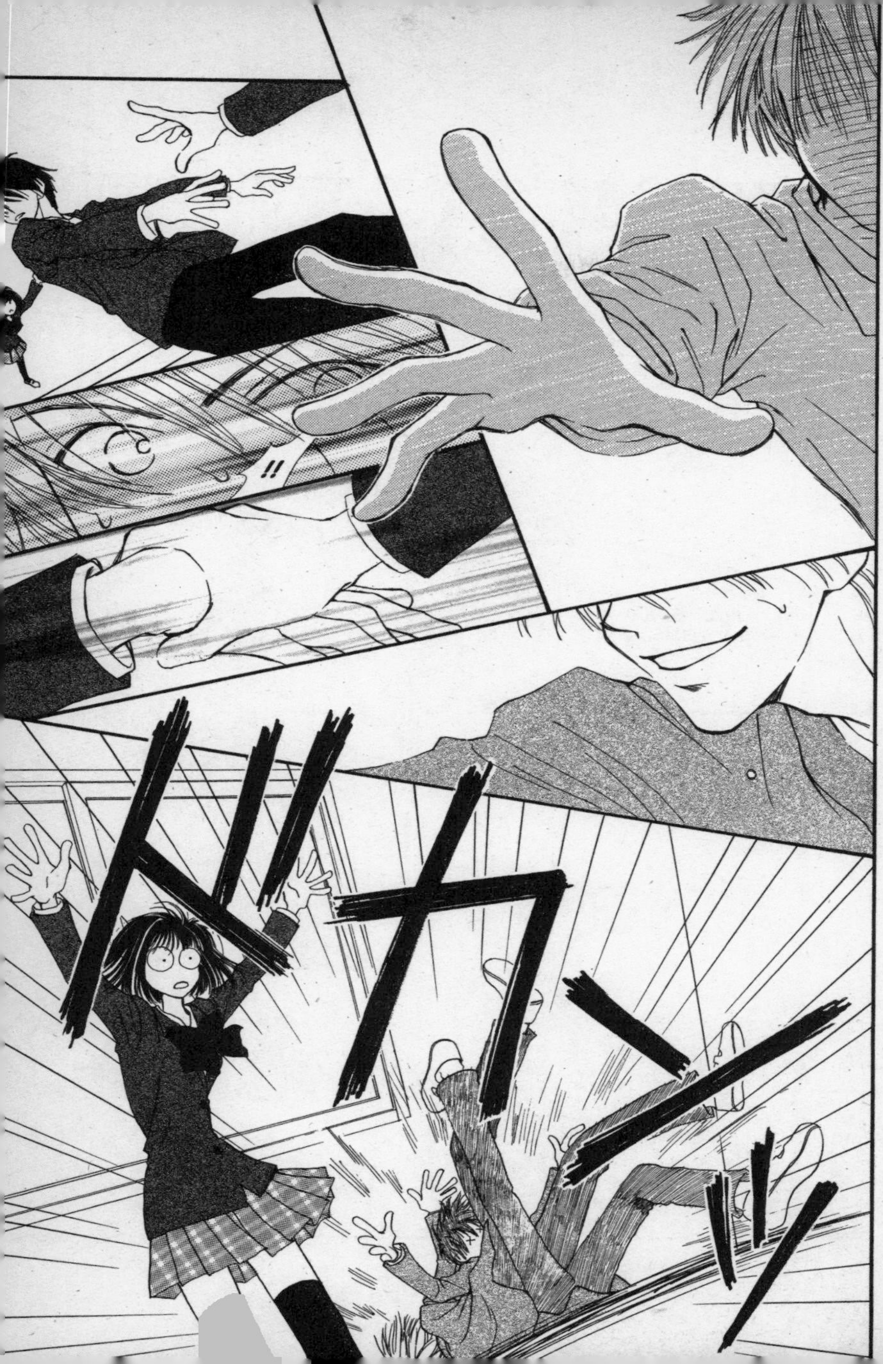
!!
ドガッ
ッ

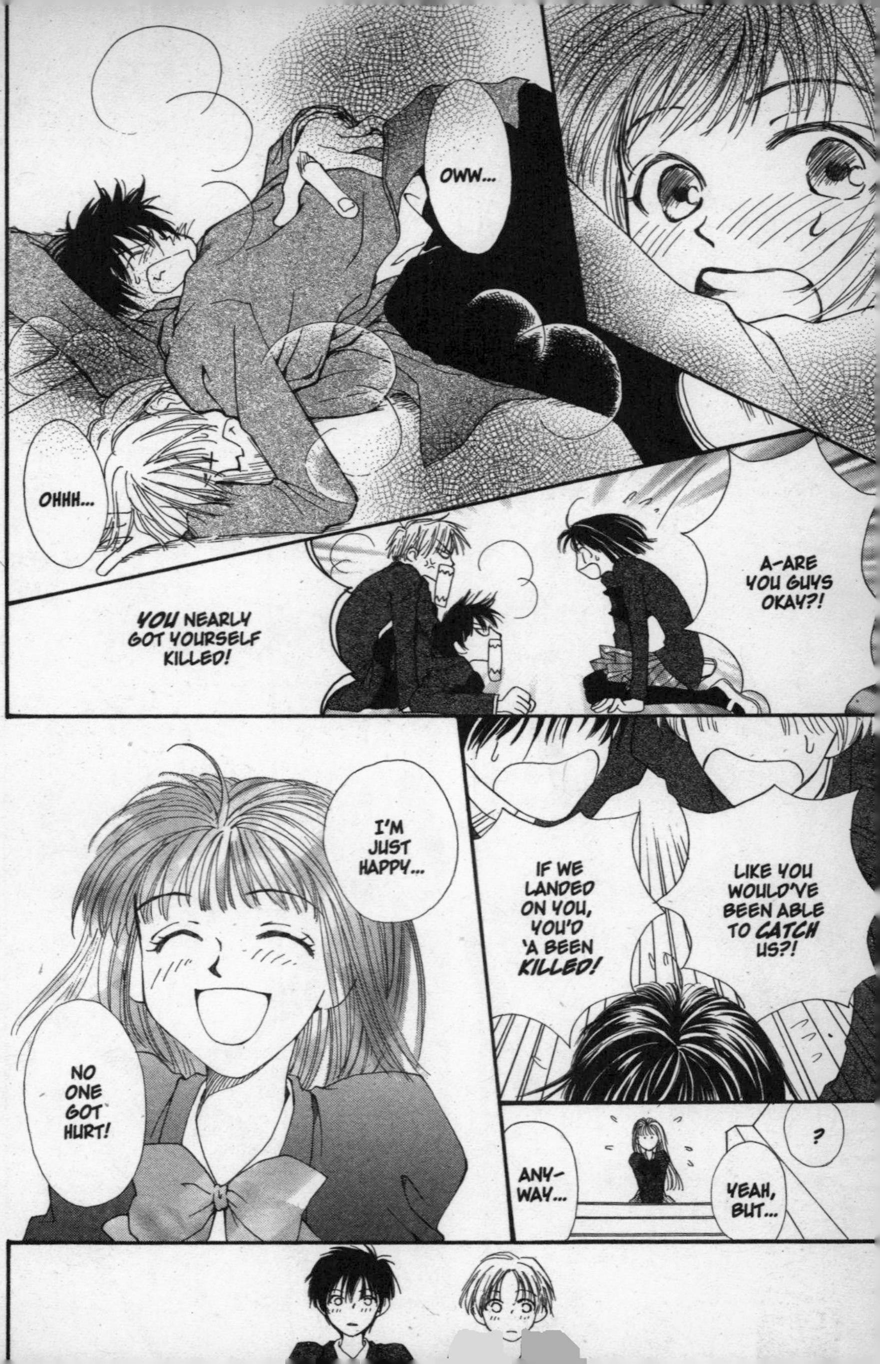
OWW...
OHHH...
A-ARE YOU GUYS OKAY?!
YOU NEARLY GOT YOURSELF KILLED!
LIKE YOU WOULD'VE BEEN ABLE TO CATCH US?!
IF WE LANDED ON YOU, YOU'D 'A BEEN KILLED!
?
YEAH, BUT...
ANY-WAY...
I'M JUST HAPPY...
NO ONE GOT HURT!

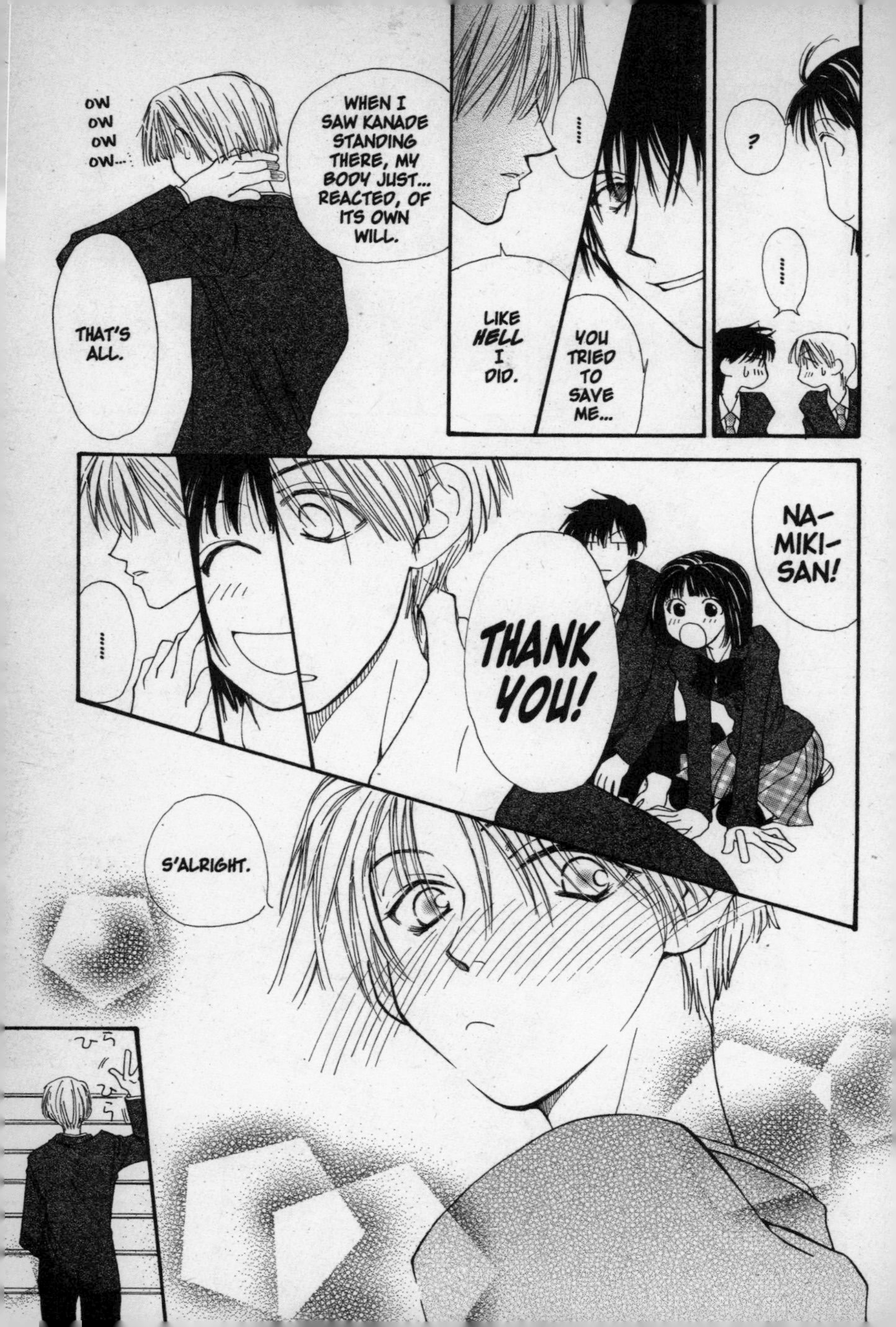
?
......
......
YOU TRIED TO SAVE ME...
LIKE HELL I DID.
WHEN I SAW KANADE STANDING THERE, MY BODY JUST... REACTED, OF ITS OWN WILL.
OW OW OW OW...
THAT'S ALL.
NA-MIKI-SAN!
THANK YOU!
......
S'ALRIGHT.

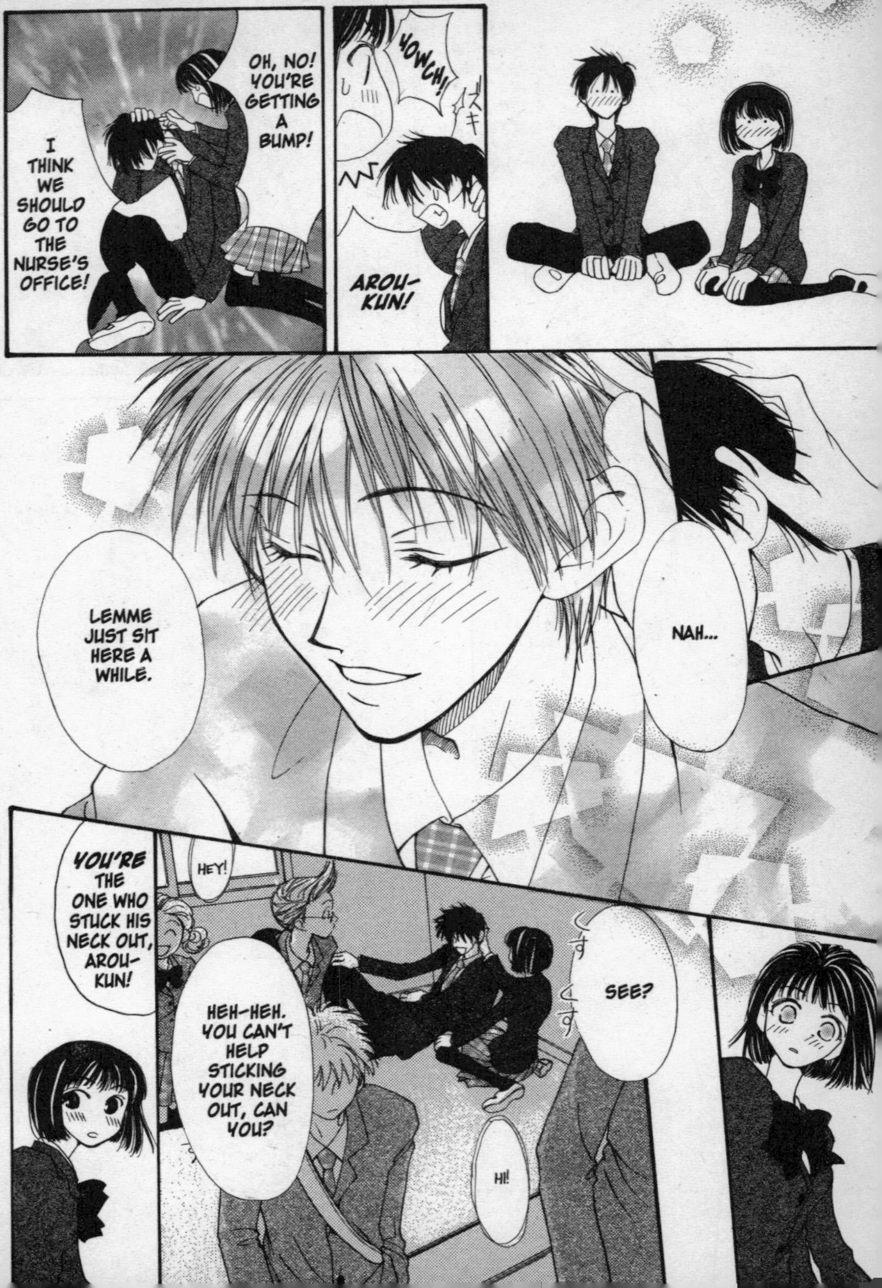
YOWCH!
ズキ
AROU-KUN!
OH, NO! YOU'RE GETTING A BUMP!
I THINK WE SHOULD GO TO THE NURSE'S OFFICE!
NAH...
LEMME JUST SIT HERE A WHILE.
くすくす
SEE?
HI!
HEH-HEH. YOU CAN'T HELP STICKING YOUR NECK OUT, CAN YOU?
HEY!
YOU'RE THE ONE WHO STUCK HIS NECK OUT, AROU-KUN!

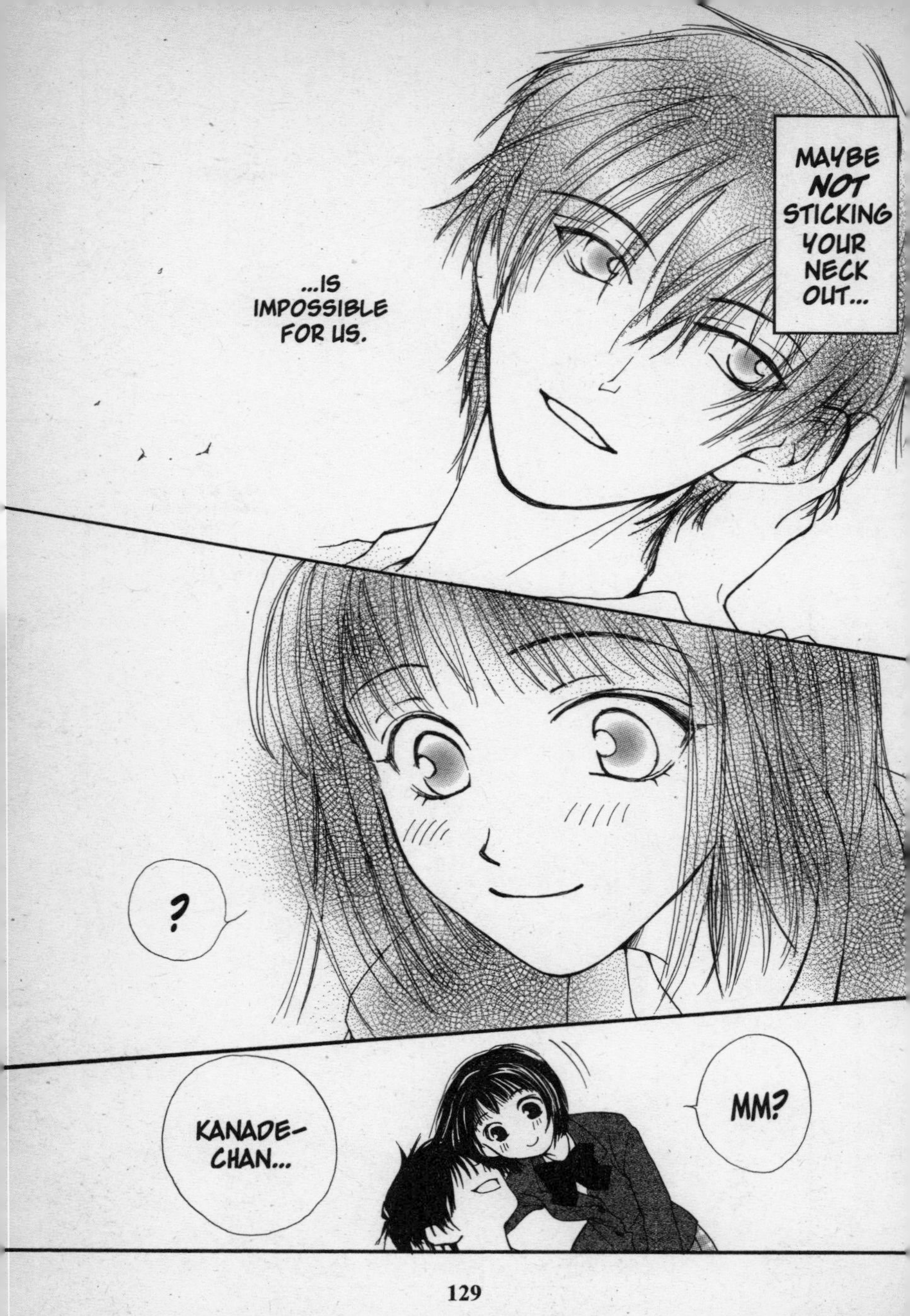
MAYBE NOT STICKING YOUR NECK OUT...
...IS IMPOSSIBLE FOR US.
?
MM?
KANADE-CHAN...

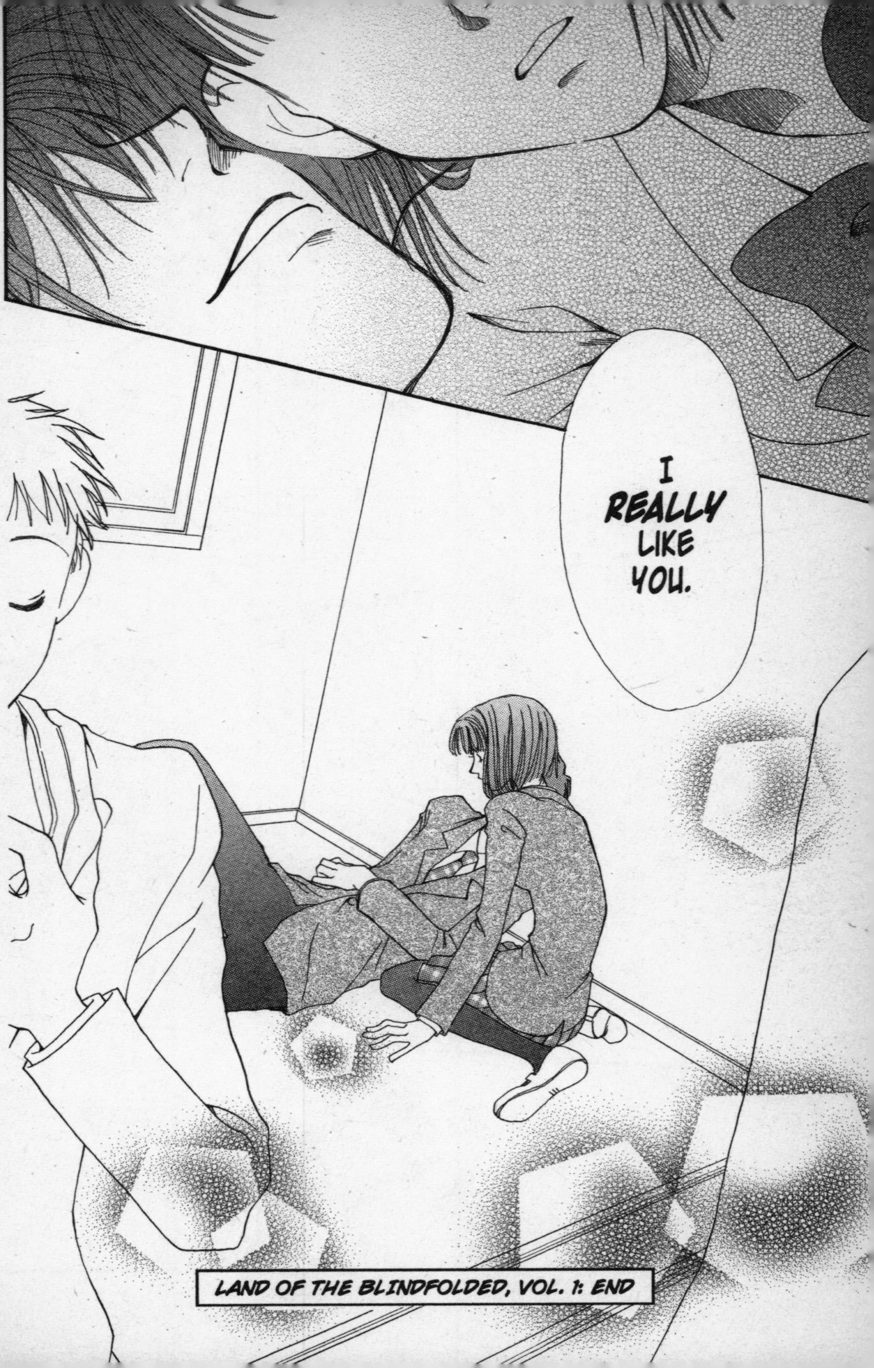
I REALLY LIKE YOU.
LAND OF THE BLINDFOLDED, VOL. 1: END

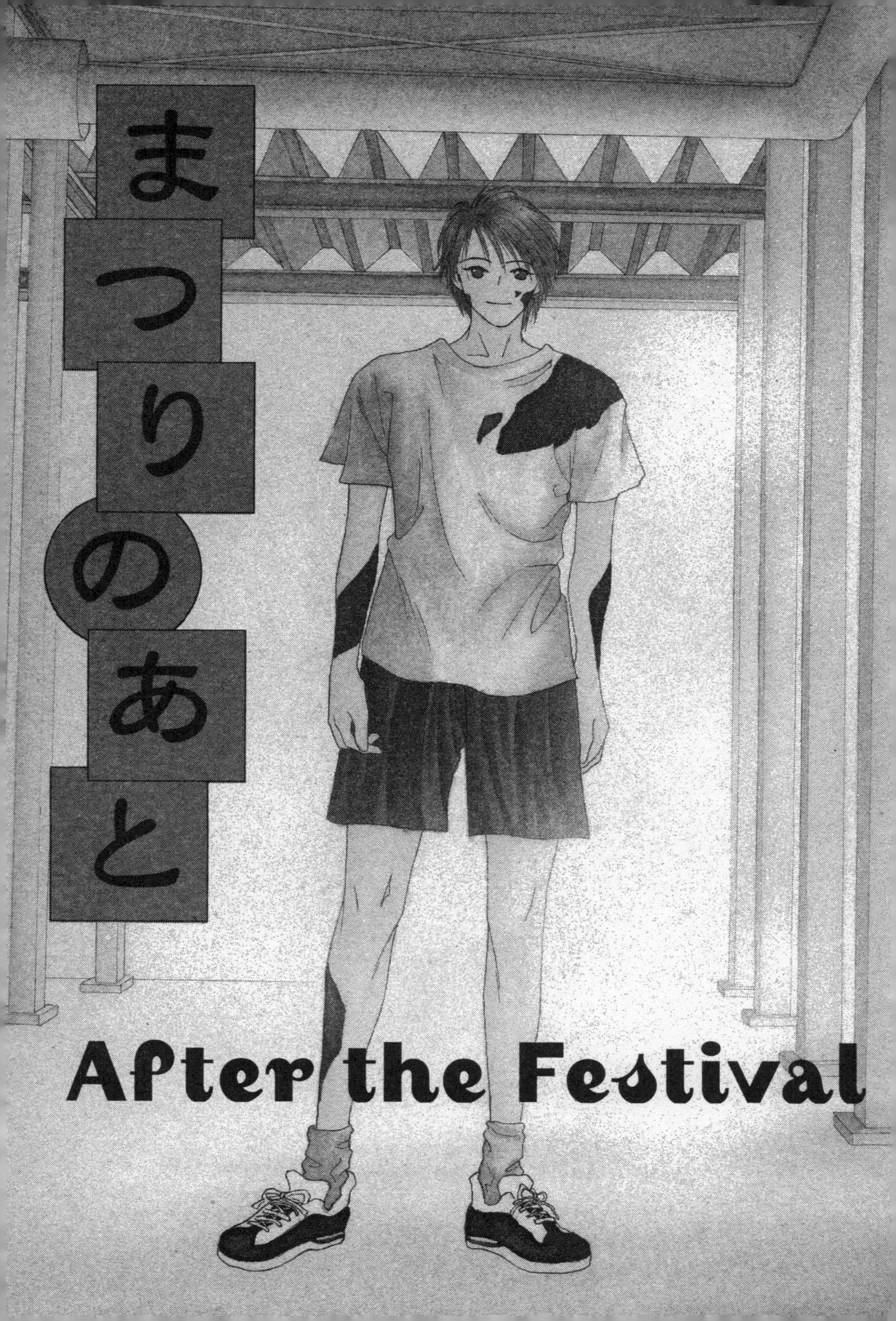
まつりのあと
After the Festival

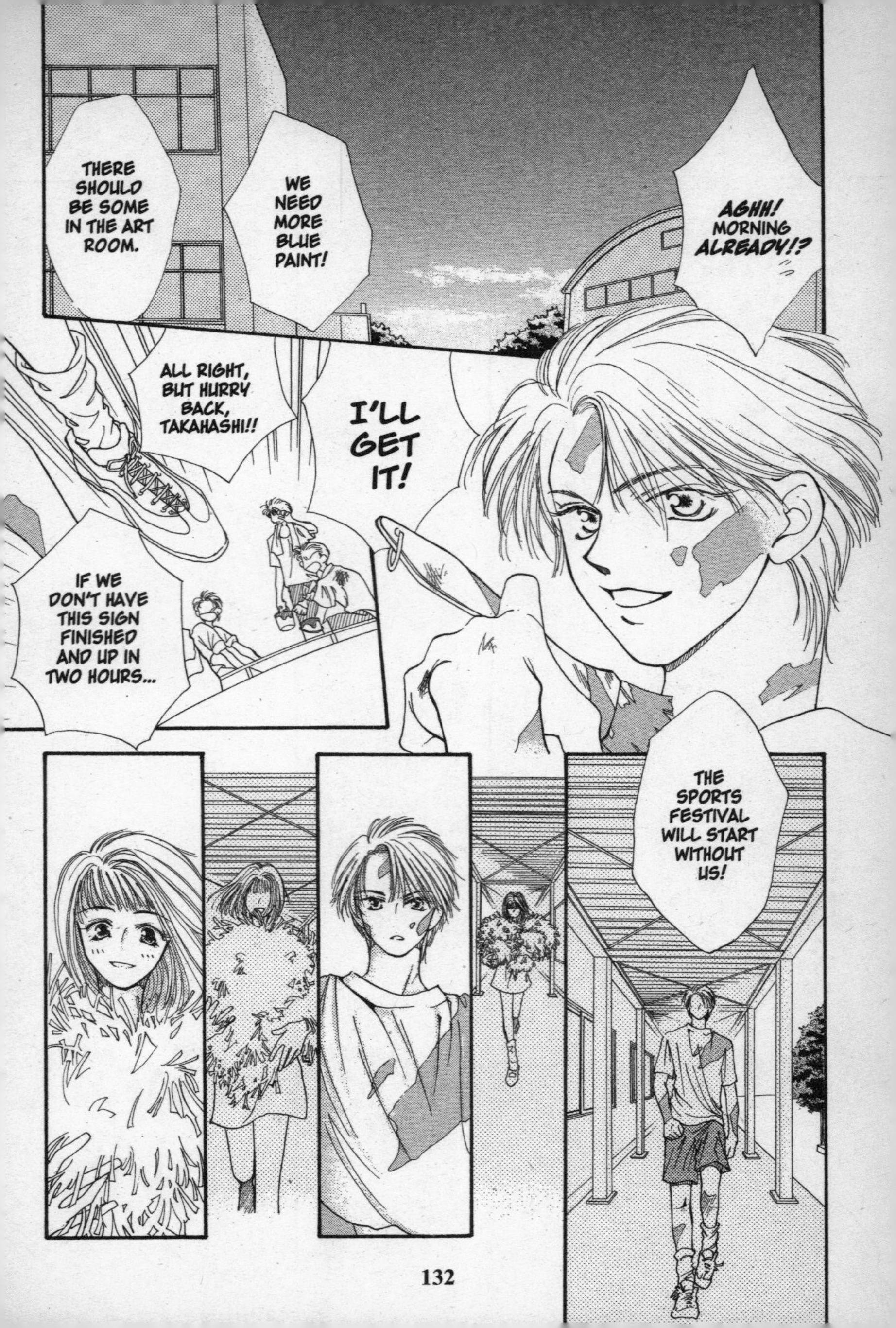
AGHH! MORNING ALREADY!?
WE NEED MORE BLUE PAINT!
THERE SHOULD BE SOME IN THE ART ROOM.
I'LL GET IT!
ALL RIGHT, BUT HURRY BACK, TAKAHASHI!!
IF WE DON'T HAVE THIS SIGN FINISHED AND UP IN TWO HOURS...
THE SPORTS FESTIVAL WILL START WITHOUT US!

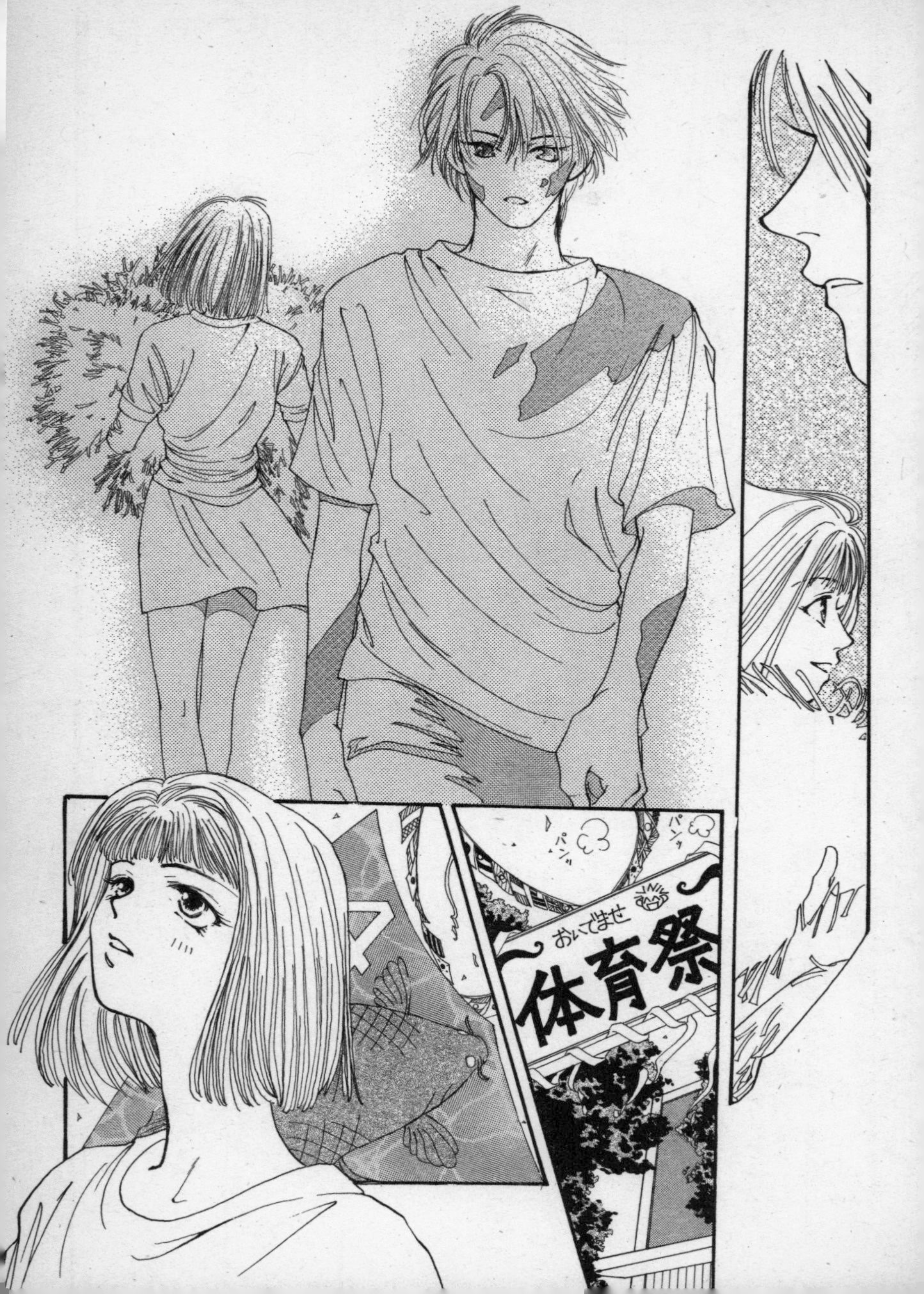
パンッ
パンッ
おいでませ
体育祭

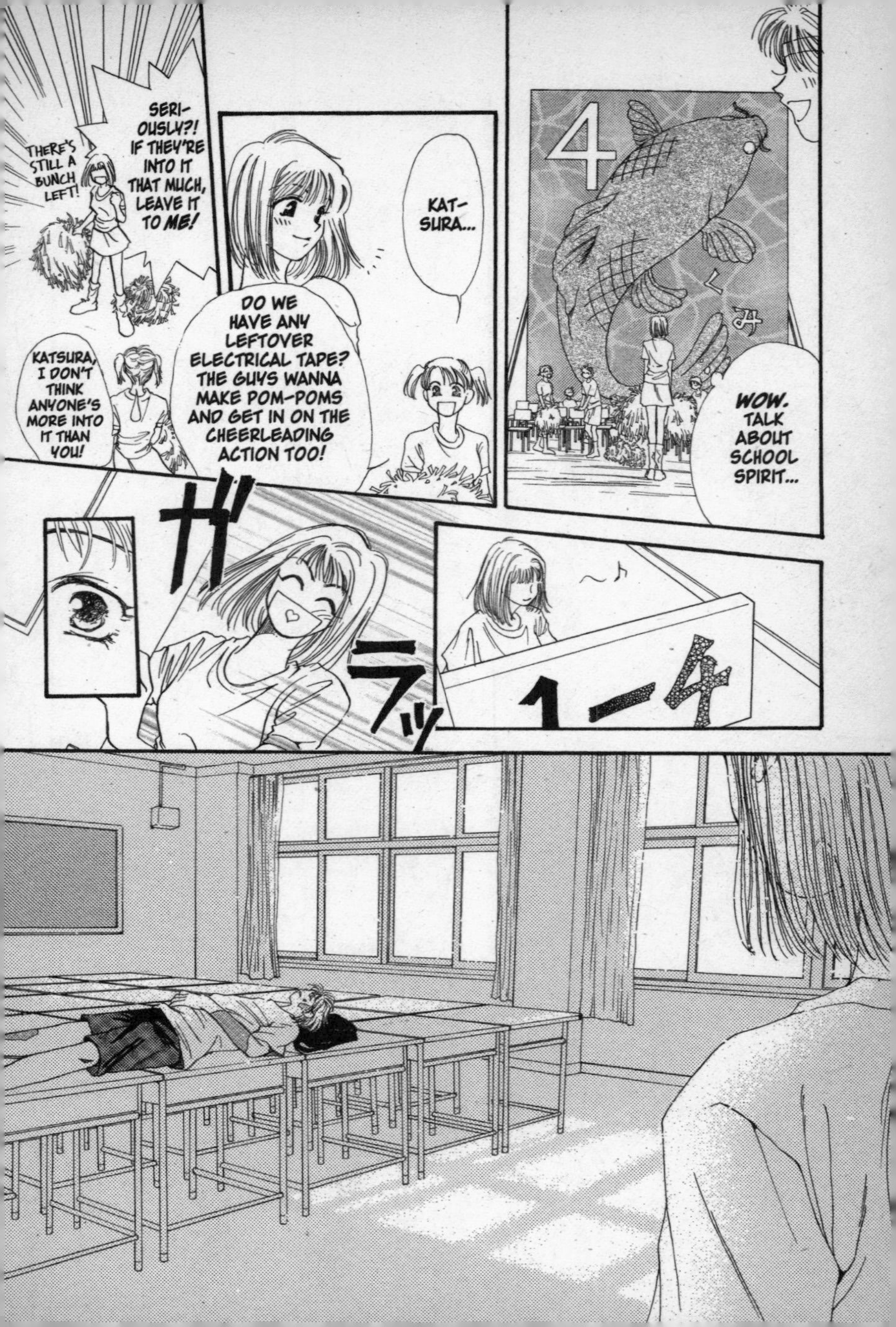
4
くみ
WOW. TALK ABOUT SCHOOL SPIRIT...
KAT-SURA...
DO WE HAVE ANY LEFTOVER ELECTRICAL TAPE? THE GUYS WANNA MAKE POM-POMS AND GET IN ON THE CHEERLEADING ACTION TOO!
SERI-OUSLY?! IF THEY'RE INTO IT THAT MUCH, LEAVE IT TO ME!
THERE'S STILL A BUNCH LEFT!
KATSURA, I DON'T THINK ANYONE'S MORE INTO IT THAN YOU!
~♪
1-4
ガ
ラッ

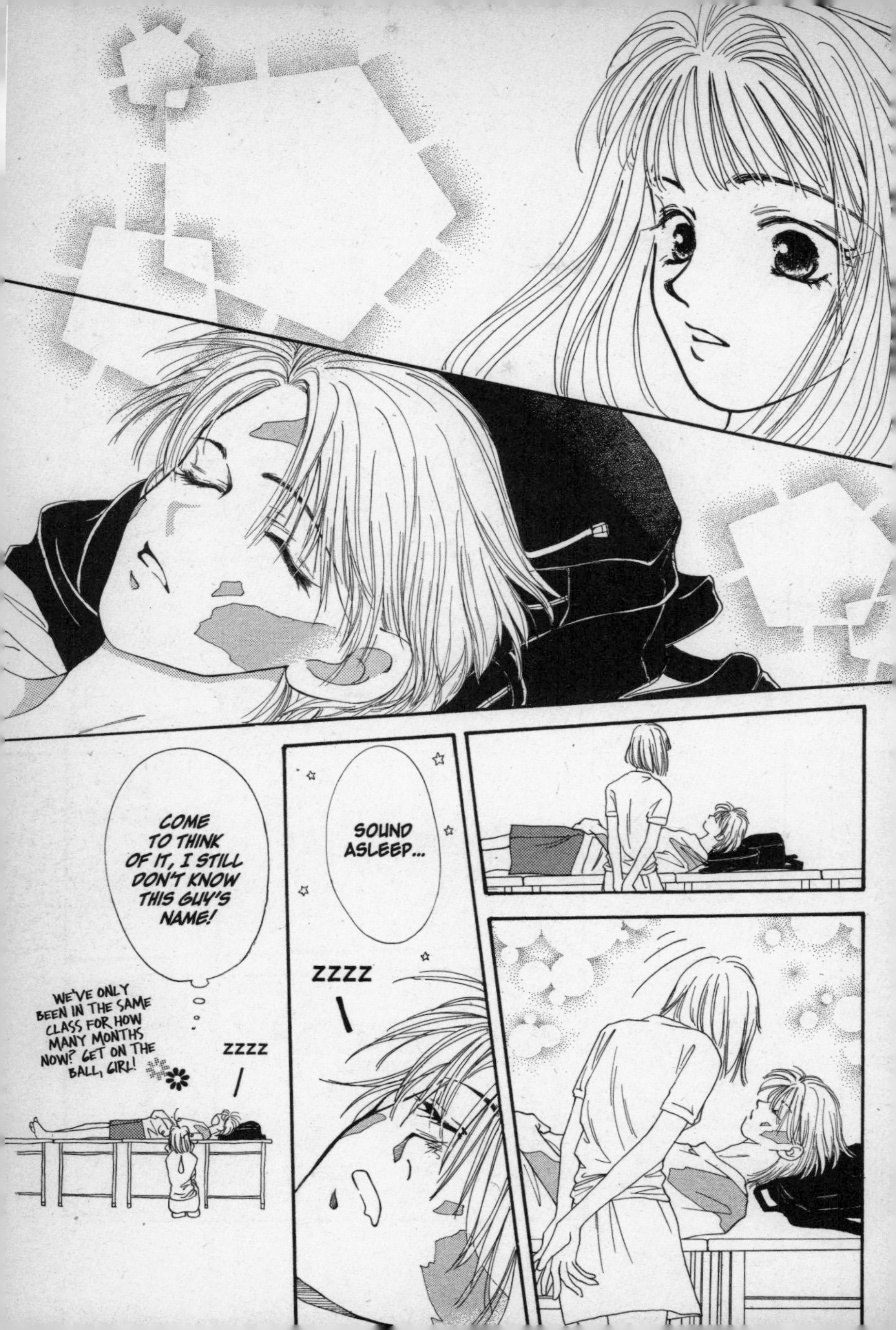
SOUND ASLEEP...
ZZZZ
COME TO THINK OF IT, I STILL DON'T KNOW THIS GUY'S NAME!
WE'VE ONLY BEEN IN THE SAME CLASS FOR HOW MANY MONTHS NOW? GET ON THE BALL, GIRL!
ZZZZ

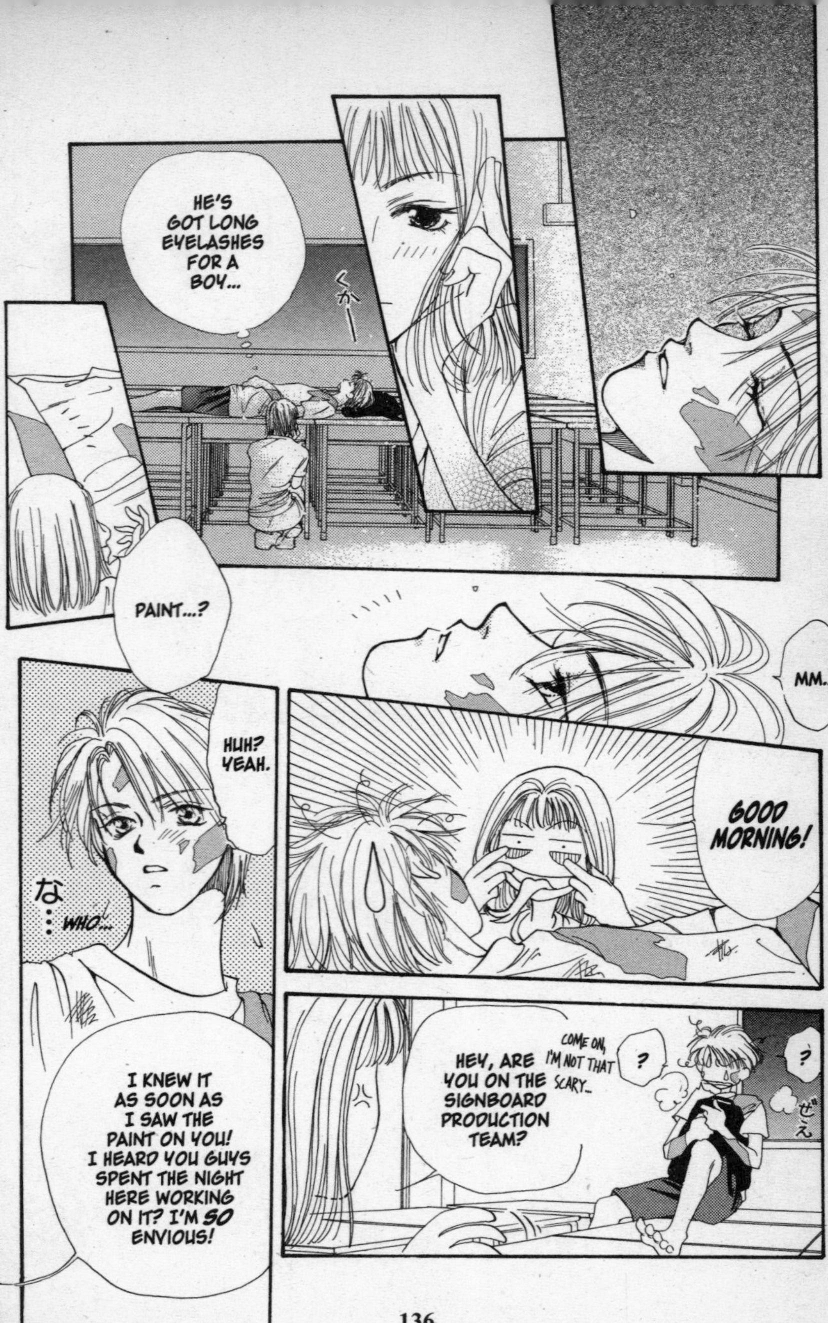
HE'S GOT LONG EYELASHES FOR A BOY...
くかー
PAINT...?
MM...
GOOD MORNING!
HEY, ARE YOU ON THE SIGNBOARD PRODUCTION TEAM?
COME ON, I'M NOT THAT SCARY...
?
?
ぜえ
HUH? YEAH.
な...
WHO...
I KNEW IT AS SOON AS I SAW THE PAINT ON YOU! I HEARD YOU GUYS SPENT THE NIGHT HERE WORKING ON IT? I'M SO ENVIOUS!

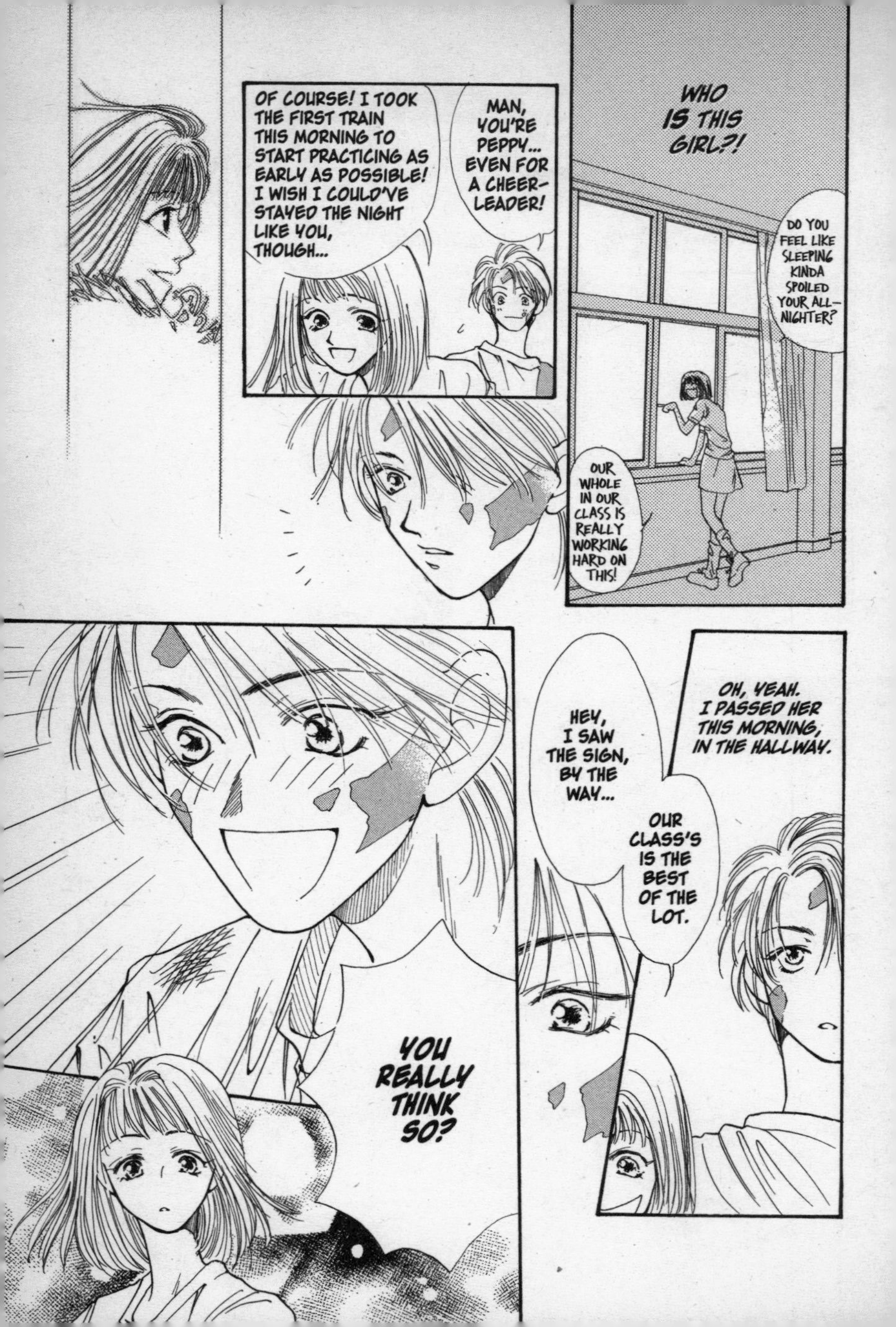
WHO IS THIS GIRL?!
DO YOU FEEL LIKE SLEEPING KINDA SPOILED YOUR ALL-NIGHTER?
OUR WHOLE IN OUR CLASS IS REALLY WORKING HARD ON THIS!
MAN, YOU'RE PEPPY... EVEN FOR A CHEER-LEADER!
OF COURSE! I TOOK THE FIRST TRAIN THIS MORNING TO START PRACTICING AS EARLY AS POSSIBLE! I WISH I COULD'VE STAYED THE NIGHT LIKE YOU, THOUGH...
OH, YEAH. I PASSED HER THIS MORNING, IN THE HALLWAY.
HEY, I SAW THE SIGN, BY THE WAY...
OUR CLASS'S IS THE BEST OF THE LOT.
YOU REALLY THINK SO?

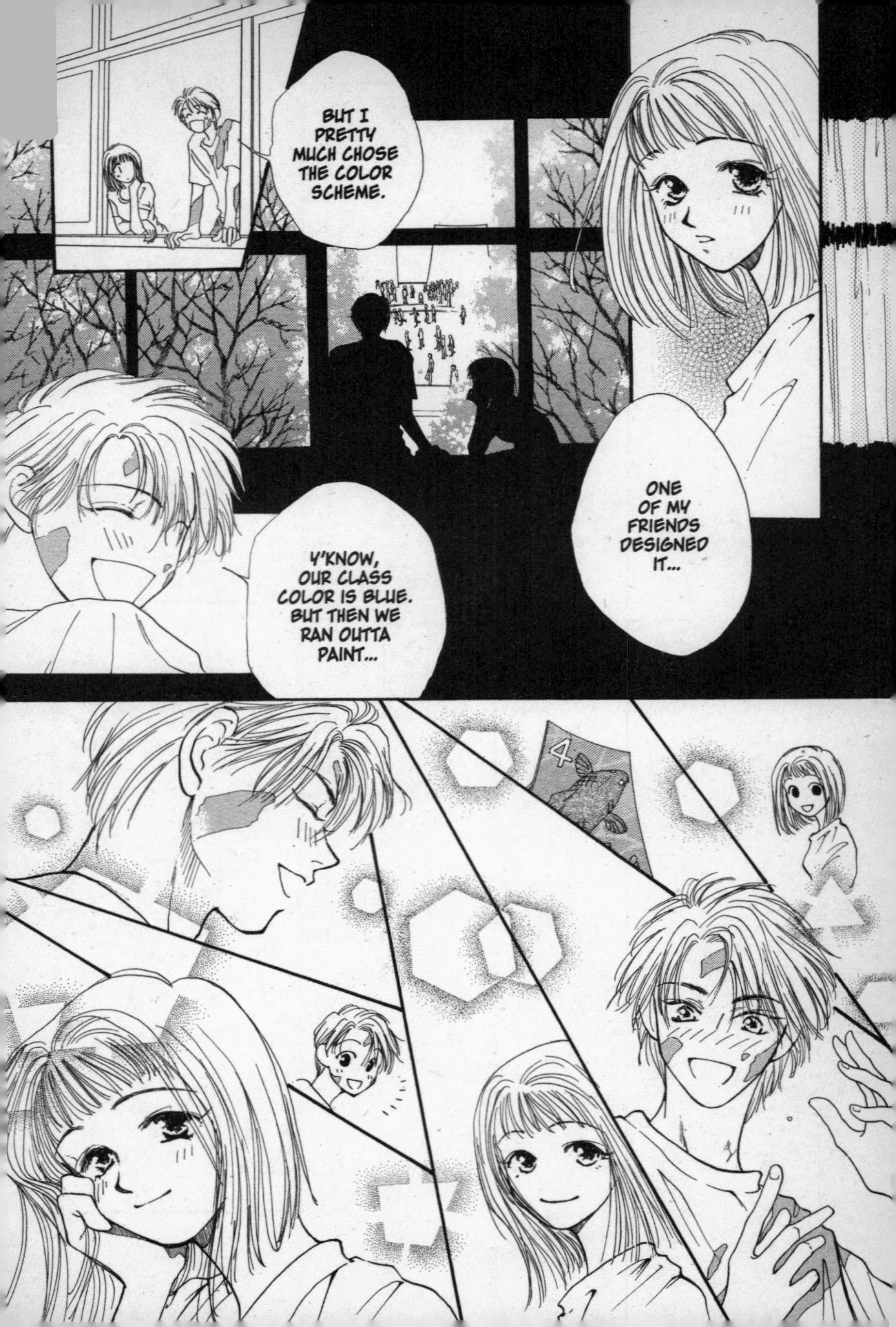
ONE OF MY FRIENDS DESIGNED IT...
BUT I PRETTY MUCH CHOSE THE COLOR SCHEME.
Y'KNOW, OUR CLASS COLOR IS BLUE. BUT THEN WE RAN OUTTA PAINT...
4

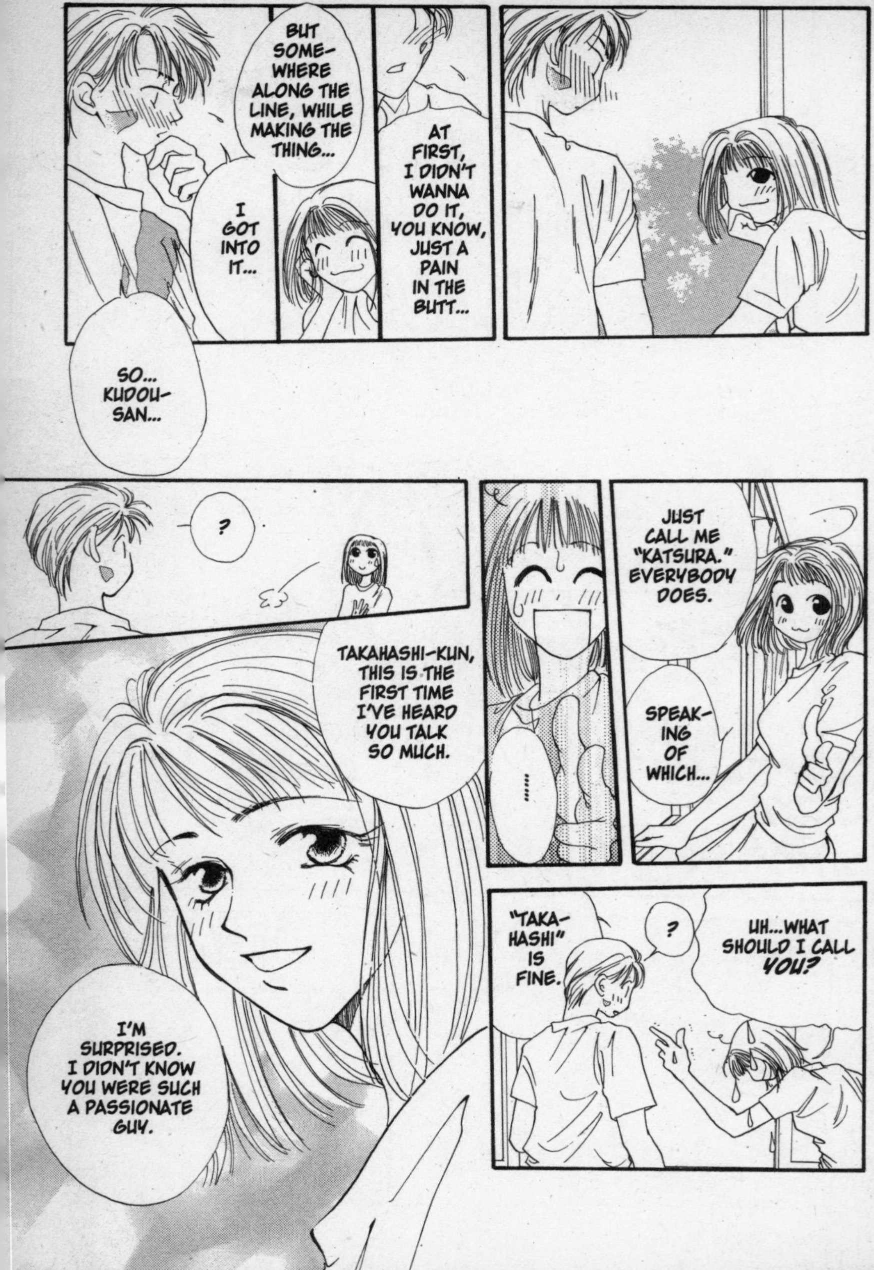
AT FIRST, I DIDN'T WANNA DO IT, YOU KNOW, JUST A PAIN IN THE BUTT...
BUT SOME-WHERE ALONG THE LINE, WHILE MAKING THE THING...
I GOT INTO IT...
SO... KUDOU-SAN...
JUST CALL ME "KATSURA." EVERYBODY DOES.
SPEAK-ING OF WHICH...
.....
?
UH...WHAT SHOULD I CALL *YOU?*
?
"TAKA-HASHI" IS FINE.
TAKAHASHI-KUN, THIS IS THE FIRST TIME I'VE HEARD YOU TALK SO MUCH.
I'M SURPRISED. I DIDN'T KNOW YOU WERE SUCH A PASSIONATE GUY.

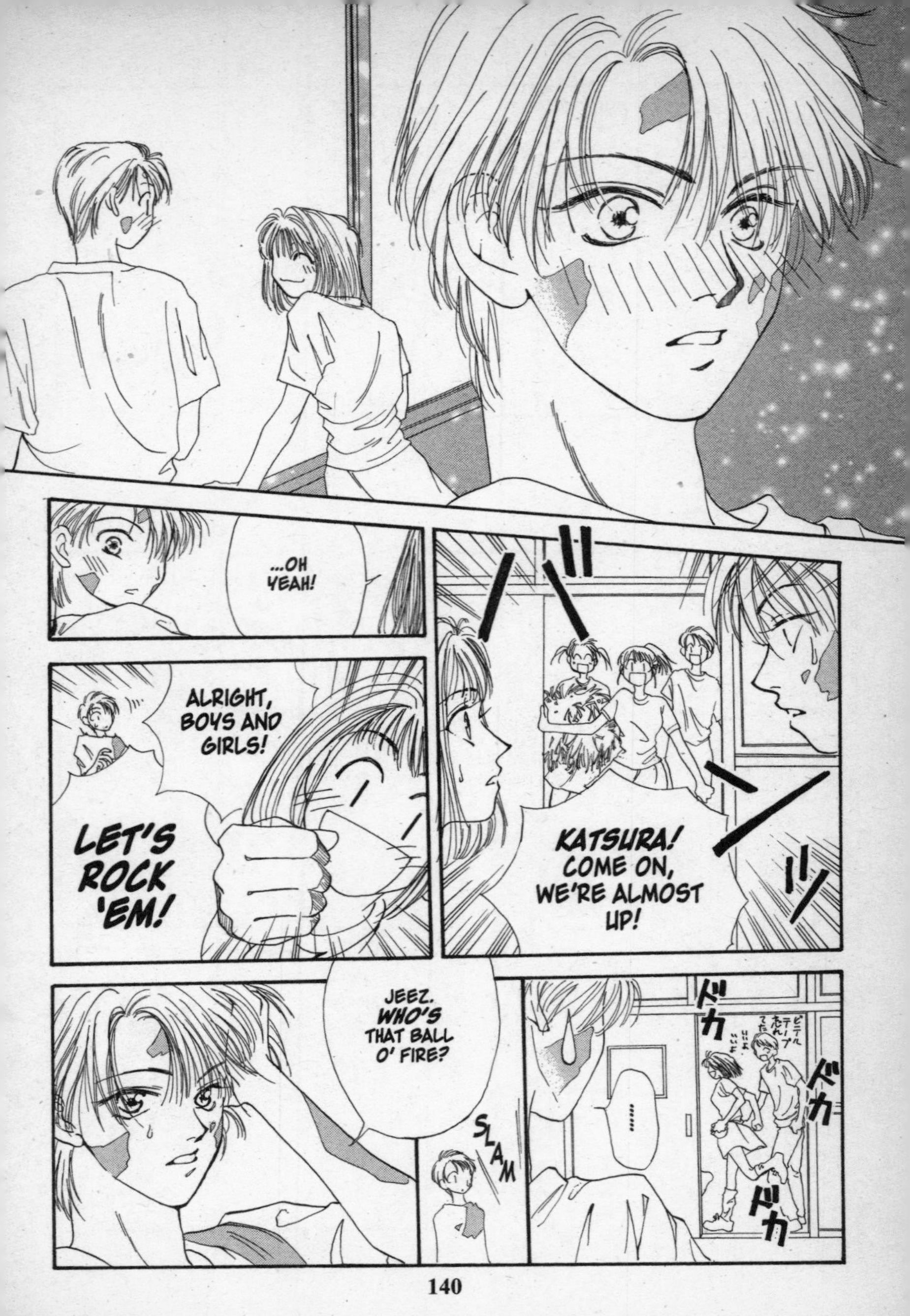
バ
ン
ッ
KATSURA! COME ON, WE'RE ALMOST UP!
...OH YEAH!
ALRIGHT, BOYS AND GIRLS!
LET'S ROCK 'EM!
ドカ
ドカ
ドカ
......
JEEZ. WHO'S THAT BALL O' FIRE?
SLAM

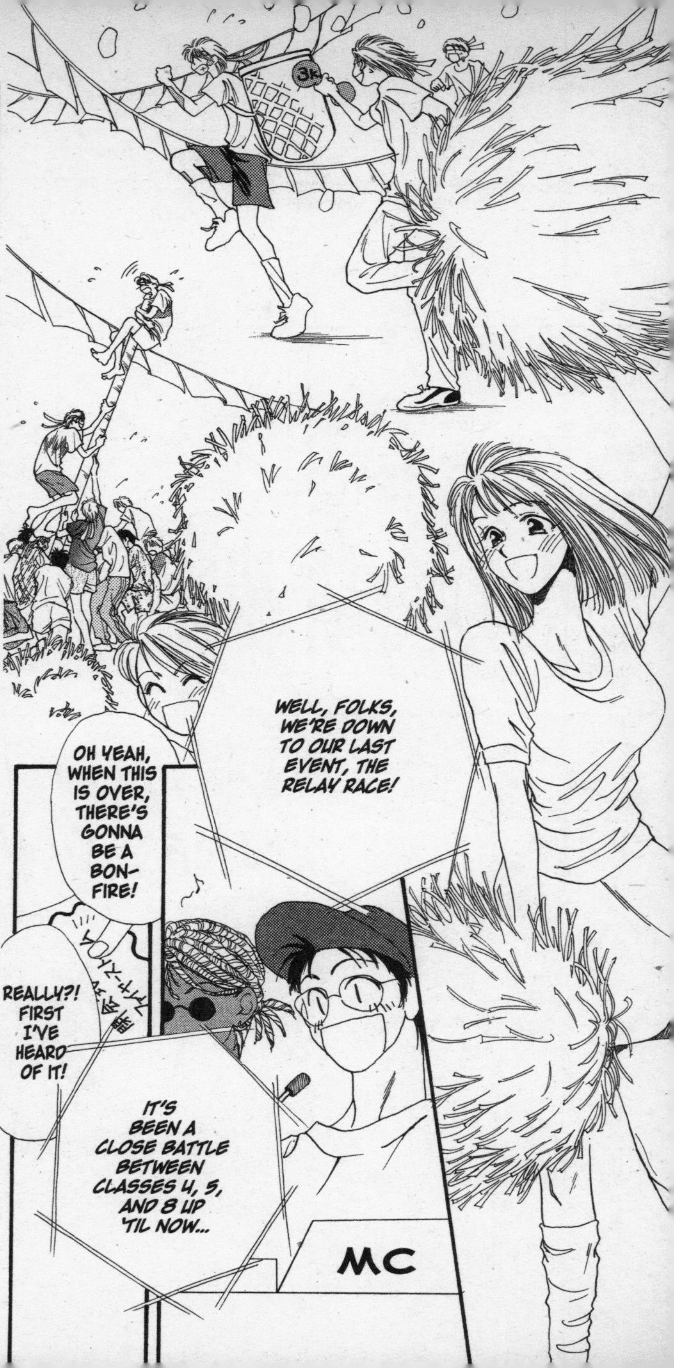
3K
WELL, FOLKS, WE'RE DOWN TO OUR LAST EVENT, THE RELAY RACE!
IT'S BEEN A CLOSE BATTLE BETWEEN CLASSES 4, 5, AND 8 UP 'TIL NOW...
MC
OH YEAH, WHEN THIS IS OVER, THERE'S GONNA BE A BON-FIRE!
REALLY?! FIRST I'VE HEARD OF IT!

Sakura Mail

No. 4

"After the Festival" was created from elements of an incident I had experienced in my high school days. Maybe this story could be called half-true? Anyway, I felt a little proud of myself for attempting to dramatize such a horrible event from my youth. Thanks to that happening, my freshman year of high school was a gloomy one indeed. As it turned out, the instigator of the incident (me) and Takahashi-kun were in the same class for all three years of high school. I always wondered if that was the teacher's plot, so that I'd be reminded every day of what happened. What actually happened, you ask? Well... I'll have to leave that to your imagination. Sorry! Anyway, I really tried my best to fashion a love story here. I'm often told that the atmosphere of my stories changed starting with "After the Festival," for which, for some reason, I have deep, abiding feelings.

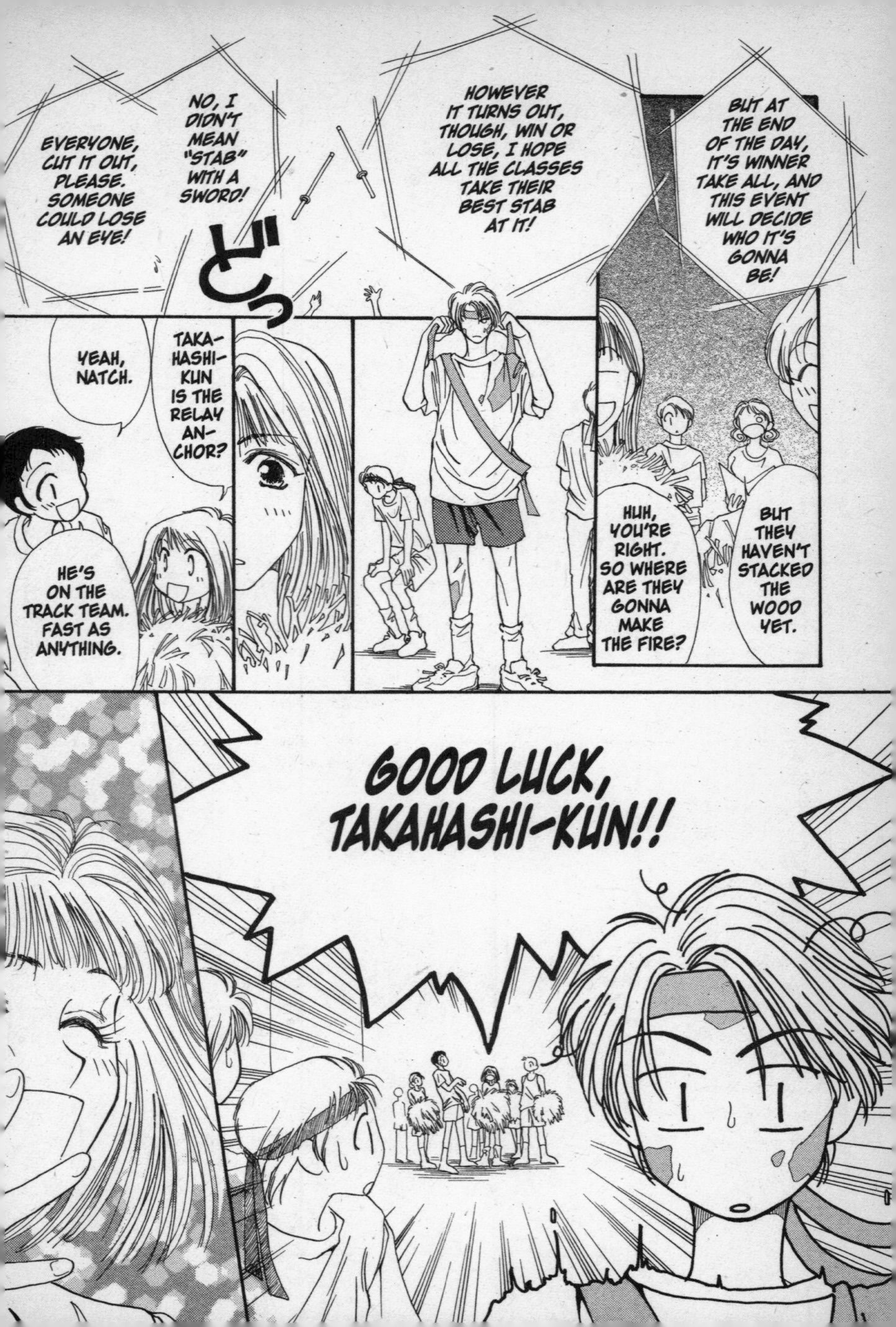
BUT AT THE END OF THE DAY, IT'S WINNER TAKE ALL, AND THIS EVENT WILL DECIDE WHO IT'S GONNA BE!
HOWEVER IT TURNS OUT, THOUGH, WIN OR LOSE, I HOPE ALL THE CLASSES TAKE THEIR BEST STAB AT IT!
NO, I DIDN'T MEAN "STAB" WITH A SWORD!
EVERYONE, CUT IT OUT, PLEASE. SOMEONE COULD LOSE AN EYE!
どっ
BUT THEY HAVEN'T STACKED THE WOOD YET.
HUH, YOU'RE RIGHT. SO WHERE ARE THEY GONNA MAKE THE FIRE?
TAKAHASHI-KUN IS THE RELAY ANCHOR?
YEAH, NATCH.
HE'S ON THE TRACK TEAM. FAST AS ANYTHING.
GOOD LUCK, TAKAHASHI-KUN!!

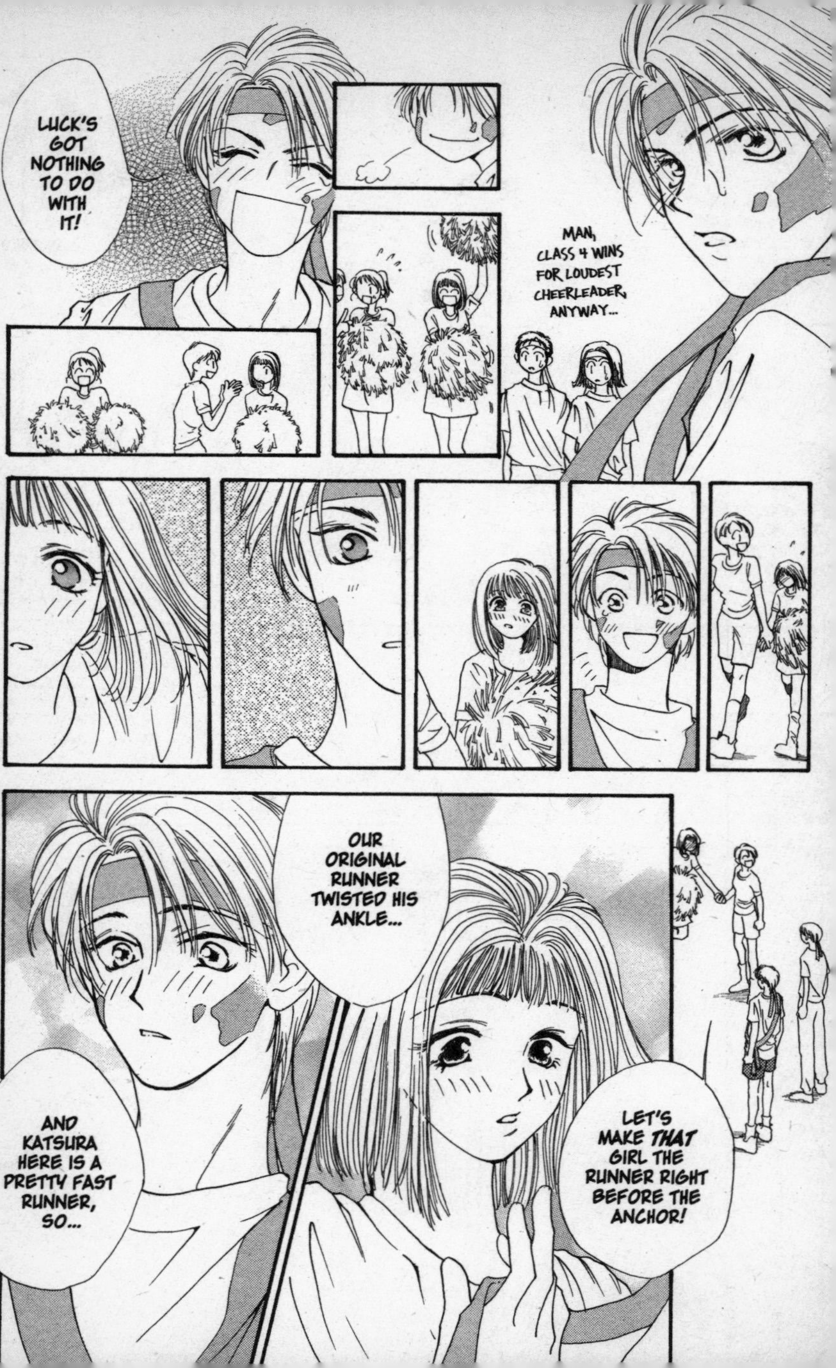
MAN, CLASS 4 WINS FOR LOUDEST CHEERLEADER, ANYWAY...
LUCK'S GOT NOTHING TO DO WITH IT!
OUR ORIGINAL RUNNER TWISTED HIS ANKLE...
AND KATSURA HERE IS A PRETTY FAST RUNNER, SO...
LET'S MAKE *THAT* GIRL THE RUNNER RIGHT BEFORE THE ANCHOR!

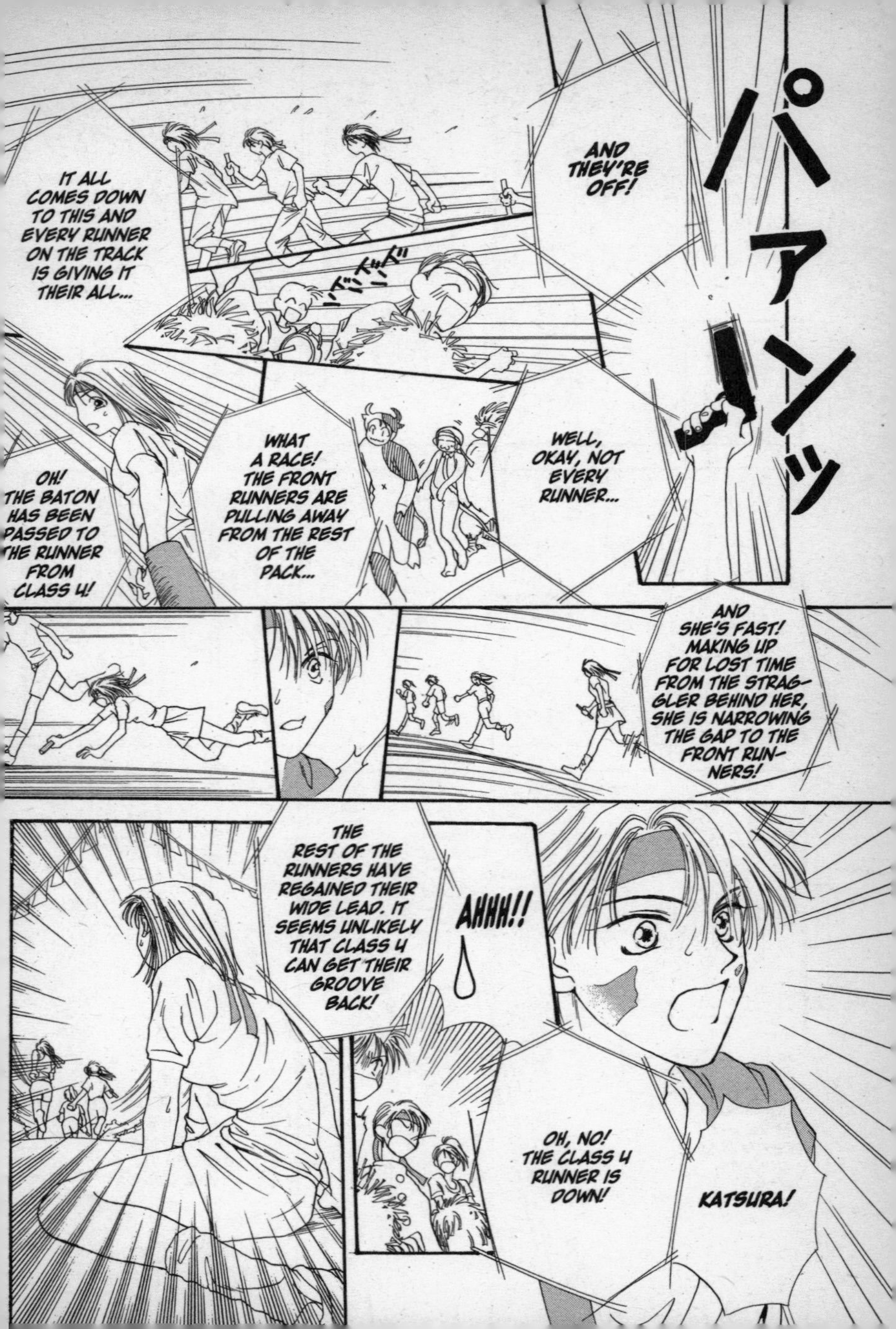
パアンッ
AND THEY'RE OFF!
IT ALL COMES DOWN TO THIS AND EVERY RUNNER ON THE TRACK IS GIVING IT THEIR ALL...
WELL, OKAY, NOT EVERY RUNNER...
WHAT A RACE! THE FRONT RUNNERS ARE PULLING AWAY FROM THE REST OF THE PACK...
OH! THE BATON HAS BEEN PASSED TO THE RUNNER FROM CLASS 4!
AND SHE'S FAST! MAKING UP FOR LOST TIME FROM THE STRAGGLER BEHIND HER, SHE IS NARROWING THE GAP TO THE FRONT RUNNERS!
KATSURA!
OH, NO! THE CLASS 4 RUNNER IS DOWN!
AHHH!!
THE REST OF THE RUNNERS HAVE REGAINED THEIR WIDE LEAD. IT SEEMS UNLIKELY THAT CLASS 4 CAN GET THEIR GROOVE BACK!

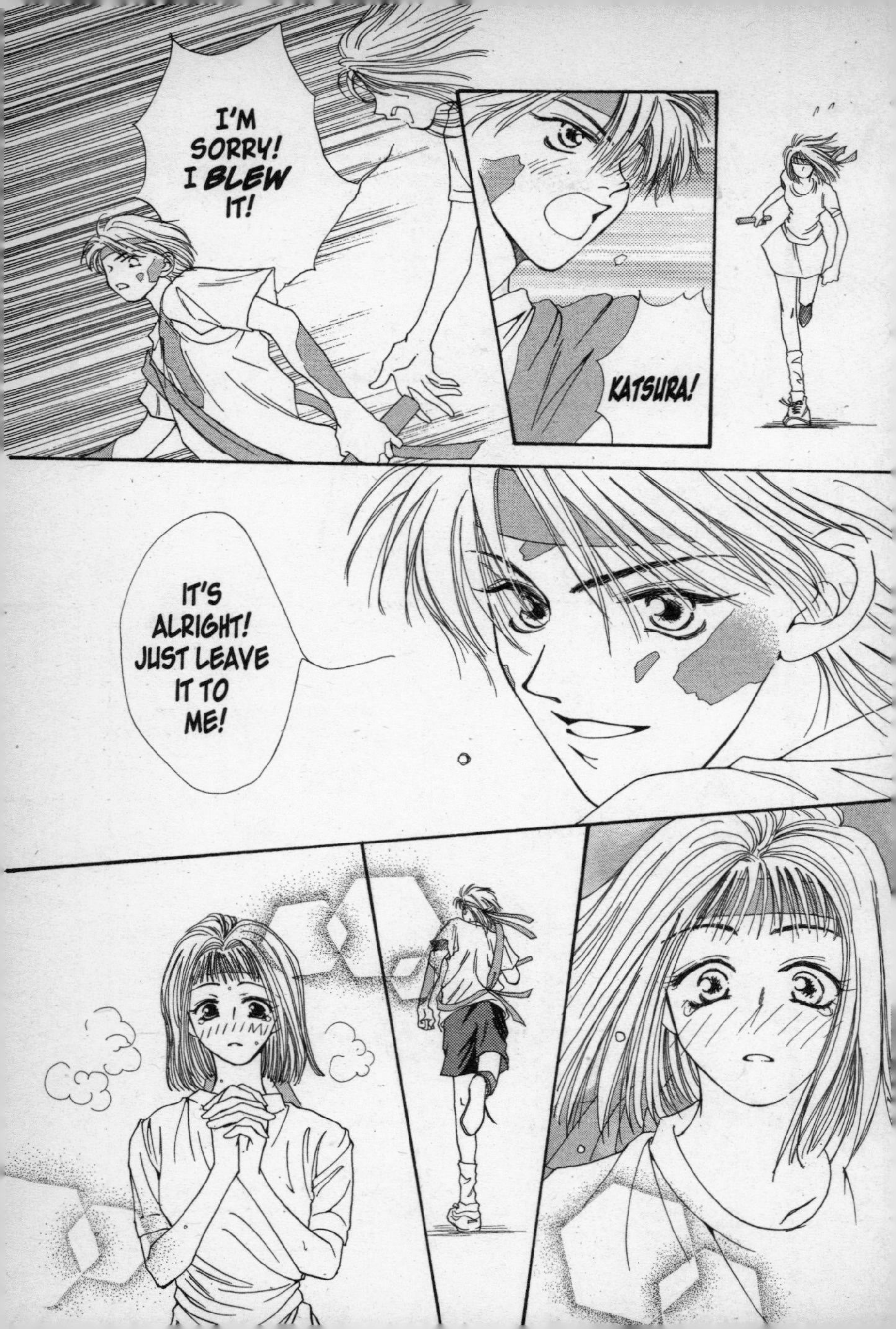
KATSURA!
I'M SORRY! I BLEW IT!
IT'S ALRIGHT! JUST LEAVE IT TO ME!

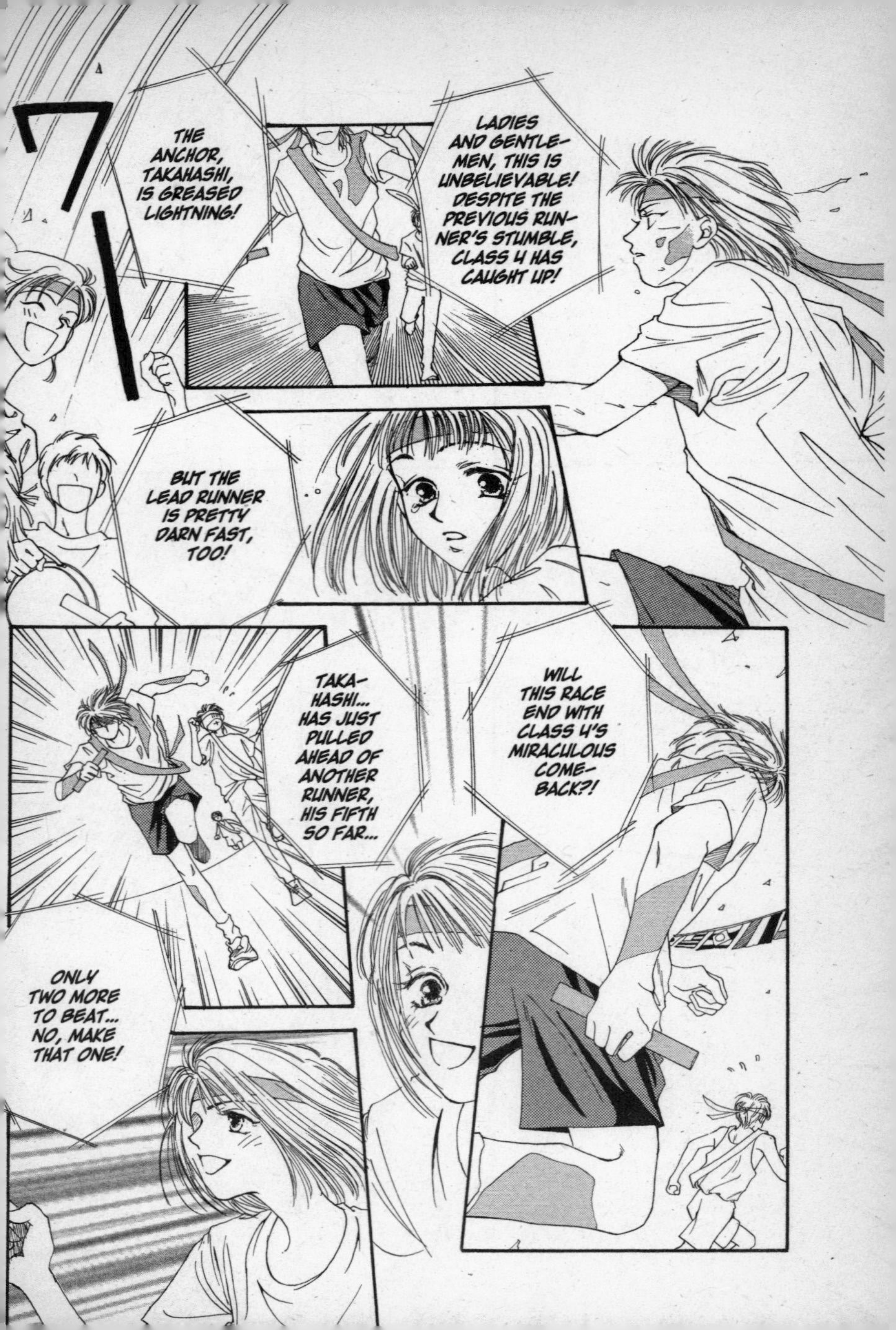
LADIES AND GENTLE-MEN, THIS IS UNBELIEVABLE! DESPITE THE PREVIOUS RUN-NER'S STUMBLE, CLASS 4 HAS CAUGHT UP!
THE ANCHOR, TAKAHASHI, IS GREASED LIGHTNING!
BUT THE LEAD RUNNER IS PRETTY DARN FAST, TOO!
WILL THIS RACE END WITH CLASS 4'S MIRACULOUS COME-BACK?!
TAKA-HASHI... HAS JUST PULLED AHEAD OF ANOTHER RUNNER, HIS FIFTH SO FAR...
ONLY TWO MORE TO BEAT... NO, MAKE THAT ONE!

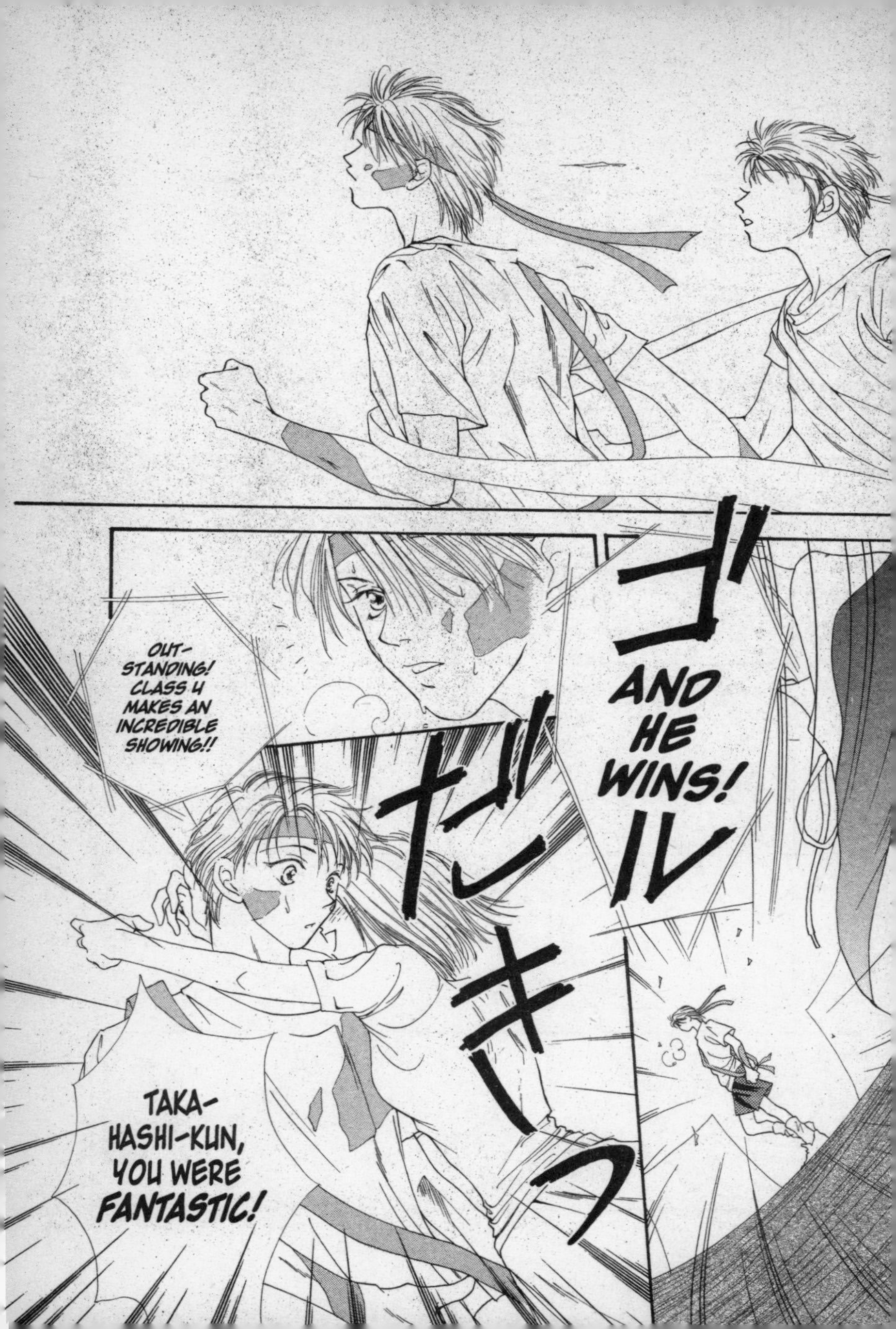
ゴール
AND HE WINS!
OUT-STANDING! CLASS 4 MAKES AN INCREDIBLE SHOWING!!
だきっ
TAKA-HASHI-KUN, YOU WERE FANTASTIC!

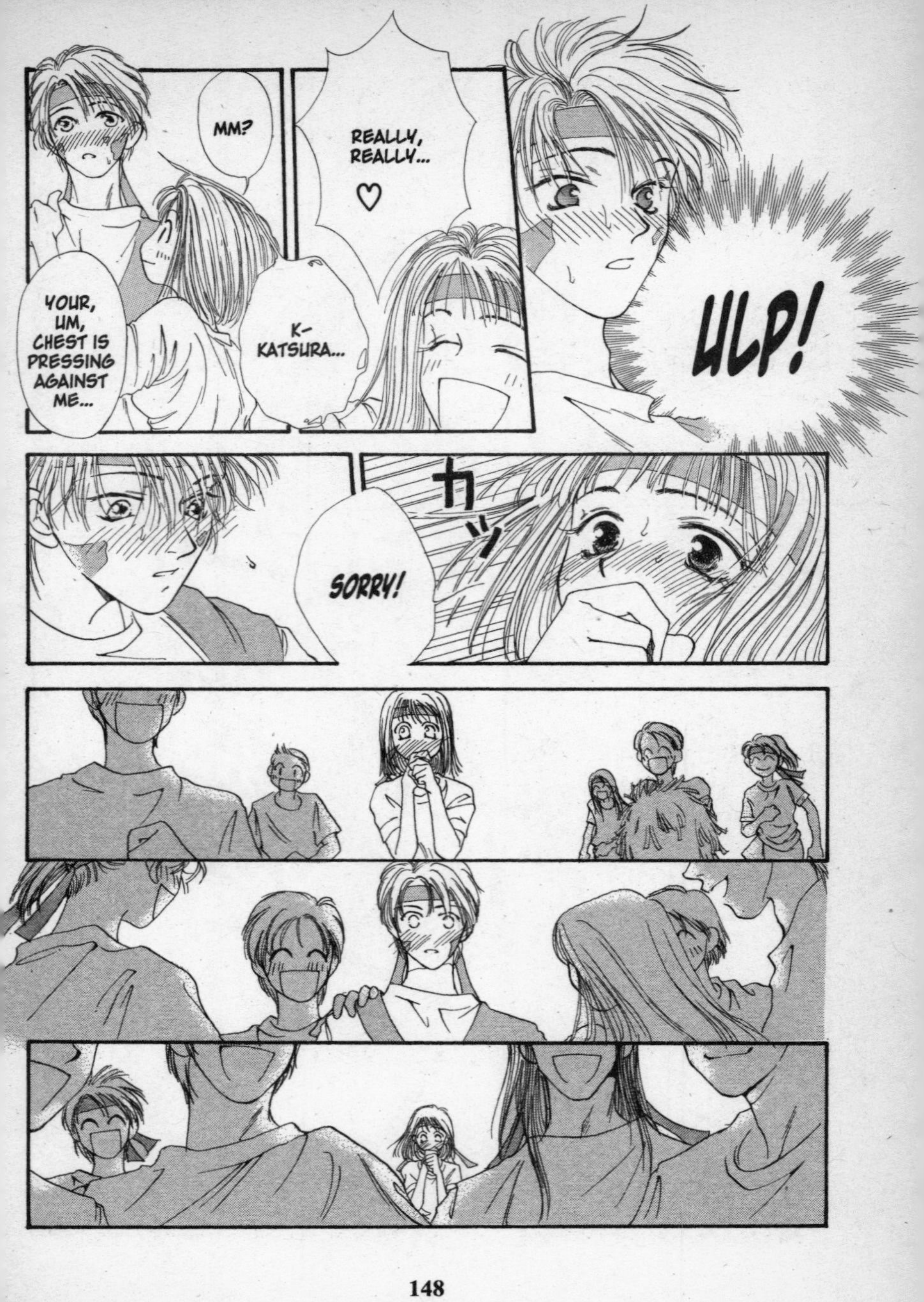

ULP!
REALLY, REALLY... ♡
K-KATSURA...
MM?
YOUR, UM, CHEST IS PRESSING AGAINST ME...
カッ
SORRY!

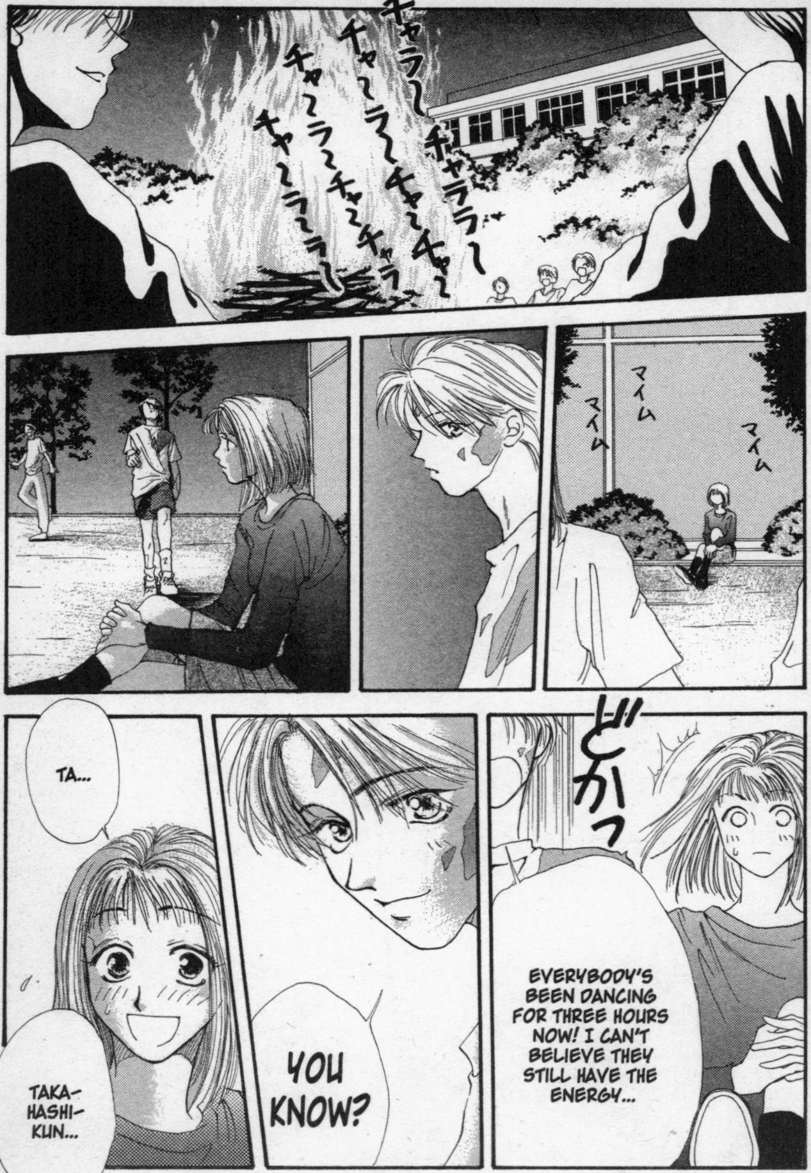
チャラ〜チャララ〜
チャ〜ラ〜チャ〜チャ〜
チャ〜ラ〜チャ〜チャラ
チャ〜ラ〜ラ〜ラ〜
マイム
マイム
マイム
マイム
どかっ
EVERYBODY'S BEEN DANCING FOR THREE HOURS NOW! I CAN'T BELIEVE THEY STILL HAVE THE ENERGY...
YOU KNOW?
TA...
TAKA-HASHI-KUN...

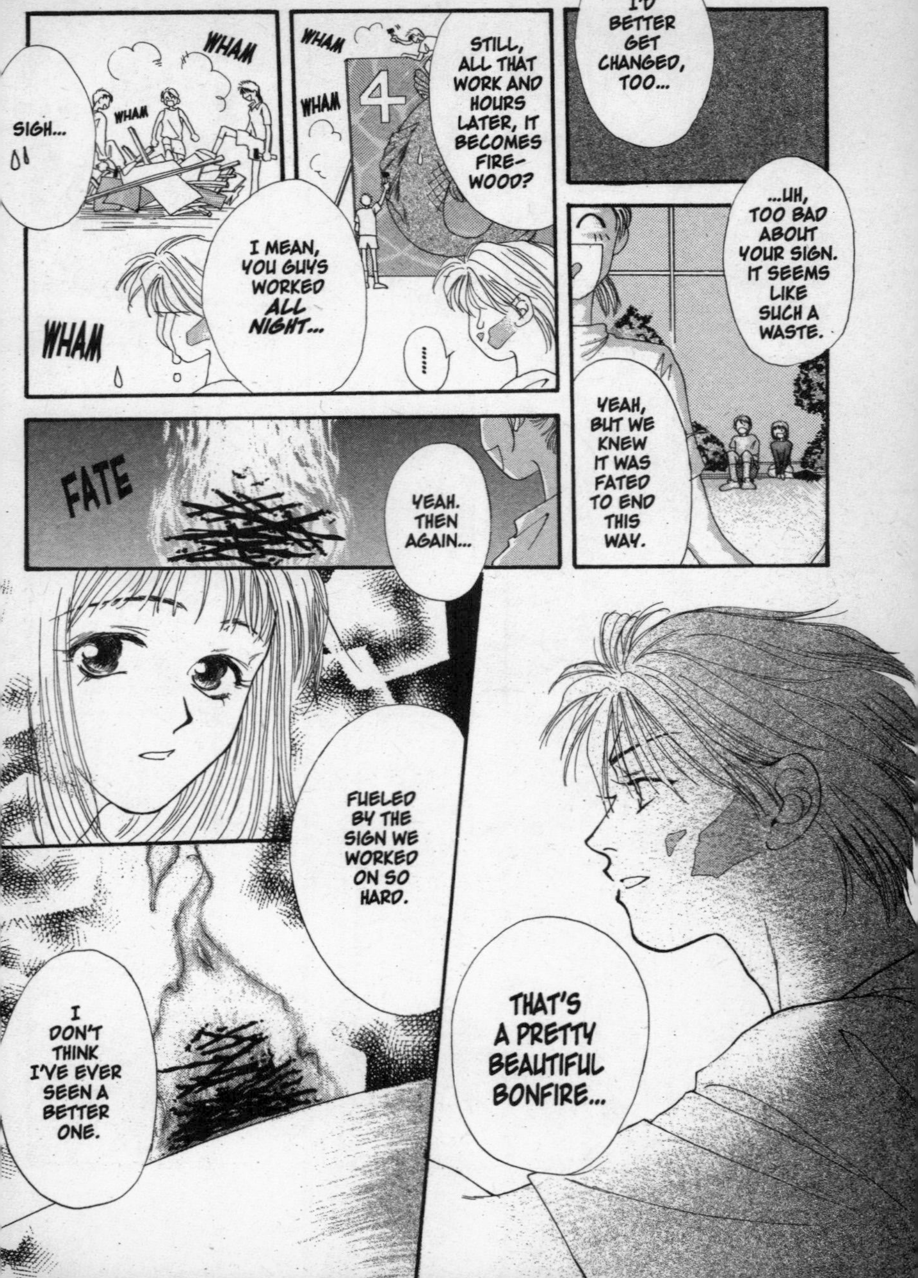
I'D BETTER GET CHANGED, TOO...
WHAM
WHAM
STILL, ALL THAT WORK AND HOURS LATER, IT BECOMES FIRE-WOOD?
I MEAN, YOU GUYS WORKED ALL NIGHT...
......
WHAM
WHAM
SIGH...
WHAM
...UH, TOO BAD ABOUT YOUR SIGN. IT SEEMS LIKE SUCH A WASTE.
YEAH, BUT WE KNEW IT WAS FATED TO END THIS WAY.
YEAH. THEN AGAIN...
FATE
THAT'S A PRETTY BEAUTIFUL BONFIRE...
FUELED BY THE SIGN WE WORKED ON SO HARD.
I DON'T THINK I'VE EVER SEEN A BETTER ONE.

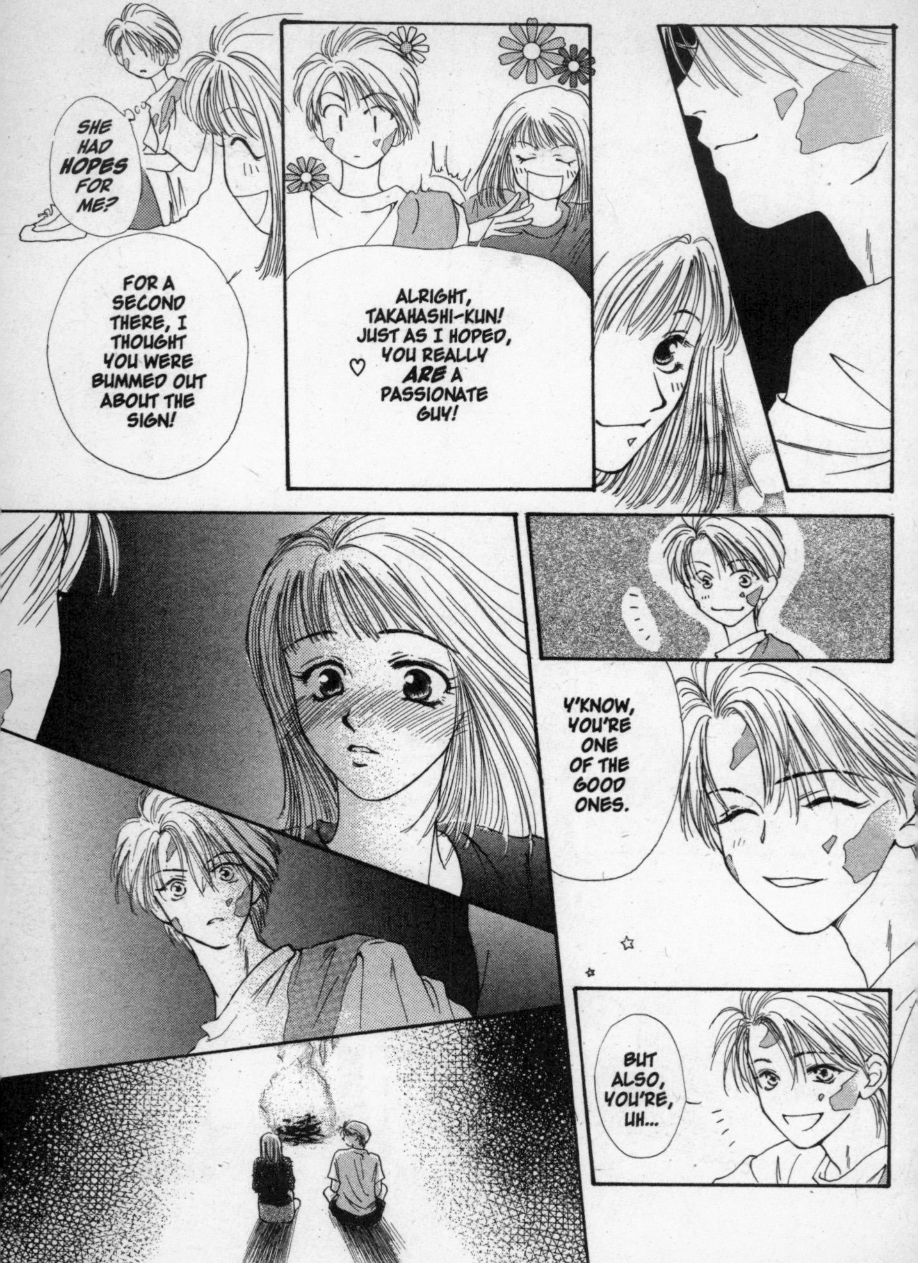
ALRIGHT, TAKAHASHI-KUN! JUST AS I HOPED, YOU REALLY ARE A PASSIONATE GUY!
SHE HAD HOPES FOR ME?
FOR A SECOND THERE, I THOUGHT YOU WERE BUMMED OUT ABOUT THE SIGN!
Y'KNOW, YOU'RE ONE OF THE GOOD ONES.
BUT ALSO, YOU'RE, UH...

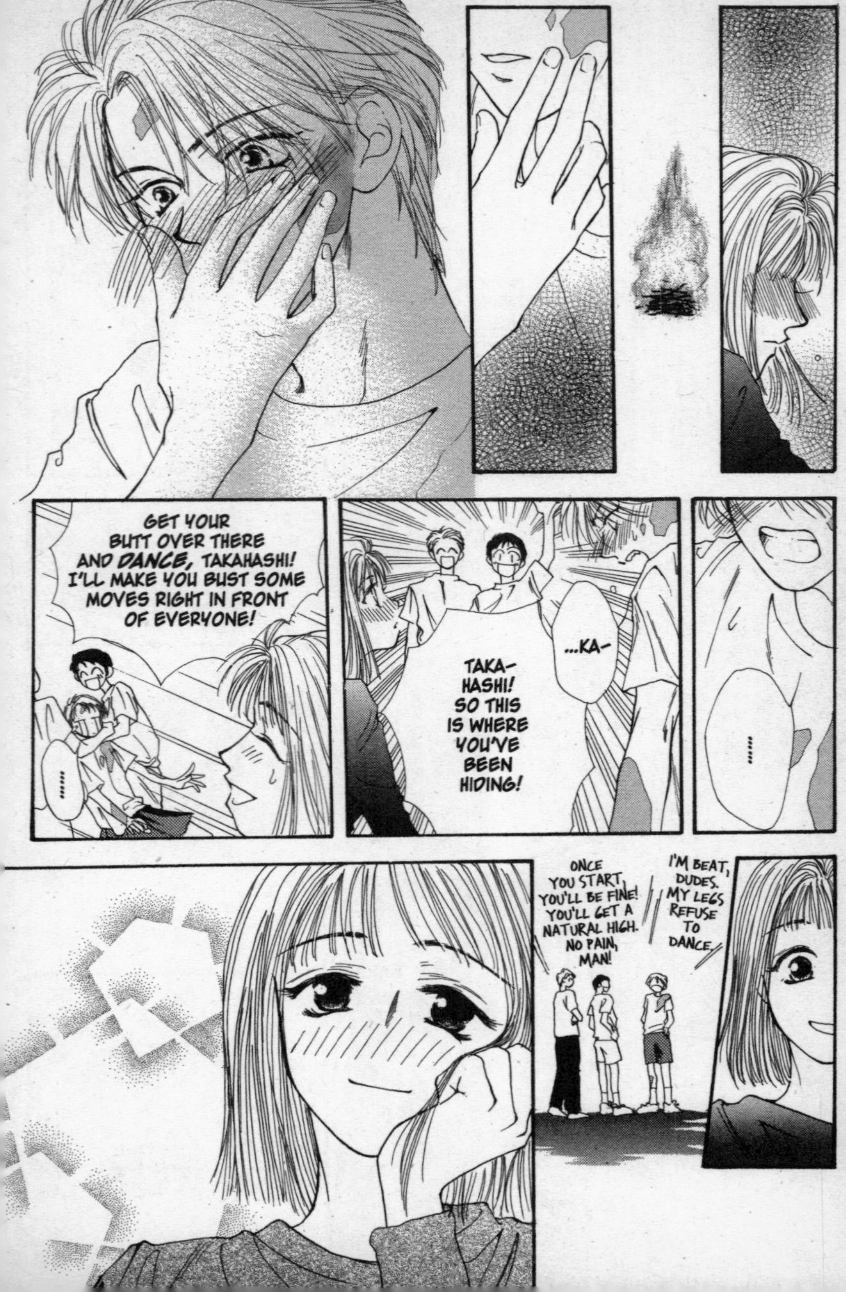
......
...KA-
TAKA-HASHI! SO THIS IS WHERE YOU'VE BEEN HIDING!
GET YOUR BUTT OVER THERE AND DANCE, TAKAHASHI! I'LL MAKE YOU BUST SOME MOVES RIGHT IN FRONT OF EVERYONE!
......
I'M BEAT, DUDES. MY LEGS REFUSE TO DANCE.
ONCE YOU START, YOU'LL BE FINE! YOU'LL GET A NATURAL HIGH. NO PAIN, MAN!

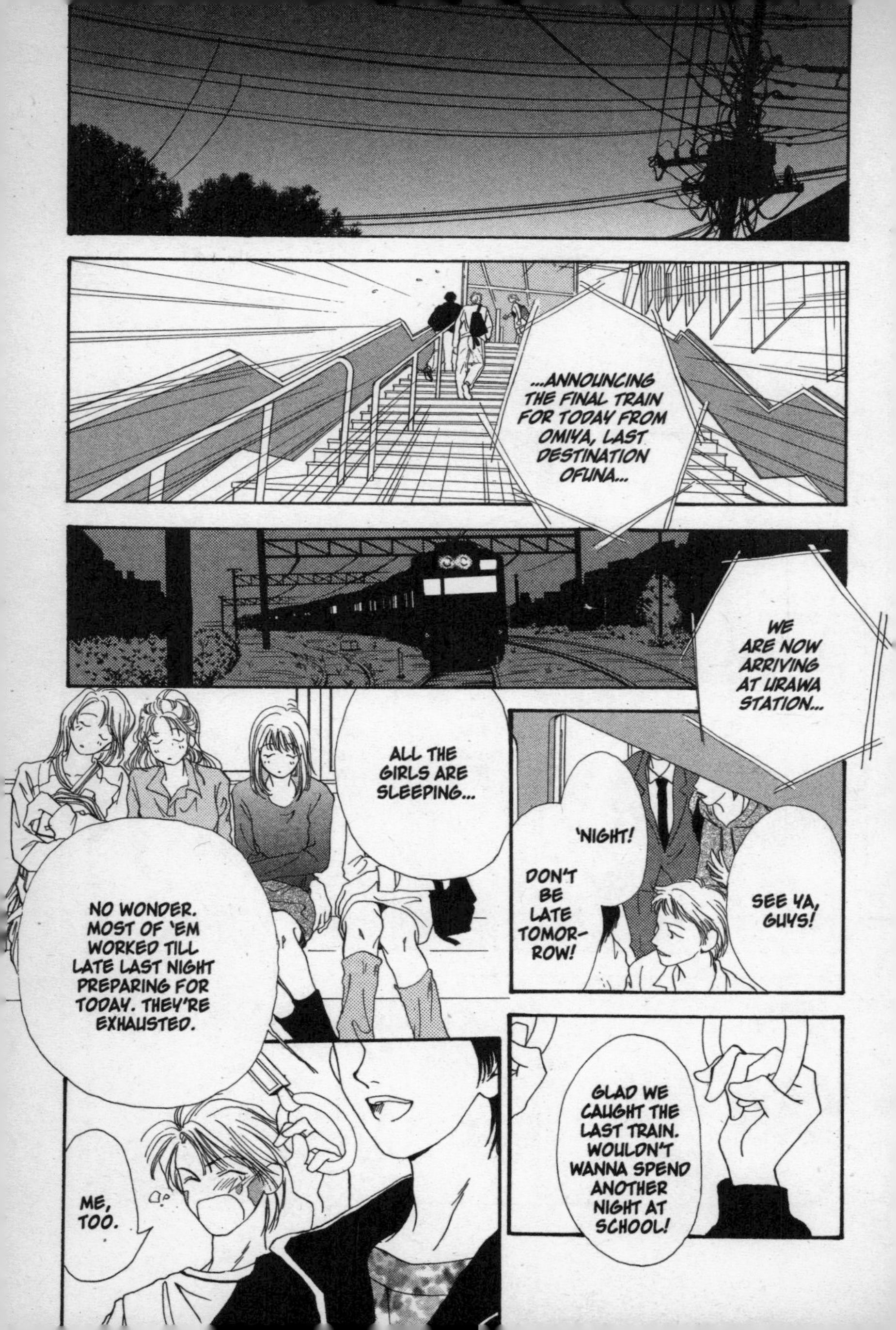
...ANNOUNCING THE FINAL TRAIN FOR TODAY FROM OMIYA, LAST DESTINATION OFUNA...
WE ARE NOW ARRIVING AT URAWA STATION...
SEE YA, GUYS!
'NIGHT!
DON'T BE LATE TOMOR-ROW!
ALL THE GIRLS ARE SLEEPING...
NO WONDER. MOST OF 'EM WORKED TILL LATE LAST NIGHT PREPARING FOR TODAY. THEY'RE EXHAUSTED.
GLAD WE CAUGHT THE LAST TRAIN. WOULDN'T WANNA SPEND ANOTHER NIGHT AT SCHOOL!
ME, TOO.

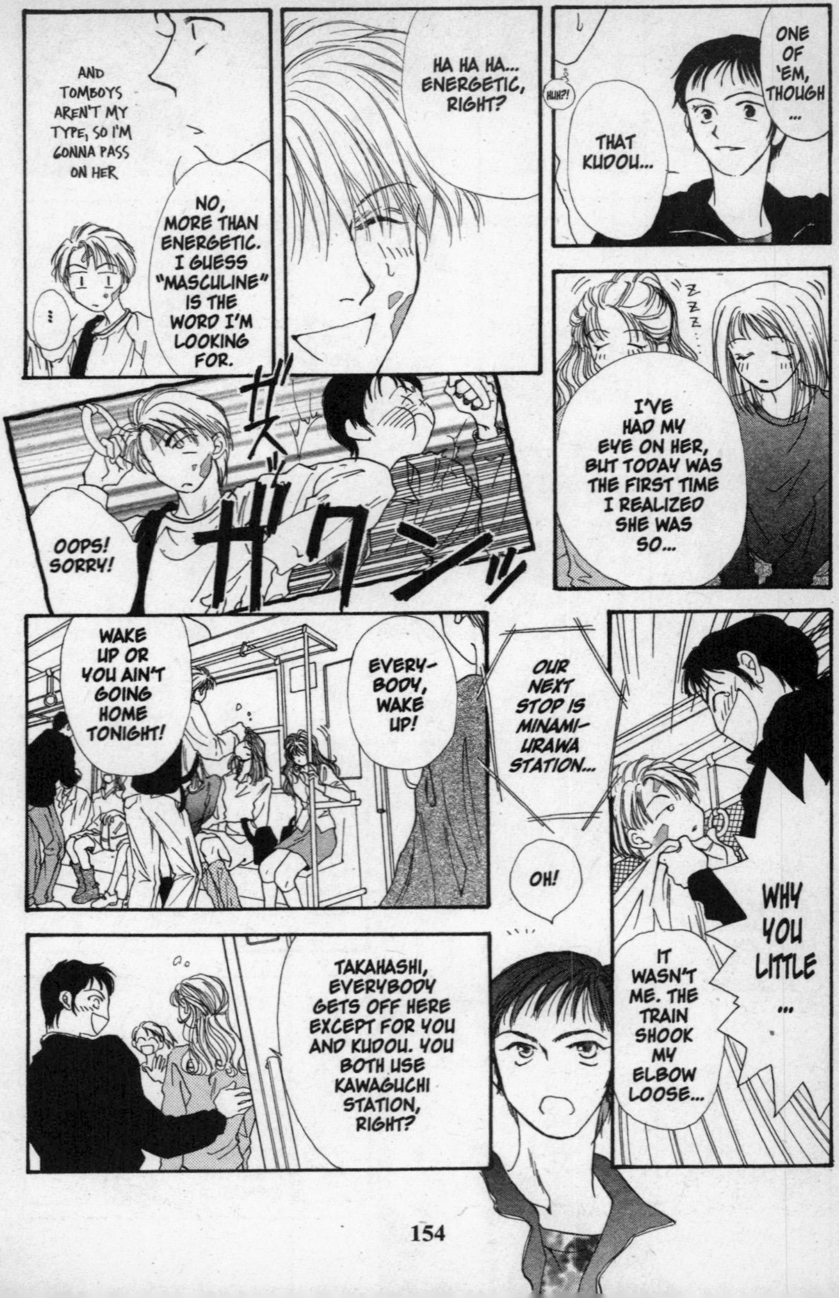
ONE OF 'EM, THOUGH ...
HUH?!
THAT KUDOU...
HA HA HA... ENERGETIC, RIGHT?
AND TOMBOYS AREN'T MY TYPE, SO I'M GONNA PASS ON HER
NO, MORE THAN ENERGETIC. I GUESS "MASCULINE" IS THE WORD I'M LOOKING FOR.
...
I'VE HAD MY EYE ON HER, BUT TODAY WAS THE FIRST TIME I REALIZED SHE WAS SO...
ガクンッ
OOPS! SORRY!
WHY YOU LITTLE ...
OH!
OUR NEXT STOP IS MINAMI-URAWA STATION...
EVERY-BODY, WAKE UP!
WAKE UP OR YOU AIN'T GOING HOME TONIGHT!
IT WASN'T ME. THE TRAIN SHOOK MY ELBOW LOOSE...
TAKAHASHI, EVERYBODY GETS OFF HERE EXCEPT FOR YOU AND KUDOU. YOU BOTH USE KAWAGUCHI STATION, RIGHT?

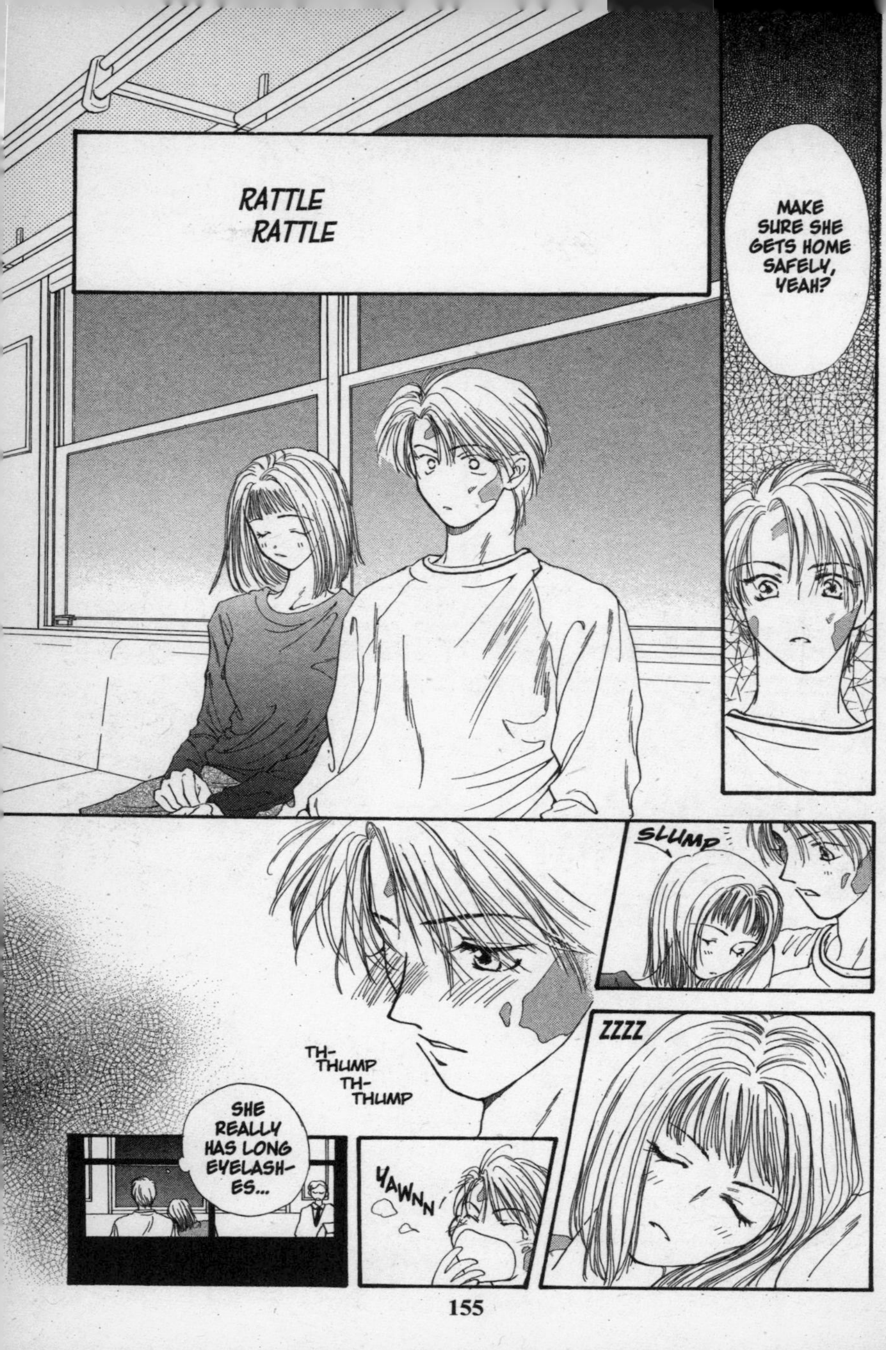
MAKE SURE SHE GETS HOME SAFELY, YEAH?
RATTLE RATTLE
SLUMP
ZZZZ
TH-THUMP TH-THUMP
YAWNN
SHE REALLY HAS LONG EYELASH-ES...

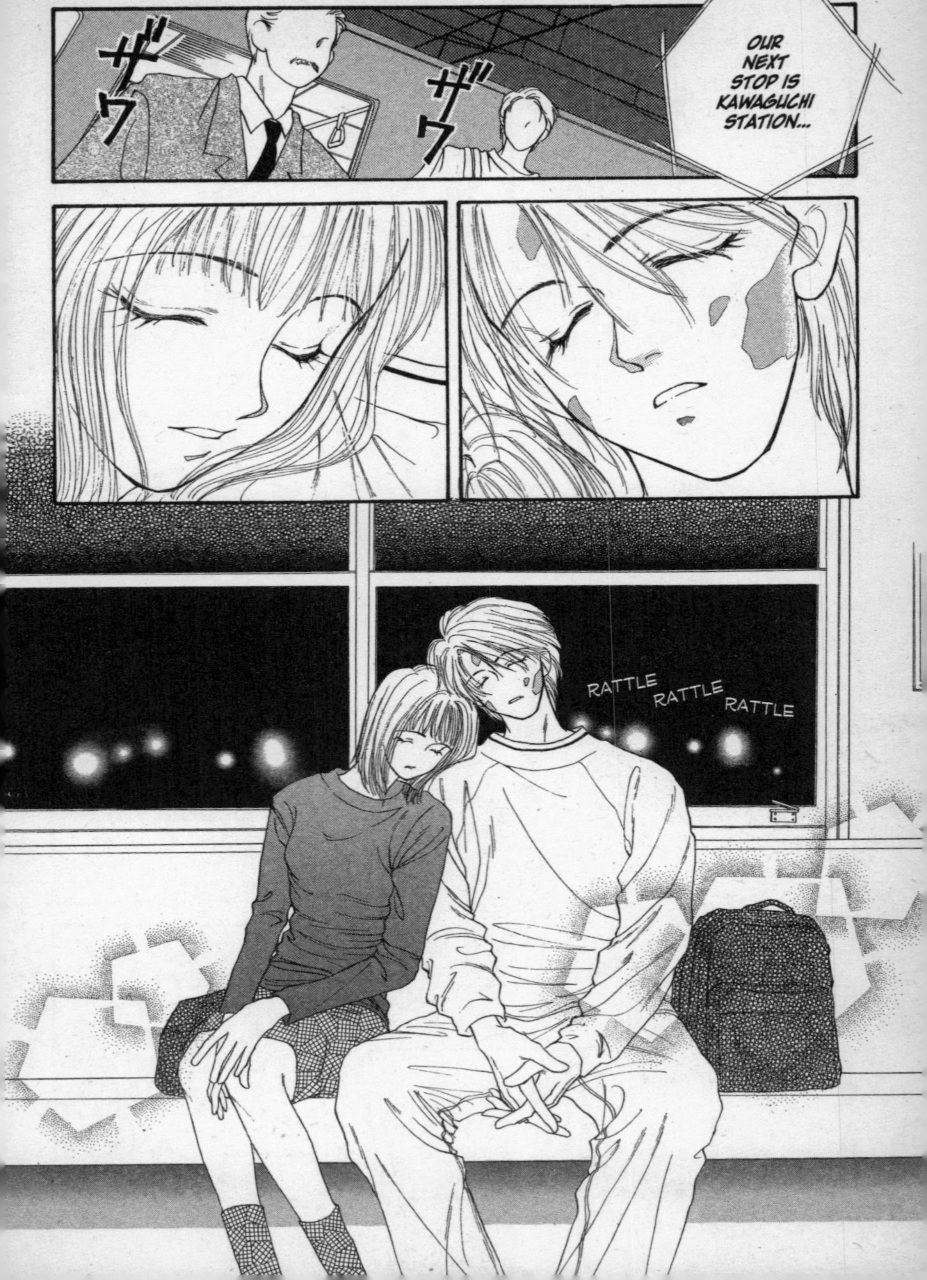
OUR NEXT STOP IS KAWAGUCHI STATION...
ザワ
ザワ
RATTLE RATTLE RATTLE

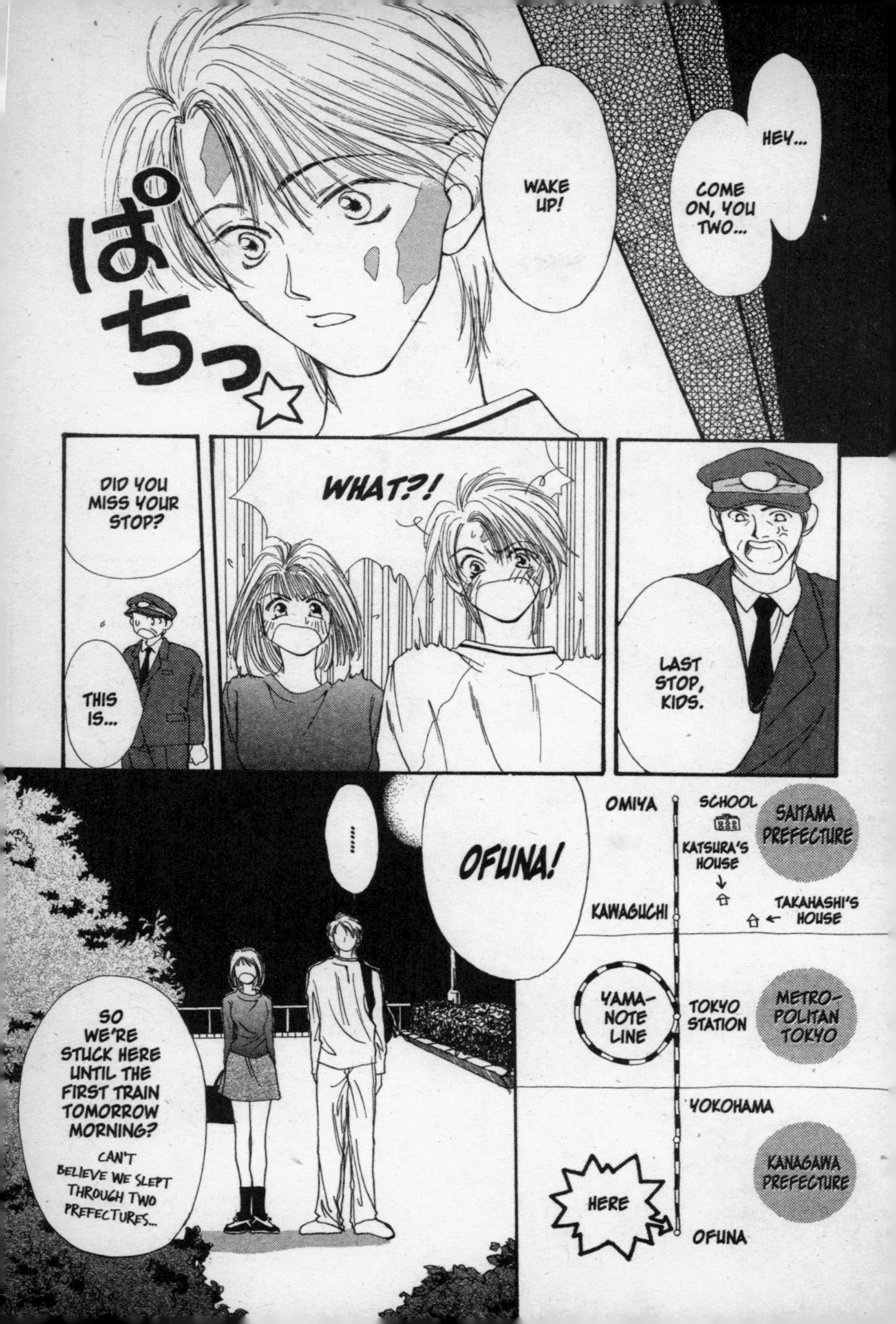
HEY... COME ON, YOU TWO...
WAKE UP!
ぱちっ☆
LAST STOP, KIDS.
WHAT?!
DID YOU MISS YOUR STOP?
THIS IS...
OMIYA
SCHOOL
SAITAMA PREFECTURE
KATSURA'S HOUSE
KAWAGUCHI
TAKAHASHI'S HOUSE
YAMA-NOTE LINE
TOKYO STATION
METRO-POLITAN TOKYO
YOKOHAMA
KANAGAWA PREFECTURE
HERE
OFUNA
OFUNA!
......
SO WE'RE STUCK HERE UNTIL THE FIRST TRAIN TOMORROW MORNING?
CAN'T BELIEVE WE SLEPT THROUGH TWO PREFECTURES...

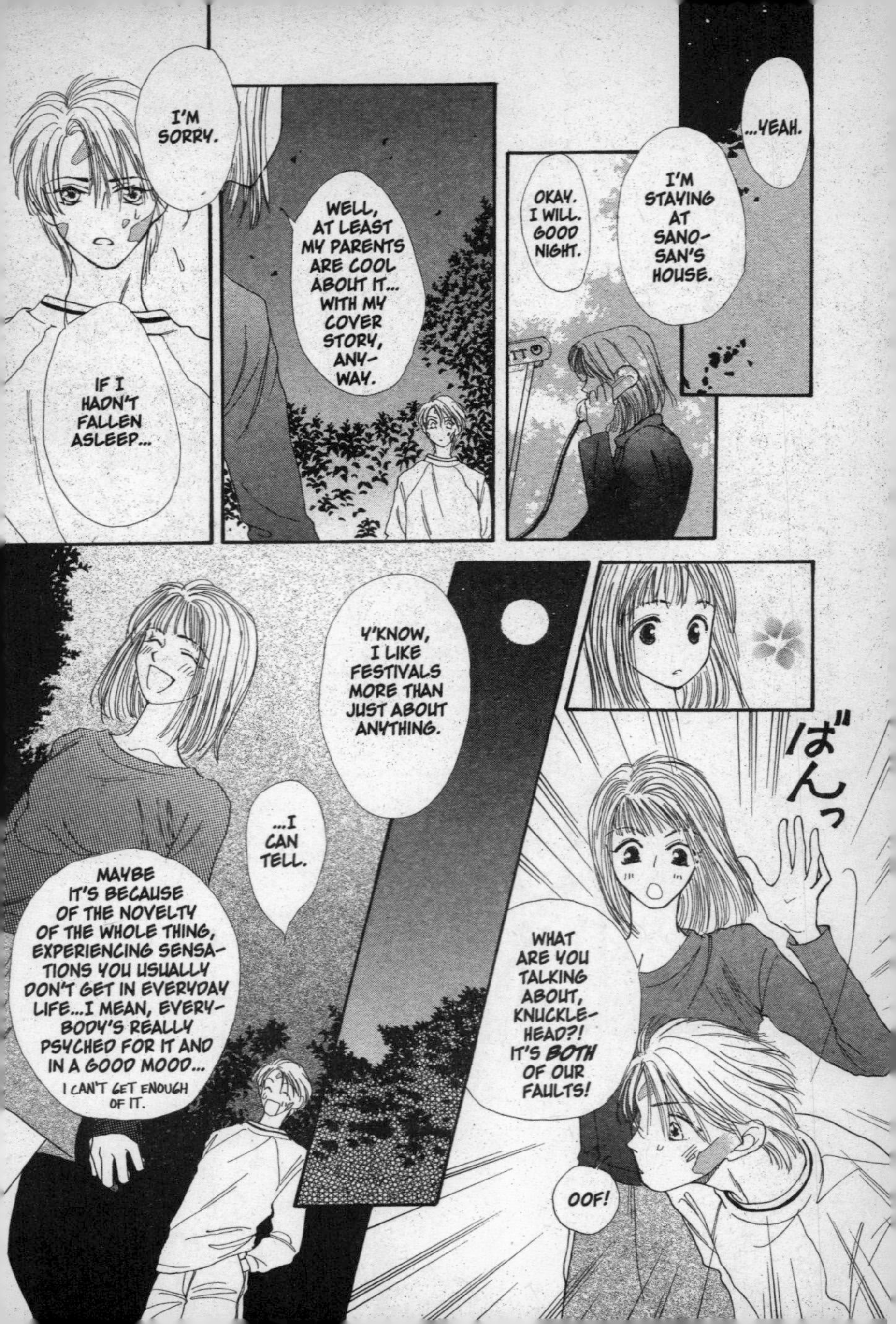
...YEAH.
I'M STAYING AT SANO-SAN'S HOUSE.
OKAY. I WILL. GOOD NIGHT.
WELL, AT LEAST MY PARENTS ARE COOL ABOUT IT... WITH MY COVER STORY, ANY-WAY.
I'M SORRY.
IF I HADN'T FALLEN ASLEEP...
ばんっ
WHAT ARE YOU TALKING ABOUT, KNUCKLE-HEAD?! IT'S *BOTH* OF OUR FAULTS!
OOF!
Y'KNOW, I LIKE FESTIVALS MORE THAN JUST ABOUT ANYTHING.
...I CAN TELL.
MAYBE IT'S BECAUSE OF THE NOVELTY OF THE WHOLE THING, EXPERIENCING SENSA-TIONS YOU USUALLY DON'T GET IN EVERYDAY LIFE...I MEAN, EVERY-BODY'S REALLY PSYCHED FOR IT AND IN A GOOD MOOD...
I CAN'T GET ENOUGH OF IT.

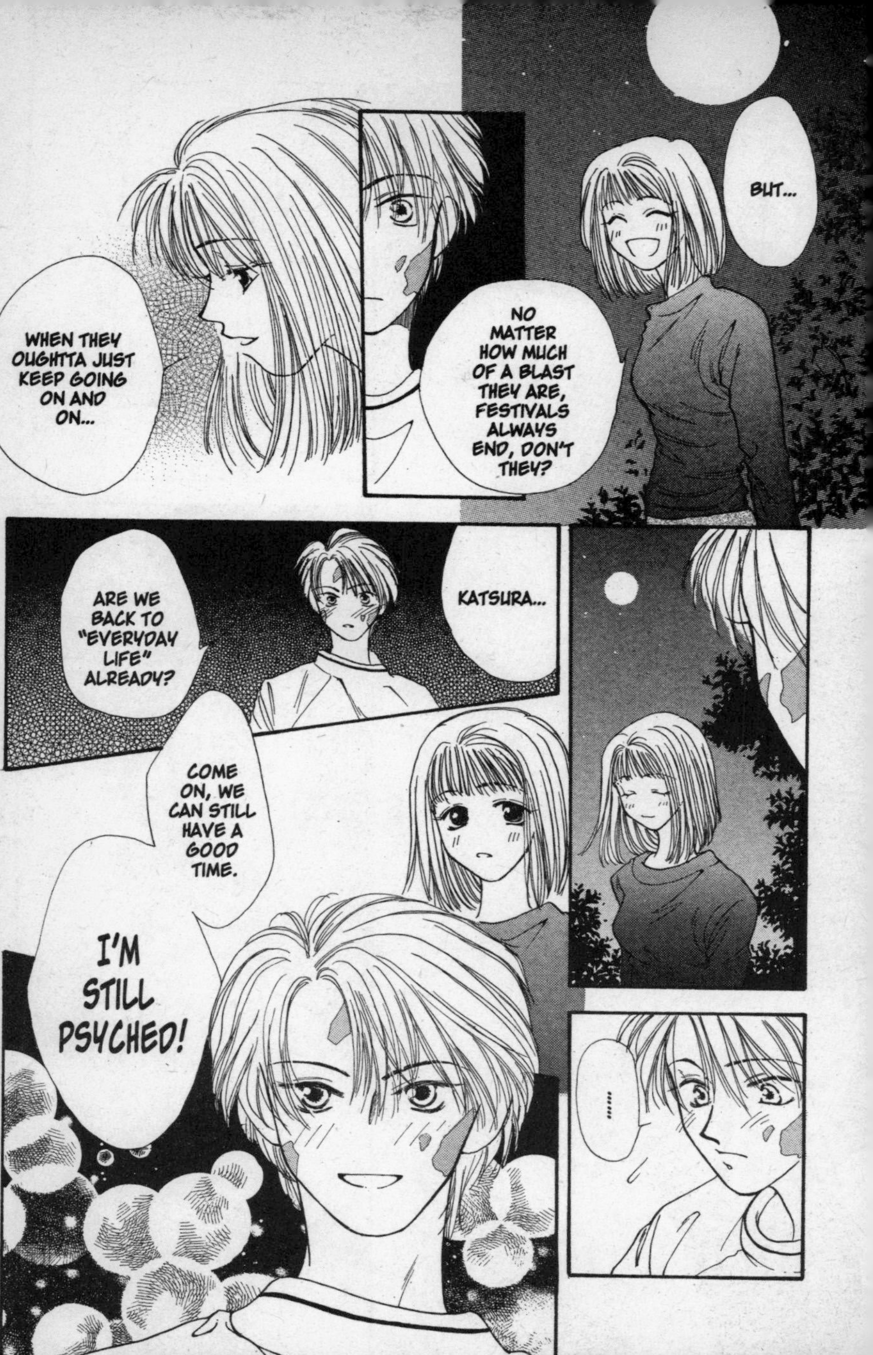
BUT...
NO MATTER HOW MUCH OF A BLAST THEY ARE, FESTIVALS ALWAYS END, DON'T THEY?
WHEN THEY OUGHTTA JUST KEEP GOING ON AND ON...
KATSURA...
ARE WE BACK TO "EVERYDAY LIFE" ALREADY?
COME ON, WE CAN STILL HAVE A GOOD TIME.
I'M STILL PSYCHED!
......

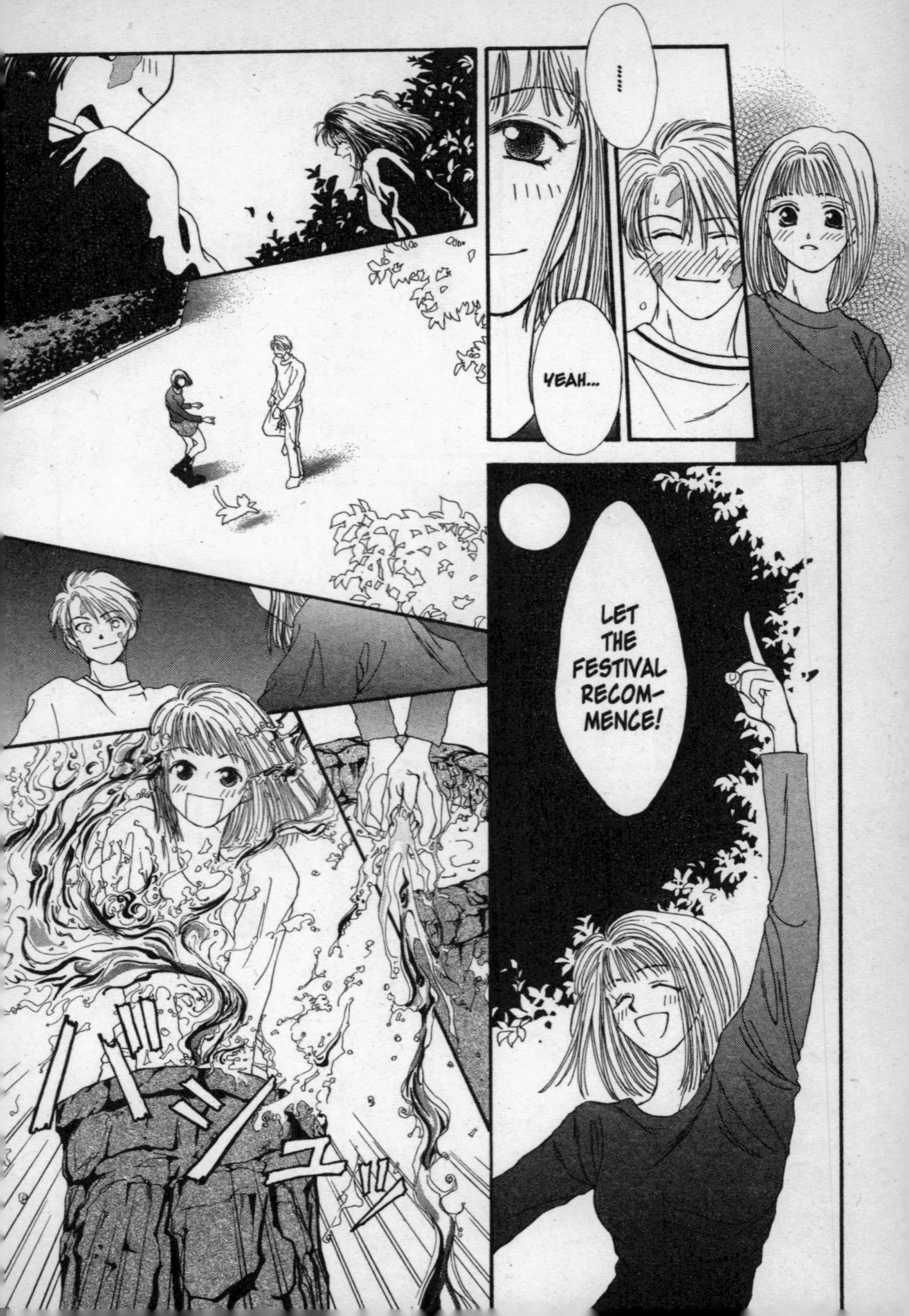
......
YEAH...
LET THE FESTIVAL RECOMMENCE!

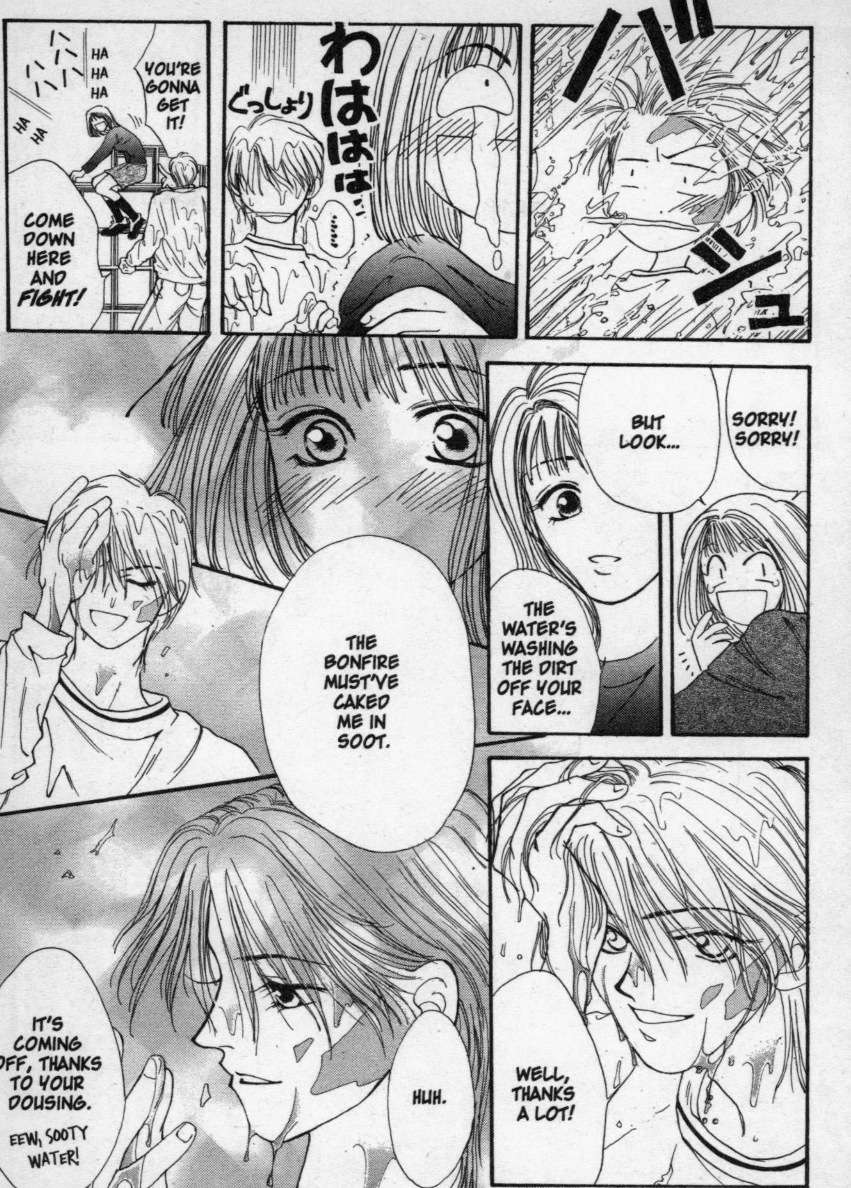
バシュ
わははは
ぐっしょり
......
ハハハハ
HA HA HA
HA HA
YOU'RE GONNA GET IT!
COME DOWN HERE AND *FIGHT!*
SORRY! SORRY!
BUT LOOK...
THE WATER'S WASHING THE DIRT OFF YOUR FACE...
WELL, THANKS A LOT!
THE BONFIRE MUST'VE CAKED ME IN SOOT.
HUH.
IT'S COMING OFF, THANKS TO YOUR DOUSING.
EEW, SOOTY WATER!

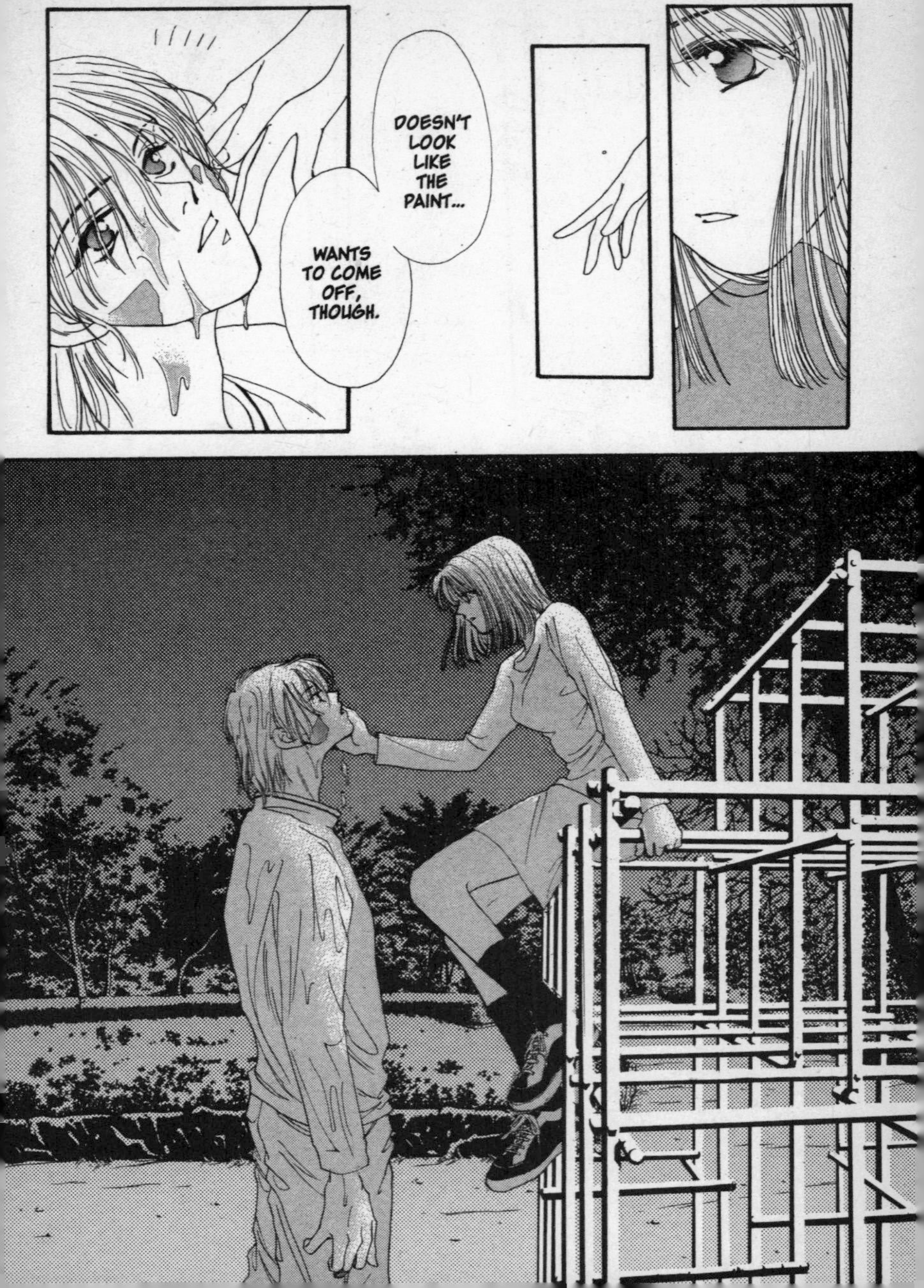
DOESN'T LOOK LIKE THE PAINT...
WANTS TO COME OFF, THOUGH.

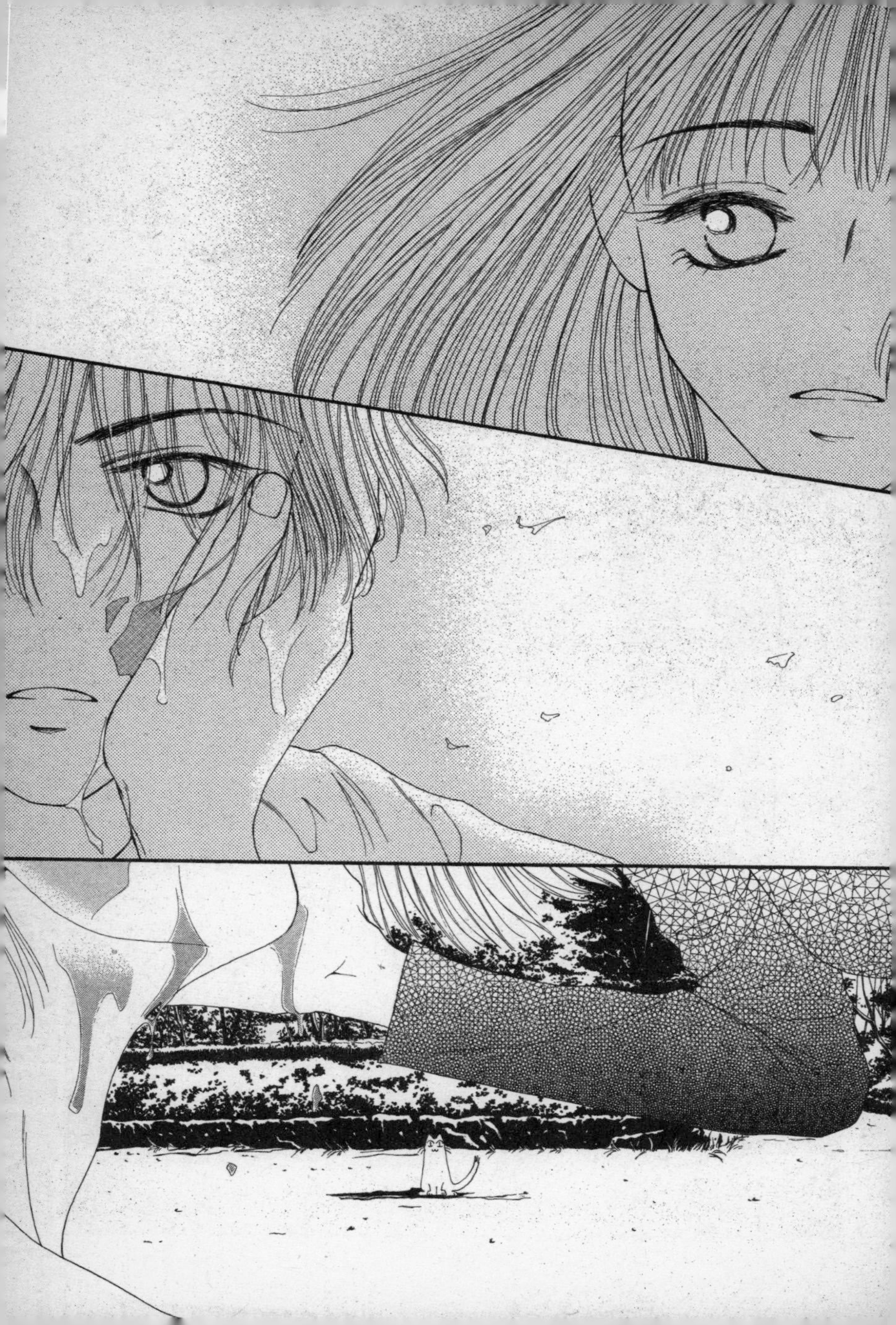

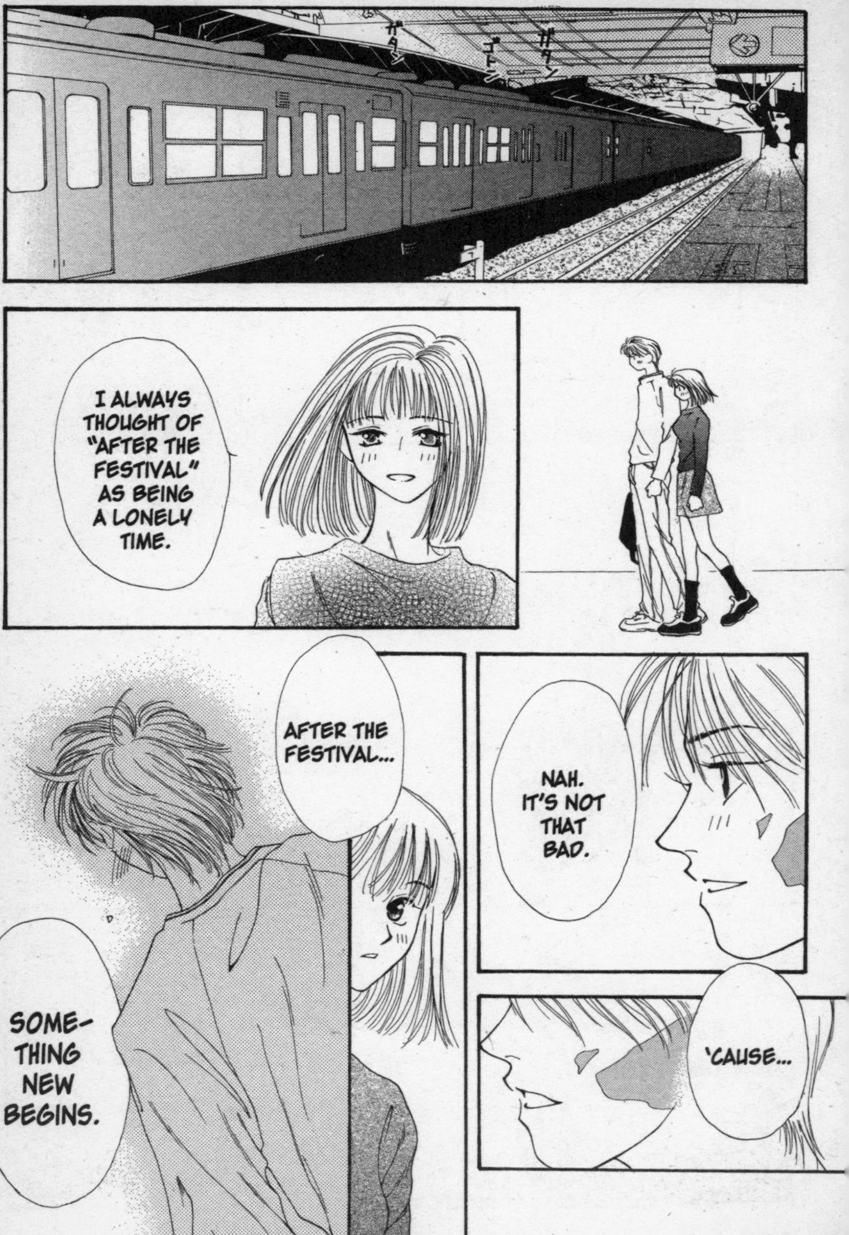
ガタン
ゴトン
ガタン
I ALWAYS THOUGHT OF "AFTER THE FESTIVAL" AS BEING A LONELY TIME.
NAH. IT'S NOT THAT BAD.
'CAUSE...
AFTER THE FESTIVAL...
SOME-THING NEW BEGINS.

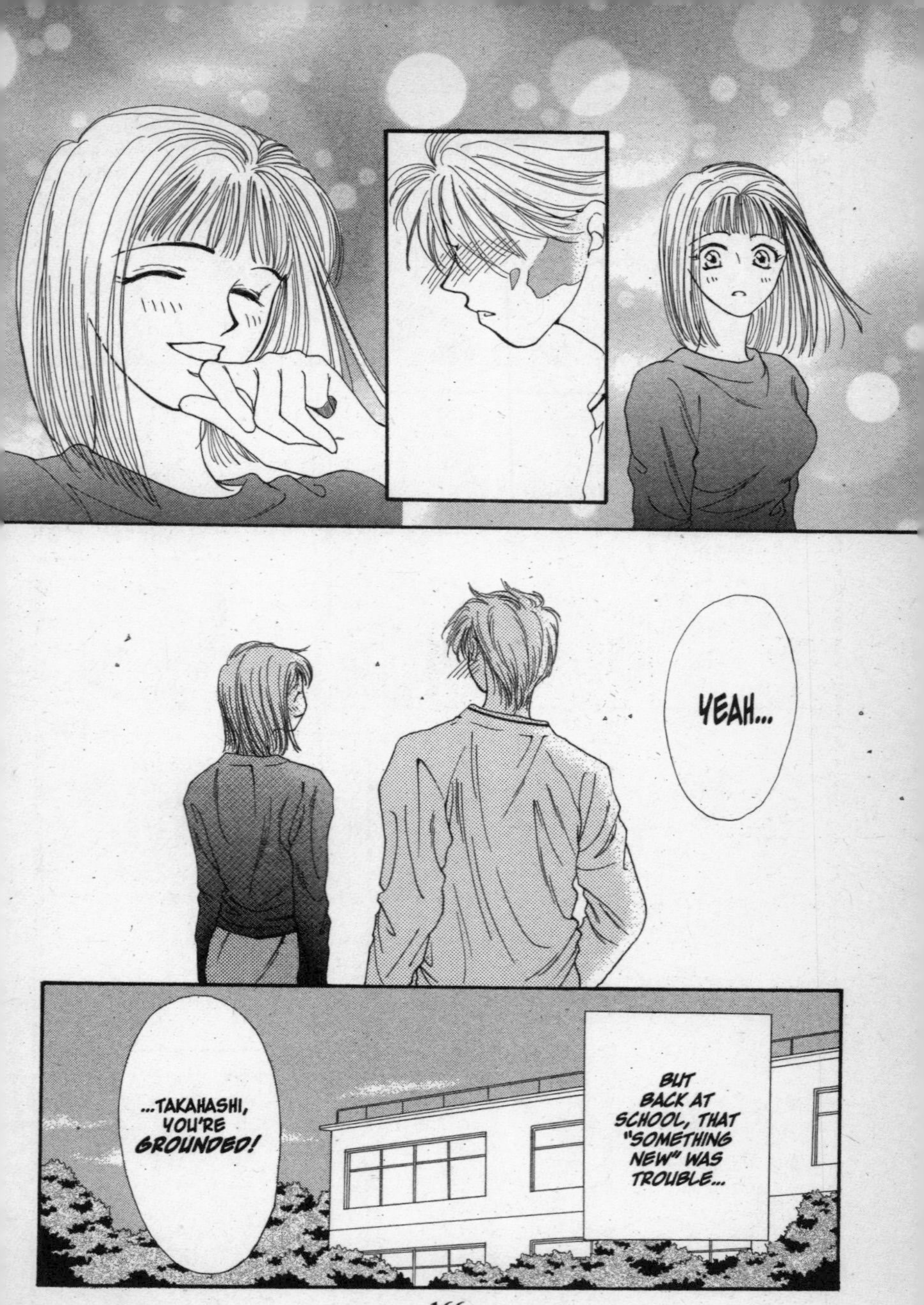
YEAH...
BUT BACK AT SCHOOL, THAT "SOMETHING NEW" WAS TROUBLE...
...TAKAHASHI, YOU'RE GROUNDED!

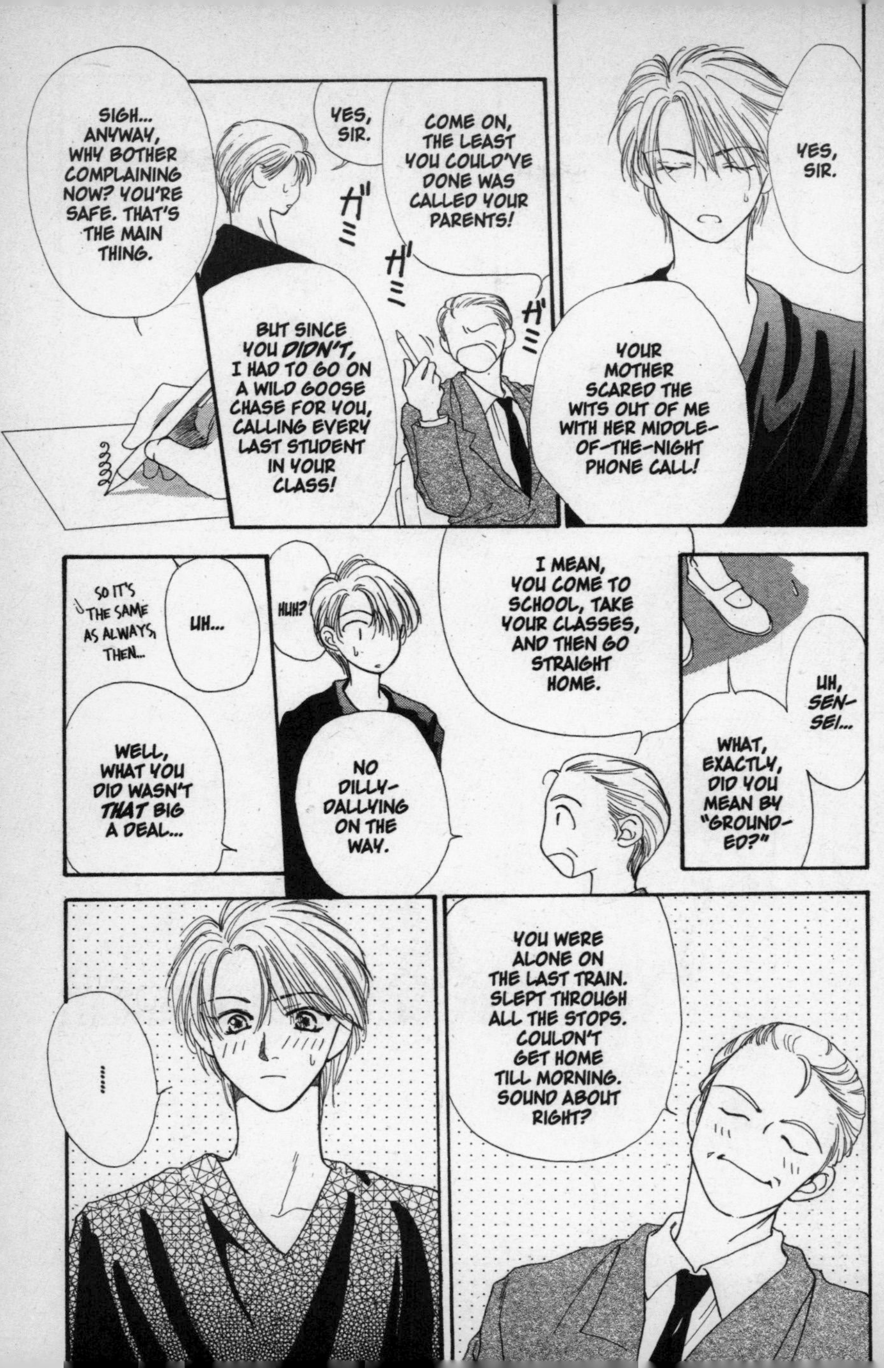
YOUR MOTHER SCARED THE WITS OUT OF ME WITH HER MIDDLE-OF-THE-NIGHT PHONE CALL!
YES, SIR.
COME ON, THE LEAST YOU COULD'VE DONE WAS CALLED YOUR PARENTS!
YES, SIR.
ガミ ガミ ガミ
BUT SINCE YOU *DIDN'T*, I HAD TO GO ON A WILD GOOSE CHASE FOR YOU, CALLING EVERY LAST STUDENT IN YOUR CLASS!
SIGH... ANYWAY, WHY BOTHER COMPLAINING NOW? YOU'RE SAFE. THAT'S THE MAIN THING.
UH, SEN-SEI...
WHAT, EXACTLY, DID YOU MEAN BY "GROUND-ED?"
I MEAN, YOU COME TO SCHOOL, TAKE YOUR CLASSES, AND THEN GO STRAIGHT HOME.
NO DILLY-DALLYING ON THE WAY.
HUH?
UH...
SO IT'S THE SAME AS ALWAYS, THEN...
WELL, WHAT YOU DID WASN'T *THAT* BIG A DEAL...
YOU WERE ALONE ON THE LAST TRAIN. SLEPT THROUGH ALL THE STOPS. COULDN'T GET HOME TILL MORNING. SOUND ABOUT RIGHT?
......

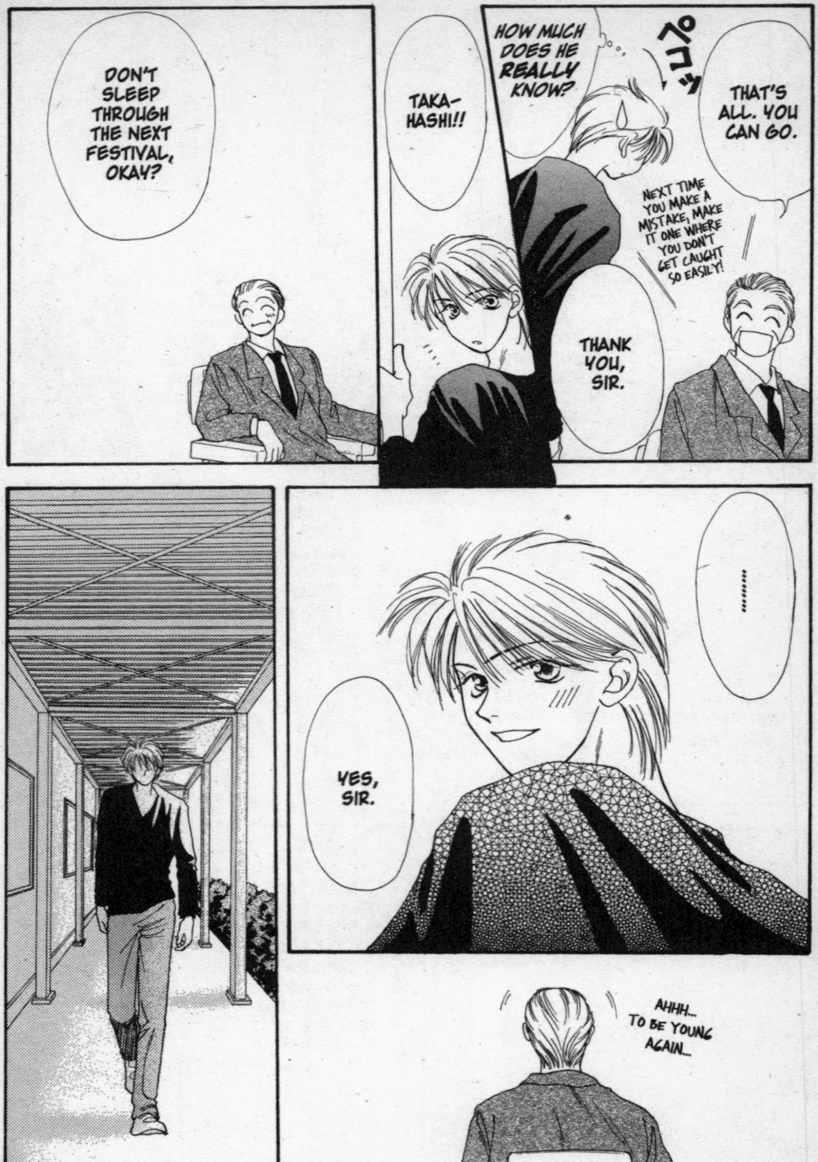
THAT'S ALL. YOU CAN GO.
NEXT TIME YOU MAKE A MISTAKE, MAKE IT ONE WHERE YOU DON'T GET CAUGHT SO EASILY!
ペコッ
HOW MUCH DOES HE REALLY KNOW?
THANK YOU, SIR.
TAKA-HASHI!!
DON'T SLEEP THROUGH THE NEXT FESTIVAL, OKAY?
......
YES, SIR.
AHHH... TO BE YOUNG AGAIN...

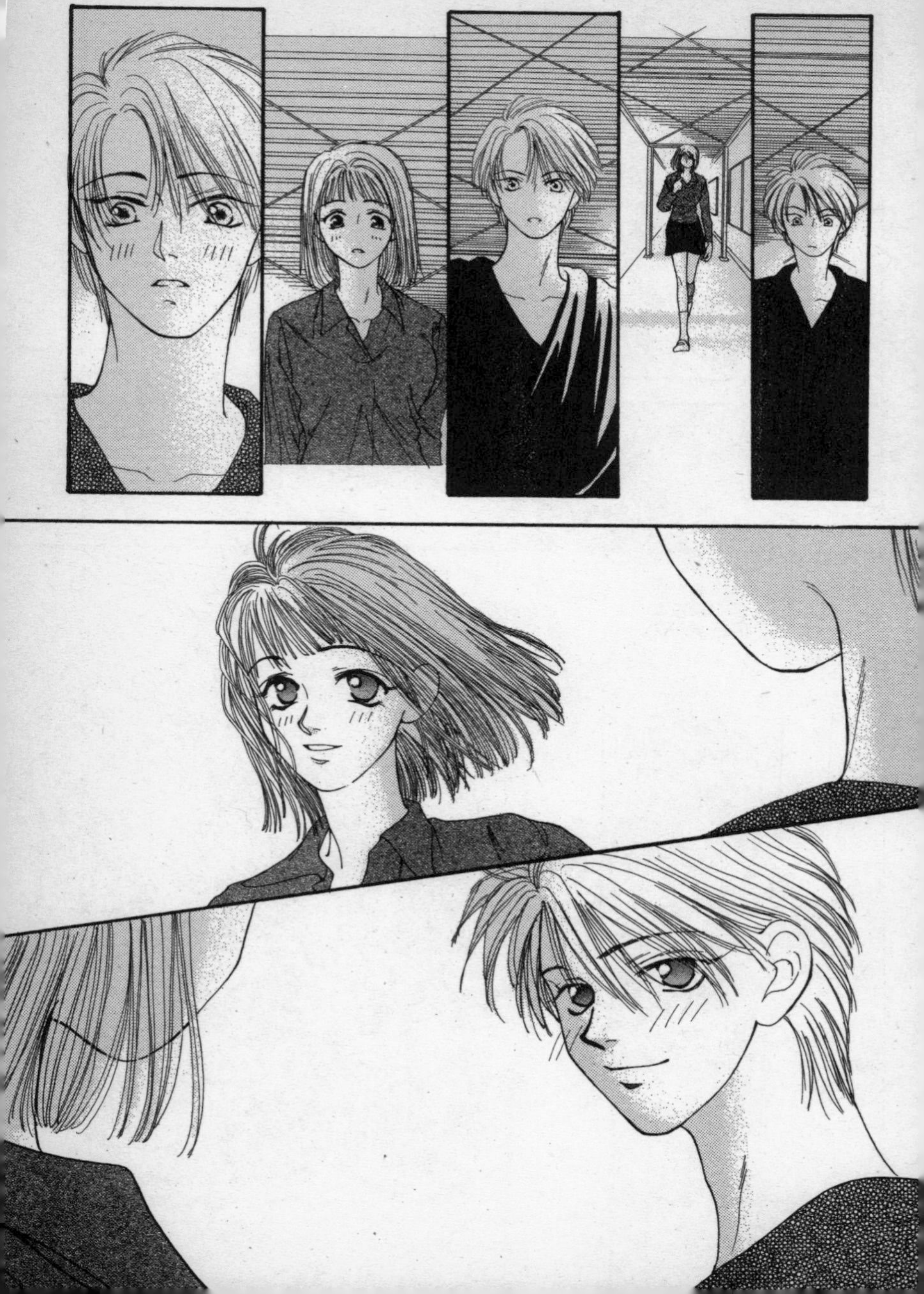

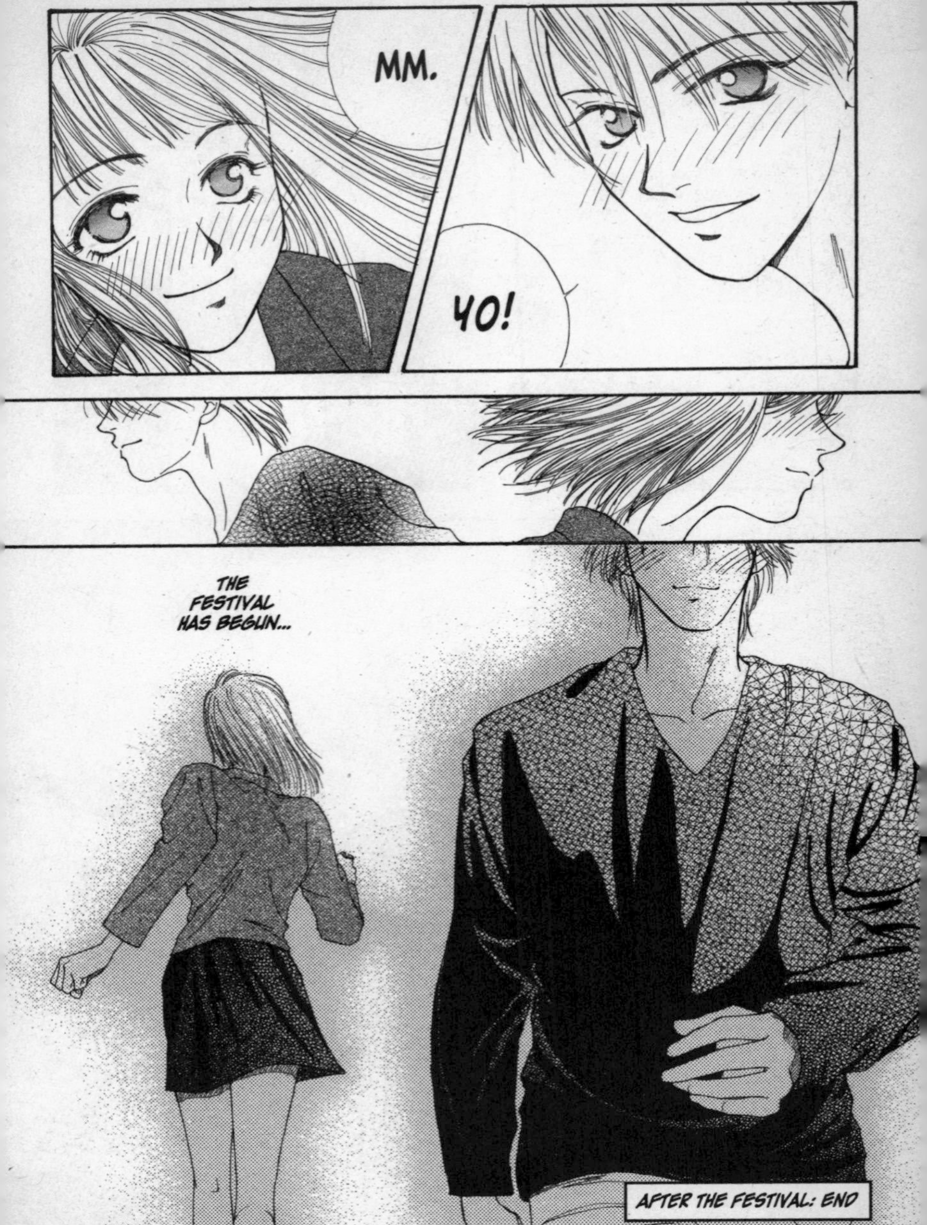
YO!
MM.
THE FESTIVAL HAS BEGUN...
AFTER THE FESTIVAL: END

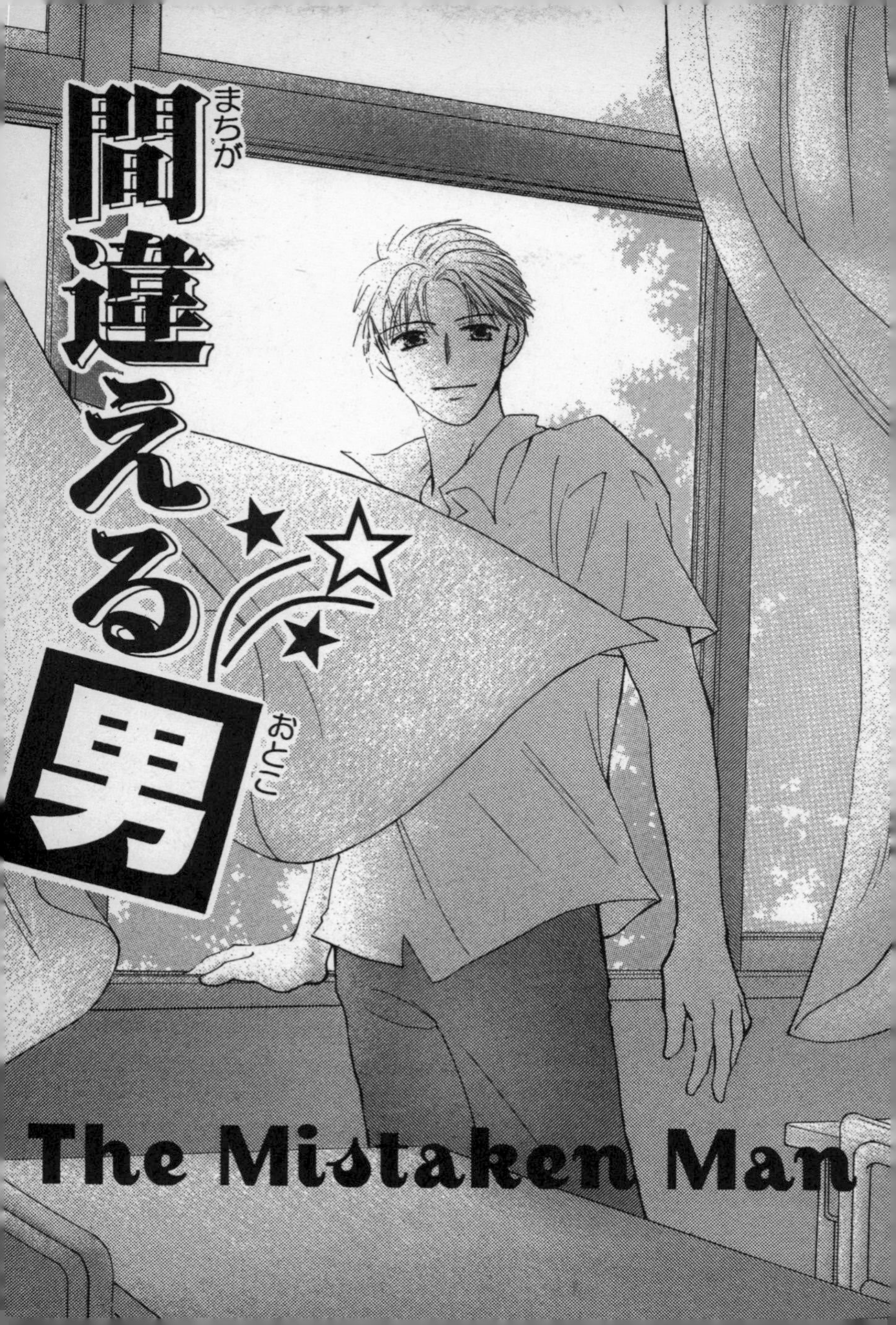
間違える男
まちが
おとこ
The Mistaken Man

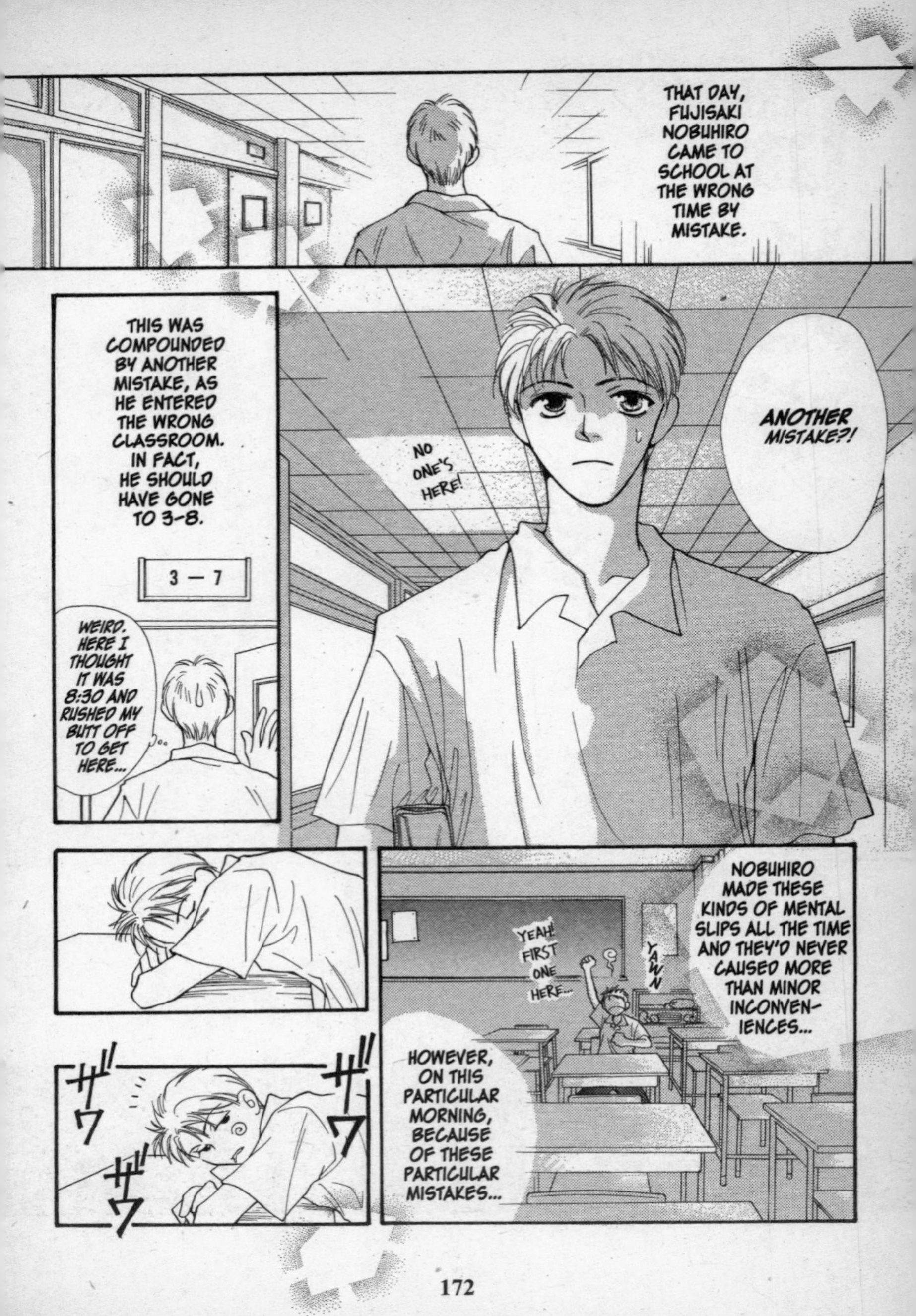
THAT DAY, FUJISAKI NOBUHIRO CAME TO SCHOOL AT THE WRONG TIME BY MISTAKE.
ANOTHER MISTAKE?!
NO ONE'S HERE!
THIS WAS COMPOUNDED BY ANOTHER MISTAKE, AS HE ENTERED THE WRONG CLASSROOM. IN FACT, HE SHOULD HAVE GONE TO 3-8.
3 — 7
WEIRD. HERE I THOUGHT IT WAS 8:30 AND RUSHED MY BUTT OFF TO GET HERE...
NOBUHIRO MADE THESE KINDS OF MENTAL SLIPS ALL THE TIME AND THEY'D NEVER CAUSED MORE THAN MINOR INCONVEN-IENCES...
YAWN
YEAH! FIRST ONE HERE...
HOWEVER, ON THIS PARTICULAR MORNING, BECAUSE OF THESE PARTICULAR MISTAKES...
ザワ
ザワ
ザワ

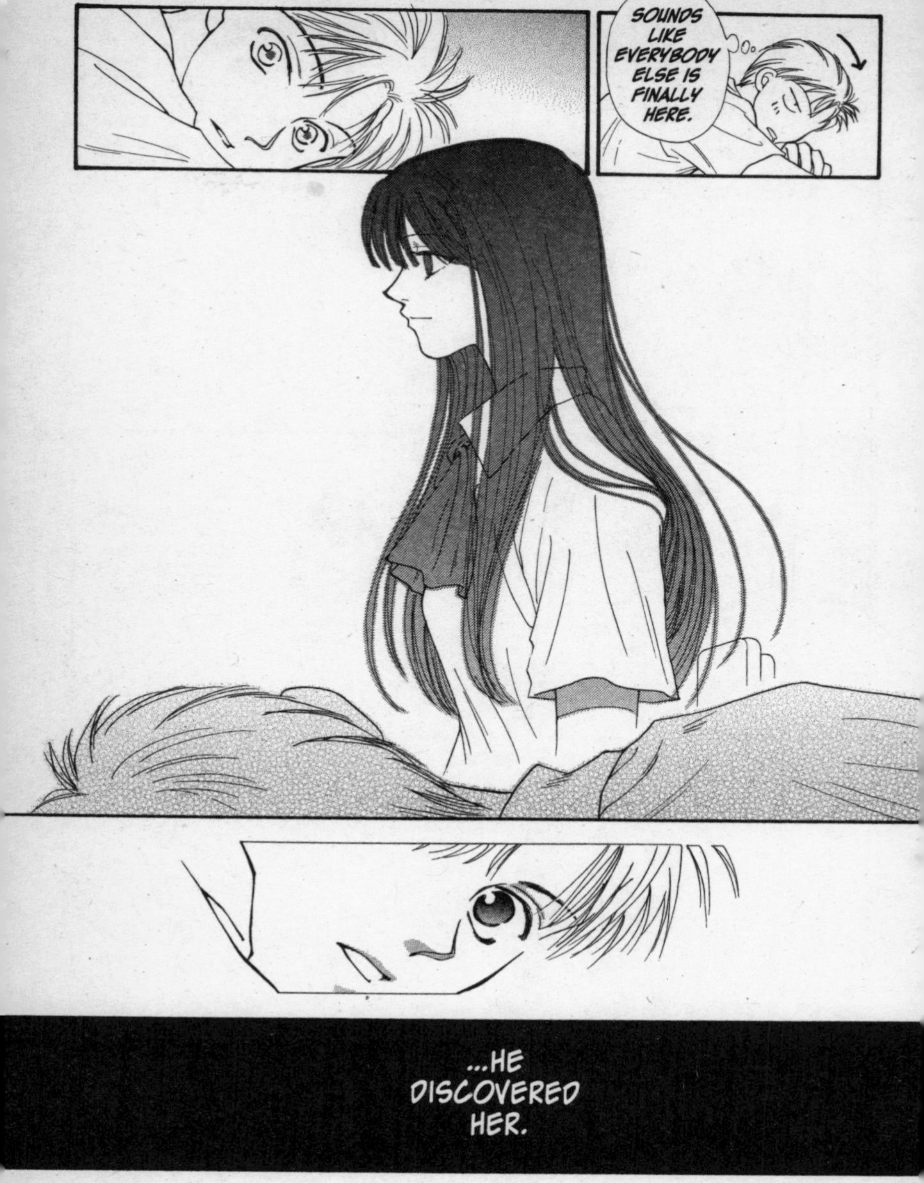
SOUNDS LIKE EVERYBODY ELSE IS FINALLY HERE.
...HE DISCOVERED HER.

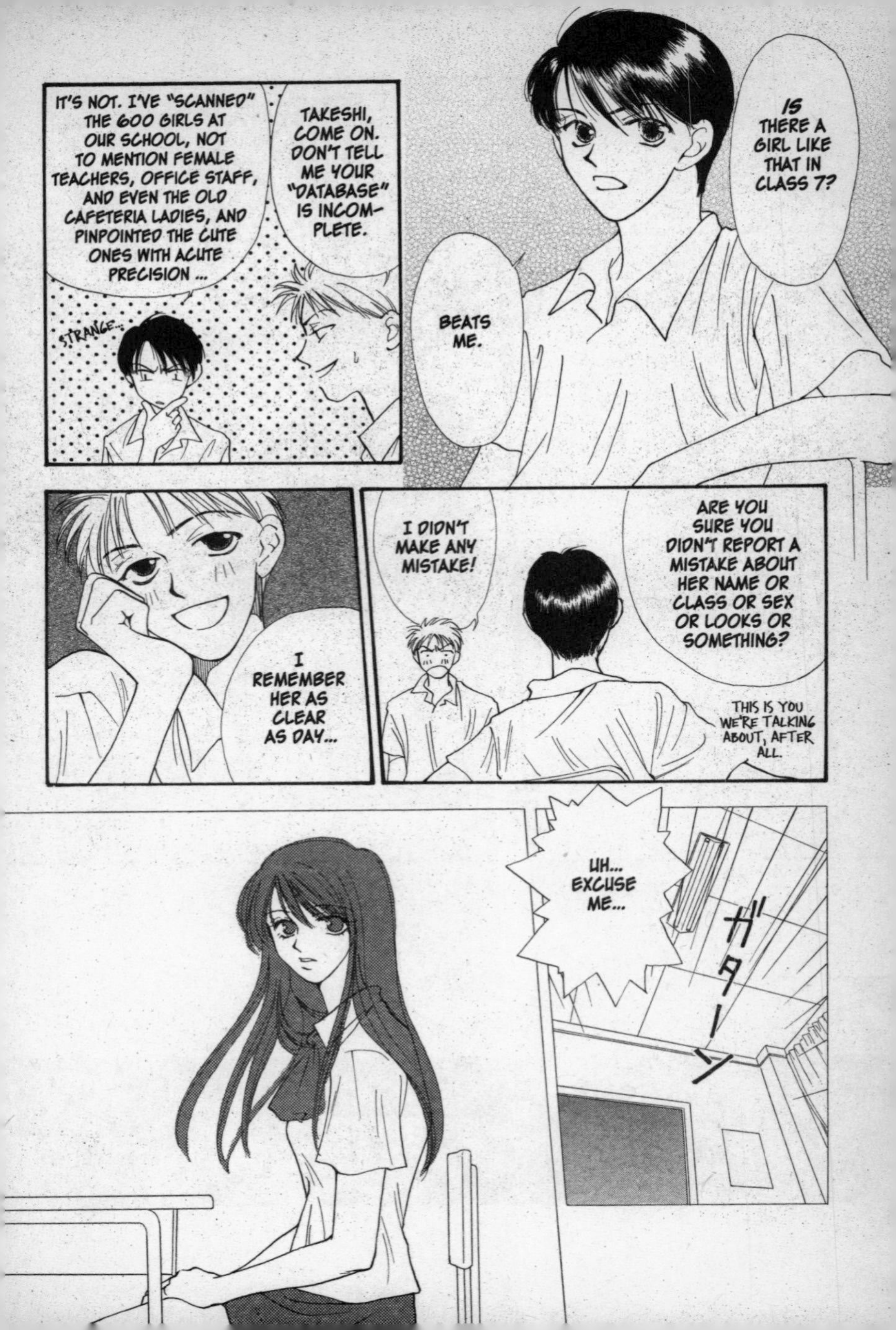
IS THERE A GIRL LIKE THAT IN CLASS 7?
BEATS ME.
TAKESHI, COME ON. DON'T TELL ME YOUR "DATABASE" IS INCOMPLETE.
IT'S NOT. I'VE "SCANNED" THE 600 GIRLS AT OUR SCHOOL, NOT TO MENTION FEMALE TEACHERS, OFFICE STAFF, AND EVEN THE OLD CAFETERIA LADIES, AND PINPOINTED THE CUTE ONES WITH ACUTE PRECISION ...
STRANGE...
ARE YOU SURE YOU DIDN'T REPORT A MISTAKE ABOUT HER NAME OR CLASS OR SEX OR LOOKS OR SOMETHING?
THIS IS YOU WE'RE TALKING ABOUT, AFTER ALL.
I DIDN'T MAKE ANY MISTAKE!
I REMEMBER HER AS CLEAR AS DAY...
UH... EXCUSE ME...
ガターン

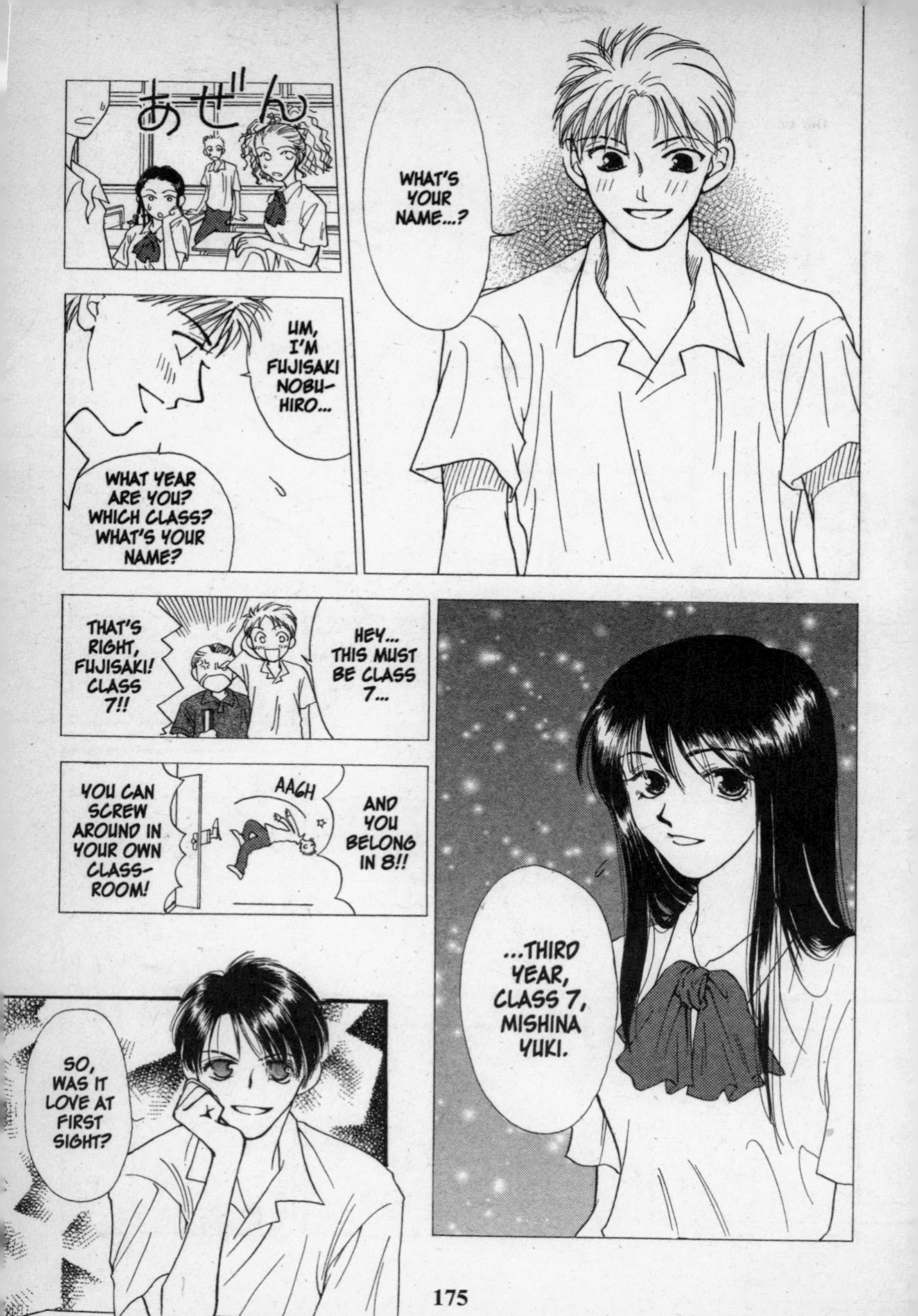
WHAT'S YOUR NAME...?
あぜん
UM, I'M FUJISAKI NOBUHIRO...
WHAT YEAR ARE YOU? WHICH CLASS? WHAT'S YOUR NAME?
...THIRD YEAR, CLASS 7, MISHINA YUKI.
HEY... THIS MUST BE CLASS 7...
THAT'S RIGHT, FUJISAKI! CLASS 7!!
AND YOU BELONG IN 8!!
AAGH
YOU CAN SCREW AROUND IN YOUR OWN CLASSROOM!
SO, WAS IT LOVE AT FIRST SIGHT?

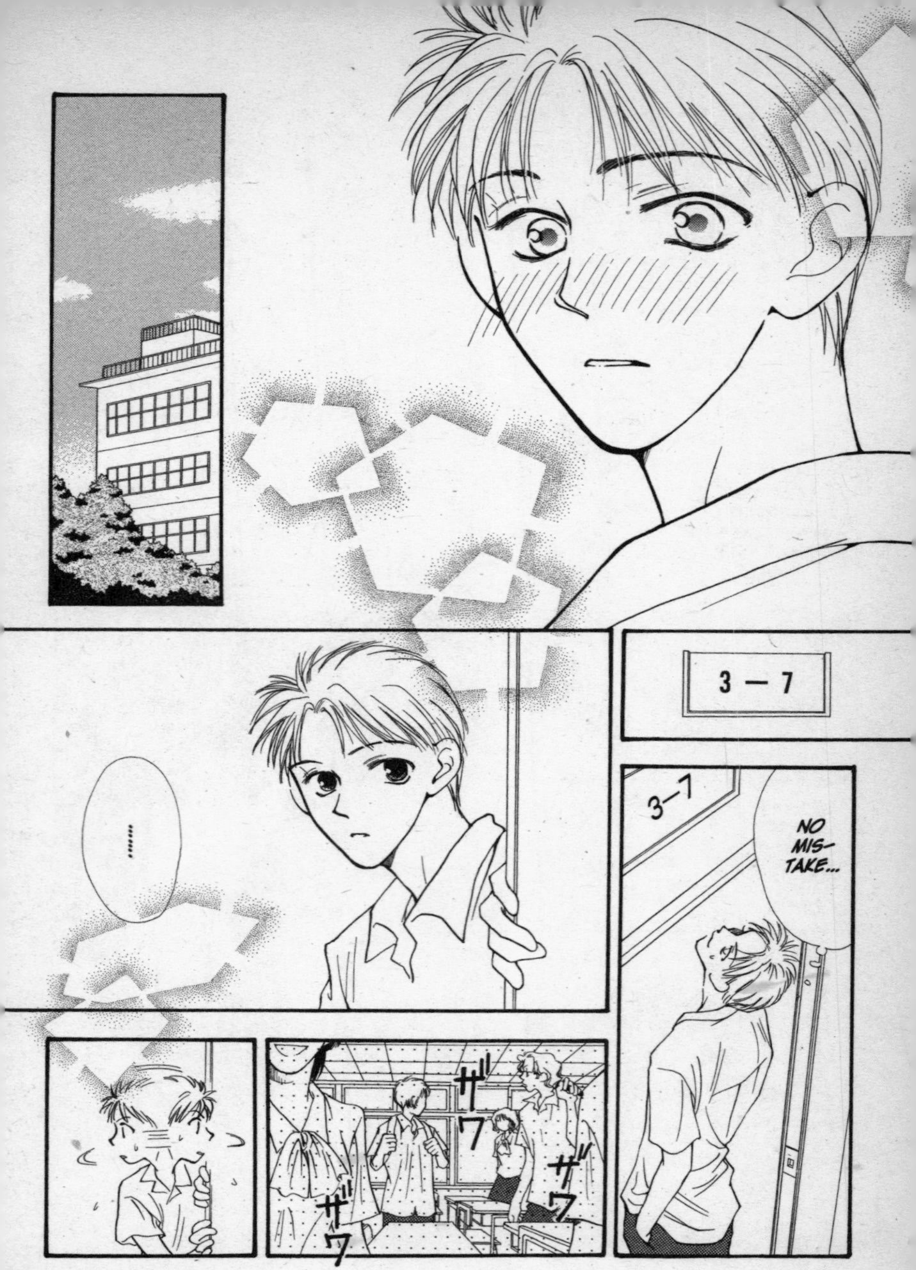
3 — 7
3–7
NO MIS-TAKE...
......
ザワ
ザワ
ザワ

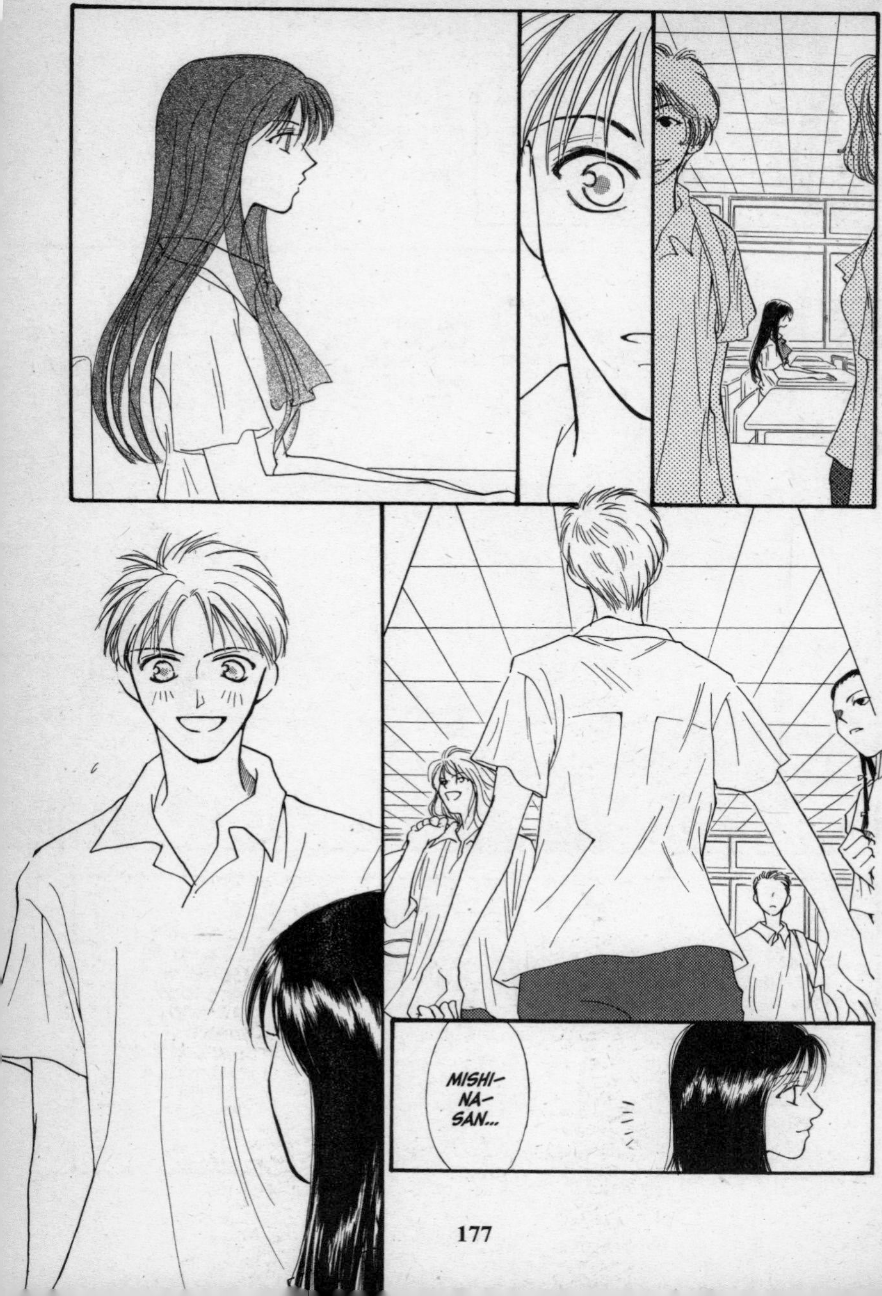
MISHI-
NA-
SAN...

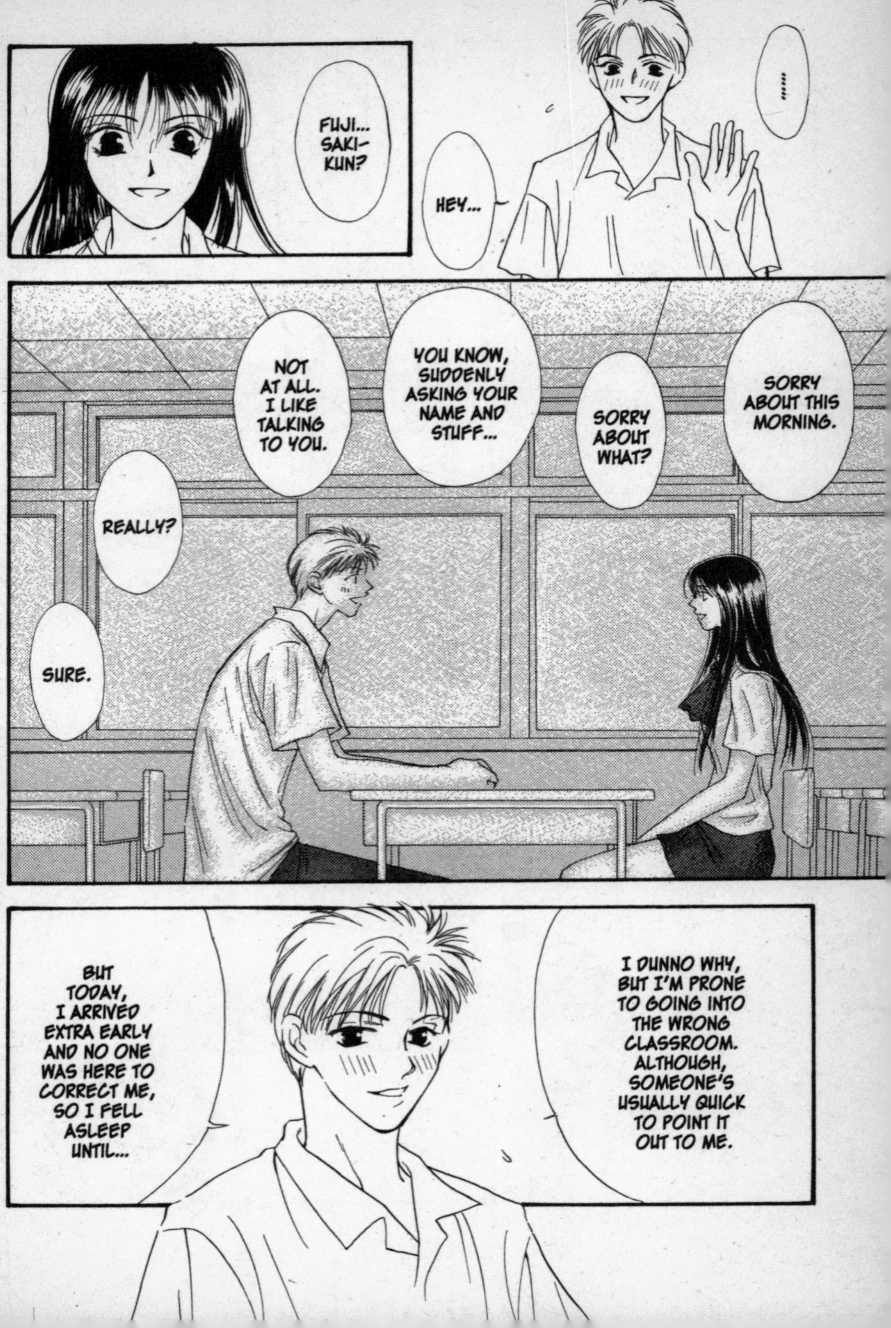
......
HEY...
FUJI... SAKI-KUN?
SORRY ABOUT THIS MORNING.
SORRY ABOUT WHAT?
YOU KNOW, SUDDENLY ASKING YOUR NAME AND STUFF...
NOT AT ALL. I LIKE TALKING TO YOU.
REALLY?
SURE.
I DUNNO WHY, BUT I'M PRONE TO GOING INTO THE WRONG CLASSROOM. ALTHOUGH, SOMEONE'S USUALLY QUICK TO POINT IT OUT TO ME.
BUT TODAY, I ARRIVED EXTRA EARLY AND NO ONE WAS HERE TO CORRECT ME, SO I FELL ASLEEP UNTIL...

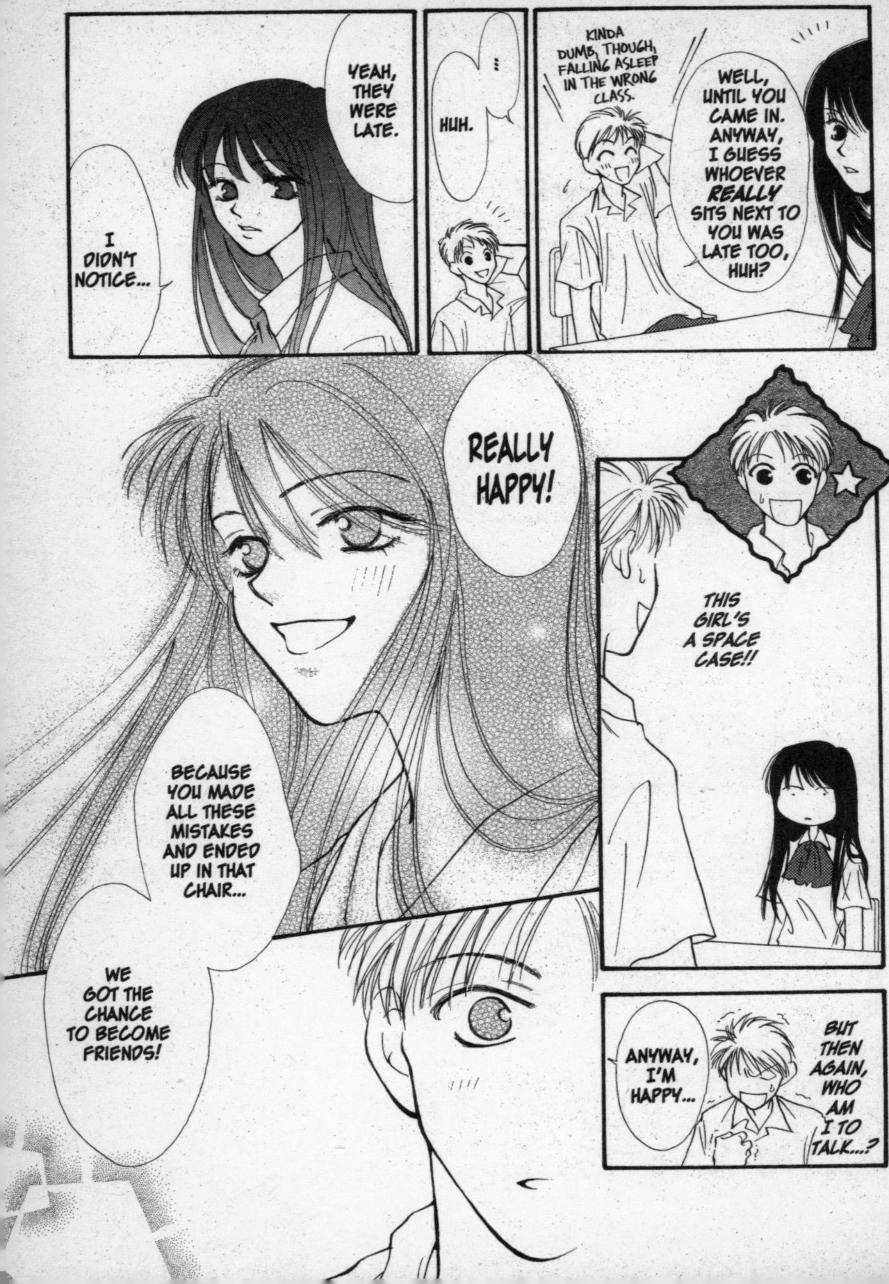
WELL, UNTIL YOU CAME IN. ANYWAY, I GUESS WHOEVER REALLY SITS NEXT TO YOU WAS LATE TOO, HUH?
KINDA DUMB, THOUGH, FALLING ASLEEP IN THE WRONG CLASS.
...
HUH.
YEAH, THEY WERE LATE.
I DIDN'T NOTICE...
THIS GIRL'S A SPACE CASE!!
BUT THEN AGAIN, WHO AM I TO TALK...?
ANYWAY, I'M HAPPY...
BECAUSE YOU MADE ALL THESE MISTAKES AND ENDED UP IN THAT CHAIR...
WE GOT THE CHANCE TO BECOME FRIENDS!
REALLY HAPPY!

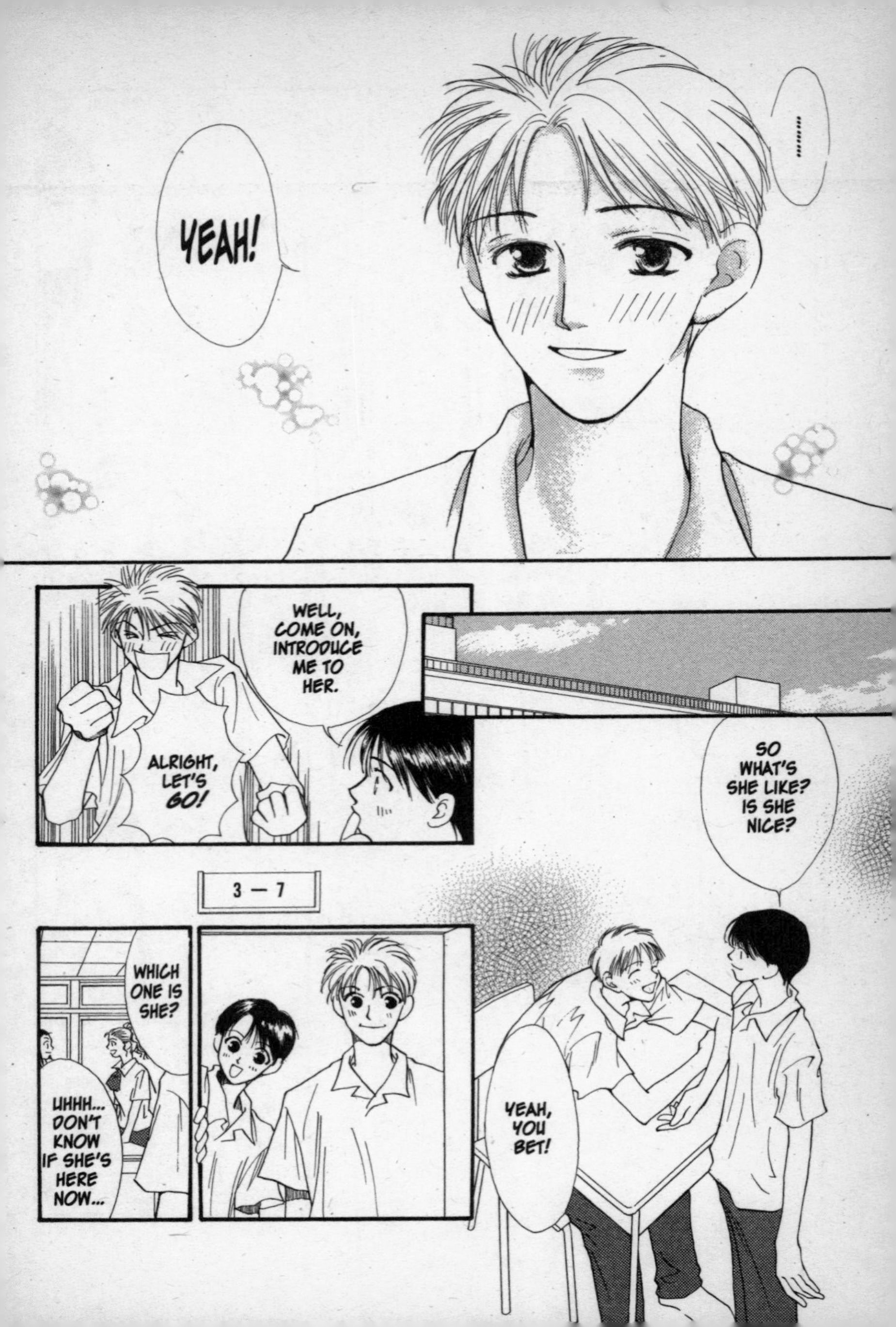
......
YEAH!
SO WHAT'S SHE LIKE? IS SHE NICE?
YEAH, YOU BET!
WELL, COME ON, INTRODUCE ME TO HER.
ALRIGHT, LET'S GO!
3 — 7
WHICH ONE IS SHE?
UHHH... DON'T KNOW IF SHE'S HERE NOW...

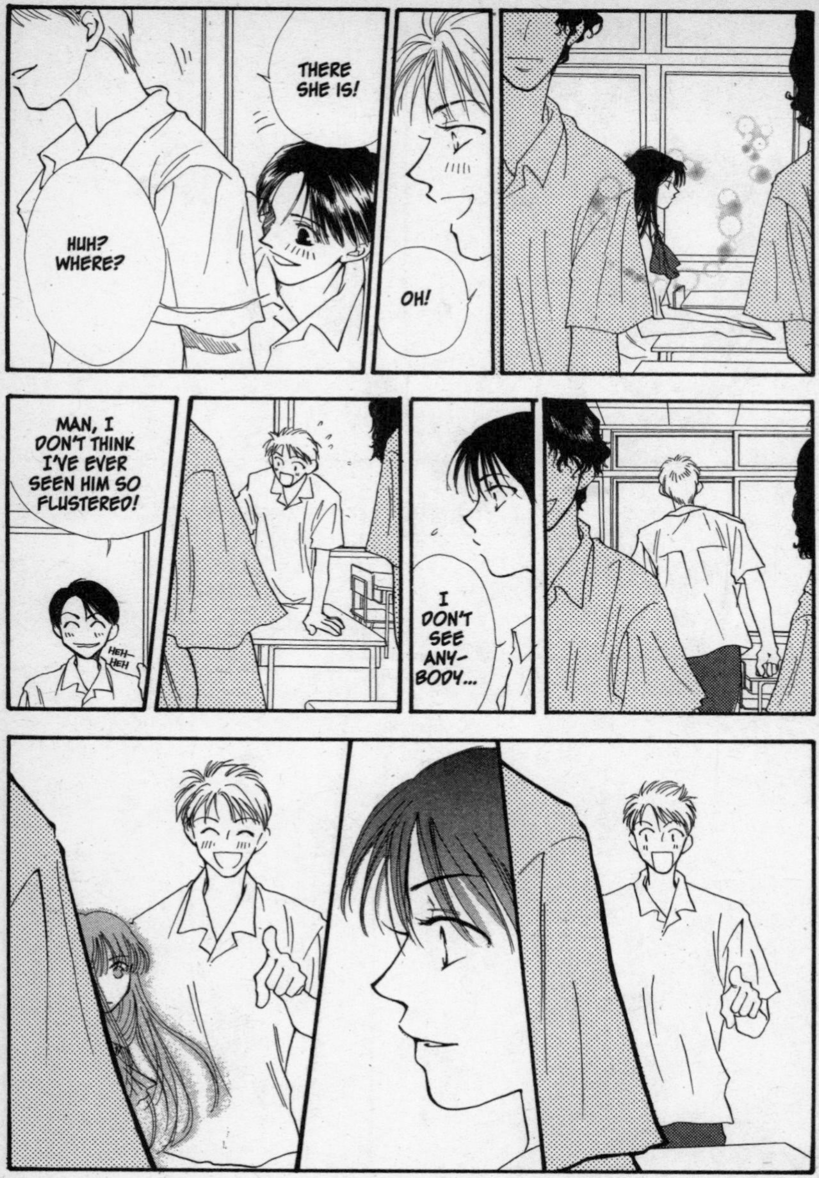
OH!
THERE SHE IS!
HUH? WHERE?
I DON'T SEE ANYBODY...
MAN, I DON'T THINK I'VE EVER SEEN HIM SO FLUSTERED!
HEH-HEH

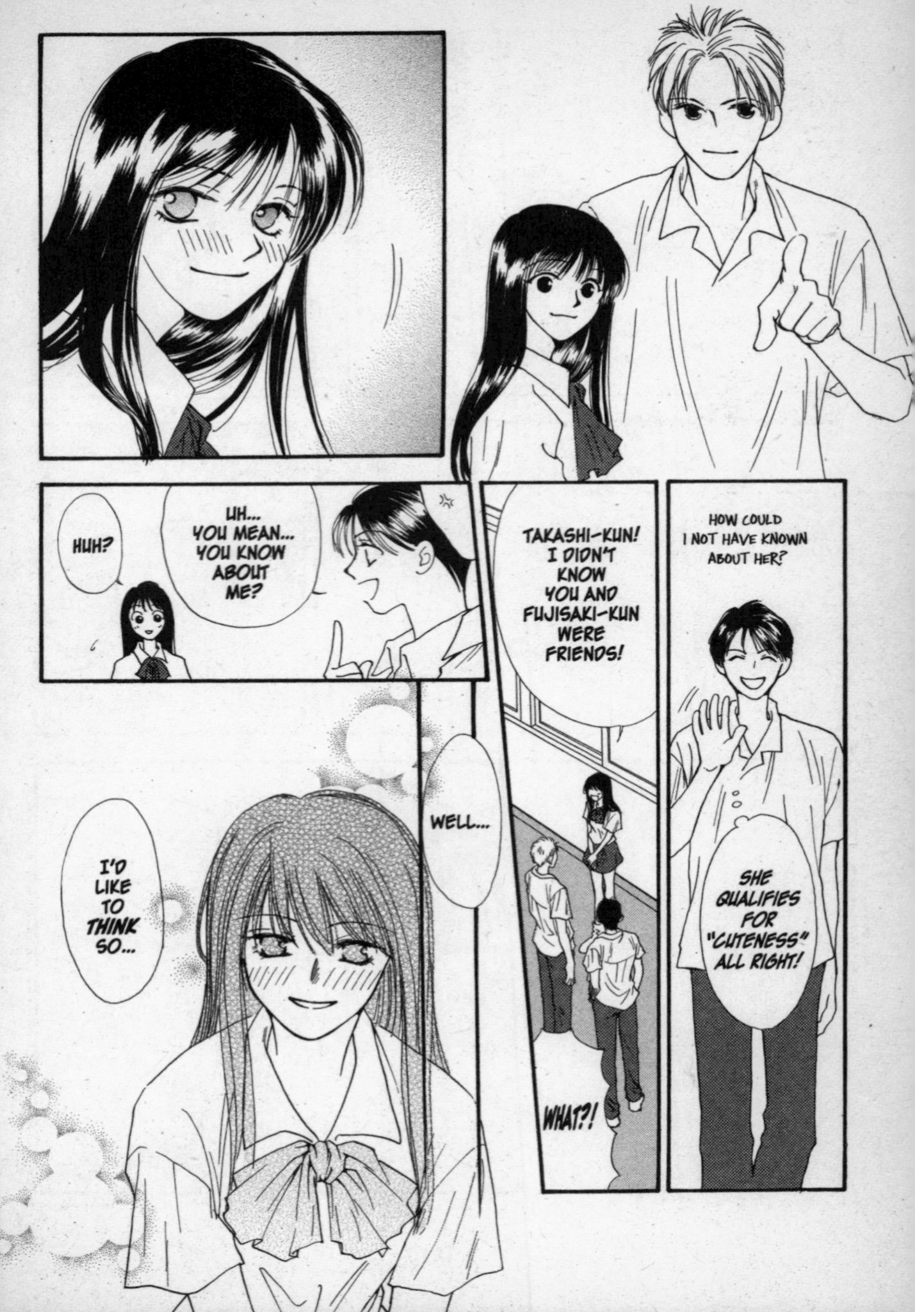
HOW COULD I NOT HAVE KNOWN ABOUT HER?
SHE QUALIFIES FOR "CUTENESS" ALL RIGHT!
TAKASHI-KUN! I DIDN'T KNOW YOU AND FUJISAKI-KUN WERE FRIENDS!
WHAT?!
UH... YOU MEAN... YOU KNOW ABOUT ME?
HUH?
WELL...
I'D LIKE TO THINK SO...

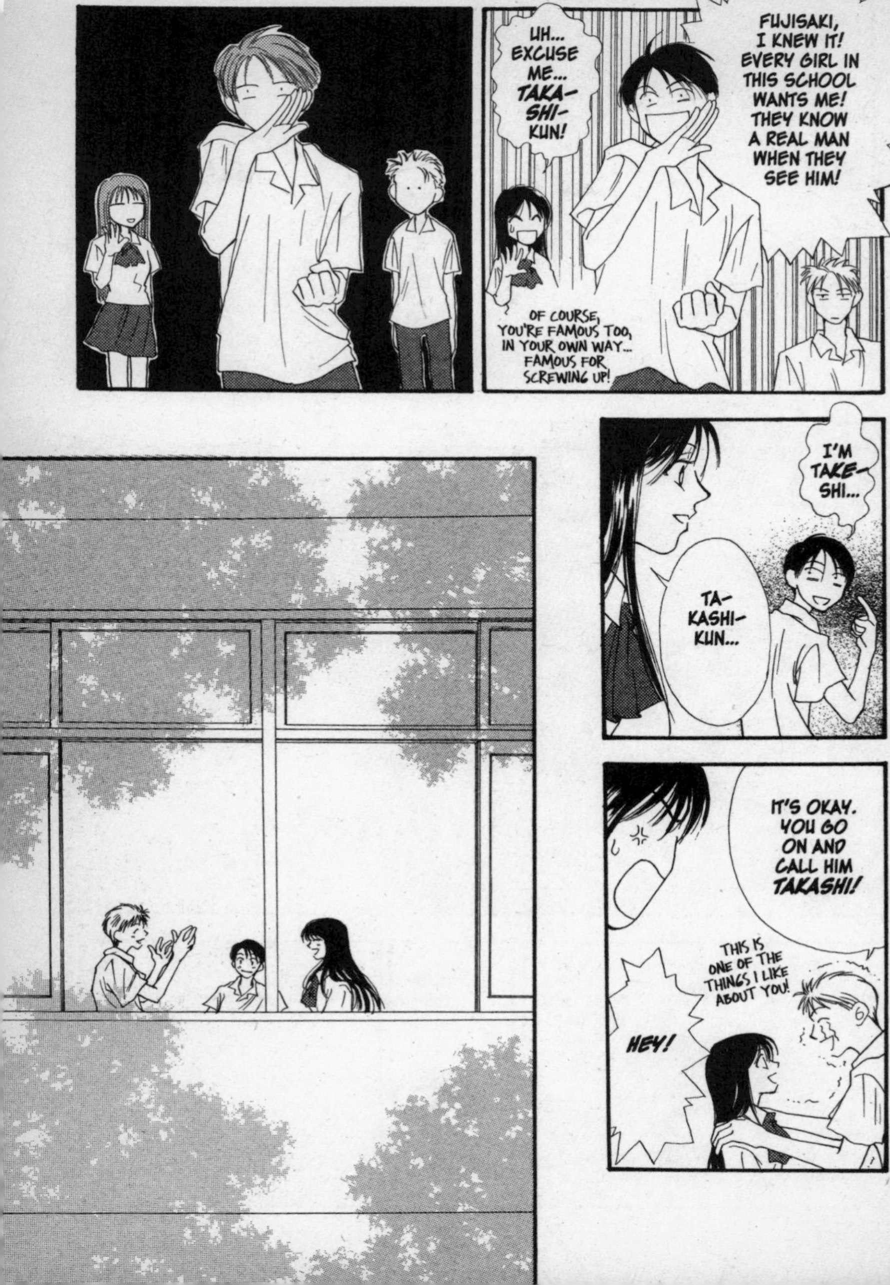
FUJISAKI, I KNEW IT! EVERY GIRL IN THIS SCHOOL WANTS ME! THEY KNOW A REAL MAN WHEN THEY SEE HIM!
UH... EXCUSE ME... TAKA-SHI-KUN!
OF COURSE, YOU'RE FAMOUS TOO, IN YOUR OWN WAY... FAMOUS FOR SCREWING UP!
I'M TAKE-SHI...
TA-KASHI-KUN...
IT'S OKAY. YOU GO ON AND CALL HIM TAKASHI!
THIS IS ONE OF THE THINGS I LIKE ABOUT YOU!
HEY!

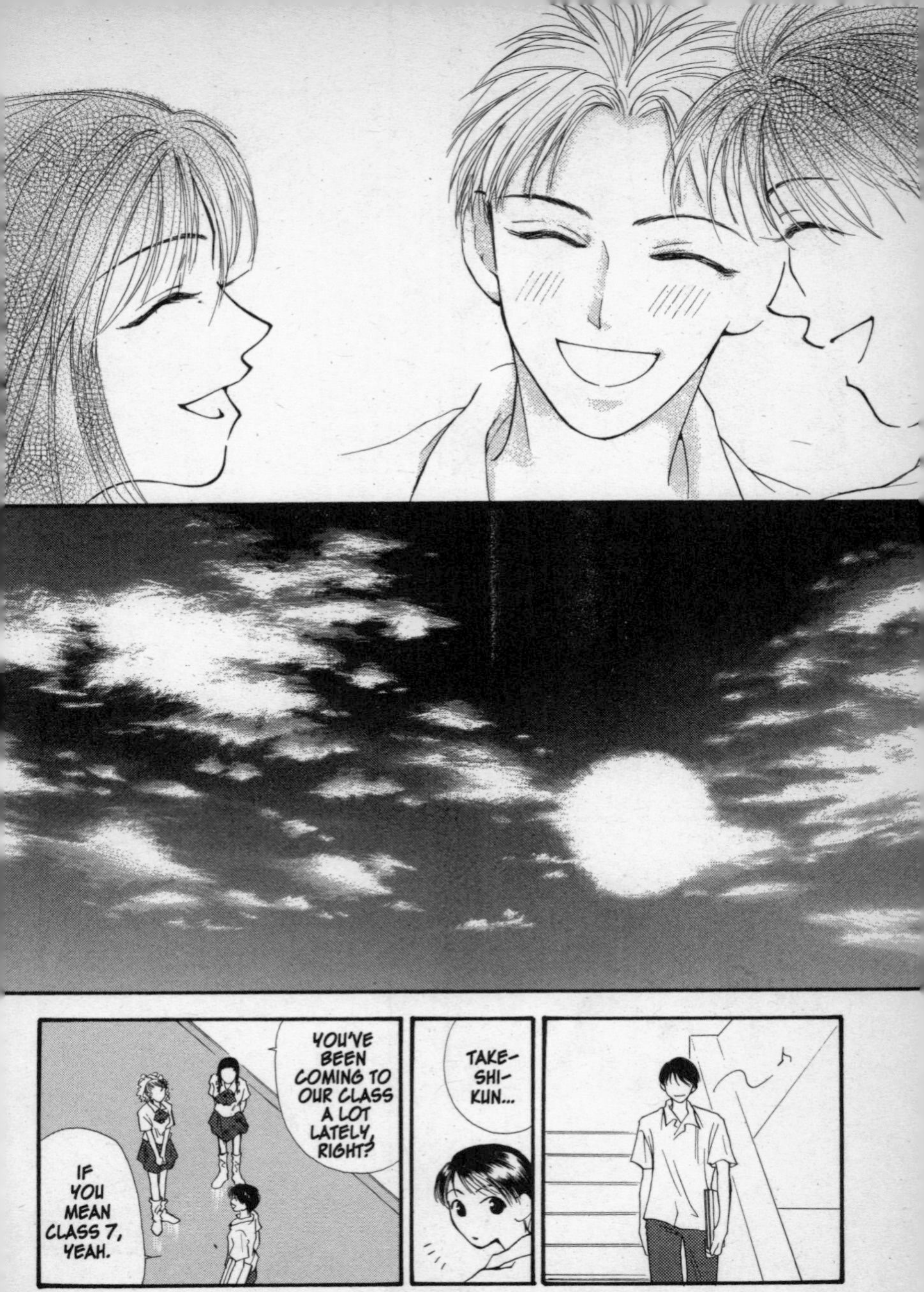
TAKE-SHI-KUN...
YOU'VE BEEN COMING TO OUR CLASS A LOT LATELY, RIGHT?
IF YOU MEAN CLASS 7, YEAH.

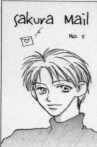

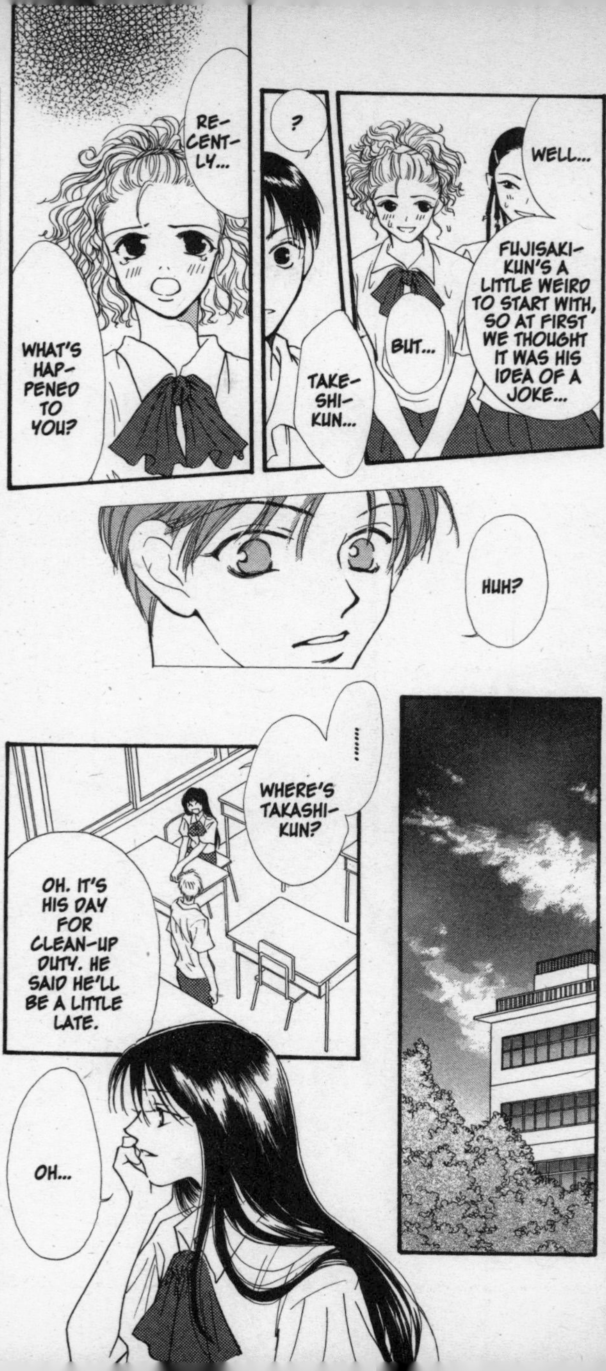
WELL...
FUJISAKI-KUN'S A LITTLE WEIRD TO START WITH, SO AT FIRST WE THOUGHT IT WAS HIS IDEA OF A JOKE...
BUT...
TAKE-SHI-KUN...
?
RE-CENT-LY...
WHAT'S HAP-PENED TO YOU?
HUH?
......
WHERE'S TAKASHI-KUN?
OH. IT'S HIS DAY FOR CLEAN-UP DUTY. HE SAID HE'LL BE A LITTLE LATE.
OH...

Sakura Mail

No. 5

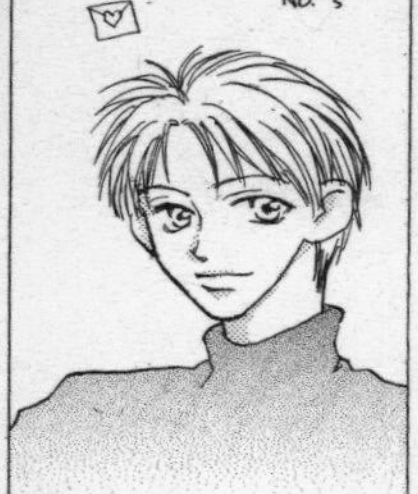

I often screw up. In fact, no matter what it is I'm trying to do, I'll always make at least one mistake. I suppose it comes from a lack of caution. And I think I fall outside the norm for blunders committed. Basic example: if there's mud outside, I'll trip and fall into it every time. I was this way as a kid. I haven't changed as an adult, and have a sinking feeling that I'll be error prone for the rest of my life. Although recently, another part of me has been calling out defiantly, "Don't worry about it! You'll get by!" And that's the part I want to share with other people who make a ton of mistakes. I wanna say: "It's OK! Roll with the blows! Even if you make mistakes, you should love yourself for who you are!" And with that, I'm out of space, so here I'll just say, see you!

-Sakura

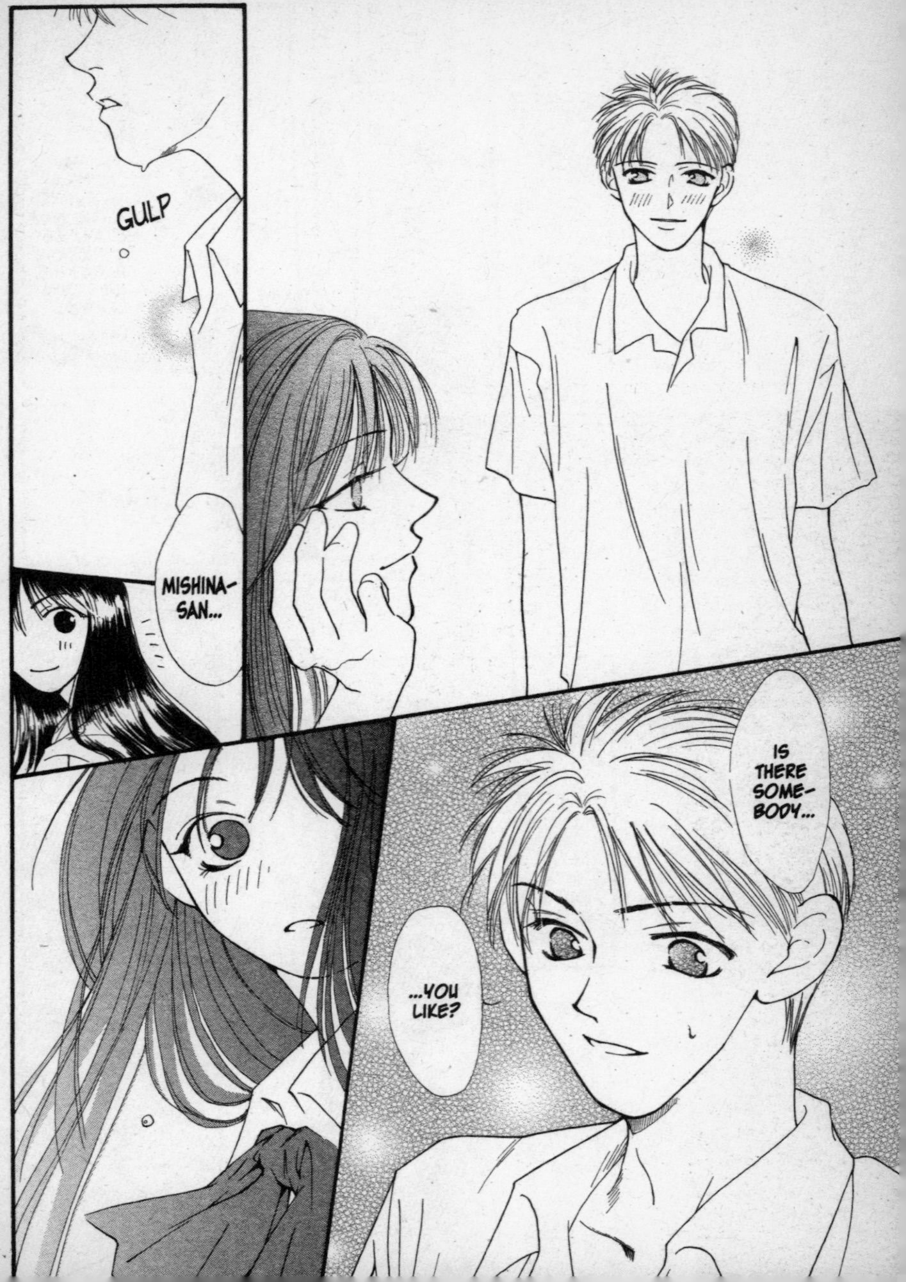
MISHINA-SAN...
GULP
IS THERE SOMEBODY...
...YOU LIKE?

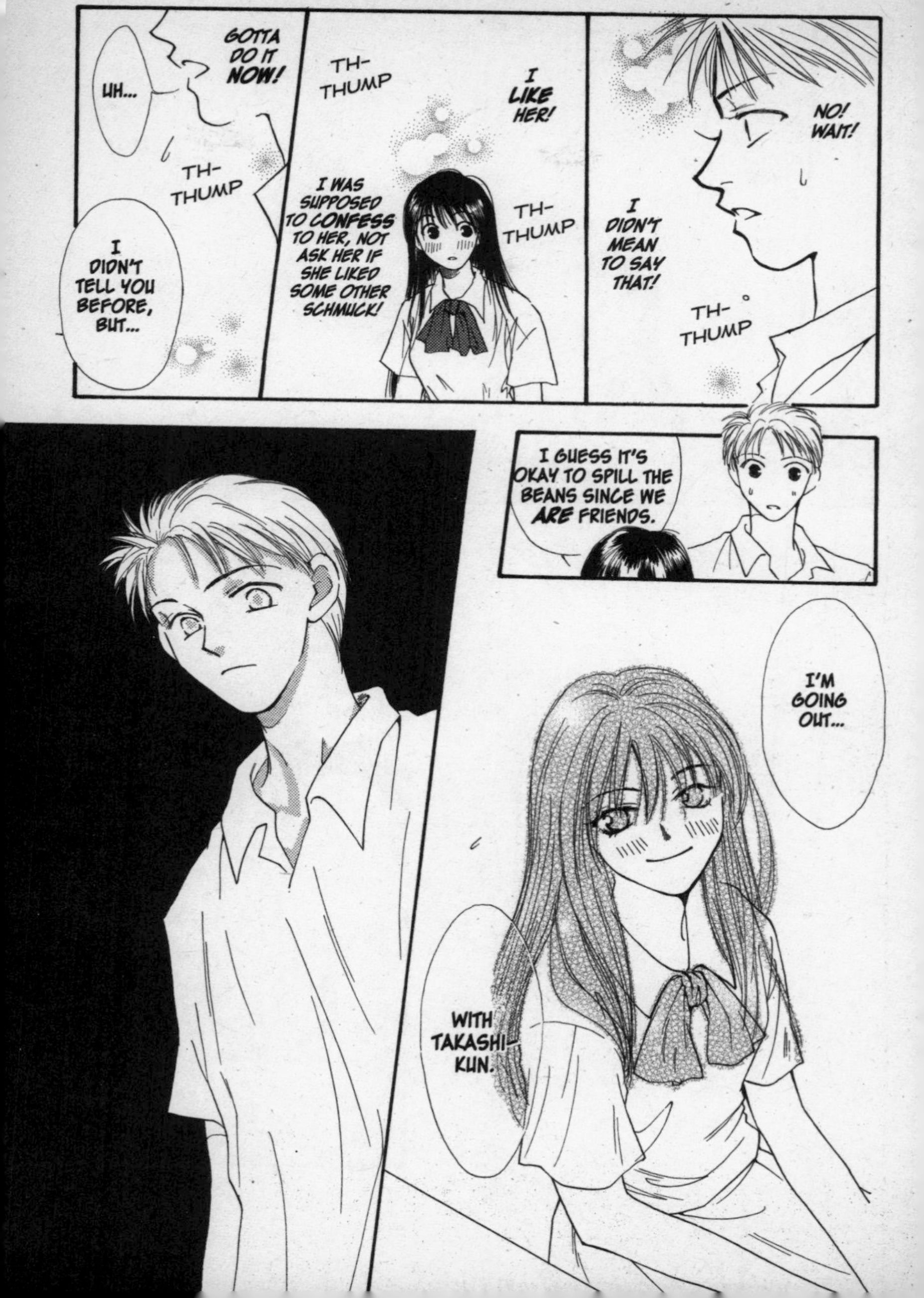
NO! WAIT!
I DIDN'T MEAN TO SAY THAT!
TH-THUMP
I LIKE HER!
TH-THUMP
TH-THUMP
I WAS SUPPOSED TO CONFESS TO HER, NOT ASK HER IF SHE LIKED SOME OTHER SCHMUCK!
GOTTA DO IT NOW!
UH...
TH-THUMP
I DIDN'T TELL YOU BEFORE, BUT...
I GUESS IT'S OKAY TO SPILL THE BEANS SINCE WE ARE FRIENDS.
I'M GOING OUT...
WITH TAKASHI-KUN.

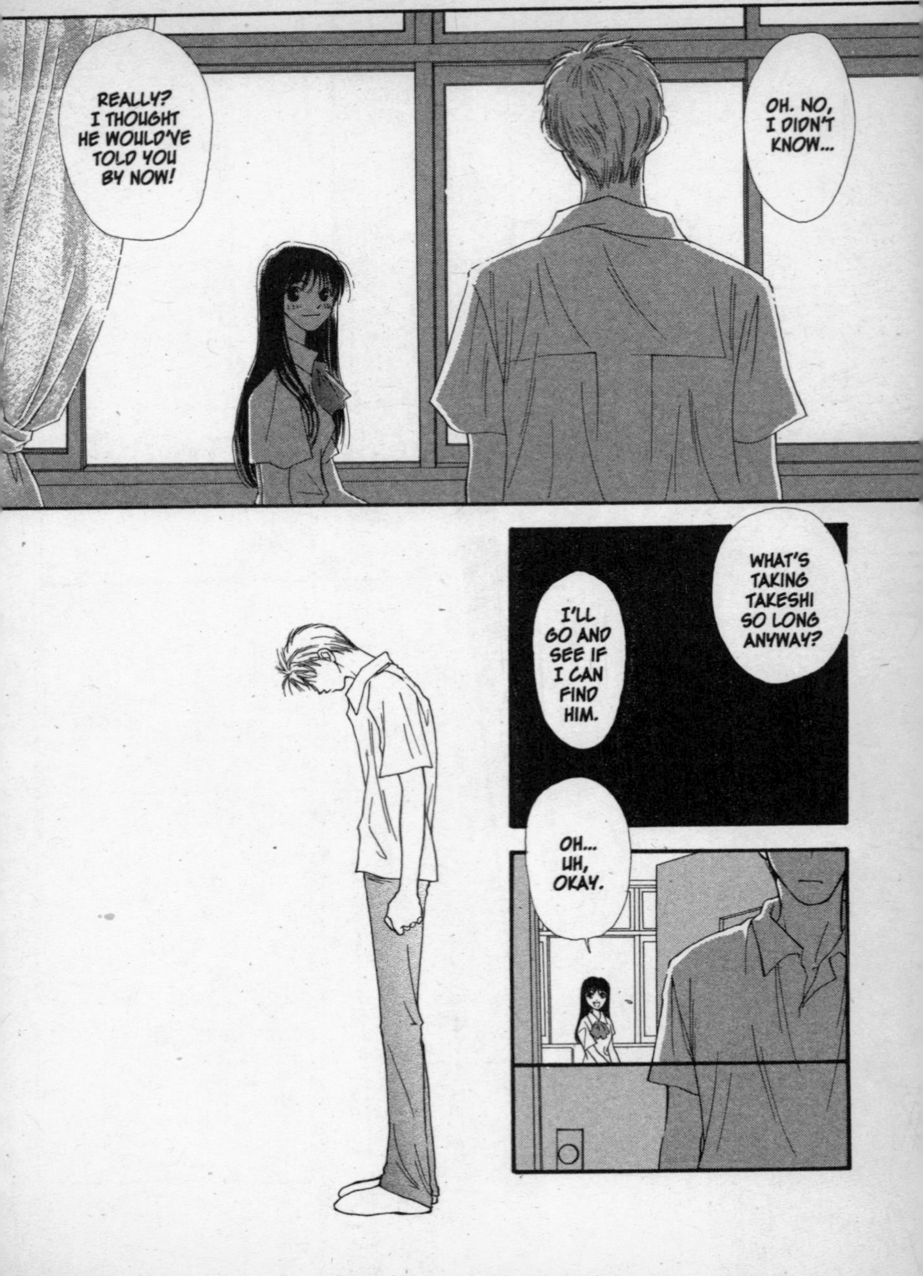
OH. NO, I DIDN'T KNOW...
REALLY? I THOUGHT HE WOULD'VE TOLD YOU BY NOW!
WHAT'S TAKING TAKESHI SO LONG ANYWAY?
I'LL GO AND SEE IF I CAN FIND HIM.
OH... UH, OKAY.

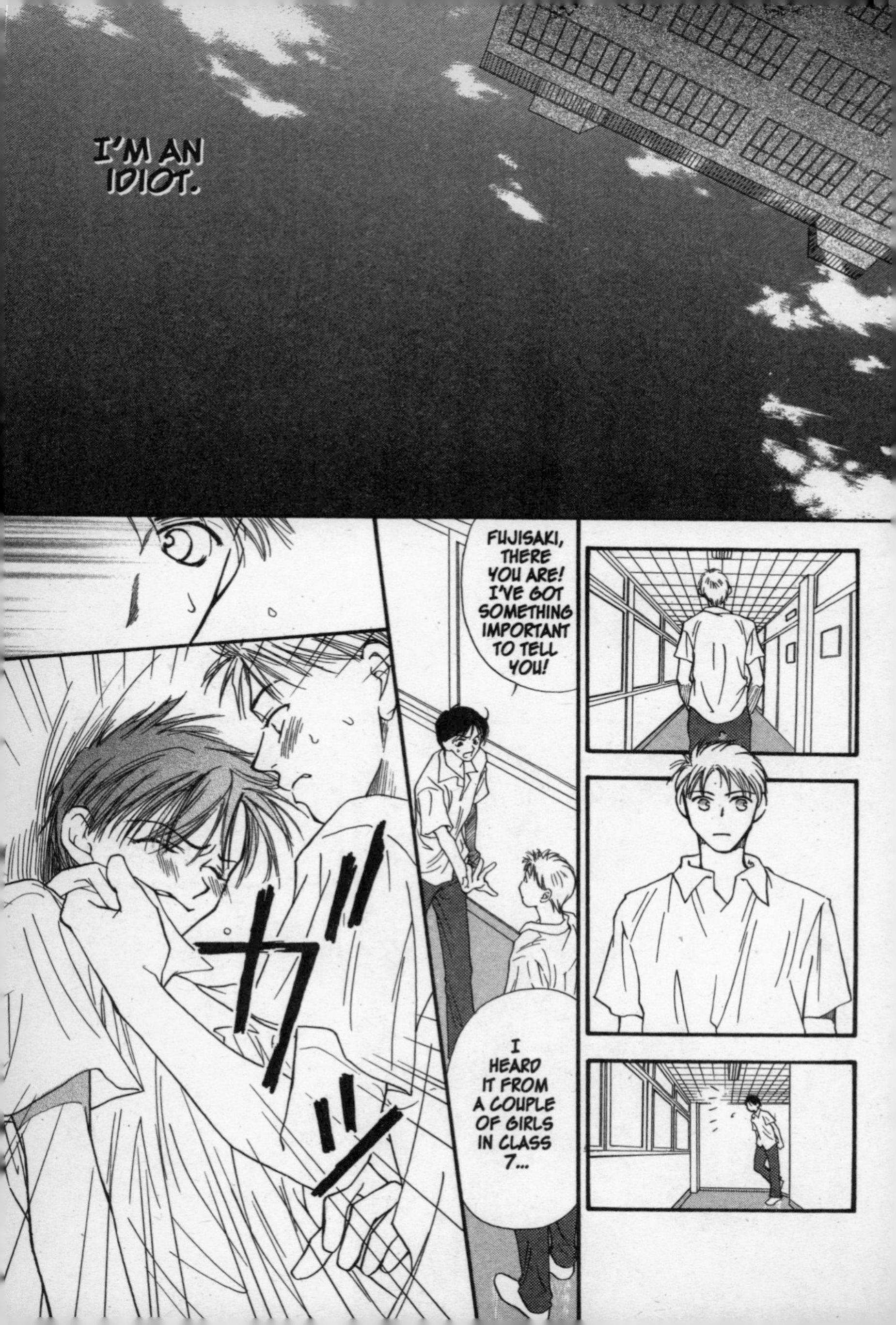
I'M AN IDIOT.
FUJISAKI, THERE YOU ARE! I'VE GOT SOMETHING IMPORTANT TO TELL YOU!
I HEARD IT FROM A COUPLE OF GIRLS IN CLASS 7...
ガッ

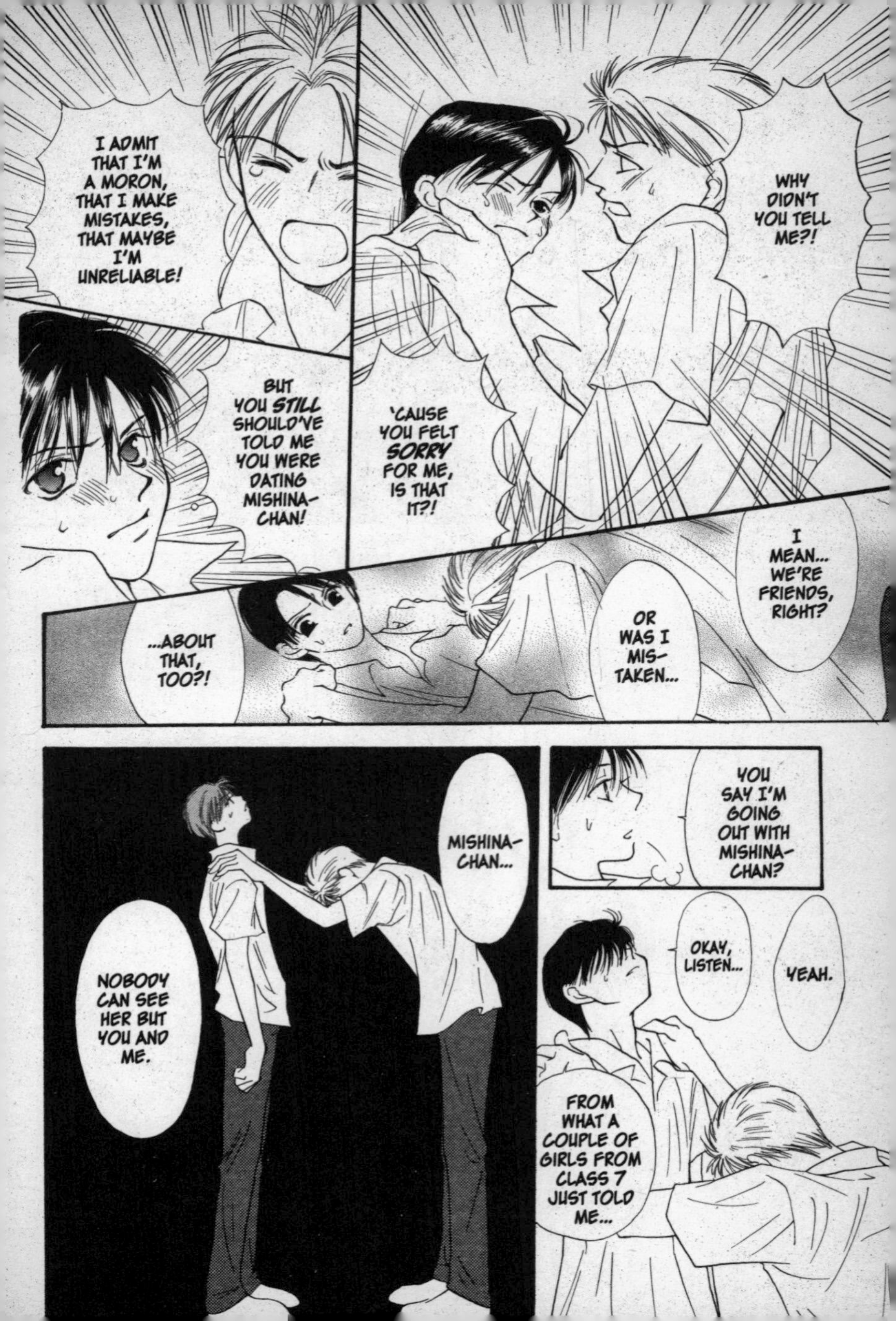
WHY DIDN'T YOU TELL ME?!
'CAUSE YOU FELT SORRY FOR ME, IS THAT IT?!
I ADMIT THAT I'M A MORON, THAT I MAKE MISTAKES, THAT MAYBE I'M UNRELIABLE!
BUT YOU STILL SHOULD'VE TOLD ME YOU WERE DATING MISHINA-CHAN!
I MEAN... WE'RE FRIENDS, RIGHT?
OR WAS I MIS-TAKEN...
...ABOUT THAT, TOO?!
YOU SAY I'M GOING OUT WITH MISHINA-CHAN?
YEAH.
OKAY, LISTEN...
FROM WHAT A COUPLE OF GIRLS FROM CLASS 7 JUST TOLD ME...
MISHINA-CHAN...
NOBODY CAN SEE HER BUT YOU AND ME.

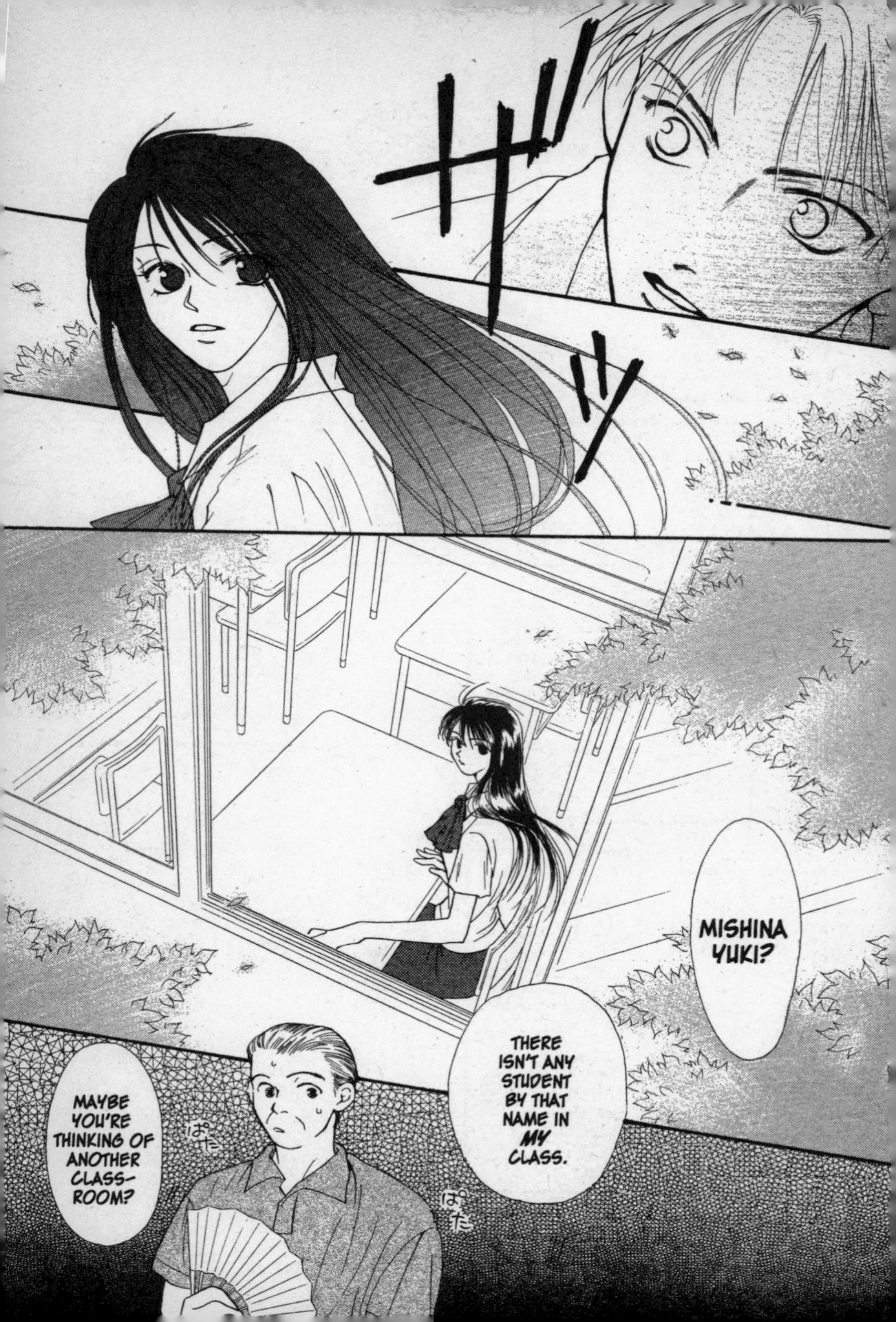
ザッ
MISHINA YUKI?
THERE ISN'T ANY STUDENT BY THAT NAME IN MY CLASS.
ぱた
ぱた
MAYBE YOU'RE THINKING OF ANOTHER CLASS-ROOM?

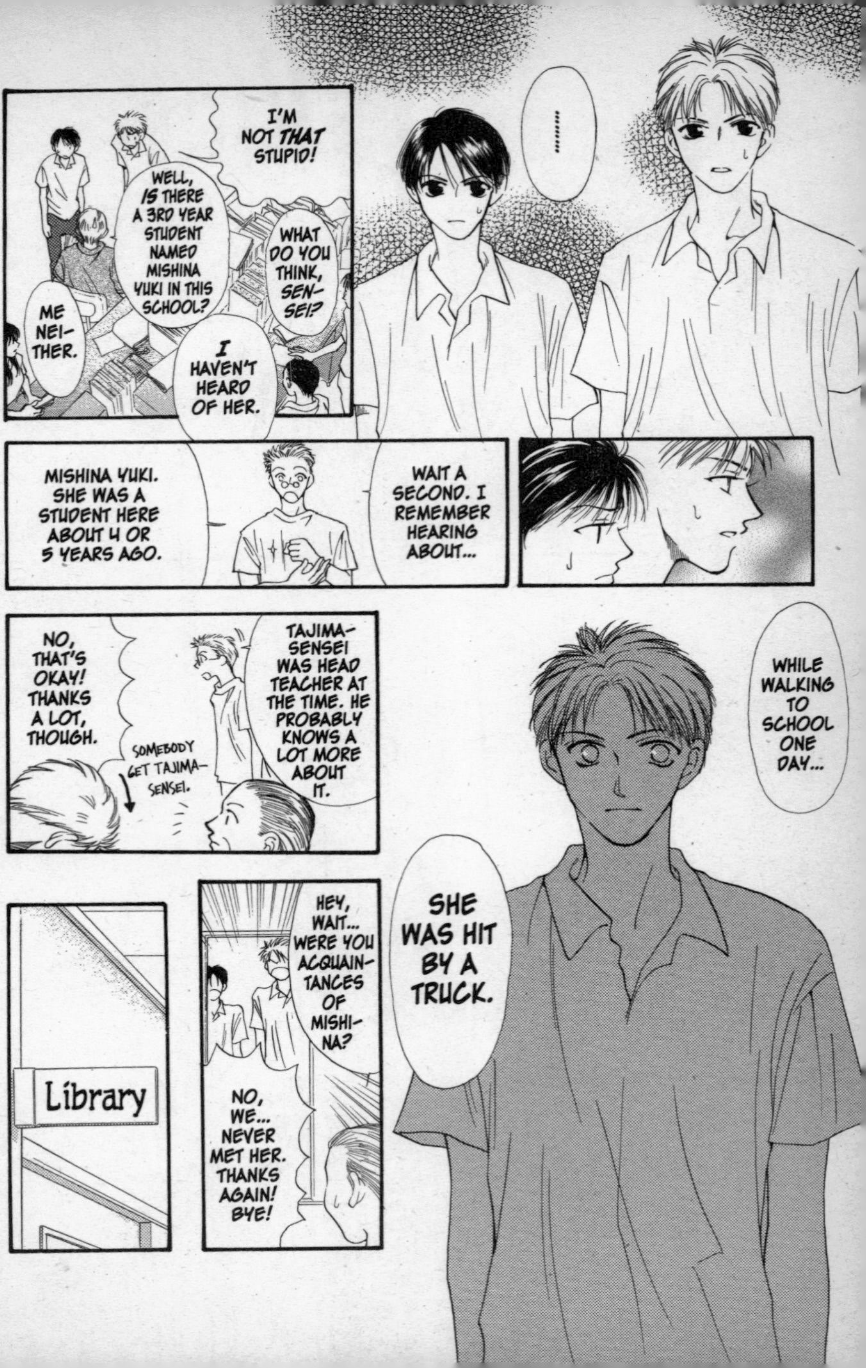
......
I'M NOT THAT STUPID!
WELL, IS THERE A 3RD YEAR STUDENT NAMED MISHINA YUKI IN THIS SCHOOL?
WHAT DO YOU THINK, SENSEI?
I HAVEN'T HEARD OF HER.
ME NEITHER.
WAIT A SECOND. I REMEMBER HEARING ABOUT...
MISHINA YUKI. SHE WAS A STUDENT HERE ABOUT 4 OR 5 YEARS AGO.
WHILE WALKING TO SCHOOL ONE DAY...
SHE WAS HIT BY A TRUCK.
TAJIMA-SENSEI WAS HEAD TEACHER AT THE TIME. HE PROBABLY KNOWS A LOT MORE ABOUT IT.
SOMEBODY GET TAJIMA-SENSEI.
NO, THAT'S OKAY! THANKS A LOT, THOUGH.
HEY, WAIT... WERE YOU ACQUAINTANCES OF MISHINA?
NO, WE... NEVER MET HER. THANKS AGAIN! BYE!
Library

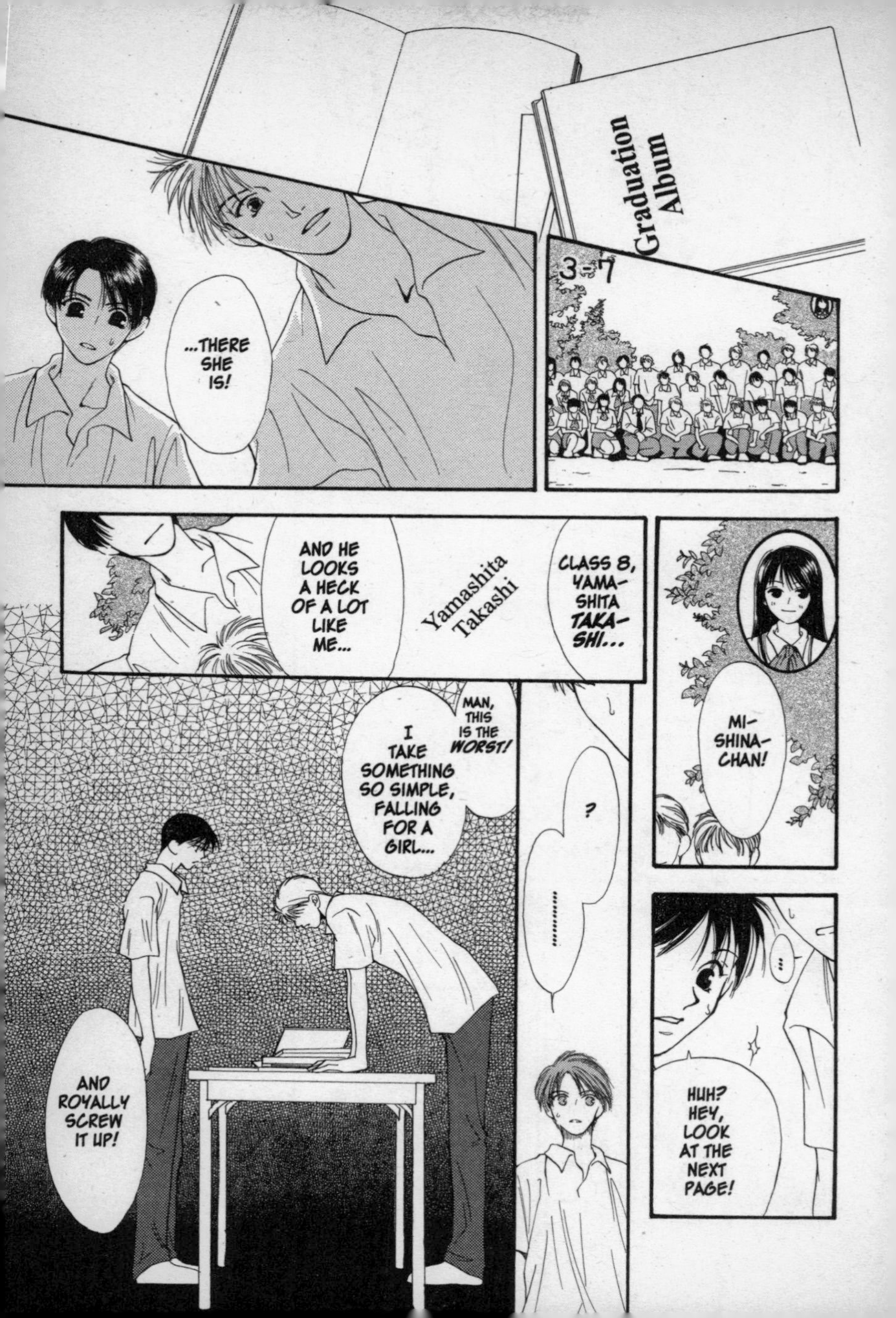
Graduation Album
3-7
...THERE SHE IS!
MI-SHINA-CHAN!
CLASS 8, YAMA-SHITA TAKA-SHI...
Yamashita Takashi
AND HE LOOKS A HECK OF A LOT LIKE ME...
HUH? HEY, LOOK AT THE NEXT PAGE!
?
....
MAN, THIS IS THE WORST!
I TAKE SOMETHING SO SIMPLE, FALLING FOR A GIRL...
AND ROYALLY SCREW IT UP!

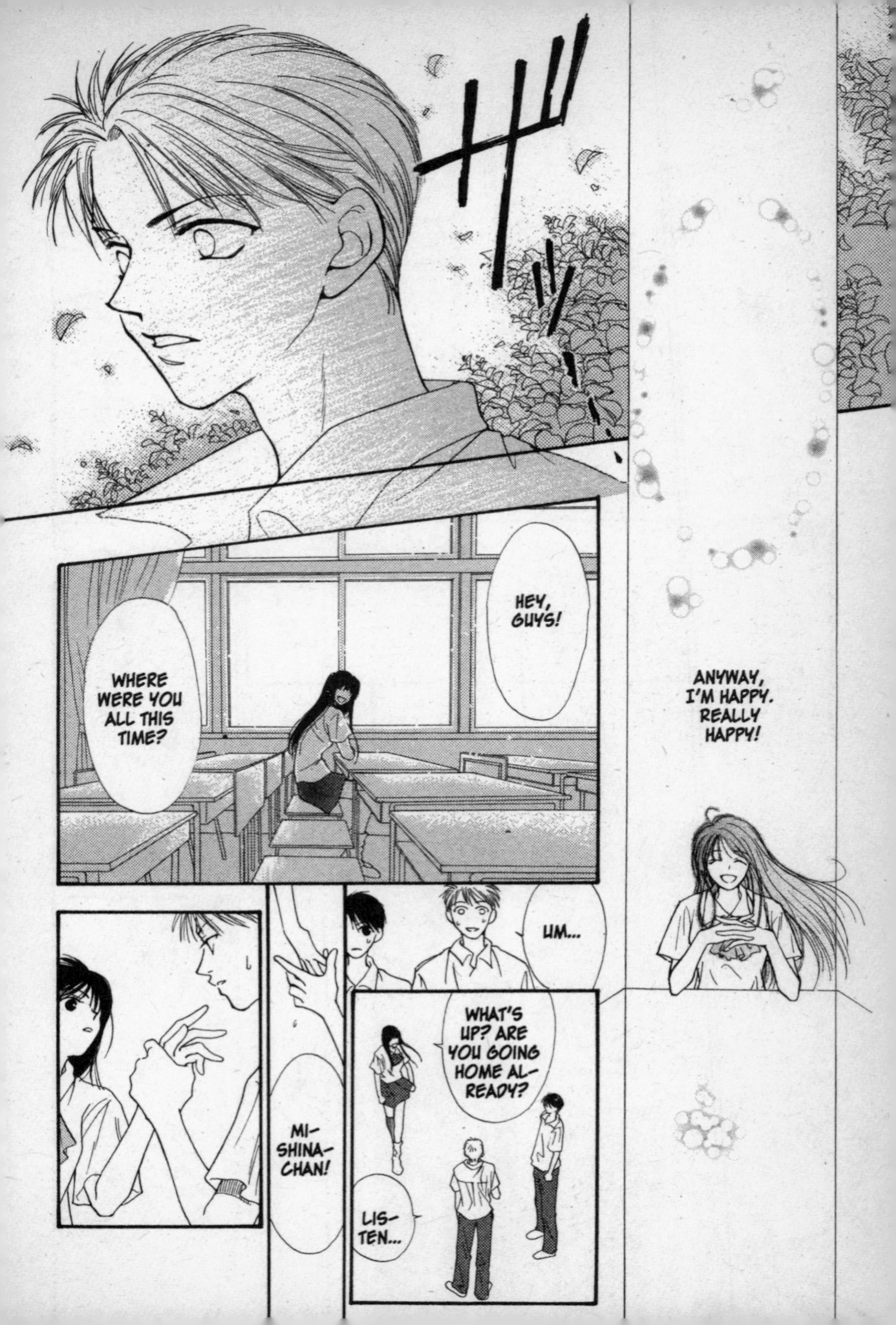
ANYWAY, I'M HAPPY. REALLY HAPPY!
ザッ
HEY, GUYS!
WHERE WERE YOU ALL THIS TIME?
UM...
WHAT'S UP? ARE YOU GOING HOME AL-READY?
LIS-TEN...
MI-SHINA-CHAN!

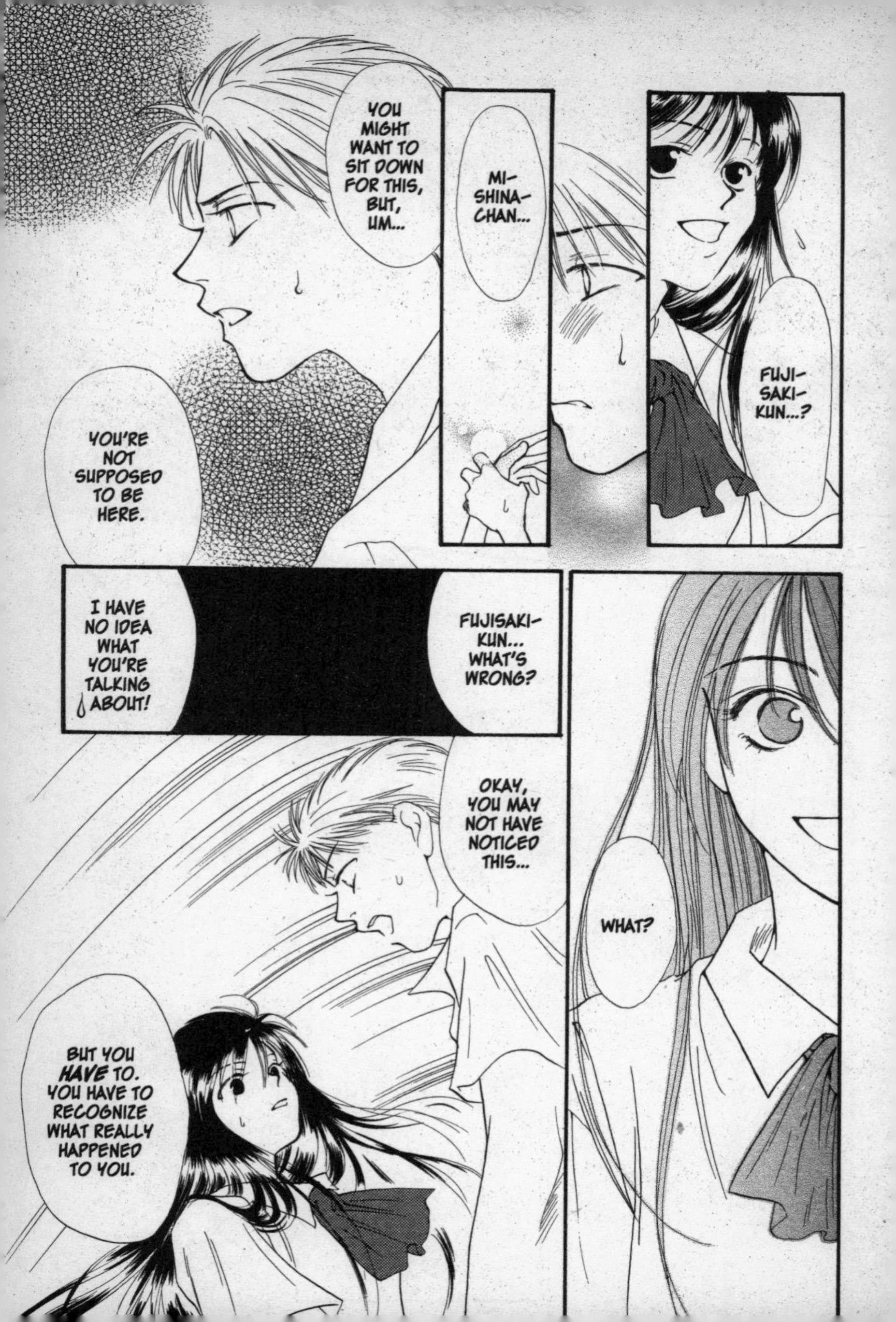
FUJI-SAKI-KUN...?
MI-SHINA-CHAN...
YOU MIGHT WANT TO SIT DOWN FOR THIS, BUT, UM...
YOU'RE NOT SUPPOSED TO BE HERE.
WHAT?
FUJISAKI-KUN... WHAT'S WRONG?
I HAVE NO IDEA WHAT YOU'RE TALKING ABOUT!
OKAY, YOU MAY NOT HAVE NOTICED THIS...
BUT YOU ***HAVE*** TO. YOU HAVE TO RECOGNIZE WHAT REALLY HAPPENED TO YOU.

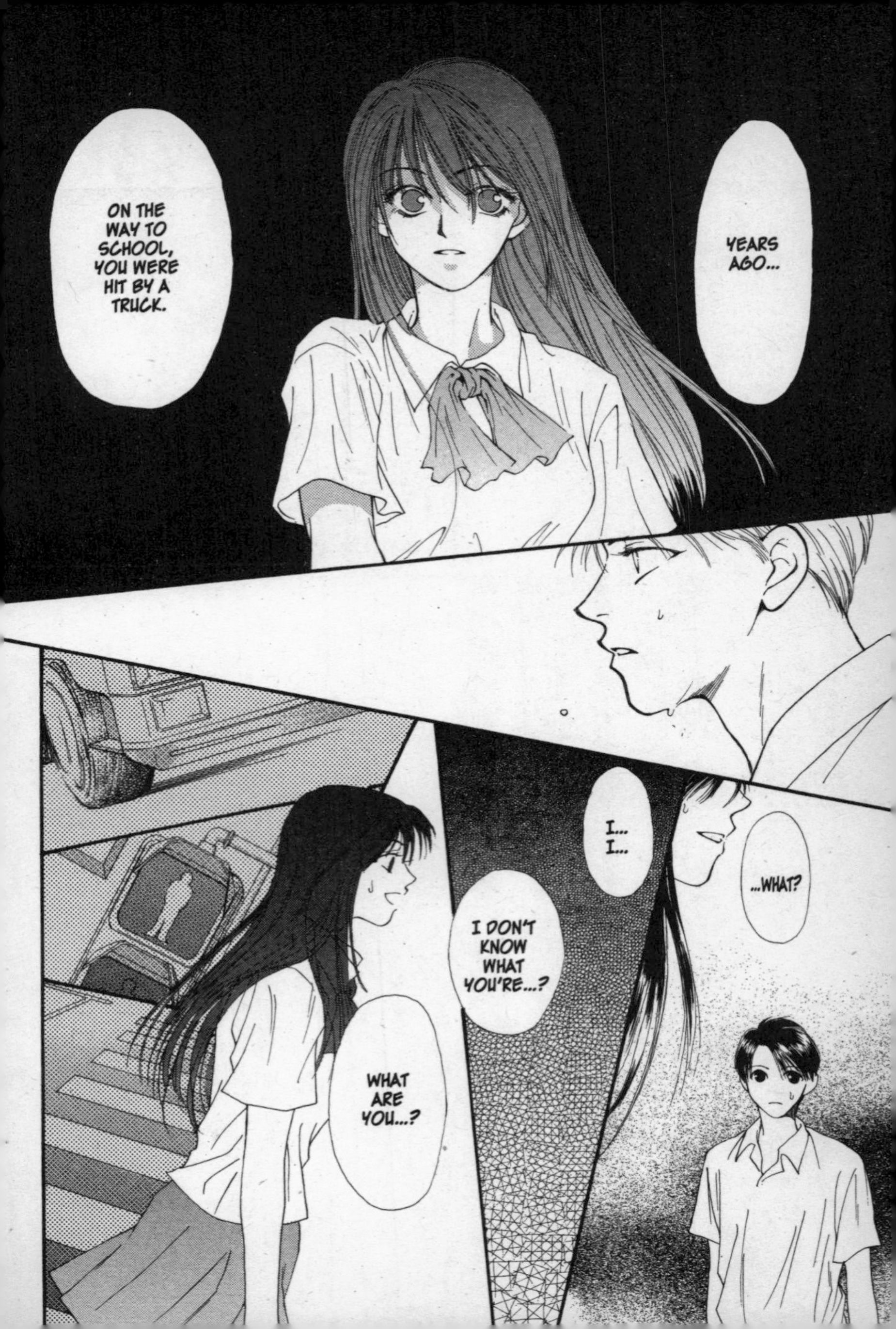
YEARS AGO...
ON THE WAY TO SCHOOL, YOU WERE HIT BY A TRUCK.
...WHAT?
I... I...
I DON'T KNOW WHAT YOU'RE...?
WHAT ARE YOU...?

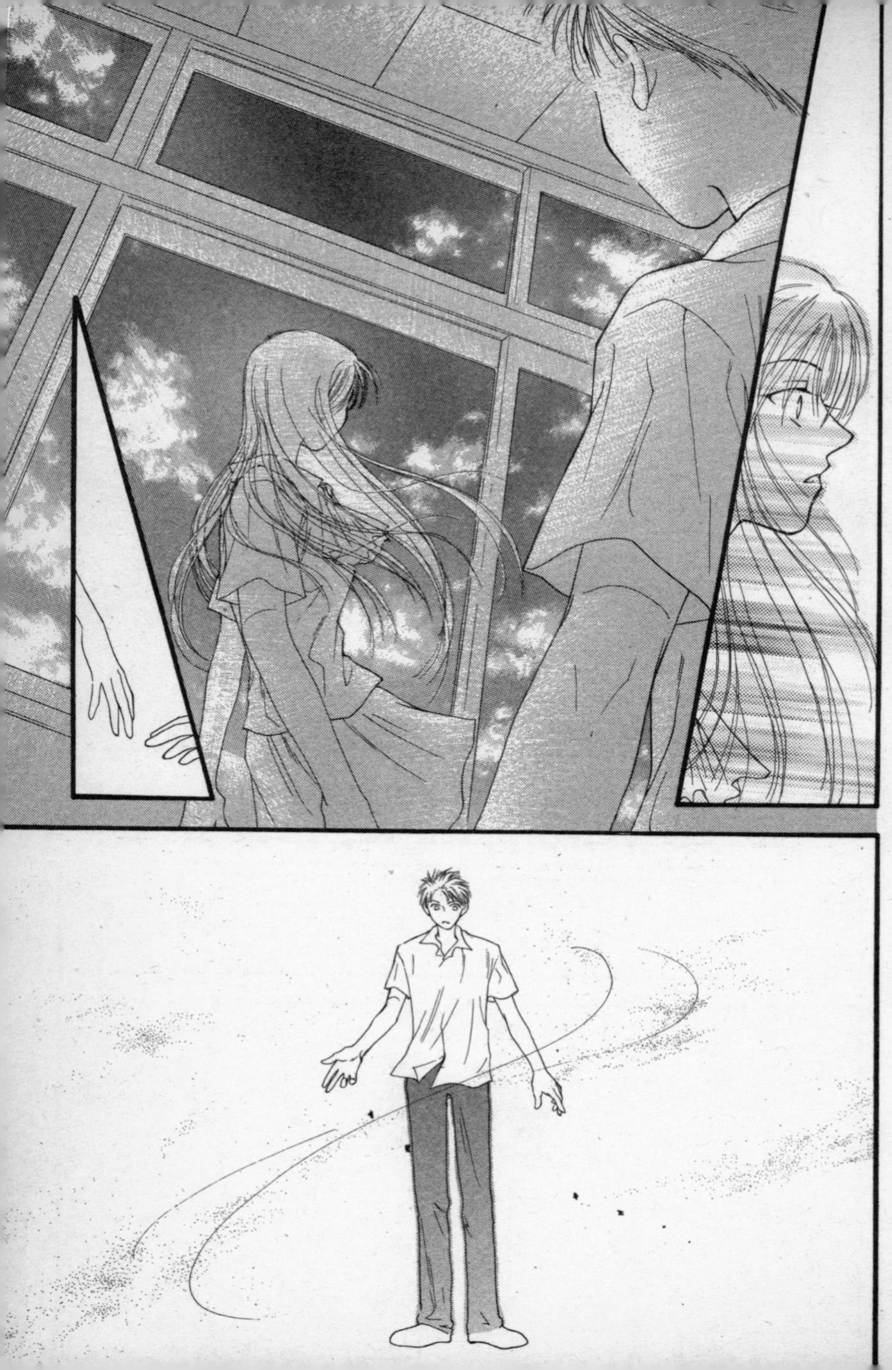

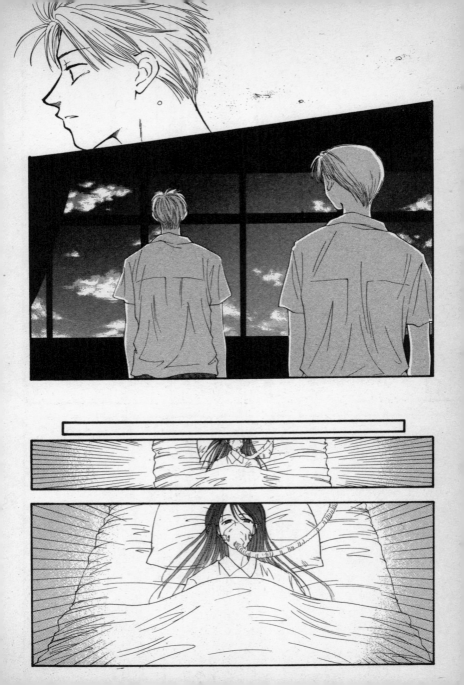

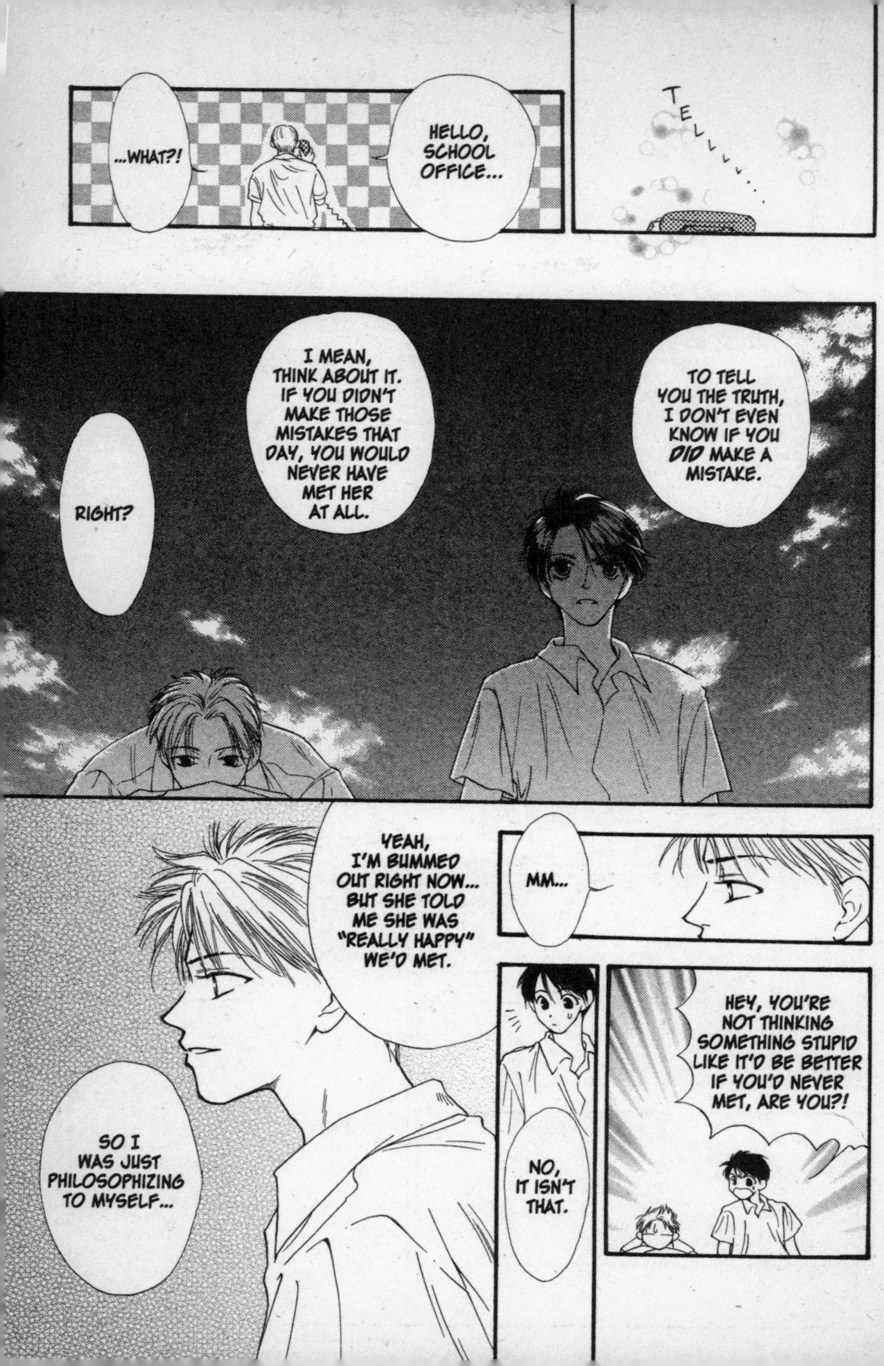
TELLLLL...
HELLO, SCHOOL OFFICE...
...WHAT?!
TO TELL YOU THE TRUTH, I DON'T EVEN KNOW IF YOU *DID* MAKE A MISTAKE.
I MEAN, THINK ABOUT IT. IF YOU DIDN'T MAKE THOSE MISTAKES THAT DAY, YOU WOULD NEVER HAVE MET HER AT ALL.
RIGHT?
MM...
HEY, YOU'RE NOT THINKING SOMETHING STUPID LIKE IT'D BE BETTER IF YOU'D NEVER MET, ARE YOU?!
NO, IT ISN'T THAT.
YEAH, I'M BUMMED OUT RIGHT NOW... BUT SHE TOLD ME SHE WAS "REALLY HAPPY" WE'D MET.
SO I WAS JUST PHILOSOPHIZING TO MYSELF...

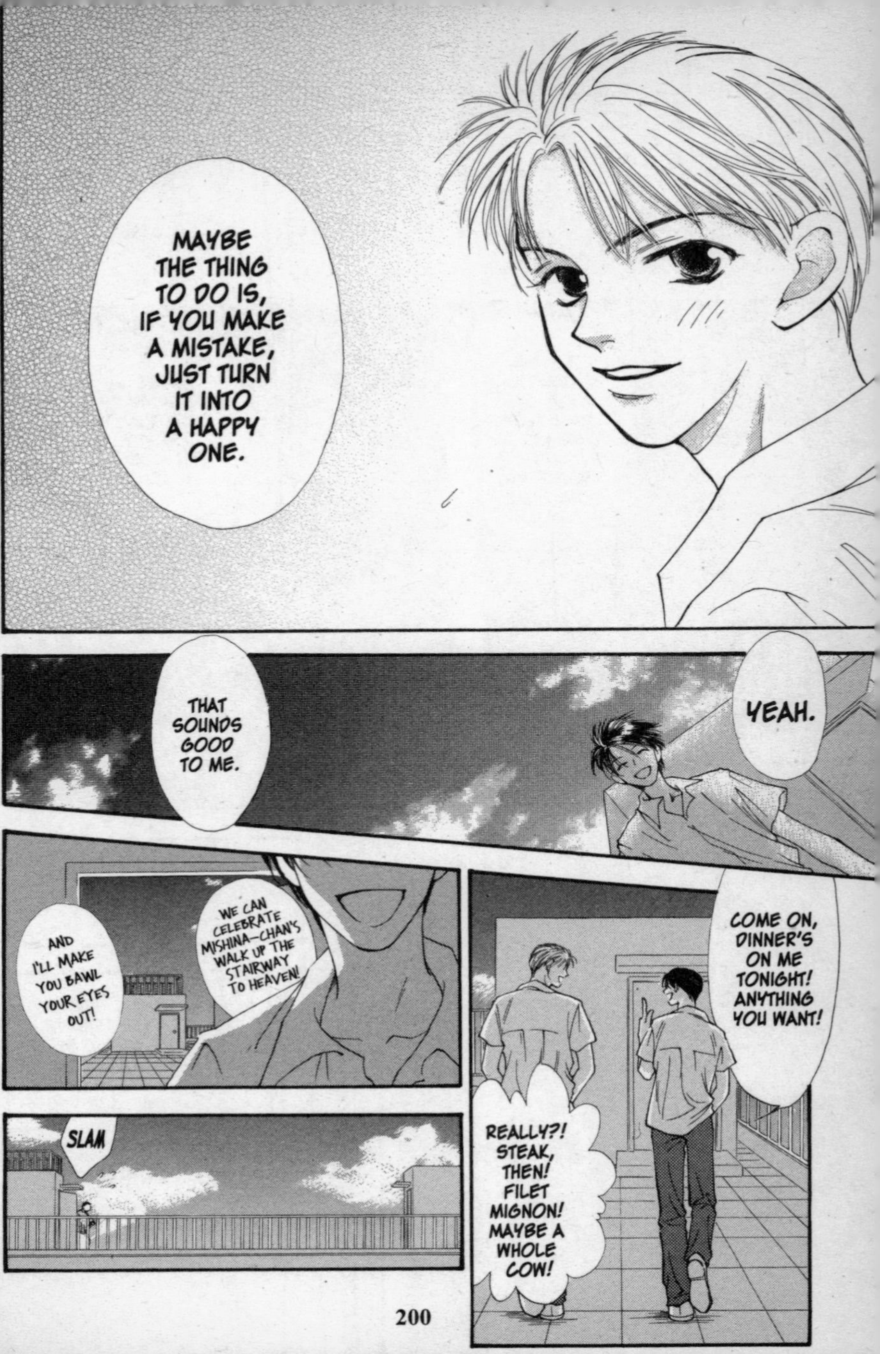
MAYBE THE THING TO DO IS, IF YOU MAKE A MISTAKE, JUST TURN IT INTO A HAPPY ONE.
YEAH.
THAT SOUNDS GOOD TO ME.
COME ON, DINNER'S ON ME TONIGHT! ANYTHING YOU WANT!
REALLY?! STEAK, THEN! FILET MIGNON! MAYBE A WHOLE COW!
WE CAN CELEBRATE MISHINA-CHAN'S WALK UP THE STAIRWAY TO HEAVEN!
AND I'LL MAKE YOU BAWL YOUR EYES OUT!
SLAM

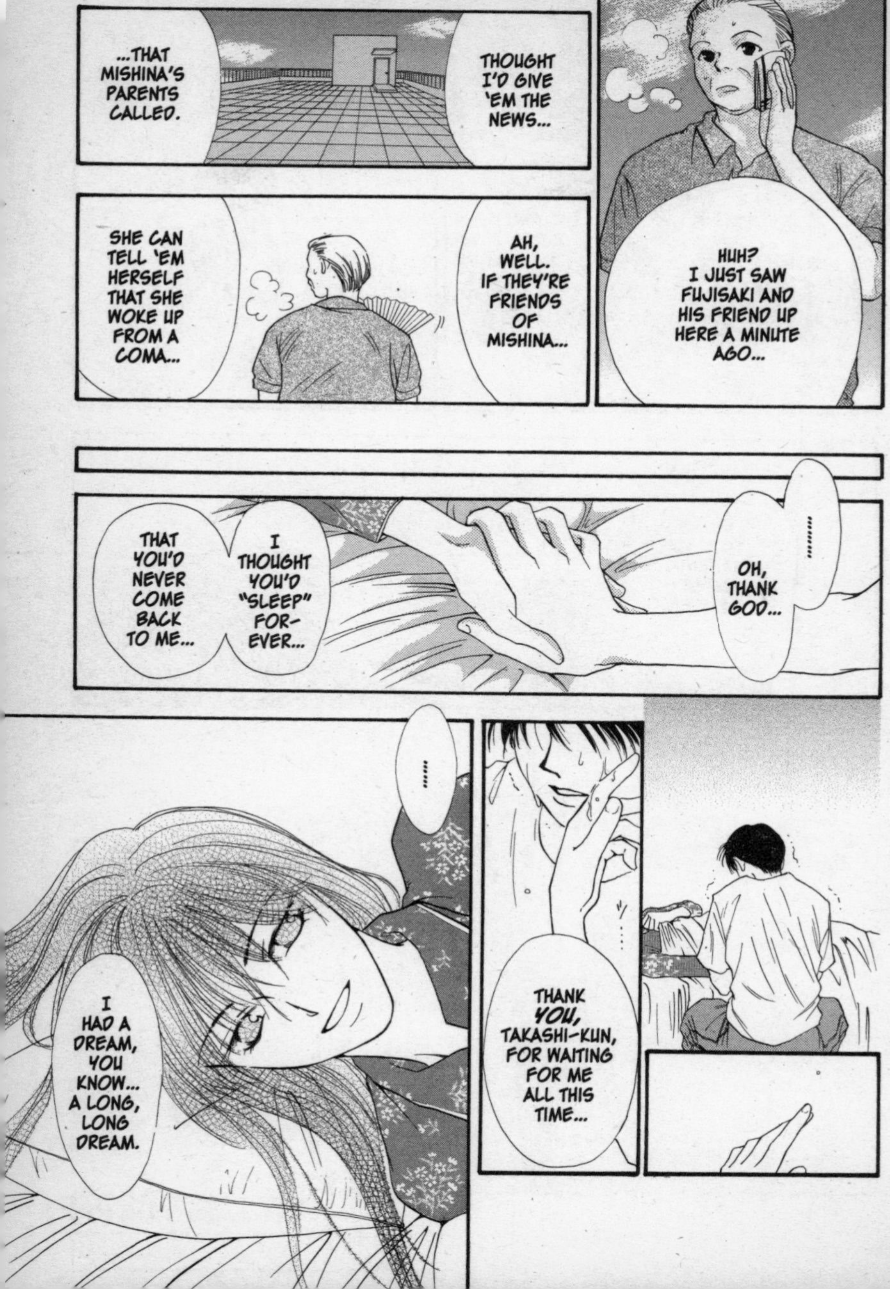
HUH? I JUST SAW FUJISAKI AND HIS FRIEND UP HERE A MINUTE AGO...
THOUGHT I'D GIVE 'EM THE NEWS...
...THAT MISHINA'S PARENTS CALLED.
AH, WELL. IF THEY'RE FRIENDS OF MISHINA...
SHE CAN TELL 'EM HERSELF THAT SHE WOKE UP FROM A COMA...
......
OH, THANK GOD...
I THOUGHT YOU'D "SLEEP" FOREVER...
THAT YOU'D NEVER COME BACK TO ME...
THANK *YOU*, TAKASHI-KUN, FOR WAITING FOR ME ALL THIS TIME...
......
I HAD A DREAM, YOU KNOW... A LONG, LONG DREAM.

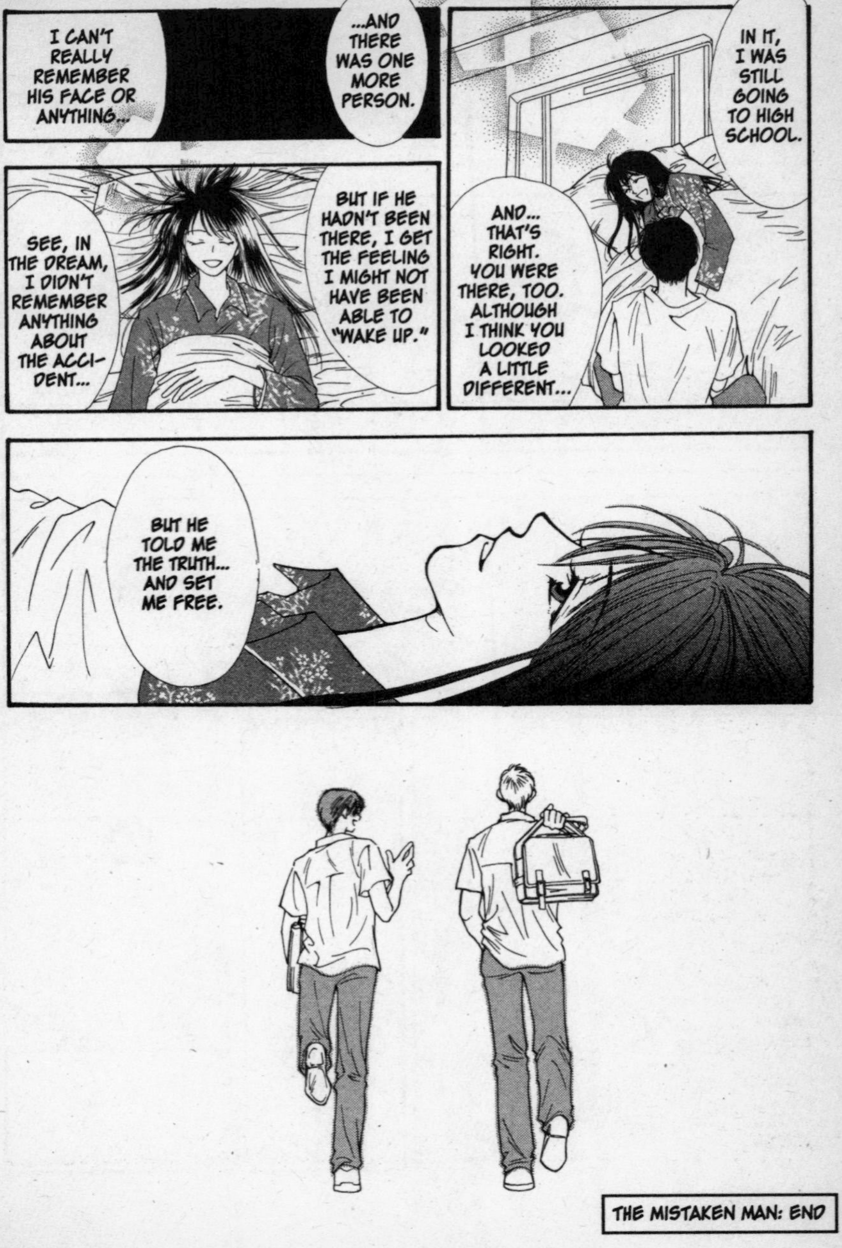
IN IT, I WAS STILL GOING TO HIGH SCHOOL.
AND... THAT'S RIGHT. YOU WERE THERE, TOO. ALTHOUGH I THINK YOU LOOKED A LITTLE DIFFERENT...
...AND THERE WAS ONE MORE PERSON.
I CAN'T REALLY REMEMBER HIS FACE OR ANYTHING...
BUT IF HE HADN'T BEEN THERE, I GET THE FEELING I MIGHT NOT HAVE BEEN ABLE TO "WAKE UP."
SEE, IN THE DREAM, I DIDN'T REMEMBER ANYTHING ABOUT THE ACCI-DENT...
BUT HE TOLD ME THE TRUTH... AND SET ME FREE.
THE MISTAKEN MAN: END

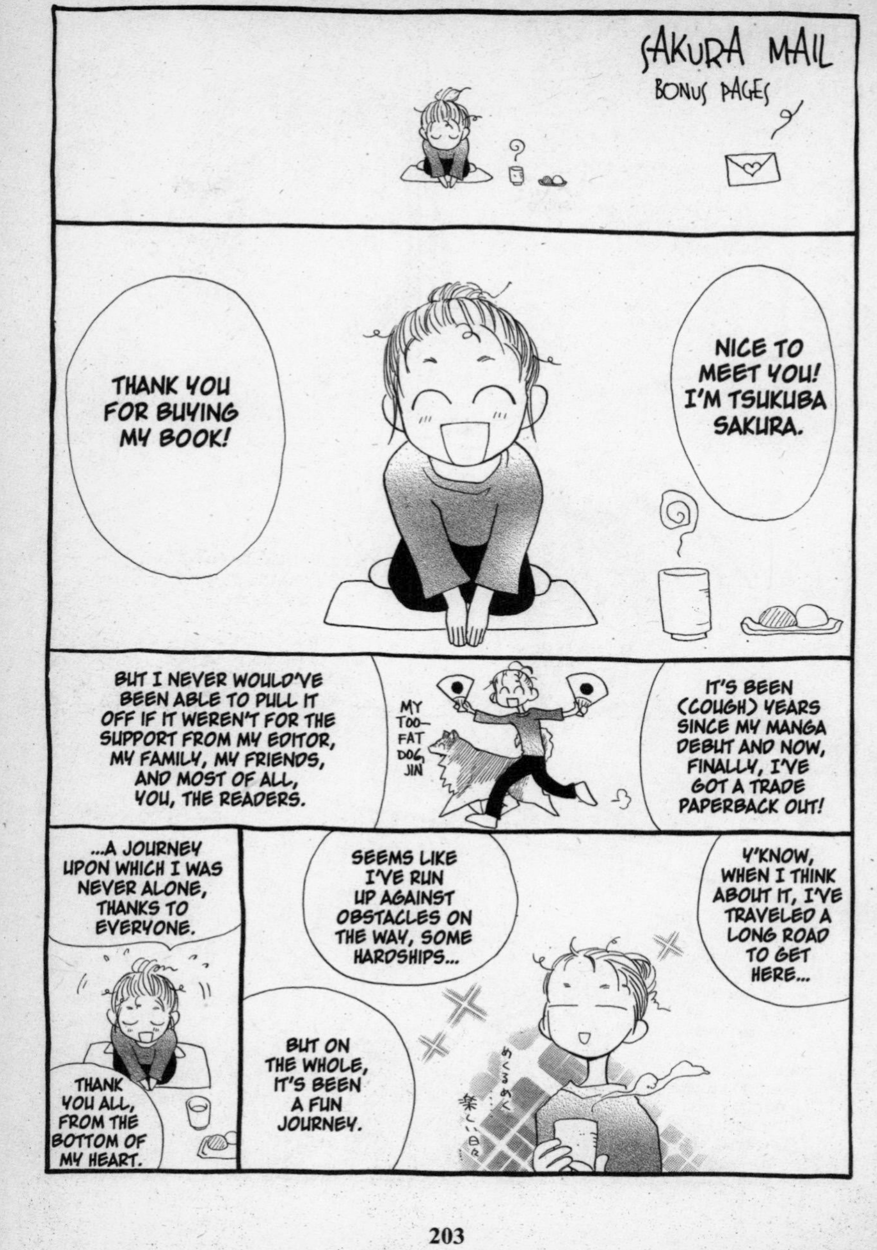
SAKURA MAIL
BONUS PAGES
NICE TO MEET YOU! I'M TSUKUBA SAKURA.
THANK YOU FOR BUYING MY BOOK!
IT'S BEEN (COUGH) YEARS SINCE MY MANGA DEBUT AND NOW, FINALLY, I'VE GOT A TRADE PAPERBACK OUT!
MY TOO-FAT DOG, JIN
BUT I NEVER WOULD'VE BEEN ABLE TO PULL IT OFF IF IT WEREN'T FOR THE SUPPORT FROM MY EDITOR, MY FAMILY, MY FRIENDS, AND MOST OF ALL, YOU, THE READERS.
Y'KNOW, WHEN I THINK ABOUT IT, I'VE TRAVELED A LONG ROAD TO GET HERE...
SEEMS LIKE I'VE RUN UP AGAINST OBSTACLES ON THE WAY, SOME HARDSHIPS...
めくるめく…楽しい日々
BUT ON THE WHOLE, IT'S BEEN A FUN JOURNEY.
...A JOURNEY UPON WHICH I WAS NEVER ALONE, THANKS TO EVERYONE.
THANK YOU ALL, FROM THE BOTTOM OF MY HEART.

Land of the Blindfolded

Character Introduction

(OR EXPLANATION, ANYWAY)

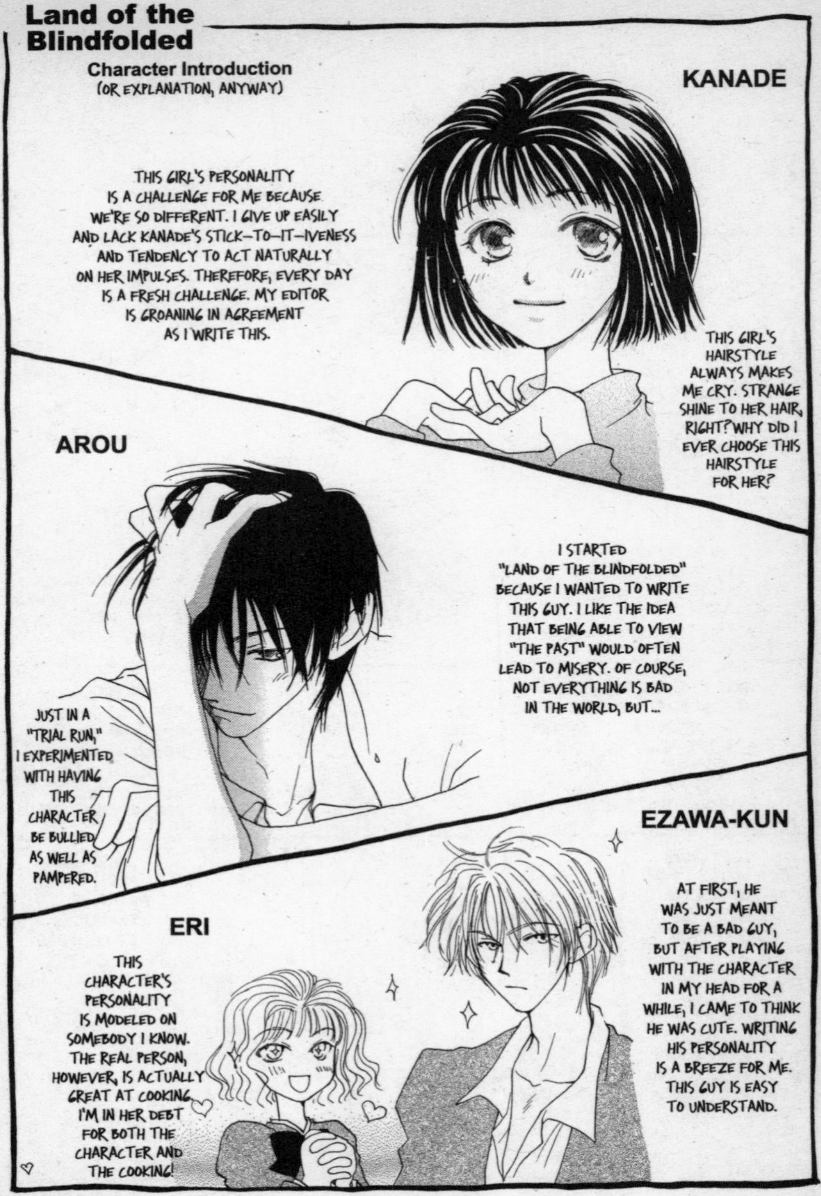

KANADE
THIS GIRL'S PERSONALITY IS A CHALLENGE FOR ME BECAUSE WE'RE SO DIFFERENT. I GIVE UP EASILY AND LACK KANADE'S STICK-TO-IT-IVENESS AND TENDENCY TO ACT NATURALLY ON HER IMPULSES. THEREFORE, EVERY DAY IS A FRESH CHALLENGE. MY EDITOR IS GROANING IN AGREEMENT AS I WRITE THIS.
THIS GIRL'S HAIRSTYLE ALWAYS MAKES ME CRY. STRANGE SHINE TO HER HAIR, RIGHT? WHY DID I EVER CHOOSE THIS HAIRSTYLE FOR HER?
AROU
I STARTED "LAND OF THE BLINDFOLDED" BECAUSE I WANTED TO WRITE THIS GUY. I LIKE THE IDEA THAT BEING ABLE TO VIEW "THE PAST" WOULD OFTEN LEAD TO MISERY. OF COURSE, NOT EVERYTHING IS BAD IN THE WORLD, BUT...
JUST IN A "TRIAL RUN," I EXPERIMENTED WITH HAVING THIS CHARACTER BE BULLIED AS WELL AS PAMPERED.
EZAWA-KUN
AT FIRST, HE WAS JUST MEANT TO BE A BAD GUY, BUT AFTER PLAYING WITH THE CHARACTER IN MY HEAD FOR A WHILE, I CAME TO THINK HE WAS CUTE. WRITING HIS PERSONALITY IS A BREEZE FOR ME. THIS GUY IS EASY TO UNDERSTAND.
ERI
THIS CHARACTER'S PERSONALITY IS MODELED ON SOMEBODY I KNOW. THE REAL PERSON, HOWEVER, IS ACTUALLY GREAT AT COOKING. I'M IN HER DEBT FOR BOTH THE CHARACTER AND THE COOKING!

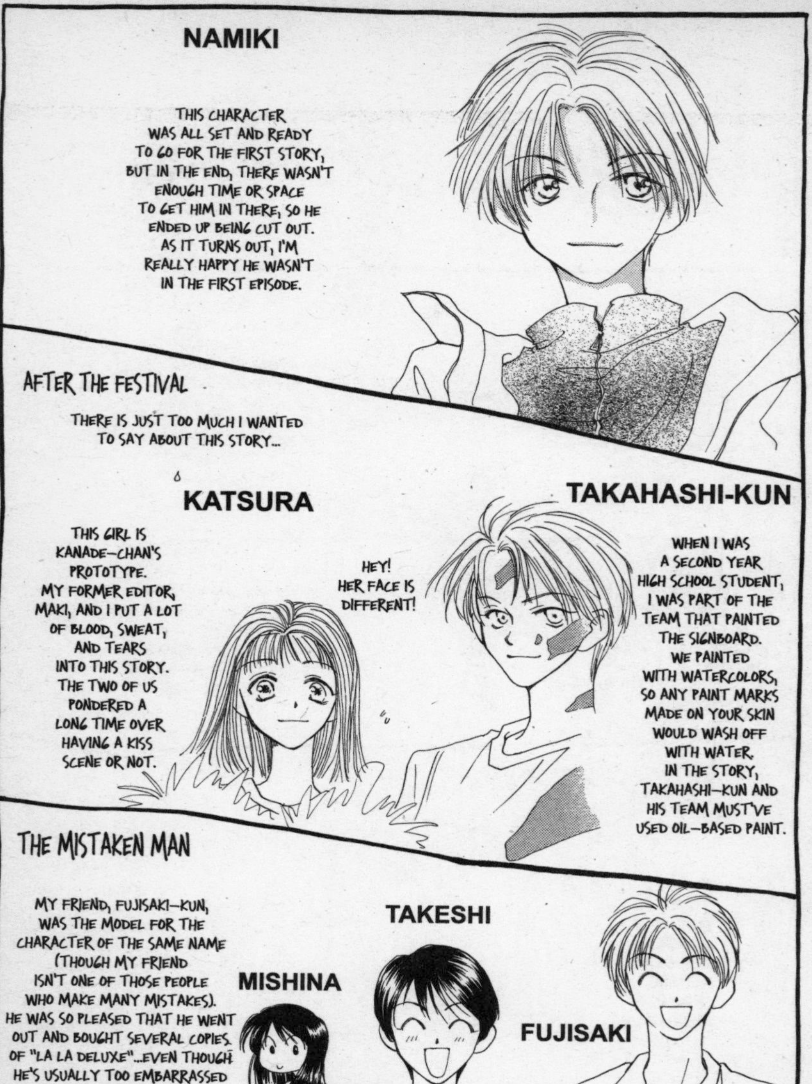
NAMIKI
THIS CHARACTER WAS ALL SET AND READY TO GO FOR THE FIRST STORY, BUT IN THE END, THERE WASN'T ENOUGH TIME OR SPACE TO GET HIM IN THERE, SO HE ENDED UP BEING CUT OUT. AS IT TURNS OUT, I'M REALLY HAPPY HE WASN'T IN THE FIRST EPISODE.
AFTER THE FESTIVAL
THERE IS JUST TOO MUCH I WANTED TO SAY ABOUT THIS STORY...
KATSURA
THIS GIRL IS KANADE-CHAN'S PROTOTYPE. MY FORMER EDITOR, MAKI, AND I PUT A LOT OF BLOOD, SWEAT, AND TEARS INTO THIS STORY. THE TWO OF US PONDERED A LONG TIME OVER HAVING A KISS SCENE OR NOT.
HEY! HER FACE IS DIFFERENT!
TAKAHASHI-KUN
WHEN I WAS A SECOND YEAR HIGH SCHOOL STUDENT, I WAS PART OF THE TEAM THAT PAINTED THE SIGNBOARD. WE PAINTED WITH WATERCOLORS, SO ANY PAINT MARKS MADE ON YOUR SKIN WOULD WASH OFF WITH WATER. IN THE STORY, TAKAHASHI-KUN AND HIS TEAM MUST'VE USED OIL-BASED PAINT.
THE MISTAKEN MAN
MY FRIEND, FUJISAKI-KUN, WAS THE MODEL FOR THE CHARACTER OF THE SAME NAME (THOUGH MY FRIEND ISN'T ONE OF THOSE PEOPLE WHO MAKE MANY MISTAKES). HE WAS SO PLEASED THAT HE WENT OUT AND BOUGHT SEVERAL COPIES OF "LA LA DELUXE"...EVEN THOUGH HE'S USUALLY TOO EMBARRASSED TO BUY GIRLS' COMICS. ANYWAY, THAT MADE ME REALLY HAPPY.
TAKESHI
MISHINA
FUJISAKI

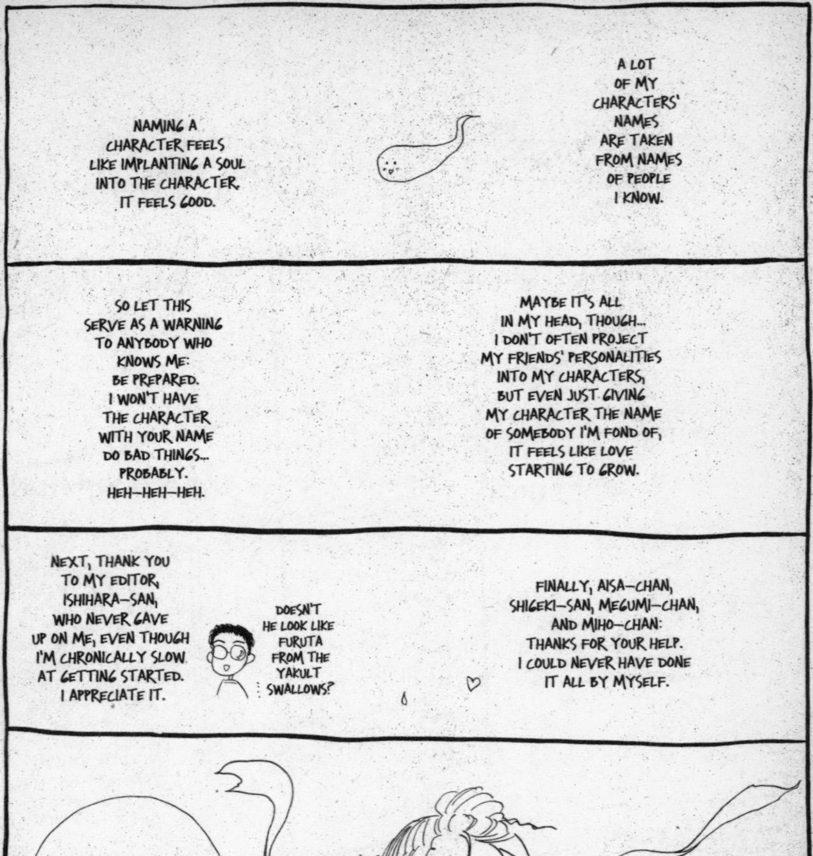
A LOT OF MY CHARACTERS' NAMES ARE TAKEN FROM NAMES OF PEOPLE I KNOW.
NAMING A CHARACTER FEELS LIKE IMPLANTING A SOUL INTO THE CHARACTER. IT FEELS GOOD.
MAYBE IT'S ALL IN MY HEAD, THOUGH... I DON'T OFTEN PROJECT MY FRIENDS' PERSONALITIES INTO MY CHARACTERS, BUT EVEN JUST GIVING MY CHARACTER THE NAME OF SOMEBODY I'M FOND OF, IT FEELS LIKE LOVE STARTING TO GROW.
SO LET THIS SERVE AS A WARNING TO ANYBODY WHO KNOWS ME: BE PREPARED. I WON'T HAVE THE CHARACTER WITH YOUR NAME DO BAD THINGS... PROBABLY. HEH-HEH-HEH.
FINALLY, AISA-CHAN, SHIGEKI-SAN, MEGUMI-CHAN, AND MIHO-CHAN: THANKS FOR YOUR HELP. I COULD NEVER HAVE DONE IT ALL BY MYSELF.
DOESN'T HE LOOK LIKE FURUTA FROM THE YAKULT SWALLOWS?
NEXT, THANK YOU TO MY EDITOR, ISHIHARA-SAN, WHO NEVER GAVE UP ON ME, EVEN THOUGH I'M CHRONICALLY SLOW AT GETTING STARTED. I APPRECIATE IT.
AND MOST OF ALL, THANK YOU, THE READERS, WHO SUPPORTED "LAND OF THE BLINDFOLDED."
PLEASE KEEP READING! I HOPE YOU LIKE THE REST OF THE SERIES.
TSUKUBA SAKURA

SAKURA MAIL — BONUS PAGES: END